Shorn Women

Shorn Women

Gender and Punishment in Liberation France

Fabrice Virgili

Translated from the French by John Flower

BERG

Oxford • New York

English Edition
First published in 2002 by
Berg
Editorial offices:
150 Cowley Road, Oxford, OX4 1JJ, UK
838 Broadway, Third Floor, New York, NY 10003–4812, USA

© 2002 Berg Publishers

Originally published in French as
La France 'virile': des femmes tondues à la Libération

© 2000 Editions Payot & Rivages

Liberté • Égalité • Fraternité
RÉPUBLIQUE FRANÇAISE

This book is supported by the French Ministry for Foreign Affairs, as part of the Burgess programme
headed for the French Embassy in London by the Institut Français du Royaume-Uni.

Published with the assistance of the French Ministry of Culture – Centre National du Livre.

Berg is an imprint of Oxford International Publishers Ltd.

Library of Congress Cataloging-in-Publication Data

Virgili, Fabrice.
[France virile. English]
Shorn women : gender and punishment in liberation France / Fabrice
Virgili ; translated from the French by John Flower.— English ed.
p. cm.
ISBN 1-85973-579-7 (cloth) — ISBN 1-85973-584-3 (paper)
1. Women—France—Social conditions—History—20th century. 2. World
War, 1939–1945—Collaborationists—France. 3. Collaborationists—France—
History—20th century. 4. France—History—German occupation, 1940-1945.
I. Title.
D810.W7 V5813 2002
940.53'163'0820944—dc21

2002012014

British Library Cataloguing-in-Publication Data
A catalogue record for this book is available from the British Library.

ISBN 1 85973 579 7 (Cloth)
1 85973 584 3 (Paper)

Typeset by JS Typesetting Ltd, Wellingborough, Northants.

Contents

Translator's Note

In relation to the specific subject with which this book deals two words are fundamental, *tonte* and *épuration*; neither has a simple translation. *Tonte*, which derives from the verb *tondre*, to mow or to shear, has rarely been used to describe the shaving of a human head except in the context with which this book deals. *Epuration* means purging, but after the Liberation of France it came to describe the attempts by the French to rid themselves of all traces and of those guilty of collaboration until an official, general amnesty was granted in 1951. Subsequently *épuration* also described this period. In order to avoid constant paraphrase therefore it seems advisable to retain these two terms.

Introduction

Throughout France, from 1943 to the beginning of 1946, about 20,000 women of all ages and all professions who were accused of having collaborated with the occupying Germans had their heads shaved. Just as the identity of those who carried this task out varied so too did the form it took. For example, among those who carried it out can be found members of the Resistance, those who took part in fighting at the time of the Liberation, neighbours who came down into the streets once the Germans had left and men whose authority depended on the police and the courts. All of them carried out this violent deed either behind closed doors – inside the walls of a prison or the home of the women so punished – or in a public square. If, in the last instance, it was the men who wielded the scissors and clippers, the population as a whole – men, women and children – were present at the event, which was both a spectacle and a demonstration of the punishment to be meted out to traitors.

The ways in which shorn women were depicted at the time, and subsequently, have for a long time caused accounts of this event to be unclear. The imposition of a punishment with distinct sexist overtones, characterized by branding or marking, has overshadowed its use for all acts of collaboration. After the war and up to the present, photographs of women with shaven heads have become the only evidence of a practice about which those who carried it out have remained silent – attention has been directed at the victims and at the act itself, leaving both what preceded and followed it (collaboration, accusation, arrest, judgement, liberation or condemnation) neglected.

This lack of information has meant that attention has been directed at the spectacular and simplified features of this practice rather than the full picture. Standard interpretations attributed the violence with which the practice was carried out either to vengeful crowds, or to those who joined the Resistance at the last minute. As for the victims themselves, they have been considered scapegoats, their heads shaved simply because they were women and for insignificant reasons. In fact, the different forms that the shaving could take militates against any single explanation. They relate to both the public and private domain, to relationships between sexes and to those between the occupying forces and the native population; their nature was violent and symbolic and amounted to a punitive measure in which elements of earlier conflict could still be sensed.

The facts as a whole can only be seen to make sense if they are studied in the context of the Occupation, Liberation, post-war years and the twentieth century in general. The standard historical view concerned primarily with how events as a whole unfolded pays scant attention to the *tontes*. Even at the time when they were most commonly practised, just after the Liberation, they were one kind of event among many whose consequences are difficult to gauge. Their interest as an historical fact does not stem from their importance simply as events, but rather from the way they point to contradictions inherent in a French society undergoing massive upheaval.

It is only possible to understand the phenomenon completely if we have a view of the country as a whole, but in order to survey its incidence geographically we have to be aware of the many ambiguities contained in the different sources of information available and to work with different scales of measurement. The examination of how the practice evolved in several departments will help define its limits and uncover differences which are sometimes buried below the surface. Studied here in detail, the departments of the Côtes-du Nord, Indre, Hérault, Moselle and Oise allow us to see how the situation differed during the Occupation and at the Liberation. For example in the Oise where Compiègne became the first German high command point in 1940, in the Côtes-du Nord, on account of its strategic coastal position, and, of course, in the Moselle, which was annexed to the Reich, the Occupation was longer and the weight of the German presence greater. In contrast in the Hérault and in the Indre in the unoccupied zone, the Occupation did not take effect until November 1942. Resistance assumed forms which were just as varied; in the Hérault the *maquis* was particularly strong in the foothills of the Massif central; in Brittany resistance fighters were more mobile and only came together in large numbers after the Normandy landings; the Indre, while not an area favoured by the *maquis* nonetheless experienced a period of intense armed fighting from June 1944; in the Oise fighting was rare and resistance remained completely underground; finally in the Moselle, which was annexed, resistance was symbolic. The ways in which these departments were liberated were also different: the Oise was liberated by Anglo-American forces in under a week, but in Moselle, Liberation occurred only after two months; the Hérault and the Indre were liberated as the result of the combination of German withdrawal and the activities of the FFI; in the Côtes-du Nord, the arrival of the Allied forces was accompanied by strong resistance activity.

liberation different

According to Henry Rousso 'one of the features that deserve to be re-examined is the tendency to make a clear distinction between legal and illegal *épuration*'.[1] The study of the *tontes* throws new light on this question. In fact they were neither trivial nor imposed by the courts. No civil court sentenced anyone to have his or her head shaved, but for any person the fact that it had happened could count heavily in later judicial decisions. Moreover, the *tontes* were sometimes carried out as a result of administrative decisions – as we shall see was the case in the Languedoc – so this punishment cannot be assessed simply as part of a rapid *épuration*. The passage from legal to illegal justice, far from being linear, was the result of a gradual transfer of legitimacy nonetheless reversible at any moment. The overlap between the two forms of *épuration* was real and the barrier between them porous.

The *tontes* equally reflect the willingness of the general public to watch traitors being punished. Whether the attitude of those carrying them out during the Occupation was a sign of their stand against the enemy, or against the policy of *attentisme,* or simply a discreet way of coming to terms with the situation, the *tontes* allowed people to state their redis-covered patriotism once the Liberation had been declared. For this reason it was essential that the *épuration* should be visible. It was as much a social as a judicial action, one 'that marks the beginning of a new age'.[2] From this point of view the sexist nature of the *tontes* was evidence of an *épuration* that was not only exclusively the result of political issues stemming from the conflict, but also the result of differing perceptions of the relationships between the sexes in a post-war society. Not only do they reflect the importance of private life and of sexuality but they allow us to examine ways in which individuals and groups interact at a time of war.

Finally this form of punishment provides us with a broader view of the way a society at war returned to peace. It goes without saying that such violence and the way it was perceived by contemporaries constitute a fundamental element in the understanding of the shift from wartime to the post-war period.[3] The shaving of women's heads was an act of violence that can be easily identified; it was executed throughout France and was experienced or witnessed by a significant proportion of the population. The way it developed allows us to study how society as a whole and the individuals within it responded to the question of violence.

For a member of the *maquis* constantly threatened by death who found himself in the position of killing a German or a member of the *milice*, the shaving of heads was a less violent act. The physical assault, however brutal, was not absolute and it was rare that a person who had been punished in this way was executed. Nonetheless, for many it was the first violent act directed at the enemy or its representative. It allowed them to move from a position of being the victims of violence to one where they inflicted it, and thereby reasserted their patriotic identity.

Even so, if the practice of violence was a precise step in the rediscovery of national identity, it was also surrounded by ambiguity. The willingness to act and so share in the reconstruction of a purified and strong national identity was paralleled by a desire to escape from war and violence. A study of the practice of the shaving of heads, on a national scale, allows us to see how there was a gradual movement towards the re-establishment of a peaceful and democratic France. Although the *tonte* as a practice was rather whimsically given up in the autumn of 1944, this did not mean that it would not re-emerge with a renewed legitimacy in the spring of the following year. In the long run, however, the picture of those who were involved illustrates the abrupt change from a desire to finish with the war and, at the same time, to have all traces of betrayal disappear. For the view of the person whose head was shaved to change from someone who was considered guilty to victim would take a long time, as would the perception of those who carried out the punishment; the latter having had a certain prestige, would eventually be seen at last minute resistance fighters and even cowards. The case of the woman in *Hiroshima mon amour* in 1960 marks the point when the idea of the people as a whole resisting began to take shape.

The single, traditional view of a woman whose head had been shaved is probably the final screen behind which the truth lies hidden. Inadequate research has resulted in the 'fixing' of images of the *tonte* and to misrepresentation. The image of a girl whose head was shaved because she slept with a German is only one example among many but it has become commonplace in images of the Liberation. It can be found in films, in books and in songs[4] as well as in numerous photographs in works devoted to this period. And in our memory we like to associate *tontes* with a particular kind of disgust. What this book tries to do is to take a well-known idea and re-examine it in the light of new research and to change the common perception from one where, instead of the act itself, the woman who has been punished holds centre stage.

The fact that there are two expressions in French whose meanings do not refer solely to this period calls for some clarification. The noun *la tondue* is the only term used for women whose heads were clipped or shaved because they were accused of having collaborated with the Germans.[5]

Women who were deported to concentration camps and whose heads were systematically shaved on arrival are never referred to in this way.[6] Nor is there an expression in the language of the period to describe the act itself. *La tonte* is the most common but there are others. The normal meaning of *la tonte* is for something to have been cut off, but not necessarily completely and it is rarely used in descriptions of human beings other than in the specific sense it has during this period. (It is more normal for the mowing of lawns or the shearing of sheep.) To retain the word *tonte* is therefore arbitrary and requires a specific definition. Head shaving was a violent and punitive act: violent because it was carried out on someone who had been detained; punitive because it related to an earlier reprehensible action. It was also a violation of a person's physical integrity.

This whole topic is burdened with multiple handicaps: sources of information hitherto considered rare or non-existent; the refusal of victims and perpetrators of this violent act to talk about it. There is also a common picture of it that adds to the general impression of the ugliness of this period and one that forms part of an historical account but that is not interested in it as a theme in its own right. And there is the problem of those who remain nostalgic for the Vichy regime whose sole desire is to create as black a picture as possible in order to rehabilitate an even more monstrous past. Historiography is only of marginal help in trying to untangle all this. Women whose heads were shaved are mentioned but are not in any way central; photographs of them are used as simple illustrations as are certain pithy expressions, but the women themselves are frequently not mentioned at all. From all of this confusion it emerges both that they were scapegoats[7] and that the phenomenon was wide-spread.[8] Works devoted to the Liberation almost all make reference to it but whereas many debates – sometimes quite polemical – have contributed to the historical reconstruction of the last fifty years they have not focused on the women themselves.

The reasons for this discretion are many but it has to be remembered that before embarking on research into a precise historical subject the historian has to conceive it as such. For various reasons that has not been the case for *la tonte* in recent decades and it has to be asked whether it has been seen as an event at all.

In historical accounts in which the military, political and diplomatic aspects of the Second World War have been dominant, references to the *tonte* have no place simply because it had no influence over the conflict and was not a political issue. At best it helps evoke the atmosphere of the Liberation of France. The reasons for this absence or perhaps the inability

ans to refer to it are many. The victims were women in a man's
ad this punishment relates to what A. Corbin has termed 'obscene
/, namely the body, pleasure and suffering. Finally *la tonte* is part
oι ᴗ ιstory steeped in memory, one of several sensitive areas that have
to be approached with caution. The practice of *la tonte* was far from
glorious and risks tarnishing the view of the Resistance. These victims
from the other side were and continue to be a source of embarrassment.

To be antifascist, patriotic and resistant does not mean that it was not
possible to have carried out certain actions which, fifty years later, shake
those who witnessed them or indeed committed them. Courage and
heroism do not mean that men were not affected by emotion, traumatic
experiences, or the weight of social appearances. Hatred, the desire for
revenge, misogamy were felt equally and at the same time as a passionate
desire for freedom. The climate of this particular episode from the past
must never be forgotten. Past and present are not the same and the
perception of the practice of shaving heads at the time of the Liberation
cannot be the same as the one we hold today.

In a simple, binary view of the period, to attribute such a practice to
the discredit of the Resistance could only bring credit to the Vichy regime
and to collaborators. But in order to conceive of Nazism as an absolute
evil is it necessary to set against it a good which is equally so? As Pierre
Laborie has made clear in the conclusion to his *L'Opinion française sous
Vichy* 'beyond any kind of explanation the dividing lines are deep'.[9] To
explain the phenomenon of *la tonte* with reference to the political and
moral choices that drew people to resist is impossible. To say that members
of the Resistance, like those who were in the police or had been deported
and like many other French men and women, organized or were present
at this practice is simply to establish the necessary facts. After that is the
question 'why?' This book is an attempt to answer it.

Part I
From Myth to Reality

–1–

Sexual Collaboration

At the Liberation a woman's shaved head was a sign to everyone of an expiatory punishment. Yet the nature of the actions for which she was reproached and warranted such a punishment are far from clear. Different documents and points of view show how wide the definition of the crime committed could be. Prosecutions were carried out according to how far the *épuration* had developed. What might be defined in court as 'indirectly helping Germany' could appear in a file forming part of the *épuration* process as 'having slept with German soldiers', 'doing business with the enemy' or even 'being an unequivocal supporter of Germany'. In his survey of the *épuration*, Olivier Wieviorka[1] has reminded us that for collaboration to be expunged required 'a clear definition of guilt' and that 'the nature of the totalitarian regime was such that the cards were mixed up from the beginning.'

As far as the women themselves are concerned, confusion is there from the start. A study of the *tonte* requires more than simply being able to establish guilt; the kind of fault committed and the form collaboration took have to be considered. Among them there is the phrase 'relations with Germans'. What that means quantitatively and the ambiguity of the phrase itself makes any investigation of the phenomenon difficult. If, for men as for women, contact with the occupiers is the *Rubicon* of unworthiness, for women it is coloured by the sexual nature – real or imagined – of their relationships. Any debate about them turns on the debauched nature of their relations. Such debate goes beyond the facts and focuses on sexual activity as a form of collaboration even though this had no influence on the outcome of the war. It has a symbolic significance inversely proportional to its real one – a distortion that is fundamental for any understanding of *la tonte*.

When, in a radio broadcast on 11 October 1940, Marshall Pétain prepared the French for his policy of collaboration, which became official a few days later at Montoire, he stated: 'France is ready to seek opportunities to collaborate in any area of activity, with all people. The choice belongs to the victor but it depends on the defeated as well . . .'. From the outset collaboration, defined by the person who initiated it, was a voluntary choice that could assume many forms.

Nearly six years later in the introduction to his account of how all features of collaboration had been repressed, François de Menthon said: 'Nazism invented a new kind of intelligence with the enemy – collaboration. With this hypocritical phrase Nazism won the support of the French; a more direct appeal for them to have betrayed their country would not have achieved this.' By attributing this initiative to the Germans (though modern historians agree that it was really French)[2] François de Menthon underlined the originality of a new situation that those responsible for drawing up laws had not forseen. The problem was particularly critical for 'those who, without being guilty of activities as defined by article 75 and beyond in the penal code, had behaved during the Occupation in a way that was not compatible with national duty.'[3]

So that this preoccupation could be addressed and appropriate judicial procedures put in place, the laws of the 24 August and 26 December 1944 were promulgated. To the crimes of high treason and of threatening national security was added that of national unworthiness, defined in the following way: 'Any French person who knowingly provided direct or indirect aid to the Germans or their allies, or who threatened national unity, or the freedom and equality of French citizens, is guilty of national unworthiness.'[4] Three judicial bodies were established: the High Courts of Justice where those of the highest political responsibility would be judged (108 in total), judicial courts for those people guilty of acts of collaboration according to article 75 and beyond of the penal code and, finally, alongside these, the civic courts where about 70,0000 people appeared.[5]

Through their work on Vichy France and on Europe under German occupation generally, historians have brought new and complementary definitions that have broadened our understanding of this period. Beginning with a classification that Stanley Hoffman in particular has termed as 'collaboration with the state' based on motivation and the ideological sympathies of the persons concerned, numerous types of collaboration have been increasingly examined. Yet the different kinds emerging from the accusations made against women whose heads were shaved, or due to be shaved, do not necessarily coincide with any of the classifications established hitherto. There was no female intellectual involved in what Henry Rousso has called active ideological collaboration, nor any woman brought before the High Court of Justice, nor did any one commit crimes reported on the front pages of the papers at the Liberation. In his study of ordinary collaboration, François Rouquet[6] has shown that it was more widespread in towns than in the country, but the real reasons for it remain difficult to establish and the scale of its seriousness very varied.

Of Which Sorts of Collaboration were these Women Accused?

Of the collaborative acts of which women were accused, four categories can be defined: political, where they had belonged to a collaborationist organization or, more modestly, had held opinions in favour of the enemy or shown opposition to the Resistance and allied forces; financial, if they had benefited from professional or business contacts; personal, if they had relationships with members of the occupying forces. They could also be accused if they had denounced someone to the occupying authorities. A fifth reason for being arrested and for having one's head shaved was to be someone from one of the Axis countries; this did not necessarily indicate collaboration but it invited suspicion. Finally no woman was pursued for having fought with the enemy. The female nurses in the *milice* or the Legion of French volunteers to fight bolshevism filled non-military positions like those of ordinary nurses or secretaries; they have been added in with those who belonged to a collaborationist party and are counted as political. Despite such variety these categories allow us to have an overview of all activities likely to result in prosecution at the Liberation. Each village could have its neighbour who joined the *milice*, its servant who worked with and joined the Germans.

The information collected on the 586 people across the country whose heads were shaved provides us with a better understanding of the reasons for which they were accused.[7]

Denunciations symbolize innumerable daily acts of cowardice during the Occupation. The thousands of letters sent to the Germans denouncing someone have been frequently studied. But they only represent 6.5 per cent of the collaborative acts of which women were accused. Such a small number does not, however, hide their motives for informing in this way. As the files consulted make clear there was an infinite variety of personal situations. Thus, for example, a woman from Machemont in the Oise claimed to have denounced a Senegalese soldier to the Germans out of fear: 'The fear of seeing a black man made me behave in such a stupid way . . . I had my hair cut off because I denounced a soldier!' In another district of the same department a financial dispute between neighbours degenerated into insults – 'Your daughter is the Boches' whore – you've grown fat thanks to them' – and ended in a complaint to the German High

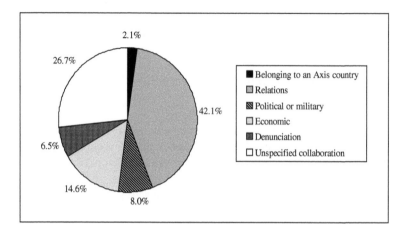

Kinds of collaboration of which these women were accused.

Command.[8] Couples and families equally used the enemy to tear themselves apart. Adultery, conjugal violence, a husband's alcoholism, mental problems were all reasons for someone or other to cause the occupying authorities to become involved in the confrontations and complexities of family life.

As it was known who the person who had been denounced was, informing in this way was often attributable to personal squabbles in a limited area. It is difficult to distinguish clearly between different motivations, but the lure of financial gain or political convictions are other traceable reasons. Nonetheless this diversity and above all the risk of a terrible and instant outcome for the person denounced puts informing into a special category defined by the action and its consequences rather than by motive. The relatively small number of cases of denunciation involving women who had their heads shaved may seem surprising. Philippe Burrin pointed to an over representation of women in cases of denunciation, quoting as examples the departments of Finistère and the Eure where 70 per cent and 66 per cent respectively of the women accused of collaboration were involved in it.[9] It has to be noted that these two departments were characterized by the number of women (42.4 per cent and 57.1 per cent) brought before the courts. Elsewhere the number of cases based on denunciation was often lower: 28.8 per cent in the Oise, 23 per cent in Charente, 17.8 per cent in the Indre and 12 per cent in the Hérault.[10]

These disparities can be explained by differences in the local situations and also by the stage the investigation had reached. It was common, in fact, for a person arrested on suspicion of denunciation to be condemned in the end for some other reason. In his work on the staff in state schools and post offices, François Rouquet has counted 7.7 per cent and 12 per cent respectively of employees punished for having informed on someone. In other words totals similar to those we have here.[11] In view of the fact that many informers were never troubled, their importance may have been overestimated.

As far as the economic sector was concerned the contrast between, say, a Louis Renault putting his factories to work for the Nazi war machine and a cleaning woman working for the Germans was very considerable. In other words we will not find a Louis Renault among women who had their heads shaved. However, it was not so much the amount of money as where it came from that determined whether collaboration had taken place. The high salaries offered by the Germans encouraged a lot of men and women to work for them and that only encouraged grievances towards those who willingly accepted. Thus a domestic working for the Germans in the Indre received 2,200 francs per month[12] – in other words more than a senior officer in the police force after eight years of service.[13] Dealing with the Germans and the resulting black market were a form of economic collaboration for which women particularly were reproached. Most of them were shopkeepers or farmers who were accused of having grown rich thanks to the occupying forces and of having profited from selling produce of which most people were deprived. Fifteen per cent of women were accused of black marketeering, trading and working of their own volition for the Germans – all of which added to the shortage of goods and reflected on a local scale the German pillaging of Europe as a whole.

Paragraph 4 of article 2 of the ordinance of 26 December 1944 provides a list, though not exhaustive, of the collaborationist bodies of which membership even without active participation, constituted the crime of national unworthiness. These bodies were the Service d'ordre légionnaire, the *milice*, the group Collaboration, the Légion des volontaires français, the Légion tricolore, the Amis de la légion des volontaires français, the Parti national collectiviste, the Parti franciste, the Parti populaire français, the Mouvement social révolutionnaire, the Rassemblement national populaire, the Comité ouvrier de secours immédiat and the Service d'ordre prisonnier. To these could be added in those departments annexed by the Germans the Nazi party and its different organizations such as the women's association, the *Frauenschaft*.

Evidence contained in the files established during the *épuration* of their having belonged to one of these organizations was the clearest sign of the political commitment of these women. Some of them were quite open about it: 'The different associations I belonged to show quite clearly my ideal', a social assistant at Châteauroux who belonged to the groups Collaboration and PPF declared to the police.[14] Others made light of their involvement, putting forward reasons that were other than political. The wife of a prisoner justified her interest in Marcel Déat's organization on the grounds that she wanted to have her husband freed: 'I learned from my sister in law that a group called the RNP was being set up in Paris to get prisoners of war back home. She said to me that she was going to find out about it because her husband was also a prisoner and that she would see to my case as well. I have heard nothing more and I have not received any party card from the RNP.'[15]

While the possession of a card of a collaborationalist organization was tangible proof, other signs of political commitment were equally condemned. A subscription to the newspaper *Signal*, a photograph of Hitler or a portrait of Pétain hung indoors, or any public comments in favour of Germany and against the Allied forces could also be seen to indicate an ideological position.

Overall, cases of political collaboration only involved 8 per cent of the women whose heads were shaved. And yet the differences between one department and another can be important: if there was only 4.5 per cent in the Oise, there was 13 per cent in the Hérault. If we take into account as well the women who had been interned, then the proportion is notably higher: nearly a quarter in the Charente and in the Indre, and 37 per cent in the Hérault. Interpreting differences such as these is problematic. They may just as well indicate how collaborationist groups were set up differently at a local level, as the political views that those responsible for justice at the *épuration* took of such behaviour.

Few women seem to have had their heads shaved simply because they were of German or Italian nationality. However, what cases there were indicate a view of war that was more patriotic than ideological. As a kind of extension of measures taken in 1939 towards people coming from enemy territories, anyone of Italian or German nationality was particularly suspect. In the Isère or the Midi, which were under Italian occupation, feelings against Italians were particularly strong after the Liberation.

Thus the prefect for the Alpes-Maritimes, anxious about the way events might develop, included in his report an account of a meeting of the Union of French Women held at Beausoleil:

> There is still very considerable antipathy towards Italians. Recently in Beausoleil there was a significant incident during a meeting organised by the

UFF. Mme Faraut, a member of the UFF, of the PCF and of the municipal delegation from Nice spoke at this meeting and at the end of this an Italian woman offered her a bouquet of flowers on behalf of Italian women. Mme Faraut thanked her, but there was a show of indignation from all the French women who were there who then left the room and made it quite clear to the speaker that they would no longer participate in any of the reunions and would not join the PCF so long as 'people continue to smile at Italian women'.[16]

The simple fact that the region had been under Italian occupation is not enough to explain such animosity. It can also be found in the Moselle where demonstrations against Italians grew towards the end of spring 1945. This hostility went way beyond that directed at nationals who supported the occupying forces. At times refugees who were anti-fascist or anti-Nazi were also bothered[17] and for some nationality alone was enough to place a person on the side of collaborators and was an expression as well of a more general xenophobia.[18]

Finally 57 per cent of women whose heads were shaved for undisputed acts of collaboration were accused of having intimate relationships with Germans.[19] The number is important but not all those women who had their heads shaved had 'slept with Germans'. This kind of relationship is not only important for establishing the facts of the collaboration, but also and above all in the way it is represented. There is only a single word for denunciation, but there are numerous expressions used when it comes to relationships with Germans. 'Relationships with Germans' is the most neutral of these phrases, but also the most frequent one and the one which soon becomes 'sexual relationships', or in a rather more discreet way 'intimate' or 'amorous' or 'sleeping' relationships. Or again it can be a 'special kind' of relationship. Yet even though it is far less used, another expression which subsequently became common is 'horizontal collaboration'. It is found in the press, in prefects' reports, in accounts issued by the police, in testimonies and in historical accounts, even if in most cases it is put between inverted commas.[20] It might be noted that in Brittany the adjective 'sentimental' is common even though it does not necessarily describe the nature of the feelings on which relationships were based. Those who carried out questioning wanted above all to focus on sexual relationships as evidence of collaboration. Thus, for example, the report from the central *épuration* committee of the Minister of Communications makes it clear than an enquiry carried out about the behaviour of a post office worker in the Pas-de-Calais 'was not able to establish beyond doubt that she had had intimate relationships with a member of the occupying forces'.[21]

The type of collaboration is what causes an initial division between the sexes. This division is relative because political and economic

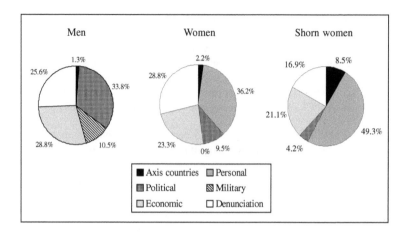

Types of collaboration in three groups of people interned in the Oise.

collaboration and denunciation are as much acts carried out by men as by women. By contrast, two other forms of collaboration have almost nothing to do with the other sex. Joining the LVF, the *milice* or the Waffen SS was something men did. Women who belonged to these organizations did not carry weapons. Unlike men, the eight women who had their heads shaved for having been members of the *milice* or LVF were put into the political category. Relationships with Germans, however, were something for which women alone were reproached. So ambiguous are the terms used to describe relationships that men also are mentioned. There is never a question of homosexual relationships and only exceptionally of relationships between men and German women. There is only one case known of a policeman who was dismissed after having sexual relationships with one of the auxiliary workers in the German army known as the 'grey mice'.[22] In the case of women in the Oise, whose heads were shaved, emphasis is placed on the sexual dimension of their collaborative actions. As that aspect of the relationships increases so anything to do with politics diminishes. Whatever reservations may be expressed, 'horizontal collaboration' and the *tonte* are closely associated.

Evidence on a national scale, as far as women are concerned, is so rare that we should take advantage of the only indication which is offered by the survey carried out by the Committee for the History of the Second World War, which has looked at departments individually.[23]

However incomplete,[24] these statistics provide the only evidence that shows the men/women split across the country. 18,572 women were charged by the courts, or 26 per cent of all those who were convicted. This figure calls for some comment.[25] The level may seem low when we consider the female population as a whole. Nonetheless, when we consider that women constitute about 10 per cent of those members of the population who are oppressed in peace time,[26] here we find a much higher percentage. A similar phenomenon has been noted for collaboration in those departments that were occupied in 1914–1918:[27] 34 per cent of all people accused of collaboration during the First World War brought before the assize courts in the Nord were women. An over-representation of women in the cases of collaboration reaches extreme proportions in seven departments (the Aube, the Eure, the Eure-et-Loir, the Marne, the Mayenne, the Morbihan, and the Territoire de Belfort) where they amounted to more than half of the number of people who were convicted.

A geographical distribution reveals a contrast between the north and the south. The departments of the Hautes-Alpes, the Indre and the Loire are the only ones of the non-occupied zone before November 1942 where the number of women convicted is higher than the national average. The other departments in the southern part of the country, where 26 per cent of all those convicted were women, are all divided by the demarcation line. This is the case of the Landes, Dordogne, Charente, Vienne, Allier, Saône-et-Loire and the Jura. Not only do all other departments in the southern zone have a ratio that is lower than the average, but it is there that we find, with the particular exception of the department of the Seine, those where the ratio is at its lowest. The departments of the Seine, the Nord, the Moselle and the Haut-Rhin are exceptions when we look at the northern part of the country as a whole. For different reasons they are all regions where the German presence was strong. Here it is a question of quantity and the important number of political collaborators who were tried and convicted – those who belonged to collaborationist organizations in Paris, or to the Nazi party in Alsace-Moselle – by comparison with other regions, relegates women very much to the background. The severity of the courts towards women was undoubtedly influenced by the length of time a region or department was under occupation though these differences are not reflected by the cartographical analysis[28] of the role of the courts at the *épuration* when the two sexes are examined.

'Sleeping with the Enemy'

As judgements were passed by the courts, contradictions in the way sexual relationships with members of the occupying forces were assessed

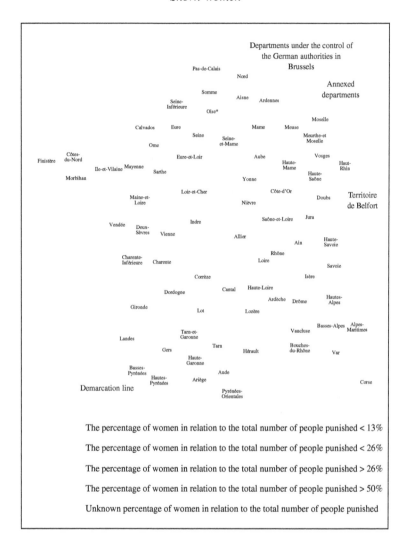

Departments under the control of
the German authorities in
Brussels

Annexed
departments

Pas-de-Calais

Nord

Somme

Aisne   Ardennes

Seine-
Inférieure   Oise*

Moselle

Calvados   Eure   Marne   Meuse

Seine   Seine-   Meurthe-et
Orne   et-Marne   Moselle

Côtes-   Eure-et-Loir   Aube   Vosges
Finistère   du-Nord   Haute-   Haut-
Ile-et-Vilaine   Mayenne   Marne   Rhin
Sarthe   Haute-
Morbihan   Yonne   Saône

Maine-et-   Loir-et-Cher   Côte-d'Or   Doubs   Territoire
Loire   Nièvre   de Belfort

Vendée   Indre   Saône-et-Loire   Jura
Deux-
Sèvres   Vienne   Allier   Ain   Haute-
Savoie

Charente-   Rhône
Inférieure   Charente   Loire   Savoie

Corrèze   Isère

Dordogne   Cantal   Haute-Loire
Ardèche   Drôme   Hautes-
Gironde   Lot   Lozère   Alpes

Basses-Alpes   Alpes-
Tarn-et-   Vaucluse   Maritimes
Landes   Garonne
Gers   Tarn   Bouches-
Haute-   Hérault   du-Rhône   Var
Garonne
Basses-   Aude
Pyrénées   Hautes-
Demarcation line   Pyrénées   Ariège   Corse
Pyrénées-
Orientales

The percentage of women in relation to the total number of people punished < 13%

The percentage of women in relation to the total number of people punished < 26%

The percentage of women in relation to the total number of people punished > 26%

The percentage of women in relation to the total number of people punished > 50%

Unknown percentage of women in relation to the total number of people punished

The percentage of women punished by the courts.

became clear. From January to April 1945, different reports and exchanges of letters indicate how points of view and sentences could vary, reflecting the different directives about the repression of collaboration. None of these directives openly declares a sexual relationship to be a collaborative act. The order of 26 December 1944 to which reference has already been made, defines in Article 2 what 'in particular constitutes a crime of

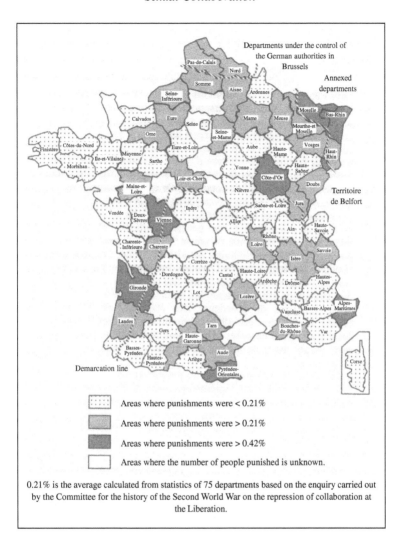

Departments under the control of
the German authorities in
Brussels

Annexed
departments

Territoire
de Belfort

Demarcation line

Areas where punishments were < 0.21%

Areas where punishments were > 0.21%

Areas where punishments were > 0.42%

Areas where the number of people punished is unknown.

0.21% is the average calculated from statistics of 75 departments based on the enquiry carried out
by the Committee for the history of the Second World War on the repression of collaboration at
the Liberation.

Areas where people were punished in relation to the population as a whole.

national unworthiness'. No one of the six types of crime envisaged includes sexual relationships with Germans.[29] It is, therefore, the non-exclusive nature of 'in particular' which allows certain people to elaborate on what constitutes national unworthiness.[30] The state authorities held two different positions. Some, sensitive to public opinion, preferred to see women who had collaborated condemned, either because that corresponded with their perception of the *épuration* or because they feared that public disturbances would occur if these women were to be released. Others, like those responsible for criminal matters in the Ministry of Justice, tended to be concerned above all about legality and did not want to see the *épuration* extended to very ordinary cases that would then threaten social stability.

In several departments, women who were accused of horizontal collaboration were systematically sent to the civic courts. That was the case for those which depended on Besançon (the departments of the Doubs, Jura, Haute-Saône, and Territoire de Belfort), on Caen (the departments of Calvados, Manche and Orne), on the regional police headquarters of Clermont[31] (the departments of Allier, Cantal, Haute-Loire and Puy-de-Dôme), and Finistère. In the case of the department of the Vosges, the prefect turned to the Minister of Justice to know whether it was 'possible to prosecute in cases of crimes against the nation, women whose behaviour with members of the occupying forces had been notorious'. He had already received two contradictory replies; two inspectors had responded affirmatively and against that the prosecutor general had said that these women could only be prosecuted in the event of their having committed offenses 'which had made contacts with the enemy easier'. The prefect then phrased his request: 'I should be obliged to you to let me know which of these two proposals is the correct one'.[32] A judgement passed at the court of appeal in Angers dated 10 March 1945, serves to confirm differences of this nature:

> Whereas X has been accused of having knowingly helped the Germans directly or indirectly, notably by regularly receiving in her home German soldiers, having had sexual relations with them, the civic court has made a note of the fact specified in this way and has applied Article 1 of the order of 26 December 1944 . . . but whereas this action as stated by the prosecution and the sentence passed do not fit with the crime as defined in Article 1; and whereas the judgement challenged has no legal basis, for these reasons: judgement annulled.[33] A case of a similar kind occurred in the court of appeal in Rennes in 4 December 1945.[34]

Such differences as these and embarrassed questions put by a number of prefects or general prosecutors give rise to certain questions put to the Ministry of Justice ordering the General Inspection of Judicial Services to request directives from the Direction of Criminal Affairs. From the point of view of the order of 26 December 1944, there is no ambiguity and the prefect of the Vosges receives the reply: 'There is no legislative text that allows people to be prosecuted simply on account of having had sexual relationships with soldiers in the German army.' Although it was aware that there was considerable pressure to introduce a punishment for the women who were supposed to have collaborated, the board for criminal affairs explicitly decided against it. It also rejected the idea of giving instructions in a circular letter because it considered it would not have sufficient legal status. The legislative approach was also rejected for three reasons. First, 'as far as this matter is concerned [sexual relations with the occupying forces], proof is particularly difficult to establish and the risks of judicial error would be all the more to be feared'. Secondly, 'it would be necessary to distinguish between women who had quite openly taken a German soldier as a partner and those who, like professionals, had not so much gone in search of a German as a man. But it is obvious that to discriminate in such a way would be very difficult, as it would be to introduce a text which dealt with it.' And the final argument that 'to apply such a text could be unfortunate in many cases, notably when a married woman or above all the wife of a prisoner of war was concerned. It seems that in the name of national interest, such licentious behaviour should be forgotten.' Whether it was a problem associated with the definition of such crimes and with demonstrating that they had been committed, or simply a concern for public order, this was the approach adopted. Nevertheless the true response seems entirely pragmatic:

> but it is possible that in certain cases the attitude of women who are guilty have made people in general feel uneasy and this in turn can threaten national unity. Assuming this might be true and in view of what consequences their conduct might produce, these women can be brought before the civic courts according to Article 1 of the order of 26 December 1944. I am of the opinion, however, that no ruling about this matter can be without its problems and it is a matter for the government commissioners alone to work out what kinds of legal pursuit should be adopted in each individual case.[35]

Concerned with the need to reaffirm the republic's legal authority, those responsible were cautious, but they were also aware of the danger that public opinion could be varied and national unity threatened. Even if it was now a distant threat, the war was not yet over and the *épuration* during the first months of 1945 was not simply a matter for the courts. During the winter, attacks on prisons and demonstrations were numerous: pressure in favour of a thorough cleansing was strong and those guilty of 'horizontal collaboration' were not spared.

Everyone on the Look Out for Signs of Collaboration

Put on one side by the Committee for national liberation and then by the provisional government, the issue of sexual relations with the enemy was nonetheless of major concern in occupied France. In July 1940 Jean Texcier lists in eleventh place in his thirty-three pieces of advice to the occupied French: 'Remember that any so-called virtuous woman who flirts with one of the occupied forces will be publicly flogged on the other side of the Rhine. When you look at her carefully therefore, take care to choose a sensitive spot and enjoy your pleasure in advance.'[36] Contrary to other 'pieces of advice' he gives, Texcier does not advocate the use of violence.[37] The relationships between French women and German soldiers quickly became the subject of disapproving commentaries and many incidents showed that sexual relationships were considered to be evidence of collaboration. In a queue outside a general store in Beauvais, one woman accused another of 'sleeping with the Boche'; a man from Villers-sur-Coudun let out the remark to a neighbour: 'your daughter is a prostitute for the Boche'; a 'list of prostitutes' was pinned to the door of the town hall in Noailles; the slogan 'go and get stuff . . . by the Boche' was pinned to the door of a woman's house in Crépy-en-Valois.[38] These four incidents which took place during the first months of 1941 in the department of the Oise show that when people wanted to get rid of the occupying forces, they wanted to get rid of their women friends as well. Insults were aimed as much at French women as at members of the occupying forces. These incidents do not simply illustrate an instant reaction towards behaviour for which there was disapproval; they also play a part in a collective memory. It was common for a woman to be challenged at the Liberation for matters which dated from long before. At Jaux (in the Oise), a woman had her head shaved because she had had drinks with German soldiers in 1940.[39] Numerous tales that create a picture of regular amorous relationships can be taken as evidence of acceptance of the Occupation.

Tracts or underground papers adopt the same attitude. Writing in the style of the Ten Commandments one witty author commands: 'Thou shalt not hide thy disgust at women who take Germans for lovers.'[40] In Corsica a 'song of the Resistance and struggle' written in 1942, calls on women of the island not to frequent Italian soldiers: 'Women of Corsica be generous, / Preserve your mother's virtues,/ The Italians never enjoyed their esteem, / Vow that they will have nothing more.'[41] Not only is sexuality seen as the outlet for one form of collaboration, it also becomes an element in what appears to be more and more like a form of Resistance. After accusations came threats, such as those in the underground press which set out to denounce collaborators. Whether they were called 'In the koll . . .', 'Sluts and Company', 'Those who betrayed', or simply 'Black list', the threats against those who had got too close to the German soldiers increased.[42]

Everyone was on the look out for sexual collaboration long before the Liberation arrived. The number of women who were arrested or had their head shaved for this reason subsequently is not surprising and is simply an expression of a feeling that was shared by the population at large, as well as by those who belonged to resistance groups. Unlike in the case of denunciation when discretion was normal, or going to work voluntarily in Germany, or collaborating for economic reasons, which generally took place in offices rather than in the open, or political commitment, which was often less publically demonstrated, to frequent German soldiers was something that could be observed every day. To be spotted walking, to be seen talking on the terrace of a cafe, or to receive visits from the German soldier were for everyone some of the many proofs of complicity. At the time of the *épuration* the reproach made against women was often expressed as 'flaunting themselves with Germans'. The importance given to 'horizontal collaboration' can be explained by the fact that it was so obvious, but it was also a factor in getting closer to the enemy.

Different Forms of 'Horizontal Collaboration'

Although sexual relationships with the enemy did not have a single nature, it is possible to categorize them in certain ways. This work has already been carried out by Anette Warring[43] for the *Tyskerpiger*, (*The Germans' Girls*), a nickname given to Danish women who had relationships with German soldiers.

It is based on the way in which their frequentation could be divided into five different types: prostitutes; those who had a discreet relationship with a German soldier whom they met by chance; women who frequented Germans in groups and who flaunted this fact publicly; those who came into contact with them for reasons of work; those for whom such relationships were merely an extension of their sympathy for Germany or for Nazi ideology.

This model differs from the usual one, which defines collaboration by motive or by the kinds of acts carried out. Here, instead, collaboration is judged according to how visible these relationships were.

Indulgence for Prostitutes

Although it has been given little attention, prostitution held an important role in the relationships between the local population and the occupying troops. In the Parisian region alone, thirty-one brothels were reserved for German soldiers, to which we should add more than 5,000 prostitutes working outside such houses and maybe as many as one hundred thousand underground prostitutes.[44] Brothels became a place where the German military presence was strong and as a result became targets for the Resistance. Attacks were made on them in Tours, Lorient Arles or again in Marseille where sixty soldiers were wounded, although we do not know what happened to the prostitutes there.[45] At the Liberation quite a few people asked questions about the money that had been made by these establishments during the Occupation. On 3 March 1945 a judge at Beauvais was quite precise about this in a letter he sent to the prefect: 'If a brothel is closed down it should not benefit from any compensation. Many of these places deserve to be sent to the committee dealing with illegal profits because they have done business with the enemy.'[46] Suspicion of this kind directed against brothels did not go unrecorded either by the law known as the Marthe Richard law of 13 April 1946.

It is not easy to be precise about the place which prostitutes had in the definition of 'horizontal collaboration'. First of all we have to distinguish between professional prostitutes whose relationships were merely temporary and those who carried on prostitution illegally, or on an occasional basis only, who were more likely to flaunt their relationships with Germans. Another difficulty arises from the fact that so many women were indiscriminately called prostitutes, whatever their relationship with Germans. Whether or not they were slang terms (*putain*, *poule de luxe*, *hétaïre*, *garce* or *courtisane*), they are found in all the sources of information on this topic, but more than describing prostitutes specifically, they were used rather to condemn any women who had sexual relationships with Germans.

In Lyon in April 1945 the prefect had released from prison, or had sent to the civic courts, twenty-seven women who by and large had been arrested for having been 'prostitutes and for having had relationships with Germans, but who had not in any real sense indulged in political activity.'[47] Nonetheless they had already been in prison for more then seven months. In the Ardennes, at Rodez (in the Aveyron), at Ruffec (in the Charente), at Saintes (in the Charente-Inférieure), at Auxonne (in Côte-d'Or), in Avéron-Bergelle (in the Gers), at Libourne (in the Gironde), at Blois (in the Loir-et-Cher), at Creutzwald (in the Moselle), at Beauvais (in the

Oise), at Saint-Omer (in the Pas-de-Calais), at Thiers (in the Puy-de-Dôme), at Rueil-Malmaison and Saint-Maur-des-Fossés (in the Seine), at Deux-Sèvres, at Albi (in the Tarn), and probably in lots of other places as well, prostitutes had their heads shaved even though it is difficult to know whether they were professionals or not.

The whole situation is made more imprecise by the significant difference between the number of women designated specifically as prostitutes and the few cases recorded in files established at the *épuration*. In the Oise[48] there are records of only four prostitutes having been imprisoned, one in the Hérault, in the Indre and in the Charente, and none in the Moselle. There are a few other individual cases that could be added as well in the Jura and in the Yonne, but they are generally so rare that they can be seen to have benefited from considerable indulgence. These nine women convicted also either got off lightly, or were not punished at all. In the case of the two Parisiennes arrested in the Oise, they were imprisoned for a few days, even though they had been caught in the company of an armed division of the German army; another woman who had denounced someone who had accused her to the *Feldgendarmerie* of having slept with the 'Boche', was condemned to six months imprisonment. This kind of indulgence was in general quite widespread. In February 1945 the Republican commissioner in Poitiers recorded that certain civil courts 'refused to have French nationality taken away from women who were professional prostitutes because it was considered that their behaviour was indeed professional and in no way political.'[49] Such leniency was also voiced by a number of newspapers such as the *Rouergue républicain*, which considered that between 'prostitution of the soul' and 'prostitution of the body', the latter 'was not the one to be condemned more'.[50] In the Hérault the writers of a tract of the national liberation movement (MLN) put in the window of its local offices a statement to the effect that 'the intellectual prositution of Dr Kollaborateur was infinitely more serious than the bodily prostitution of a young woman who had been abandoned'.[51] The most revealing case of the role played by such ambiguity comes from the departmental committee of the Liberation in the Pyrénes-Orientales. In September 1944, the committee decided in fact 'that with the exception of prostitutes working in recognised brothels, women who had had sexual relationships with Germans should have their heads shaved. They would also be as well obliged to undergo a twice weekly visit to the doctor, during the period of six months, in the same way as professional prostitutes.'[52] In this way, all of those women guilty of 'horizontal collaboration' were categorized as prostitutes even though the prostitutes themselves were spared the punishment of having their heads shaved. The ambiguity is obvious. The immorality of which they were condemned relates both to their relations with the enemy and to their sexual behaviour. In this way they were not subject to the social control that the CDL wanted to impose. The official confirmation of professional prostitutes' activity meant, in fact, that they did not have to be recategorized at the Liberation.

Reactions could then be very varied and the degree of fraternization seen in a contradictory way. The professional nature of prostitutes' relationships with the enemy could be taken as evidence of an absence of real feelings and they would be treated leniently. In contrast, in other cases the frequency of contacts can explain why prostitutes were punished by having their heads shaved.

To Love the Enemy

To tackle the subject of love stories is not easy. In most cases the sentimental dimension of these relationships is blotted out and the number of occasions when they can be seen to have been based exclusively on love are rare. Certainly women would use love as an excuse. The woman who was interned in the camp at Jayat at Charente 'claims that it is not a crime to have had relationships based on love with a German when one has had difficulties with one's husband, and in any case matters of the heart have nothing to do with politics.'[53] The young girl from Saint-Clément in the Yonne defended herself when she was interviewed by the police:

> I met a non-commissioned German officer. I became his mistress. He sometimes came to the house to help my father when he was ill. When he left, he left me his *Feldpost* number. I wrote to him and had my letters taken to him by other Germans because I could not use the postal services in France. I wrote to him for two or three months but I do not have his address anymore. I can assure you he is the only German with whom I had any relationship.[54]

Some files do mention stable relationships – 'they were considered to be a regular couple'[55] – or a project of marriage and recognise the entirely sentimental nature of the affair. And yet the possibility of a true love story between a French woman and a German man is something most people found difficult to conceive. Luc Capdevila[56] has already shown in his study of 189 women who were persecuted for sentimental collaboration after the Germans had finally surrendered in the Lorient, the contrast between the number of lovers these women actually had and the common image of sexual behaviour that had become completely out of control.

Nearly half of the women said they had had only one lover. His study is corroborated by the fact that in most of the accounts of the period dealing with relationships with Germans, women are considered to be motivated solely by immorality, desire, thoughtlessness, or a love of Germany. In August 1944 a condemnation was published by *L'Appel de la Haute-Loire*:

> in most cases there was no trace of love whatsover in these relationships. Quite often German officers would use these girls as sources of information for the Gestapo. As for these generous love goddesses, it is not for the fine eyes of the German officers that they put the lives of their compatriots in the hands of the Gestapo.[57]

Any relationship between a German man and a French woman could only be thought of as one between a person whose country had been occupied and an occupier. Photographs of couples used as evidence for conviction in files at the time of the *épuration* were, for those people who figured in them, no doubt the record of a real relationship, but the presence of a German uniform would wipe out any other meaning such a photograph might have for the members of the committees.

The context in which statements and testimonies feature in the files of the *épuration* clearly did little to advantage true feelings. It is rare to find archives of a private nature such as correspondence, private diaries or photographs. Exceptionally such documents will testify to true feelings of love, such as a photograph in which a German soldier in uniform[58] can be seen to have his arm around the waist of the woman who is accused, or again the letter written in clumsy French in which a soldier announces his departure and the beginning of a long separation:

> My dearest Jeanne, first of all we got orders that we were going to leave during last night, but we are still here today. But we will leave tonight. I can't forget you and the hours we spent together. Jeanne, violent fighting awaits us, but I will have the happiness of God, who has not wished that we should once be separated . . . and so I am leaving you with my heart full of your face and very distressed. A thousand, thousand kisses and do not forget your [illegible – probably his first name].[59]

In testimonies of love and affection, the war is never completely absent. And yet sentimental relationships did exist despite the extremely difficult circumstances in France between French women and German soldiers and beyond the Rhine between French prisoners of war and German women.

The study of such a phenomenon has been completely neglected by historians of the twentieth century and especially by those of the periods of war. This can be easily explained given the need to study the political, military, ideological and social aspects of the Second World War. And yet even though love holds such an essential place in the life of any individual, it has still remained unexplored as a subject. Understanding why and how thousands of people experienced such relationships would bring an extra essential element to our understanding of societies at war. Studying the way in which conflict can upset private intimate relationships, or how on the contrary such relationships can create, even if only temporarily, moments of escape, would allow us to understand far better the impact of such crises for each individual. This is a vast and unknown area still remaining to be explored.

Pro-German Sympathy?

To demonstrate sympathy for the Germans in a public manner was a point of no return in any consideration of relationships with the enemy. From a legal point of view 'Sexual relationships . . . by the way in which they are flaunted and are scandalous . . . can be considered to be an act of real propaganda.'[60] Articles in newspapers and testimonies also bring out the importance of this. To be seen with a German once and for all destroys any opposition between real intimacy and 'collaboration', and any private relationship is considered politically significant. The same is true also for women who were employed by the Germans. If the majority of testimonies, whether forming part of an accusation or a defence, deals with the reality of the situation, professional relationships obviously attract suspicion. There were many women who, without actually working for the Germans came into contact with them – shopkeepers, waitresses, or sales persons. It was not what contribution such commercial or professional relationships made to the German economy that was important, nor how frequent private relationships were, but how they were perceived publicly as evidence of real sympathy for the Germans.

Sexual Relationships and Political Contact: Women in Favour of the Nazis

It is difficult to trace the development of women who were in favour of the Nazis over the whole period and to know whether their opinions dated from the period before the Occupation, or whether they were a result of it. Furthermore, any traditional representations of the way in which women were politically committed often blur the distinction between a choice based on feelings and one that is based on politics. The account of a court session in the Hérault that appeared on 27 October 1944 in the daily paper *Midi libre* offers an example of this:

> This young woman who is in the dock and who has a scarf around her head in order to hide her shorn head from the public was *a champion of the collaboration in all its forms.* In 1941 she became the mistress of a German soldier. She joined the Collaboration group in Sète in July 1942 so that she could stay close to the man she considered to be her fiancé. 'Love has no barriers' she declared. She was a shorthand typist and 'the Germans' girl' in various businesses run by the Boche and in other pro-Nazi propaganda organizations. After having subsequently been the mistress of two German officers, she fell into the arms of the General Commissioner of the PPF and on this occasion, so that nothing could be between her and the one she loved, she joined the Party. Condemned in 1944 to three months imprisonment for abortion, she changed her address and identity once she came out, but alas not her way of life. This accused woman, who seems to know how to play the game, is defending herself against the charge of having collaborated with the Gestapo. We have reports, however, accusing her of having denounced Vaillant who made anti-German speeches. This accusation cannot be proved. In spite of that in an indictment which is supported by the general public, the commissioner for the government has asked for a sentence of hard labour for life. This is the sentence which the court is pronouncing.[61]

To take a lover and to join a party or organization were often seen to go together. The ideological choice is only one of the many facets of the commitment entered into by women who had collaborated. To work for the Germans, to belong to a collaborationist organization, to have sexual relationships with Germans, to express sympathy for them, to indulge in threats of denunciation – all of these could amount to creating the picture of women 100 per cent committed to collaboration and often described as '100 per cent German' or '100 per cent Nazi'. No matter how serious the crimes for which they were sentenced and how heavy the penalties, the accusation of having had a sexual relationship remains integral to the idea of female collaboration.

Fantasies Associated with Female Collaboration

At the Liberation, the fact that a woman had slept with a German was considered to be an act of collaboration and punished accordingly, even though in a strict sense sexual relationships did not constitute a threat to the rest of the population and had no influence either on the way the war developed or on the daily circumstances of the Occupation. The gap between the reality of the event and the way in which it was perceived is particularly clear. I have shown that one of the reasons for this is the way in which it was seen publicly, but that is not the sole explanation. The majority of the documents that I have been able to consult reveal a view of the collaboration that is not simply sexual, but sexist, and forces us to consider it from a cultural point of view.

The language in which female collaboration is discussed is quite different from that dealing with men. It reflects an image of women who are incapable of acting on their own initiative, either because they follow the man with whom they share their lives, or because of something in their nature. Without being referred to systematically the idea of female irresponsibility indicates an attitude still prevalent six years after the law of February 1938 cancelling the Labour Code.

In Montpellier at least twenty-three women were arrested simply because they were the wives of collaborators. Alongside the husband who belonged to the *milice*, who was an agent for the Gestapo or worked for the Germans, we find the image of a collaborationist couple joined as much in crime as in marriage. Husband and wife appear to benefit together from their collaboration, whether they are at the head of a business that profits from its dealings with the Germans, whether they simply display their pro-German feelings, or worse, whether they act as informers for the Gestapo.

Submission to the husband's will is rarely offered as extenuating evidence and the best case was that of a woman who belonged to the *Frauenshaft* at Richemont in the Moselle. She was 'influenced by her husband who belonged to the SS and was one of its most fanatical members in the commune.'[62] That did not prevent her from having her head shaved when she came back from Germany in June 1945. While the wife would in most cases follow the husband, marriage implied complicity and shared commitment and in turn led to similar punishments. We have the example of a trial of a collaborationist couple at Feuquières in the Oise: 'Madame collaborated more intimately with these gentlemen since they passed the pox on to her which she then naturally enough gave to her husband (were they not married under the system of sharing their property?) . . . and so she had her head shaved at the Liberation and in good company. M. and Mme should be punished in an exemplary way and made to take their undesirable presences out of France at once.'[63] Everything here comes together perfectly. Venereal disease, more than a punishment for reprehensible behaviour, stigmatizes a relationship with Germans and then rebounds onto the husband.

At Carcassonne the attempted lynching of a member of the Legionary service directly involved his wife:

> Yesterday evening at about 20:30 in the Café Calmet, there was an incident which occurred during the Sunday dance . . . X was brutally hit in the face and so was his wife who was trying to protect him. The person who attacked him having shouted: 'Get him outside! He's a member of the *milice* and a collaborator' the crowd tarred and feathered him. He managed to escape, however, and get back to his house pursued by about fifteen other people. Cobble stones were thrown at the front of his house and two windows were broken.[64]

This woman was struck because she tried to protect her husband, even though no other accusation had been made about her. The fact that they were married took precedence over the facts and turned her into a collaborator as well.

The violence directed at women on account of their attitude towards their husbands reflected a state of exceptional tension. It did not signify a different perception of marriage, but nonetheless underlined a view that refused to see women as individuals in their own right.

Another illustration of the misogynistic and secular way women were perceived can be found in the explanations given for their behaviour.[65] The prosecutor in the court in Montpellier claimed in the case he was making against three young women who had belonged to the *milice* in the Hérault that 'women will always be inferior'. Carelessness, greed or immorality, seen as natural, were always offered in explanation of women's actions, however serious, and were taken into account before any opinions they might hold. In any representation of women who collaborated what is always present is the idea of the 'weaker sex'.[66]

At the centre of many acts of collaboration was money. The German mark, hugely overvalued,[67] gave German troops important purchasing power, which was all the more acute in a period when goods were in short supply. Whether it was to pay for denunciation, to pay a prostitute, or to provide a salary for a voluntary worker, 'German money' became one of the proofs of having been compromised. Questioned by the police in the Oise on the 'conduct and morality' of a young girl in his commune, the local gamekeeper offered as proof of her behaviour that she had boasted of having got a 'hundred franc bill'.[68]

Depending on the witnesses, greed was denounced in a variety of ways. On a platform set up for the purposes of a *tonte*, a notice read:

'shame to those women who are in love with the mark';[69] a woman from Grenoble was reproached for 'being too fond of money'.[70] At Troyes a brochure issued by the CDL recalls the fact that 'women who for a few marks did not fear to dishonour themselves'[71] had been arrested, and at Evreux, *L'Eure libérée* condemned a woman who had gone so far as to denounce 'her husband who accused her of spending too much money'.[72] In such denunciations of women we find as well the misogynistic representations of the woman who overspends, the values brought by the Resistance[73] and the working class, which rejected money,[74] but we also find at a more profound level the presence of a Judaeo-Christian morality and of the sin of greed. In an article issued by the CDL in the Lot-et-Garonne collaboration is no longer evoked: 'An old popular song has come back into fashion – the one that used to be sung some twenty years ago: 'They've all had their hair cut.' It concerns all of those who from vice or from greed have given up all moral sense and dignity. *It is not true to say that money does not smell.* But the exhibition made of these dreadful creatures is unhealthy and should stop. All they deserve is total scorn.'[75] When he writes about the women in Agen who had their heads shaved, the author offers only greed and vice as the reasons for their behaviour during the Occupation and the sole punishment or disapproval that he offers is a moral one.

A third reason given for these women's behaviour is their easy or deplorable morals. In descriptions of women of 'doubtful morality', it is common to find mentioned facts that have nothing to do whatsoever with German presence: 'The woman L who is of easy virtue (she had a child before her marriage and a second one with a lover in 1943, during the time her husband was a prisoner of war), is said to have been the mistress of the Bosch.'[76] Immorality encompasses everything whether it be sexual relations before marriage, adultery or frequenting German soldiers. To denounce behaviour of this kind in such a way reveals a moral stance that is not entirely free from ambiguity. The natural immorality of women is in some way revealed and confirmed through their relationships with Germans. The account of a visit paid to the prison of Montluc at Lyon gives us a picture that is a long way away from that of somewhere where people were in prison for collaboration:

Montluc is no longer Montluc . . . As for the area where the women are housed it seems to be a matter for the police responsible for moral behaviour. When we go into their cells we are met with little laughs and nudges. In the courtyard where the women prisoners exercise – some of them hide their shaved heads by wearing turbans – there are outbreaks of talking and laughter.

When our photographer was getting his equipment ready, they all rushed off like birds.[77]

The importance of misogynous stereotypes tends to obscure the political dimension of women's collaboration.

It is as difficult to unravel the interwoven complexities of moral condemnation and punishment as it is to estimate the influence of the male view of these women. The young woman member of the *milice* mentioned above who was described as being 'eternally inferior' was sentenced to two years' imprisonment with reprieve by the court of justice in Montpeller. Did the judges treat her leniently on account of her lack of care due to her young age and to her sex, or because of her actions or because her involvement with the *milice* was limited to being a nurse? In this way female nature is put forward as an explanation for the way a lot of women behaved towards the occupying forces and yet the courts punished a more significant number of women at the moment of Liberation than in peace time. The irresponsibility of women is only a partial excuse for their behaviour, but the way in which it is discussed adds to the confusion when the acts which they have committed are being defined. Such ambiguity goes some way to explain the choice of a punishment that combines moral humiliation with a sentence passed for strictly political reasons.

Suffering versus Pleasure

The gap between the symbolic importance that has been attributed to sexual relations with Germans and their total lack of influence on events can only be understood if we look at the way people at the time imagined them. How otherwise is it possible to explain that a visit to the cinema or a bouquet of flowers could become factors in cases brought against women? Out of the daily picture of French women and German soldiers being together, a multitude of facts emerge that were open to exaggeration and different interpretations. Stories and fantasies could give rise at the same time to a picture of suffering, of dignity and of hope and one in which treason would lead to the withdrawing of citizens' rights. As the Home Secretary Pierre-Henri Teitgen declared in April 1946, those who had collaborated had betrayed France 'in her soul'.[78]

Recent work has highlighted how difficult daily life during the Occupation could be and the tragic appearance it often had.[79] Certainly there were discrepancies between departments where there were no shortages of food, those where people were starving and those in between; rural areas and towns were set against one another and finally social inequalities became more marked at a time when certain people had enough money to allow them to continue to live comfortably.

However, the constant reduction in rations and in the number of available workers, the fact that adolescents were becoming physically weaker, that there was a rise in infant mortality and an increase in the number of cases of tuberculosis, were the realities of a situation, which, as Dominique Veillon has said, was evidence of 'a population in a bad way'. The situation worsened during the first months of 1944 and any hopes that there would be a rapid improvement once the country had been freed soon gave way to the reality of the situation during the winter of 1944–5 and the realization that hardship was continuing.

The reality of the suffering experienced helps explain the accounts of the lives led by women accused of having collaborated and the charges brought against them. The many evocations of material advantages and of privileges provide us with the negative image of daily misery. The list of products obtained from the Germans tells us as much about the way in which people imagined the lives of these women to have been as the frustrations that they themselves experienced. At a time when supplies were the principal occupation, food became a major concern. Others were those typical of times of hardship and a part of the well-known picture we have of the Occupation – a sack of coal, cigarettes or a pair of stockings.

Taken in isolation, accusations appear derisory, but each item of food or clothing mentioned in this way was for those involved proof that another way of living during the war was possible. Two opposing images of these dark years emerge: on the one hand the threat of the morrow when it might not be possible to have heat, to eat or to provide clothes for children; and on the other, a carefree and abundant life in which the threat of the following day simply did not exist.

Overall these differences in day-to-day life were part of a larger picture in which, while the country as a whole had suffered, the lives of a few changed. That many women accused of collaboration at the Liberation had known difficulties themselves in just the same way did not mean that they would not be excluded. The German presence blurred social reality; privileges that resulted from it overcame class conflict and drew instead a new barrier between those who had profited and the rest. Women in particular were targets of accusations of collaboration directed at the French bourgeoisie and a number of articles at the time condemn 'a particular high society woman, a shopkeeper who could not make hardship her excuse'[80] or 'those grand lovers whose position in society gave them impunity'.[81] Nonetheless in most cases a neighbour who was denounced for privileges she had received had enjoyed them not as the result of her social origins, but thanks to her relationship with the enemy.

Each bread ticket, each bar of chocolate, implied the disgrace that came with the comforts brought by the enemy. At Luchon in the Haute-Garonne, one witness was in no doubt, having watched the goings on of a local woman that '[her German lover] had a bag that was heavily laden and certainly full of food'.[82] At Ligny-le-Châtel a market gardener declared about a neighbouring family reputed to be collaborators that 'nothing was lacking in that house, the most disgusting things happened there'; and another: 'I often went there to get Champagne which they drank with Germans'.[83] The dividing line can be found everywhere and is explained as much by the insistence on the need to remain dignified as by the many examples of relationships with the enemy.

The news sheet issued by the CDL in the Haute-Loire made this opposition quite clear:

> A very large majority of women have been dignified and have kept their distance and even those who were tortured by hunger and have been left to their own devices refused to recognize the presence of enemy soldiers and those wearing a German uniform. Others, far fewer in number, have let themselves go. Too bad. Stained by their relationships with Germans they will be considered as if they had the plague. They deserve what happens to them.[84]

Any doubtful behaviour allowed people to drag up reputations that certain women had before the war, to expose what went on in their private lives and to condemn their behaviour. Comings and goings, the sound of riotous parties or simply of music, scenes watched furtively or through half opened doors were developed into stories in which fantasy and imagination played as much a part as reality. In this way people invaded the private lives of these women and invented stories full of debauchery and sexual excitement. An agricultural worker from the Yonne recalled 'having seen [the village primary school teacher] give French lessons to the German officer while her sister was sitting on his lap. This took place in the shoe shop.'[85] The dressmaker from a village in the Var related how 'One day I saw the three young primary school teachers in the village enjoying themselves, laughing and joking with German officers and dressed in swimming costumes they played at soaking themselves in the school playground.'[86] Descriptions that emphasize dress and behaviour are many and taken together they create an overall image of a completely dissolute life. The woodcutter from the Oise stated to the policeman who came to question him: 'In 1940 I took some photographs of Mme X at the time when she was in her shop garden and posing in a way that suggested bad behaviour. I cannot show them to you. I hid them in 1940 and since then I have not been able to lay my hands on them.'[87]

Different degrees of importance can be attributed to sexual behaviour. Like food, it is an element in any description of collaboration, but given that it was essentially pleasurable and something not shared by all, it was seen to be particularly serious. Accusations are not made simply in terms of undignified or unworthy behaviour; other accounts have more specific points to make. The physical union between the French women and the invading forces and Franco-German couples is denounced. Seen to be the absolute outcome of collaboration, it is resolutely rejected. Cross-breeding between victor and the vanquished is seen to be the beginning of the end of the nation. Questioned by police in the Oise about the goings on of a particular woman, a witness said that he had 'heard it said that in the course of one debauched evening Germans had poured Champagne over the head of the girl and that the soldiers licked it as it flowed down her body.'[88] How is it not possible to see in this account the pornographic metaphor of the country which had willingly given itself to an enemy, allowing the enemy to pillage and debauch it?

Not to have shared in the common suffering, to have behaved in an undignified way and not to have hoped in the future were all features of treason. More than a simple acceptance of the situation, sexual relationships were a confirmation of the positive submission to the conqueror, bringing with them the risk of acculturation and the loss of national identity. 'Not one of these women, as they swooned in the arms of the Germans, thought for a moment of the suffering of others, any more than when they drank Champagne with them, did they hope in the eventual victory of France.'[89] This extract taken from an article published in the *Patriote de l'Eure* entitled 'a bombshell' perfectly reflects the point beyond which any women guilty of having made approaches to Germans, however serious, were guilty of treason. We are not considering things in a legal way here with the necessary accumulation of hard facts, but rather an image of betrayal on which the identity of a new liberated nation would be built. As Luc Capdevila has stressed 'the collaborator is more than a traitor, he is someone who has renounced his principles because he has denied his identity'.[90]

The shaving of the heads of women accused of collaboration was an initial punishment, however serious their actions. It was also symbolic in that it marked a break with an enemy most people rejected. But there is a third feature that makes it a more complex matter, namely the way it and the women concerned have been represented *a posteriori*. The *tonte* is gradually seen as the only and exclusive punishment for women who had relationships with Germans. The shaved head becomes extra proof, albeit temporary, of their sexual guilt, as was the *fleur de lys* branded on the shoulders of prostitutes during the Ancien Regime.

Whereas the link between the *tonte* and sexual relationships was recognized at the time, it has since then become more significant to the point where it has resulted in a specific and dominant image of *la tondue*. How we are to measure this shift is not easy. If we concentrate on its symbolic significance, the actual event behind it loses some of its reality and instead feelings and the need for revenge emerge as influential factors. It is important to make it clear that *the shaving of heads was not a punishment for sexual collaboration, but a sexist one*.

The victims of it are far from being the only women whose love lives were crushed by the war. Certainly there were among them a number who had collaborated, but that is not enough to explain why so many people, whether or not they form part of the Resistance, were so violent towards women.

−2−

Where and How Many?

From Ajaccio to Lille, from Quimper to Colmar, everywhere throughout France women had their heads shaved. Certainly there were differences. There was no single regional factor that was strong enough to prevent the practice being carried out. And the practice took place as much in the most important of towns as in tiny communities in which there were only a few dozen inhabitants.[1]

Three Characteristic Departments

Out of the ninety departments in existence at the time, three – the Oise, the Côtes-du-Nord and the Indre – are worthy of particular attention. First of all, at the moment of the Liberation, they were the places where the practice was most widely carried out. After that is the fact that in the coastal area of the Côtes-du-Nord, the industrial area of the Oise and the military base at Martinerie in the Indre, there was a strong German presence. This factor is important. Unlike the other two departments, the Indre was in the non-occupied zone until 1942, which leads us to speculate that the Occupation was not a determining factor when it came to the practice of *tontes*. Only in the case of the legal *épuration*, which was much more severe on women in the north of the country, can that claim be made. Above all it was at a local level that the presence of the Germans – and what that implied in terms of personal, professional or physical relationships – which affected how the *épuration* was carried out locally. Finally whether the practice of shaving of heads took place or not, in the smallest of the communes in these three departments, it is the principal towns that stand out. This is accentuated by the first arrests organized by certain Resistance groups and the *tontes* that eventually occurred, particularly in the regions where the *maquis* existed as in Brittany, or where there was, as in the Indre, a strong contingent of the Resistance army. These elements created the right conditions for the practice, but they did not determine how it developed; nor is it possible to work out a geographical distribution.

The Oise and the Importance of Industrial Zones

In the department of the Oise forty communes witnessed *tontes* and ten others are referred to in testimonies even though it is not possible to know whether women actually had their heads shaved or whether they were simply threatened. At her trial in March 1945 a shopkeeper from Barbery said: 'I did not want to stay in the area any longer because people had threatened to cut my hair off.'[2] The fact that she clearly escaped from the anticipated punishment does not tell us anything about whether the same was true for other women in the commune. Where reference is made to the *tonte* in fifty communes in a department in which there were 698 means that it occurred in 7% of them only. Such a proportion might seem small, yet this sample contains the most populated communes – those of Beauvais, Compiègne, Creil, Senlis, Clermont, Noyon. Between them these fifty together account for a third of the department's population.[3] When we examine where they are situated it is particularly interesting that we come up with the main geographical divisions of Picardie.

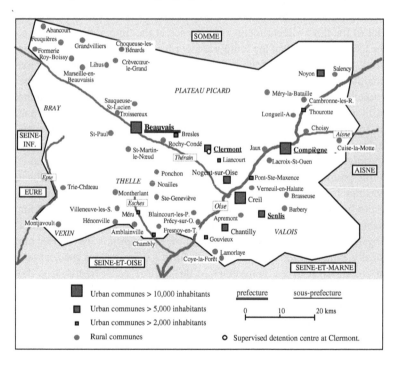

Places where the *tonte* took place in the Oise

Although two-thirds of these communes have a population of less than 2,000 and statistically qualify as rural, the towns and industrial centres had an important place. First there is the valley of the Oise, which crosses the department diagonally from north-east to south-west. Since the nineteenth century a whole series of industrial sites have grown up along this traditional route from Noyon to Chambly, with a particularly dense area south of Compiègne. All these industrial towns witnessed *tontes*: Liancourt, where a Saint-Gobain factory was built in 1940; Creil, specializing in railway materials; or again Noyon, where there was a centre for mechanical engineering. Outside of the valley itself, other communes where the practice took place are those of the industrial towns of Vexin, Méru, Trie-Château and Amblainville, or again the rural ones where there was a high population of working-class people and which are to be found along the Thérain, from Marseille-en-Beauvaisis as far as Creil, without forgetting the town of Beauvais itself. The contrast is marked between these places and the vast agricultural expanses of the Picardie plateau to the north, or the Valois in the south-east, where there are few references to the *tontes* having taken place.

There are various reasons why the department should be divided up in this way. First we have report from the prefect Yves Perony dated 30 September 1944 in which he wrote that 'the arrests made during the first few days and the rather brutal changes made to local councils caused people in the agricultural part of the department to be a little uneasy.' The differences in reactions can be seen as a kind of extension of the war itself which not everyone has experienced in the same way. If the agricultural richness of the Oise meant that the department as a whole did not suffer too much from hardship, Jean-Pierre Besse has nonetheless noted that there were considerable differences between both the country and urban centres that retained strong links with the hinterland (Beauvais, Compiègne, Noyon, Clermont), and working-class communes where the population had been built up by successive waves of population movements and that had few links with the countryside.[4] We can see therefore that those parts of the department that suffered most from hardship were the ones where the German presence was strongest, namely the major industrial and urban centres. It was also there that the Resistance was most active. If the Front national was present right across the department, the Organisation civile et militaire (OCM), whose ranks were swelled by fighters from the Libé-nord movement, was more important around Creil and the principal urban centres. Furthermore, the FFI took part in resistance activities before the arrival of Allied forces at Chantilly, Compiègne, Creil and Beauvais.[5]

All of these factors shed light on how the practice of shaving heads was carried out across the departments, yet even if it was most common in urban and industrial areas, rural areas were also affected. More than two-thirds of the communes were rural and 13 per cent of the women who had their heads shaved owned smallholdings or worked on the land. Although less than half the female population worked on the land this figure reminds us, if there were need, that rural communities were by no means spared.

The Department of the Côtes-du-Nord: The Importance of the Maquis

In Brittany the shaving of heads began before the Liberation in the rural areas of the Argoat where the *maquis* was principally active. Given the strong German presence in the coastal regions the breton *maquis* developed more easily in the inner regions of the department, particularly towards the south-west. In this particular region, Carnoët, Locarn, Lanrivain, Glomel and Mûr-de-Bretagne witnessed the practice of head shaving before the arrival of the Allied forces, as did the region of Guingamp and four other communes further to the east of the department.

With the Liberation the practice became more common in those places where the German presence had been heaviest, namely in the towns and in general along the coast: Perros-Guirec,

Tréguier, Lézardrieux, Bréhat, Paimpol. The *tonte* was practised in most of the ports of Tréguor as well as in the two towns in which there were more than 10,000 inhabitants – Saint-Brieuc (36,674 inhabitants) and Dinan (12,737 inhabitants) – and more or less all the principal towns. Nonetheless, rural communes accounted for 80 per cent of the places where it occurred. We should not forget that the places where people in this region lived were widely scattered which helps explain the existence of rural communities with a population of nearly 4,000. Any attempt to estimate the number of hypothetical cases is also made more difficult by the fact that each of these communes was divided into a number of hamlets.

As in the department of the Oise, the strong German presence here along the coast coincides with the places where the *tontes* were carried out at the Liberation. The fact that in sixteen out of the sixty-two communes, the first incidences of the practice in the Côtes-du-Nord occurred before the Liberation, reveals that the Resistance already had a hand in inflicting this punishment.[6] We shall return to this matter in Chapter Four.

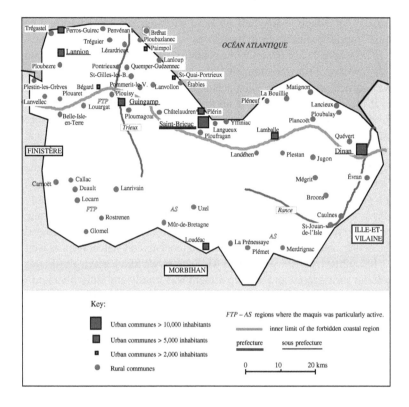

Places where *tontes* took place in the Côtes-du-Nord

The Department of the Indre and the Heaviest German Presence

The situation in the Indre was a distinctive one because, out of the 248 communes, only fourteen appear to have witnessed *tontes*. We can note six of the ten urban communes in the department: the prefécture at Châteauroux and the three sous-préfectures at Issoudun, Le Blanc and La Châtre, two other less important towns of Buzançais and Déols and eight rural communes. Between them these sixteen areas are spread across the whole department and account for 32 per cent of the population. Elsewhere, in other words more or less in all of the rural communes, there was nothing or nearly so. A number of factors explain this imbalance. First of all, the concentration of German troops around Châteauroux and the military base of La Martinerie. There a number of women were employed as servants, laundry workers, maids or cooks. It is one of the reasons for which nearly half of those working in administration who were imprisoned came from this town.

The second factor relates to the conditions under which the department was liberated. From the moment of the Allied landings resistance activity was particularly intense.[7] The secret army and the FTP shared control over the southern, eastern and north-eastern reaches of the department. From the month of July 1944 women accused of collaboration were arrested and had their heads shaved, sometimes in the main square as at La Châtre on 9 July. Even so, the fact that the *maquis* was present did not mean that these areas did not suffer from reprisals exacted by the German troops. However, from 19 August they left the department and the prefecture and the other towns of the department were immediately taken over by the Resistance forces. The situation remained uncertain, however, for German columns coming up from the south-west crossed the department on several occasions and reoccupied Châteauroux as well as Issoudun from 28 August to 11 September 1944 when the Elster column surrendered and the department was finally and fully liberated.

The ongoing uncertainty of the situation had a direct influence on the way the *épuration* developed. Women had their heads shaved in public in the main towns of the Indre immediately after the first liberation and more generally after the second on 12 September 1944. Many women also had their heads shaved during the time they were imprisoned. Arrests continued to be made throughout the summer. Some people were released and then arrested again. Others, however, remained in prison but were transferred to different places as events changed. Given the circumstances people arrested by the FFI were quickly moved into prisons.[8] In Châteauroux, the Rue des Mousseaux was designated as a place where interrogations took place, the barracks as a transit centre and the Bordessoulle barracks as a prison. In the south-eastern part of the department in the area under the control of the *maquis*, the camps at Pouligny Notre-Dame and Lourdoeux-Saint-Michel also acted as places of internment before the Liberation, as did the one further west at Saint-Hilaire. A number of testimonies recall that in these places women had their heads shaved. Three women who lived in the commune near Châteauroux were transferred to the town and there had their hair shaved off. The first, a cleaner from Plusiers, was arrested on 21 August 1944 and then transferred to the Bordessoulle baracks. The second, a market gardener from Montierchaume, was arrested on 23 August 1944 and had her hair cut off the following day at the Bertrand baracks. The third and last example is that of a shorthand typist from Déols whose hair was shaved off in the rue des Mousseaux a fortnight after her arrest on 7 October 1944.[9]

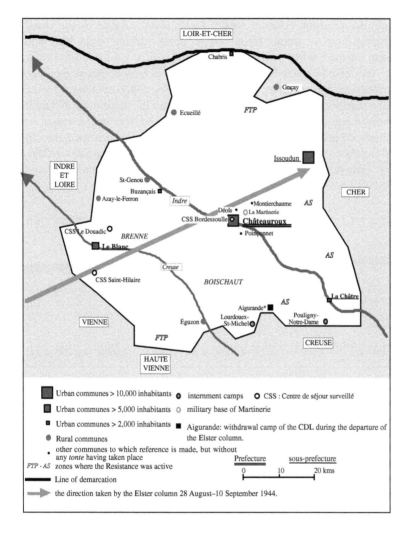

Places where the *tontes* took place in the Indre

The same phenomenon would be seen elsewhere in the Indre; the préfecture, main centres and even smaller places became centres where *tontes* were carried out. On the one hand women who were arrested in nearby communes were transferred to these places with a view to their being interned; on the other, people left to look for women who had been accused of compromising themselves with the enemy and who were still at liberty in nearby villages. In the Indre, therefore, the practice was centred on urban communities, a fact also confirmed by the small proportion of all women (around 6 per cent) working on the land who were interned or had their heads shaved.

The main lesson to be drawn from all this is what it tells us about the underlying organizations. In the Indre the FFI police dominated by the secret army carried out most arrests. It was also in charge of the different internment camps up to the time when the prefect insisted that all prisoners should be transferred to supervised detention centres at the end of October 1944. These were at Le Douadic for men and at Saint-Hilaire for women. In this way any decision to shave off a woman's hair would be taken at a court martial and would be recorded.

```
FFI                                              27 août 1944
  -:-
Secteur I
  -:-
  P C

Madame..... Maîtresse avouée du chef de poste allemand de
Gracay

Sanction : Cheveux coupés et relaxée


(tampon : une croix de Lorraine entouré par la mention FORCES FRANÇAISES DE
L'INTERIEUR)
```

Part of an FFI courts marshall record in the Indre, 27 August 1944.[10]

The fact that the departmental FFI police took overall responsibility for administering punishments sometimes provoked protests. The section of the national liberation committee at Issoudun challenged the decision taken by the departmental committee for having freed a woman who was known to have been the mistress of a member of the *milice* who was shot at the Liberation: 'The people in this little commune are upset. They thought that the FFI had settled the matter but it seems that the woman has not even had her head shaved and has been shown every consideration.'[11]

The Situation in the Towns

Of the twenty-two towns[12] with populations of more than 100,000 at the time, Strasbourg is the only one where there is no mention of a *tonte* having taken place. However, to claim that no woman had had her head shaved there would be risky. In fact the prefect of the Bas-Rhin records in a report dated 15 May 1945 the case of women in the department who had their heads shaved, but without giving any indication of the precise place.[13] National police reports of the same date record that young girls had their head shaved and that there were a number of demonstrations against 'women sympathetic to Germans' in the three former departments which had been annexed.[14] Finally, a fortnight later, several women had their heads shaved at Mulhouse during the night of 31 May and 1 June.[15] More than one assumption can be made encouraging us to imagine that in the Alsation capital, as elsewhere, women had their heads shaved. In any case neither the particular situation of Alsace-Moselle, nor the importance of Strasbourg itself, can explain why this should not be so. The problem created by the fact that there are no records also applies to less important towns in such built up departments as those of the Nord, Pas-de-Calais, Rhône, Seine and the Seine-et-Oise. If we look at a map of the whole of France showing towns with a population of more than 30,000 and where *tontes* were carried out, the special case of the Pas-de-Calais becomes clear.

Out of twenty towns with more than 10,000 inhabitants only Arras (the prefecture), Béthune and Saint-Omer experienced *tontes*. There are mentions made of them in other less important communes, sometimes in the same urban area; there was nothing at Lens, but four women had their heads shaved at Courcelles-lès-Lens on 4 September. In departments where there were so many towns that no single one acted as a centre, it is likely that there is no record of any *tontes* having occurred other than in local memory. However, the relatively important place which this subject had in the regional press suggests that the practice was quite widespread. In the Catholic daily paper *La Croix du Nord* as in *La Liberté du Pas-de-Calais* reports suggest that the practice was not so much exceptional as general. The turban is reported as a feature of the post-war landscape ('Turbans are now the classic headdress for women whose heads were shaved at the Liberation')[16] and the act of shaving itself as an essential part of the Liberation: 'Here is the Liberation! Without making the slightest distinction, one part of the local population wants punishments carried out instantly. Those women accused of being unworthy must be humiliated! – The sentence? – Off with their hair.'[17]

A similar situation existed in the former Department of the Seine where, if the liberation of Paris has been much talked about and studied, that of neighbouring districts has largely been forgotten. In this enormous department with a population of nearly five million, sixty-six communes out of ninety-one had over 10,000 inhabitants. If we find a much more

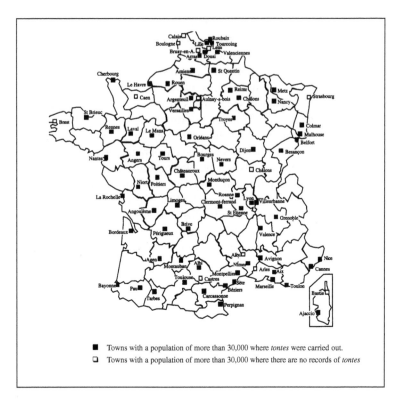

Towns where *tontes* were carried out with a population of more than 30,000 (excluding the department of the Seine).

significant number of towns where cases of heads having been shaved have been recorded – 30 per cent as against 10 per cent for the Pas-de-Calais alone – it is largely due to an archive established from the beginning which contains reports requested by the head teachers and sent to the Teaching Authorities, describing the circumstances and consequences of the Liberation for their schools.[18] In this way, mixed in with a list of the damage suffered by schools in the Seine Department with comments about pupil numbers and teaching staff, we find an account of the shaving of the head of a caretaker in a school in the eighteenth *arrondissement* and the use made of the playground at the Lamartine group of schools at Gentilly for public *tontes*, or again the report that a woman whose head had been shaved was released to the crowd in the Rue des Corbillons in Saint-Denis. Together with a number of others, these documents give us a picture of the Parisian connurbation enclosed between the Arc de

Triomphe, the Hotel de Ville and the Montparnasse district and where everything happened, including head shavings. Like many villages, each district of Paris and a number of neighbouring ones celebrated their freedom and shaved the heads of female collaborators.

The more important the town, the easier it is to trace the accounts of women accused of collaboration who had their heads shaved. However, in the main, records are too general and since the files do not specifically mention this punishment, the victims are difficult to identify. At Beauvais where *L'Oise libérée* for the 2 September 1944 reports the shaving of eighty-four women, there are only three files which refer to women specifically from that town.[19] That can be explained as much by the irregular nature of references to shaving as by the fact that women were brought into the town from nearby villages to have the punishment inflicted.

The pull of a town centre on the surrounding countryside is not unique to Beauvais. It is found in a number of towns which formed the political centre of their region at the moment when they were liberated. As a member of the FTPF remarked forty years after the events, women were regularly rounded up:

> In Saint-Rémy (he was referring to Saint-Rémy-de-Provence) we were conscripted to go and round up girls who had taken refuge in other villages at the Liberation because they were frightened of having their heads shaved. So we set off with a lorry to arrest them. Once we were in Saint-Rémy we sat them down on chairs in the middle of the town square. Their hands were held so the hairdressers could get on with their job. They were really scalped. Shaved with clippers until nothing remained. Once it was all over we put them together to lead them through the village.[20]

... in the Countryside

Compared with those areas with a high urban population the situation in the countryside is even more uncertain: 213 rural communes, of which the smallest had only eighty-three inhabitants, is not very significant in view of the tens of thousands that existed. What use should be made of fragmentary pieces of information obtained for certain districts from the publication many years later of a book of memoirs or personal diaries? If Gertrude Stein's diary informs us that at Culoz in the Ain 'the village is upside down because girls who compromised themselves with Germans during the Occupation are going to have their heads shaved'[21] or if the abbot Marcel Basseville's diary tells us that at Sissy in the Aisne 'things are happening . . . before they left to fight at the front the local Resistance members insisted on giving a lesson to two young women . . . after having shut them up for forty-eight hours in premises in the Rue de Châtillon, they gave them a 'perm' free of charge and let them go again',[22] what can be done about the numerous places for which nobody has provided any history?

With some exceptions certain witnesses – people who went about the surrounding countryside regularly – can provide a better overall picture. For example, a vet from Doudeville in the Caux wrote in his diary on 3 September 1944: 'In nearly all the villages where the women were singled out for their misbehaviour or for having been guilty of denouncing people, heads were shaved.'[23] Such witnesses are rare, however, and in most cases it is a single general remark that tends to group all the villages of a region into a place where the punishment was carried out. Thus in the Rouergue on 28 October 1944 *Le Patriote rouerguat* exclaimed that 'the smallest wigmaker of the most humble village would become one day a valued executer of justice'. *La Libération de l'Aunis et de la Saintonge* explains the importance assumed by the phenomenon in a different way: 'What a story! In a small village children are playing at being in the "Maquis" . . . armed to the teeth with wooden swords they take possession of an orchard, raid the chicken run and let the rabbits out . . . then they 'shave' three little girls.'[24] Obviously no reliable interpretation is possible after such an anecdote as this and the location remains very imprecise. When children copy the behaviour of adults, however, and incorporate into their games a scene which they saw or heard talked about, when they borrow from what is real to enrich their imagination – the swords are made of wood, the prison is a chicken run, but the shaved women are indeed little girls – it is possible to see how influential such a practice was and how it could catch on.

20,000 Shorn Women . . .

In the wake of a *tonte* there is neither corpse, tomb, grave nor inquest over a disappearance, nor reports at the police station of discovered bodies. Nor are there classified files in the judicial archives. Even though the Minister of Justice kept a record of his actions, the Minister of the Interior enquired how many people were interned, and, from 1946, the Police and the Security Department were sent to work out the number of summary executions that took place, nobody seems to have asked how many individuals had their heads shaved.[25] For people who were interned, condemned or executed at the time of the *épuration* there are reliable facts, but no precise estimate has been made of the number of heads that were shaved.

Something like 1,200 references give some idea of how the practice was unequally spread across 623 areas from the whole of France. The range of people who were generally concerned can range from 2,255 to 4,569. This difference may be explained by the difficulty of knowing the precise number of women whose heads were shaved in any given town or a village. Certain references are quite perplexing. What should we make of a 'line of women with shaven heads taken by lorry loads towards the Montluc prison', noted by Georgette Elgey[26] in her diary for 4–7 September 1944. According to the prefect of the Rhône department, 2,000 people were arrested during the month of September 1944.[27] The only man/woman ratio available is for women punished by the courts, and is 12 per cent. If we apply this to persons taken in for questioning, 240 women would have been arrested in the Rhône – plenty enough for there to have been 'lorry loads', but on 18 October 1944 *Le Patriote* noted in an account of a visit to the women's area of the prison that 'A few had their heads shaved and hid them under scarves.' This is an extra piece of vague information since it has to be asked whether what was counted were the heads or the scarves. On the one hand 240, on the other just a few and only four women identified by name in the archives available for consultation as having had their hair shaved. The range is immense and there is no merit in reckoning the truth simply to be somewhere between the two extremes.

Another distinction that has to be made is between references to the act of shaving and women who had had their heads shaved. Quite a few cases are indicated by the files on named individuals and a reference to a single person having 'had her head shaved at the Liberation.' In contrast nearly all of the descriptions of the practice itself use the plural. At Sète *Le Midi libre* described a local woman guilty of collaboration who arrived at the court wearing a scarf. This is the only mention of an individual known for this town, and yet a police report notes: 'By order of the local Committee for National Liberation 18 women recognised to have had intimate relations with soldiers in the occupying army were brought together today at 18:00 hrs on the central Esplanade. In front of a large crowd their hair was cut off with clippers.'[28] In smaller districts it is often by putting together the number of individual cases that we can estimate the collective nature of a *tonte*; at Amblainville in the Oise department,[29] for example, five different reports drawn up during November and December 1944 allow us to count at least five women who had their heads shaved.

Departments	No. of women whose heads were shaved	Total population	Percentage of total population (%)
Côtes-du-Nord	281	527 000	0.05
Hérault	280	461 000	0.06
Indre	50	245 000	0.02
Moselle	114	450 000	0.03
Oise	286	397 000	0.07
Total in Indre and Oise	336	642 000	0.05
Total of the five departments	1,011	2,080,000	

The number of *tontes* carried out in the five selected departments. The Indre and the Oise have respectively the lowest and the highest rate in the sample.

Depending on the regions examined the uncertainties are too numerous and the discrepancies too great to pretend that any exhaustive survey would be possible. However, by opting for a statistical projection based on the five best known departments a general view can be offered. By considering the incidence of head shaving only in these departments (which is far from the total picture), it is possible to estimate the number of people whose heads were shaved in relation to the overall population – 0.02 per cent in the Indre and 0.07 per cent in the Oise, giving overall an average of 0.05 per cent. In towns for which there is numerical evidence, the ratios are often the same or higher. In Albi, Annecy and Creil group photographs allow us to make a precise count, giving us respectively ratios of 0.03 per cent, 0.10 per cent and 0.39 per cent. At Clermont-Ferrand and Sète police reports provide numerical evidence and an identical proportion of 0.06 per cent. A police commissionaire's testimony in Evreux and in the account Elsa Triolet gives us of what happened at Montelimar, indicate almost twice as many in these two towns: 0.05 per cent and 0.03 per cent.[30] In relation to the French population as a whole this leads to an estimate of 23,215 people who had their heads shaved, but if this number is compared to the number of females aged fifteen and above (16,665,000) the proportion of women who had their heads shaved is 0.12 per cent, or in other words slightly more than one woman aged over fifteen out of every thousand.

The estimate of 20,000 women who had their heads shaved is in line with other figures to do with the *épuration;* for example it is more or less the same as that of 19,452 women punished at the Liberation in seventy-six departments, obtained from the departmental enquiries carried out by the Committee for the History of the Second World War.[31] The similarity between the two groups supports the general scale proposed even if it is possible at a local level to find important divergences. In the Côte-du-Nord the legal *épuration* was relatively moderate and the percentage of people who were punished (of both sexes) was lower than the national average. Yet this department was noteable for a particular harshness towards women: 327 women were punished by the courts out of a total of 742 people (namely 43 per cent) and 281 women had their heads shaved. By contrast in the Moselle department the 556 women (out of a total of 3,243 people, namely 17 per cent) condemned by different judicial processes represent five times the number of those who actually had their heads shaved.[32] Without being able to establish a numerical link between these two types of punishment on account of the differences between regions, we can note that on the scale of the country as a whole we have more or less the same proportion of women affected by the two forms of *épuration*. Finally, as far as summary executions are concerned, there were overall twice as many people who had their heads shaved as there were executed. Clearly, it is easier to shave someone's head than it is to shoot him or her.

... But a Few Men as Well

The fact that the victims of this punishment were women seemed to me to be so obvious that the discovery of the first case of a man having had his head shaved in St Etienne came as a real surprise. *La tondue* could just as well be a man and a photograph of two looters with their heads shaved being led through the streets of St Etienne underlined once more the need to get away from the popular image. How is it possible to know whether a man who had been manhandled, beaten up or physically abused had his head shaved or not? On the 5 June 1945 at Vichy there was an incident when the guarded transit camp that had been set up at the showjumping centre was evacuated. Demonstrators grabbed hold of several of those who had been interned, some of them had their heads shaved and a member of the *milice* was hanged. According to the detailed report by the principal commissioner of police 'two of the demonstrators cut off the hair of four women and a man'.[33] Now the general prosecuter may simply have repeated the police report, but as far as the commissioner for the Republic was concerned it was a question of four women, while the deputy prefect for Vichy only talked of 'three women prisoners'. Is it the case that it seemed so impossible for a man to have had his head shaved at this point that any mention of it was corrected as having been an error by the staff working for the commissioner for the Republic and the deputy prefect? Paradoxically, the atypical nature of the shaving of men's heads is more likely to cause them to be overlooked than to bring them to our attention. Overwhelmingly, victims were female: 96 per cent of a sample taken by name of 614 people whose heads were shaved and 98.4 per cent if account is taken of the total number.[34] Between thirty-five and fifty-five men had their heads shaved among whom twenty-two can be identified individually.

Twenty-five communes have been listed where the shaving of men's heads took place. Seventeen departments were involved; in six of them (Aveyron, Côtes-du-Nord, Indre, Isère, Loiret and Moselle) this took place in at least two communes and approximately half of the references are to the area to the south-west of the Massif central and the region around Lyon.

As far as the district of Laguiole is concerned, on 28 October 1994, *Le Patriote rouergat* tells us that justice meted out by the *maquis* resulted 'in the shaving of all or part of the head for women depending on the importance of the offence, and for men shaving of the beard and if no beard a moustache, and if no moustache all of the hair and if there is no hair on the head the shaving of all bodily hair.' The precise nature of this exercise, the cutting of head hair for women and of all bodily hair for men, depending on the offence committed, indicates that the *tonte* was carried out in a particularly systematic way. By drawing up a number of different punishments based on normal judicial procedures, such distinctions forbade any improvization and ensured that both sexes would be treated equally.

At Vichy the man who had his head shaved did so at the same time as his four female fellow prisoners, just as at Romans, Caulnes, Châlette-sur-Loing, Agen, Bambiderstroff, Boulange, Craon, La Mure, Orléans men and women also had their heads shaved at the same time. In the remaining places men alone had their heads shaved. At St Etienne a photograph and then an article that appeared successively on 14 and 20 October 1944 in the daily paper *L'Espoir* indicate that five men had their heads shaved, two for looting and three for denunciations. It has to be noted that no article in the regional press talks about women and yet there were plenty who had their heads shaved in the first days following the Liberation.[35]

In the departments of the Indre, the Haute-Garonne and the Tarn-et-Garonne, young people who refused to join in the struggle against the

Key:
○ shaving of men's heads probable
⦿ shaving of men's heads: Ⓢ men only, Ⓜ shaving of heads threatened (Luchon)
＊ unknown commune

Geographical distribution of men's heads having been shaved.

Germans had their heads shaved. Once the Liberation came the coexistance for FFI fighters and a population desperate for peace and for fresh supplies was not without incident. As the reports issued by the prefect's office make clear, the former were increasingly resented. Complaints multiplied about overzealous checks, the FFI's sloppy appearance and the squabbles they caused. On the one hand we find a fairly traditional opposition between the native population and soldiers merely passing through, and on the other the complete rejection of a group of people accused of sustaining disorder and of making it appear as though the war was still going on. At Bagnères-de-Luchon (Haute-Garonne) a brawl on the 11 March 1945 necessitated the intervention of the police. A first witness to this event drew attention to the increasing gap between the FFI and the local population: 'since their arrival the FFI fighters stationed at Luchon have provoked a certain discontent among local inhabitants by their conduct, their language, by the people they mix with and by the way they check people in an irregular and impolite way.' On 10 March a squabble between civilians and the FFI about a road check ended in insults and threats on the part of the civilians. Two other accounts reveal the way in which the young people of Luchon were threated by the FFI: 'my son said to me that during the afternoon several FFI members said to him and to some of his friends that they would cut their hair off'; 'One of the soldiers walking past my house said that he wanted to cut off the hair of all the young people in Luchon.'

At Issoudun 'young people from good families' had their heads shaved at the Liberation because they had not joined the FFI. Such actions caused the CDL to protest: 'Official statement by the CDL. Shavings – we have learned that members of the FFI have shaved the heads of people from Issoudun. We very much regret that this incident has taken place without approval of the CDL; it will not happen again under such conditions.' Such disapproval was not recorded as far as the women who had their heads shaved on the same day were concerned. In the department of Tarn-et-Garonne 'several men and non-commissioned officers who refused to leave to join the Resistance were bullied by their comrades. Having led them through the streets of the town they shaved the heads of these cowards'.[36] In the second battalion of the FFI forces in the eastern part of the Indre one man complained to the President of the local liberation committee about the brutal behaviour of his commanding officer who had accused him of 'having taken a motorcycle from one battalion to another'. He talked of having been beaten, of having had his head shaved and of the threat of being shot.[37]

Carried out on their own comrades or on other members of the civilian population, the shaving of heads of 'cowards' was an extension of the same punishment carried out on women accused of collaboration. It shows how easy it was to be able to resort to this practice. The symbolic significance of this can be understood in different ways: as far as young men of an age to fight are concerned, it reminds us of the shaving of a conscript's head but also associates those who refused to leave, or who did not join the FFI, with those women for whom it was a special and a particularly vindictive punishment. The way in which this form of punishment caught on in French society allowed for all kinds of imprecision. If it did not indicate a specific case of collaboration, it could be used to denounce a lack of courage, or of a lack of masculinity and fighting spirit.

Nonetheless the shaving of men's heads remained marginal. Visually and symbolically, the sight of a man's shaven head does not have the same impact as a woman's. In the period 1944–5 the association of shaved heads and collaboration was standard as far as women were concerned; in the case of men it was not. For men the difference between a normal hair cut and a shorn head was less important.

For men to have their heads shaved like women can certainly be considered a mark of humiliation, an attack on their virility. Official reports, however, never make mention of it – unlike the case of women – and the strictly local nature of it does not have any corresponding national significance. One final point: at no time are their sexual practices mentioned. No man had his head shaved for having had sexual relations with a German woman or German man. Masculine sexuality remained a private matter. Men enjoyed an implied sexual freedom and if a woman's body could be reappropriated, a man's remained the object of silence.

Men, then, were equally subject to having their heads shaved, but not in significant numbers. For this reason, and contrary to the grammatical rule which argues that the masculine form should be used, we will continue to use *tondue* in its feminine form.

Twenty thousand people then had their heads shaved in the whole of France. To put forward a number for the first time involves a certain responsibility. This figure is open to all the mistakes, rough estimates and criticisms that could arise from the mixed nature of the sources used, the way the calculation has been carried out and the kind of forecast that has been made. In the future this figure may be revised up or down. It is not intended to be the last word on the subject, but rather to allow other more detailed pieces of research to be added to it. Nonetheless, it is supported by a large number of reliable facts and that is the intention: to destroy provisionally the image and indeed the myth surrounding the *tondue*, and to return to the historical sources; to define this subject according to factual reality so that the general view of it will no longer be based on emotion but clearly rooted in space and time.

Part II
1943–6: The High Season

–3–

During the Occupation

Normally it is thought that the practice of shaving heads is associated with the moment when the Liberation burst on France, giving the impression that the phenomenon lasted only for a short time. Nothing could be further from the truth. If the practice in fact reached a peak with the Liberation, archives show us that it lasted for three years. It began in 1943 during the Occupation and finished in 1946 immediately after the war had finished. By situating it in this way in a period of a few years, a myth becomes an action that only continued for a short while and prompts a number of questions – about the way it developed and also about the identity of those who carried it out. In 1943 it could not have been carried out by those who joined the Resistance at the very last moment. Women could not have had their heads shaved during the few months that followed the Liberation in the same *sous-préfecture* without at least the tacit agreement of the local authorities; nor could others have had their heads shaved simply on account of an initiative taken by those who had been deported and had now returned from the camps of Germany for reasons of jealousy or local quarrels.

Between 1943, the date of the first reported incident and March 1946, the date of the last one, 636 examples have been precisely dated and situated in 591 towns or villages.[1] But what was the pattern? Were there times when more were carried out than others?

From the evidence we have it was at the end of the summer of 1944 that the practice was most frequent: nearly 500 incidents occurred during the months of August and September. We should not forget that on 15 August 1944 when the Allies landed in Provence, they were also still fighting with Germans around Falaise in Normandy. Surrounded, the Germans surrendered on 20 August. A month later, 500 kilometres away, Nancy was freed and the Allied front became fixed along the Moselle. At that point, 90 per cent of France was free. Nonetheless, the high point of the summer of 1944 should not be allowed to overshadow other moments when the shaving of women's heads was frequent. The first was the months just before and just after the summer during which an

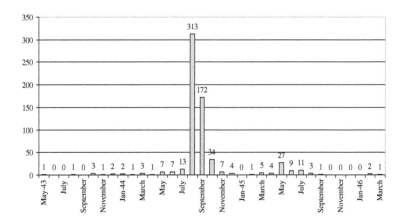

Monthly distribution of recorded *tontes*.

increase, followed by a decrease can be observed. A second is for the end of the spring and beginning of summer in 1945 when fifty or so references draw attention to a specific and isolated period when the practice was carried out. Finally a third emerges from the contrast between the slow growth in the number of references to the practice during the Occupation and the way in which such references rapidly disappear after August 1945.

It is difficult to divide these events up into neat periods because local circumstances are often at odds with what took place on a national scale. The symbolic dates of 6 June 1944, 25 August 1944 and 8 May 1945, however memorable and evocative they may be, are not very useful in making clear distinctions between what happened before and afterwards. The end of the Occupation began on 6 June 1944 with the Allied landings in Normandy, but the German presence remained a reality for most French people, certainly for a few weeks and indeed for several months. 25 August 1944 saw the surrender of the German commander Grossparis, but nearly all the days between June and September 1944 witnessed the Liberation occuring in different places. Finally, the capitulation of the Third Reich put an end to the Second World War in Europe, but this did not amount to the same thing for people in La Rochelle, or Saint-Lô or in some town or other in the south west of France. For some people, the Liberation was already something that belonged to the past; for others it was still very much a matter of the present.

Further problems are also created by the time the Liberation itself lasted. Although it was recognised by everybody, for some it was a precise turning point, but for others it lasted a considerable time. Each town had its 'day of Liberation' but in most cases this day represented a whole period, however short, which included the first struggles that took place, the final departure of the Germans and then the arrival of the Allied troops, with or without the Resistance fighters,[2] and the first days when the new authorities took over. With this in mind it makes more sense to talk about 'days of Liberation' an expression that makes it possible to move away from the idea of a single celebratory day, at local or departmental level on the one hand and on the other the idea that on a national scale the Liberation could be considered to stretch from the Allied landings in Normandy to the end of the war,[3] or to the end of the provisional government and the departure of General De Gaulle on 20 January 1946.

The *épuration* is normally divided into three periods: up to 6 June 1944 while France was still occupied; from 6 June to the Liberation, a period of continued fighting; and finally the post-Liberation period with two stages varying in length according to regions.[4] The first, during which France remained fragmented, when the powers of those who had belonged to the national Resistance and those of the GPRF were far from clearly defined. So urgent were the steps to be taken for the *épuration* to be in place that they could not wait for the legal framework drawn up in Algiers. This period could last for a few hours, but could also extend to a few months, as for example in the municipality of Béziers where law and order were not properly established until February 1945. The second period of the post-Liberation phase, when overall national authority was restored, finished in October 1945 with the legislative elections and the end of the provisional government. The *épuration* continued over a much longer period, however. Peter Novick[5] has selected the date of 1949 as an end point, a year in which the last trial took place before the High Court of Justice on 1 July and when on 29 July the vote was taken that officially abolished with law courts.[6]

The history of the shaving of heads is not contained neatly in any one of these periods. Its pattern depended on periods when the practice was widespread, the way in which it developed and the differences between regions. For each place, therefore, we have to be clear whether women had their heads shaved while the Germans were still present, on those days celebrating the Liberation, or immediately after. The end of these days of celebration came a week after the departure of the Germans and given such a period it is possible to take in, more or less, all of those things that happened and that were characteristic of the time – the take-over of the town, the widespread arrests of people suspected of having

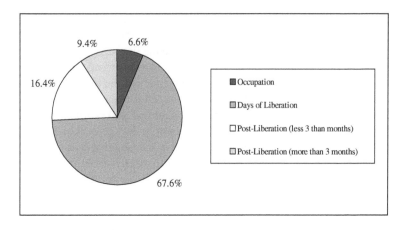

Distribution of *tontes* recorded by periods.

collaborated, the celebration of the Liberation itself and then the resumption of normal activities. Once these days were over those incidents of head shaving that took place in their immediate aftermath should not be seen to be related in any way to those that were carried out after a significant break. This break is one of three months after the Liberation.

From 1943 through to the Liberation few *tontes* occured – 42 cases or 6.6 per cent of the total number – but in a sufficiently regular way to be significant. Given the particularly harsh circumstances of the Occupation, they already anticipated an *épuration* which was to come.

In July 1944 we come across references to the practice linked to the first days celebrating Liberation: initially in Normandy and then throughout the rest of France as and when places were liberated. In La Rochelle and St Nazaire, as in the Channel Islands, women had their heads shaved following the German surrender on 8 May 1945. The surrender of the remaining pockets of German troops on the Atlantic coast put an end to this period, often of short duration locally, but which could be as long as a year for the country as a whole. Two-thirds of the incidents are concentrated in these few days: an important proportion, and one that modifies the feeling given by the high number of cases reached in August and September 1944. Many women were indeed shorn during these two months, but in those places that had been liberated over a period of a few days or a few weeks.

Once the days of celebrating the Liberation were over the number of cases is much reduced. Nonetheless, the 17 per cent that did take place during this period emphasize the fact that it was more a diminution than a complete disappearance of the practice, and behind this general trend it is possible to discover local situations that were very varied. Certain towns can be considered to have been quite slow: women who had collaborated and who were spared at the moment of the Liberation would be punished a few days later by some kind of unconscious mimicry. At Tournon in the Ardèche four or five women had their head shaved more than three weeks after the departure of the Germans. The weekly paper, the FTP *Assaut* gives an account on 25 September 1944:

HAVE YOU SEEN WOMEN WITH SHORN HEADS? It is never too late. Tournon should also have its shorn women. Justice has just been done. Last Saturday at the request of the local committee, the hairdresser for the FTP company billeted in our area got his clippers to work on some sumptuous heads of hair . . . after this sacrifice had been made the women were lead in a cart through the streets of Tournon with the jibes of the local people being hurled at them. And the day finished in front of the girls' *Lycée* with a resounding rendering of the *Marseillaise* sung by a chorus made up of the local people and our courageous FTP.

Not only is the way in which this *tonte* took place similar to many at the Liberation, but the author of the article underlines the local pride which has been rediscovered to such a degree that the expression 'justice has just been done' can be applied as much to the women themselves as to the town.

Elsewhere the practice went on uninterrupted during several weeks. In Béziers it was regular at least until the middle of November, in other words nearly three months after 22 August, the day on which the town was liberated.[7]

Finally, the punishment could be applied sporadically to women who had in the first instance had been 'forgotten'. In most cases evidence of the practice once the days celebrating liberation have passed is rare. Arrests were still made, but women who were interned did not necessarily suffer this punishment. The gradual return to peace, underlined in many reports, came about as a more organized *épuration* was established. Nevertheless, throughout the autumn of 1944, scattered cases of the practice cannot be considered to be merely residual, but rather examples reappear in circumstances that were markedly different and reflect dissatisfaction with the official processes of *épuration*. In twenty-five departments there were about fifty cases of heads being shaved; in nineteen others there were demonstrations and even attempts at lynching, although it is impossible to know whether or not they were connected.

So numerous, extensive and frequent were they – they occurred in between a quarter and a half of the departments in France and were recorded by several prefects in, for example, the departments of the Jura, the Vosges and Saône-et-Loire – that it shows that there was indeed a second wave of this practice.

The changing pattern plotted up to this point, however, not only reflects a quantitative change; it was integral to a period during which the different forms of punishment, like everything else that was at stake, were changing.

From First Threats to First 'Tontes'

It was in June 1943 that we find the first mention of a *tonte*: 'A group of young people sickened by the way in which certain women – new style procurers – behaved with the German army rabble, they shaved their hair off. They will be more discrete from now on and especially so if they are aware that what they have done is going to be made widely known.'[8] This took place in Pau, the *préfecture* of the Pyrénées-Atlantiques – Pau which had only experienced the presence of the Germans for a few months because it had been in the unoccupied zone until 1942. The punishment was meted out therefore extremely quickly.

This text, published in the first underground number of the *Populaire du Midi,* does not explain why this form of punishment was chosen. By talking of these women as 'procurers', however, it quite explicitly attributes a sexual nature to their behaviour. Finally, it also makes clear the dual purpose of the action of these young people: to punish a particular way of behaviour, but also to issue a warning. Precociousness, sexual connotations, evidence and the punitive and preventative nature of the punishment – these features will often be standard in the first evocations of *tontes.*

From July 1940 Jean Texcier anticipated that any women who had relationships with the occupying forces would be punished physically. Other threats followed. In an underground pamphlet dated 29 August 1941, the idea of branding or marking in some way is clear even if it would be long in coming. What is also noticeable is that despite several technical difficulties the artist has taken care to present the portrait of 'a seductress' – flowing hair, lipstick, earrings, bare neck and a fur collar.

A month earlier in July 1941 a text appeared that considered the different punishments which would be reserved for 'traitors and collaborators'. It is not possible to know how widely distributed it was, but the

Vittel, ce 29/8/4I

C'est ainsi, qu'un jour, seront marquées au front les françaises indignes qui fréquentent les sales boches .- Tous les collaborateurs seront aussi flétris avec ce signe diabolique. Français, à vos postes ! ayez l'oeil ouvert sur tous les agissements louches de ces loques de français. VIVE LA FRANCE LIBRE .

Underground pamphlet, *Vittel*, 29 August 1941.

text was published in February 1942 in the eleventh number of the *Defense de la France* with the following comment: 'This article was written in July 1941, we believe that it is useful to publish it now, however, so that French people maintain their indignation and do not forget it in the future.' It predicts branding and physical punishment with particular violence:

> You so-called French women who have given your bodies to Germans, will have your heads shaved and you will have a notice put on your backs: 'Sold to the enemy'.[9] You too, you unworthy creatures who flirt with the Germans will have your head shaved and you will be whipped, and on all your foreheads the swastika will be branded with a red hot iron.

The fact that there is no reference to a precise case of this kind and the use of the future tense, gives this text the nature of a warning, but from 1943 onwards threats and accounts of the shaving of heads increase in number.[10]

From that date other cases of *tontes* take place throughout the country. In the Gard in August 1943,[11] and then in Roanne, where nine women had their heads shaved in October because they had worked for German businesses.[12] In November in the department of Finistère young people shaved the head of the girl from Plouhinec. Finally, in December, *Le Pilori*, the voice of the movement France d'abord, confirmed that the practice was being carried out:

> Another delicate and even painful point is the conduct of certain women or girls who display more than simple interest in the occupying forces. In some country areas or in small towns several women had their heads shaved by young people who were indignant about their behaviour, and were sometimes even covered in mercurochrome or in ink . . . It was a good way of doing things. In bigger towns it was more difficult, but it would be possible to warn those who were guilty by letter and say to them that after the Liberation the committee of public safety would not forget them . . .[13]

From 1943 it is clear then that the practice of shaving heads was widely known across all of France. With the exception of Brittany, all the cases took place in the former non-occupied zone. There the German occupation occurred in a context in which public rejection of the occupying forces and of collaboration was already clear, contrary to the situation in the northern zone, where in 1940 the occupation appeared to be the logical and inevitable outcome of defeat.

At the end of 1943 on 6 December the *maquis* surrounded the town of Nantua. A couple who kept a hotel and who were collaborators had their heads shaved, were plastered with swastikas and led through the streets of the town. Uniformed members of the *maquis* had marched past the war memorial and had chosen this punishment to mark their passage through the town. Another form of branding 'aimed at dissuading eventual criminals' had been adopted in the department of the Ain two months before and used against the village postman in Matafelon: 'he was arrested during his rounds by a group from Chouegat, undressed, tarred and feathered and forced to carry on with his rounds done up in this ridiculous fashion and mocked the whole while by his fellow citizens. The next day a stuffed dummy dressed in the postman's uniform was hung from the bell tower of the church. The warning was effective, the postman was quickly moved to another district.'[14] Subsequently carried out elsewhere in the region, it gave rise to a particular name – the 'matefelonnage', based on the name of the original village.

Having at first signified simple refusal and then outright rejection of the occupying forces, the practice of shaving heads became a way of causing fear, of letting the enemy know quite clearly that any form of collaboration would be punished and that the price would be paid in blood and tears. In the department of the Ain it was not only something carried out by a handful of people, but was organized by members of the *maquis*. Although the *tontes* did not belong to any particular military tradition, its practice by certain Resistance groups became more frequent from the winter of 1943–4.

The Case of Corsica

At the risk of interrupting the flow of this story, but in order to respect chronology, we need to make a digression in order to see how matters developed in Corsica, the first department to be liberated nearly a year ahead of the rest of French soil. The Liberation began on 9 September 1943 with a call made by the *Front national*, and finished on 5 October after the arrival of free French troops from Algiers. From the beginning of the uprising women were arrested. There was a list of names, drawn up at the end of October, of individuals of both sexes who were put behind bars by the administration from 9 September onward. Out of 160 persons only fifteen women, several of them were Italian, were accused of having had relationships with either Italian or German soldiers.

In addition to these few cases the relations between Corsican women and the occupying forces would appear, if we are to believe a report drawn up by the Commissioner of the Interior dated the 30 May 1944, to have assumed more important dimensions. Estimating the Italian presence to be about 80,000 men, it condemned the attitude of Corsican women: 'It is certain that the ease with which contacts were made thanks largely to the similarity of dialects, made an increase in relationships much more possible. These became a real scandal and were denounced in all the towns across Corsica.'[15] Just how widespread it was is not known, but the carrying out of the shaving of heads has been reliably vouched for.[16] In March 1944, *Le Patriote* refers to it as a fairly moderate punishment. It seems nonetheless to have reached sufficient proportions for a special delegation from Bastia to make its opposition known. One of its members, Dominique Paoli, representing the *Front national* disapproved of 'this persecution to which women and girls are subjected

– 69 –

to on the pretext of their having collaborated horizontally with the occupier'.

Thus there appeared from the end of 1943 not only a punishment, but a name for it – horizontal collaboration. Subsequently as liberation took place we find both of these in the 89 other departments of France. Whether what happened in the island had any influence on the rest of France remains uncertain. The mainland press made no mention of it and the fact that *tontes* occurred at an earlier date in Corsica does not necessarily lead us to link them. Once again the event itself defies analysis and must remain subject to speculation.

An Act of Resistance?

In 1943 when the first *tontes* took place, French people had clearly distanced themselves from the Vichy regime. The rounding up of Jewish children, forced recruitment of men to go to Germany to work (the STO), increased rationing and repression that was becoming more and more brutal, all contributed to make the political nature of the collaboration clear. Increasingly resistance to the occupying forces could no longer be something that was a separate struggle against the collaborators. As Pierre Laborie has stated 'it can confidently be said that from the summer of 1943 the government's programme was completely at one with Germany's. Public opinion was at its most hostile stage.'[17]

For anyone who gave hiding to a labour conscript, listened to Radio Londres, or was known for his anti-fascist opinions, the collaborator presented a danger that increased daily. Because he knew persons and places, the collaborator was an extension of the repressive German and French forces that were incapable of controlling the population efficiently alone. The longer the war continued the more collaborators were seen to be traitors. By taking action against them, and by eliminating the most dangerous ones among them, their threat was reduced. Such actions were also a way of making an impression on those who still remained undecided. They also helped isolate those who were most committed to collaboration and to ensure that those who were still lukewarm did not rush to the side of collaboration. Finally all possible demonstrations of hostility towards the occupying forces and their henchmen were intended to instill in the population at large the hope in, or for, a final victory.

As the armed struggle intensified so did the increase in the practice of head shaving and consequently invites questions about the ways in which forms of violence directed at the various people accused of collaborating might be linked. Several cases of the practice carried out during the Occupation were similar to underground activities, for example. We know of five examples from the correspondence records of local police stations – in each case there is a succinct report simply based on facts. All five have as a common feature, namely the fact that they took place at night between 9.00 p.m. and 1.30 a.m. They were also carried out by a group of individuals, normally between three and ten in number, who were armed and masked. These actions had a double purpose: to punish collaborators by shaving the heads of the women (and in one case of a husband) though there is no mention of any other violence; and at the same time to collect money, food and clothes, a list of which is given on each occasion at the police station. The political nature of the activities is only mentioned on two occasions; on one there is talk of a terrorist attack and on the other of husbands who were reputed to be collaborators. In all of the other cases it was simply a matter of 'armed robbery'.

Clearly these cases can be interpreted in completely different and opposing ways. Either they were cases of armed robbery by groups taking advantage of the general confusion of the period in order to become rich; or they were activities carried out by the local Resistance with the phrase 'armed robbery' simply being used an expression to make it sound as though it was a deliberate criminal act. The propaganda disseminated by Vichy and by the Nazis regularly resorted to assimilating the Resistance forces as well as the Allies to groups of criminals. In this case the shaving of heads was simply the extension for one of many actions directed against the dwellings of those people who had collaborated. What this represents is not violence on a small scale, or a refinement or channelling of violence, but on the contrary, one of the ways activities against the Occupation could be seen to be increasing.

If they are compared with the many acts of sabotage, the collecting of information, the provision of an escape route, or the killing of German soldiers or collaborators, then the acts of head shaving were few in number. Just as much as the practice put its stamp on the Liberation, so it would appear to be completely absent from Resistance activities, at least as the history of them would subsequently suggest. However, it is not only its similarity with more militant activities which makes it necessary to put it into perspective. It was indeed sometimes claimed to be an act of resistance.

The first number of *Femmes Françaises*,[18] which appeared in January 1944, explained to 'French mothers' how to protect their sons:

French mothers, defend your sons against the females of the Gestapo . . .
Explain how they should resist these revolting bitches of the Gestapo. First
never reveal their true identity and introduce themselves to them under a false
name. Then pretend to accept all they are offering, get them into a trap, punish
them severely, shave off their hair down to the skin, and finally take their
identity card. The photograph will help identify them and punish them later
when the time comes. A number of fine young men have been deported and
even shot as a result of the actions of prostitutes working for the Gestapo. Say
it, repeat it to yourselves, you will then steer them clear of one of the most
serious dangers threatening us at the moment.

The *tontes* were not intended simply as a warning but was shown to
be a real way of helping protect those who had decided to join the
Resistance. Progressively the distinction between the acts of shaving
heads and those of the Resistance generally became more and more
tenuous. In *La Marseillaise,* the underground paper of the MUR in the
South-East, which appeared in February 1944, the shaving of the heads
of two women, female accomplices of an informer, is referred to in an
article along with other actions (attacks, executions, sabotage, skirmishes)
in an article entitled 'Spirit of the Resistance'.[19]

In a communiqué issued by the FTP in the department of the Haute-
Saône in which there are details of actions carried out between 26 July
and the middle of August 1944, in other words in the period that preceded
by one month the liberation of the department as a whole, we find the
two associated once again in the same way. The list includes eight
executions (six collaborators, of whom two were women and two were
members of the FFI found guilty of looting), six train derailments, six
different attempts at sabotage, five attacks to recover material and seven
on German soldiers. The list ends with a note on *cheveux rasés* ('shorn
hair'). The names of three women from Lure are given, together with the
following warning: 'It won't be long before it's the turn of others.' After
that there is a general statement:

> This communiqué is eloquent enough; no others are required to make people
> of the Haute-Saône aware of the active part the FTP are playing in the struggle
> to free our country. We can only repeat: Weapons! More Weapons! Still More
> Weapons! For our courageous FTP fighters.[20]

This example from the Haute-Saône reflects the shift to 'widespread
resistance of a revolutionary nature'. Everywhere, and to different
degrees, resistance action was intensifying. There were cases of places
which were freed temporarily and pressure on those who collaborated

was growing. Arrests were made in areas that had in part been freed. In the Charente near La Rochefoucault, in an area which was under the control of the *maquis,* five women were arrested and had their heads shaved between 31 July and 5 August 1944, even though Angoulême would not be liberated until 1 September. In the Indre at least twenty or so women were arrested in the month before the Germans left Châteauroux on 18 August. Among them at least one had her head shaved publicly at La Châtre on 9 July.

Although it was carried out during the Occupation, could the shaving of the heads of women who had been suspected of having relations with the enemy, be considered an act of resistance? Today historians agree to define resistance in the first place on the basis of action. And yet the motives for and the outcome of such action continue to prompt a number of questions. Pierre Laborie offers three criteria that according to him, provide

> the basis for a first definition: one, the desire to harm an enemy who can be identified, who is in occupation or who is assisting the occupying forces, and by organizing matters in such a way as to prevent the enemy, by all possible means, of achieving his objectives; two, by being fully aware of actively resisting; three, by being involved in actions which were basically unlawful.[21]

That the underground press should claim that women who had relationships with Germans formed one group of collaborators among many, shows quite clearly that they were an identifiable enemy. As for wanting to do damage, the press targeted these women, who by being punished were publicly exposed, as much as the Germans for whom any challenge hindered them in their pursuit of complete domination. The practice of shaving heads, often carried out at night by masked groups, and often likened to more recognized acts of resistance, was, by its violence, evidence of a willingness to break the law in the period of the Occupation.

At the same time, it is difficult to see how it could be a way of preventing the enemy from realizing its objectives at a time of war. One of the major paradoxes here is the disproportion between the significance of the practice itself and its total failure to have any effect on the course of the war, any more than the increase in relations between German soldiers and French women can be said to have been one of the aims of the occupying forces. Some recent work[22] has in fact shown, on the contrary, that one of the first priorities of the Wehrmacht was the prevention of venereal disease, and that its aim, although it was quickly abandoned, was to limit the sexual relationships of German soldiers to those with prostitutes under its own control.

Even though it was seen by those who carried it out and by numerous witnesses as an act of resistance, the shaving of heads was hardly that at all. The majority of these testimonies come certainly from the period of the Liberation, but it is difficult to know whether those who were responsible for the practice during the Occupation thought they were carrying out an act of resistance. Besides the hatred of the women concerned, the act expressed the hatred of a collaboration as it was reflected in the relationships, real or imagined, between French women and Germans. The ambiguity remains, however, and all the more so as it extends into the Liberation when relations between those who had resisted and those who simply shaved heads become confused. Clearly, however, there is in the statements that accompanied this practice a wish to appeal to French people as a whole. It brought together everyone to punish those who had already betrayed.

The roots of the causes for the impressive increase in the practice of shaving heads at the Liberation can be found, then, during the period of the Occupation. But the practice was not as widespread nor as brutal as the *Grande Peur* at the time of the French Revolution had been for example. At the Liberation the shaving of heads was already a legitimate practice. It did not take its victims by surprise and was an answer to the expectations both of those who carried it out and the rest of the population. But it is clear that, although it was not known about for a long time, the fact that the practice had already existed during the Occupation shows that something widespread and fundamental had already begun to develop. It was not the spontaneous event it has far too often been alleged to have been.

The Explosion of the Liberation

Like all pivotal and crucial dates, the Liberation fixes our attention. The passage from war to peace was not a question simply of a few hours: the wounded had to be cared for, the dead buried, the population had to be re-fed, the enemy had to be seen off and traitors had to be punished. By concentrating on the 'moment' of liberation, the practice of shaving heads can only be explained as the spontaneous reaction of the masses who indulged in some kind of expiatory act that had no effects other than for the women who were the victims. As we have seen, the practice was known at the Liberation as a form of punishment deemed quite natural for those women accused of having collaborated. But this idea of 'spontaneity' should not be allowed to hide the decisions that shaped the way in which the practice developed; the anonymity of the crowd should not obscure the reality of those who individually or collectively took part in different ways in the carrying out the act; the euphoria of the moment should not be allowed to isolate the event within something much longer and within a period in which the political interests were high.

To Shave: a Matter of Instant Urgency

The transformation of the word 'liberation' into a proper noun gives the event an apparent uniformity that hides many differences. The way in which the towns and villages of France were liberated was very varied, due as much to the importance of the struggles that took place and the length of time they lasted, as to the parts played respectively by those who freed them (Allied forces, FFI, local population). If we compare the accounts of three places that were liberated – Chablis in the department of Yonne liberated by the *maquis*, Bapaume (Pas-de-Calais) by the Americans, and Bologne-Billancourt (Seine) as a result of a local uprising – we will be able to situate the practice of shaving heads in the sequence of events.

Chablis, and the Arrival of the Maquis

Chablis, which is a large rural community in the Yonne, was liberated on 25 August 1944. The main towns in the department like Auxerre, Avallon and Sens, had already been freed by this date, but the Wehrmacht continued to have an important presence in the region in order to allow the withdrawal of their troops coming up from the south-west of France. By 12 September 1944, their threat disappeared when the Allied armies, which had landed in Normandy and in Provence, joined forces at Montbard, fifteen kilometres to the south-east of Chablis.

The community was liberated by the FFI. An account of this is described in the *L'Yonne républicaine* on 27 September 1944:

> On 25 August the FFI take the town, install their headquarters in the town hall and organize guardrooms . . . Having taken these precautionary measures, then, outside the town hall and in front of a jubilant crowd they shaved the heads of eight young people who, during the Occupation, had made it quite clear that they liked the Boche . . . On 2 September different arrests were made. During the night of 25–26 August swastikas were drawn on three buildings. The Mayor and the Commander of the FFI forces publicly condemned these actions.

A police account confirms that these events took place and also shows that the FFI had carried out a reconnaissance of Chablis on 23 August but had had to disappear before the arrival of German lorries. As far as the shaving of heads is concerned, the president of the local Liberation committee makes it clear that they were carried out due to the pressure of public opinion.

Bapaume, Liberated by the Americans

In the small town of Bapaume the arrival of the Americans on 1 September 1944 marked its liberation 'without a single shot being fired'. After the jubilation with which the first armed American column was welcomed at 4.30 p.m., and while two other columns were crossing the town, the local Resistance fighters organized themselves into two groups. 'The first group, accompanied by two hairdressers, ran through the town looking for young women or girls whose conduct with the occupying forces had been deplorable so that they could cut off their hair.' During this time 'the FFI began to clear up the immediate surroundings and brought in prisoners'.[1] German soldiers and women who had collaborated were all pursued at the same time, the former being disarmed and shut in the police station, the latter having their heads shaved and being taken through the streets. The day Bapaume was liberated finished with the announcement of a curfew to last until 6.00 a.m. the following morning.

Boulogne-Billancourt, and the Uprising

Like many towns in the immediate vicinity of Paris, Boulogne-Billancourt took part in the capital's uprising. A relatively complete account, dated 15 September 1944, was given by the headteacher of the boy's school:

> Boulogne did not begin to show much reaction until Saturday 19 August when the French flag was flown over the local police station. On the afternoon of the same day the local population, in a vindictive mood, had free reign and several women had their heads shaved in the square in front of the town hall. 20 August was a calm day and in the evening notices were put up announcing that an armistice had been signed. These same notices were torn down later in the evening. It was only on Monday 21 August that the first groups wearing the FFI armbands appeared and there were two of them. They were almost completely unarmed; the first group managed to get some weapons from two Germans who surrendered of their own accord and in whose lorry they found a sten gun, a few rifles and some cartridges. The second group found weapons in the Claude-Bernard and La Fontaine schools which were abandoned by the Germans on Thursday 24 . . . This was a war carried out by groups of snipers who immobilised the enemy forces and prevented them from withdrawing . . . The barricades began to be put up during the day on 24 August and in the evening of the same day, around ten o'clock the first tanks of the Leclerc division came into our town. They arrived from the Pont de Sèvres along avenue Édouard-Vaillant . . . On Friday 25 throughout the day firing continued intermittently between the Germans and the voluntary forces on the Right Bank who were lying in wait behind the walls and trees, etc. In the end the Germans gave themselves up to the Americans on Saturday 26 August.[2]

Chablis, Bapaume and Boulogne-Billancourt differ from one another in terms of population,[3] how long it took for them to be liberated and by whom. Against this, what they share is the way in which the population took part, the way in which the events developed in military style and by the shaving of women's heads. Whether this practice had been anticipated by the local Resistance people in Bapaume, had been organized by the FFI who responded to the request of the local population in Chablis, or whether it was carried out by the locals themselves in Boulogne-Billancourt, it was integral to the process of liberation. Like the military measures that had to be taken, the practice was a direct result of the various tasks to be carried out. Women whose heads were to be shaved were not persecuted instead of the Germans, but at the same time. In Boulogne the punishment that was organized and took place outside the town hall as much announced the Liberation as brought it to an end and, with the raising of the French flag above the police station, marked a kind of starting point to the week. If it is difficult to know who was responsible for the initiative, it is nonetheless possible to ascertain that the FFI troops appeared in the same way as other military operations appeared, afterwards.

What sense should we give to the urgency and the speed with which women had their heads shaved in many of those towns which were freed? The threats and the shaving of heads that took place during the Occupation anticipated those of the Liberation when the sense of relief and victory would be closely associated with the need to punish traitors. Final threats, swastikas, other inscriptions, the departure of the collaborators, were all a kind of countdown for the event everyone was waiting for. The urgency of the practice to shave heads can only be understood if it is placed in the context of the Liberation. It was not only a feature of a better future in a country which would be cleansed, it was also an essential element in the liberation itself, in the sense that it allowed everyone to become part of the struggle for the recovery of his or her country. Finally, how can we explain the speed with which it was carried out without seeing it as something to which all people subscribed? The desire to punish the guilty people in a way that people felt appropriate seems to have been widely shared. There was no risk involved in carrying it out against women who were neither armed or protected, and the ease with which it could be done was an encouragement for it to be extended even further.

Resistance Workers of the Last Minute

The shaving of heads that took place during the days of liberation was carried out by groups of people in most cases and was often a public event. Contrary to what happened during the Occupation in which, as we have seen, a limited number of people was involved, here it is a question of a large group that cannot be defined and in which the roles played by individuals are impossible to pin down. Individual involvement is difficult to establish precisely, and all the more so when it forms part of collective and constantly changing action.

If the 'shaver' is simply the person who wields the clippers, there were many others who were also involved in the practice: women, children, men. Amongst the last of these, some wore armbands and/or were armed, others not. Men in uniform could also be present, whether they belonged to the local or national police force, or were soldiers. The possibility of working out what their motivations and actual roles were simply from their appearance, makes any understanding of this event difficult. Who could know whether someone wearing an armband was a Resistance fighter of the 'first hour' or of 'the twenty-fifth', whether the person who was wielding the clippers had volunteered, or had been requisitioned, whether a particular person among the onlookers was beyond reproach? And the appearance of fake resistance fighters (also known as last-minute resistance fighters) has been mentioned in accounts of the Liberation.

In the revolutionary spirit of the Resistance (in particular communist resistance) and with De Gaulle's 'appeal to fight the enemy by all possible means'[4] it was inevitable, when a country was being freed by 'its people' that differences between them would disappear. If in this way the country as a whole 'had the sense of participating and even of being the principal actor in the Liberation'[5] and in having free France recognised by the Allies, it was not without influence over the ways individual behaviour would be judged subsequently.

What could be more revealing than the necessary addition of the adjective 'authentic' to the confused picture of the 'Resister' in the autumn of 1944? It is as though the description 'Resistance fighter' was not a sufficient guarantee of the commitment it suggested; as though the precocity of having joined the Resistance was not in itself proof of an individual's sincerity. Even those who had made the choice to join once the course of the war had changed direction after the battle of Stalingrad were not always free from suspicion.

Without going back over the ways in which people were engaged in Resistance activities during the Occupation, and leaving on one side therefore those who, whether under Vichy or under the Occupation, took the decision to enter the Resistance, it has to be noted that there was no single type of anti-Nazi activity that extended beyond the chronological limits of the Occupation. Those who had been able to avoid being deported or executed increased their activities as the Liberation approached. Among those activities was the aim of encouraging the largest number of French people as possible to join the Resistance in order to see off the enemy. They were also joined by those who responded to the call to rebel. It has always been easy to make fun of the belated commitment of such 'rebels' in towns where the population was more active in fighting the Germans than in others. Certainly to build a barricade in August 1944 did not carry with it the same risks as becoming part of a resistance network in 1942. Even so, when Paris was liberated, nearly 3,000 of the FFI troops and the local population had been killed and 7,000[6] wounded, and if the enthusiasm and the joy of the rebels were real enough, the war was no less so. If questions can be asked about the authenticity of some Resistance fighters, they can also be asked about those who stayed at home until the very end of the war.

Not without a certain irony do we find accounts of the considerable increase in the strength of the FFI from 100,000 men or so in June 1944 to 400,000 in October of the same year. However, many had participated in the final struggles of the war: 120,000 joined the new French army; 25,000 others fought in the region of the Alps; 75,000 were brought together under the leadership of General de Larminat who was in charge of the French forces in the west of the country. In all 20,000 FFI soldiers payed for their involvement in the Resistance with their life and 14,000 of the First French Army met death pursuing the war into Germany and continuing to fight against Germans in those small pockets where they had remained on the Atlantic coast. As Jean-Pierre Rioux has emphasized 'a significant element of the youth of France took part in these activities.'[7] They could be Resistance fighters, rebels, participants in some kind of action – but for all of them it was a way to share in the war against Nazi Germany. Another image quickly began to emerge, however, namely that of the last-minute resistance fighters. These were a mixture of those who had found an easy way out or opportunists or even former collaborators who managed to turn their coat just in time.

Who were they? The naming of them in this way appeared once the liberation became effective and indicates a considerable gap between those who took part in the Resistance and those who did nothing. In Normandy at the beginning of August, the newspaper *Renouveau* condemned

> those expressions of Resistance which are a mere caricature of what really happened. You will notice with what eagerness these fakes undertake cleaning up operations . . . This brunette woman sold a few hours happiness to this Gerry? Who is to say, in fact, that she did not do France a service? You have shaved her head and that will be enough, no doubt, in the same way that the Russian army will not stop its advance because of the drop in temperature.

In Charleville in the Ardennes, people deplored 'seeing too many armbands on suspect arms.'[8] The resistance authorities had enough to do with people who were wearing unchecked armbands without having to bother with real criminals. Charles d'Aragon recalls, not without irony, the way in which he took action

> against a group of men who under the supervision of a former seminarist were courageously shaving the heads of prostitutes. I grabbed hold of the clippers and scissors. The look on the faces of those there taking pleasure in the spectacle was dreadful; it is sick to see how in towns everywhere, people are emerging to watch public executions. The next day the hairdresser came to the prefect's office to claim back the tools I had confiscated from him.[9]

Serge Ravanel also explains how women who were having their heads shaved were transported naked in carts through the streets, exposed to the view and the shouts of the crowd. Resistance fighters have told me how they had been present at such scenes and powerless to do anything against a raging crowd of people. That had nothing to do with the Resistance.[10]

Yves Farge, the Republican commissioner in Lyon, records in one of his first reports that

> during the first days of the Liberation a number of arrests were carried out by anybody, and under any circumstances . . . and in a number of cases by people who had no right to wear the FFI armband, simply to take personal revenge or to indulge in all kinds of degrading activities.[11]

An in-depth study of these last-minute resistance fighters remains to be carried out, but it is already possible to focus on how they were viewed. Accounts we have from the period itself highlight the cracks in the facade of national unity and the divisions that would develop between those who resisted and others. The first symptom of the syndrome, one might be tempted to say. Nonetheless, whether we are talking about a group activity, a state of mind, a myth, or all three at once, these last-minute resistance fighters should not be thought of as being solely responsible for carrying out something which the myth of the Resistance has otherwise blotted out. What might have appeared quite unacceptable, if we are talking about a single definition of the Resistance and something that could only degrade it, assumes a quite different meaning when all the many and various factors are taken into account.

nd Resistance Fighters: from Suspicion to Union

ount of their huge size, the crowds that gathered at the time of the
ation have remained a point of reference for a long time. Even if
memory of May 1968 has tended to overshadow them, many demonstrations have been given the splendid title of 'the most important
demonstration since the Liberation'.[12] In all likelihood exaggerated and
even distorted by the way in which the period of the Liberation has been
represented by memories of those days, the evidence we need in order to
have a precise idea about which elements of the population took part in
these demonstrations is lacking. However, after the Occupation period,
during which people were withdrawn and concerned for their individual
existence, the Liberation saw them come out together. All other things
being equal, the French came onto the streets in large numbers. All kinds
of expressions describe the size and single-mindedness of these demonstrations: 'considerable', 'vast', 'coming from all sides', 'countless', 'like
holiday crowds', 'so thick that it was impossible to move about'. This
'crowd', emblematic of the Liberation, is an expression not only of
freedom, but also of life. What a contrast there is between on the one hand
the pictures of French people crowding onto the public squares in towns
throughout France, and on the other of a few persons who managed to
escape from fighting or air raids who came back to look at the ruins of
their former homes!

The importance we can attribute to the crowd can be seen as well by
the different images we have of it. Many photographs taken at the time
when women's heads were being shaved reveal a population made up of
all kinds of different people: men and women, children, old people,
civilians and members of the military are all there, and it is even possible
to see how they responded in different ways. Nearest to the woman who
is having her head shaved, we always find men – not too many of them –
on the whole young, with a number of them wearing an armband and
carrying a weapon. They comprise the first group in charge of the victim,
and are often holding her by the arm. In the second group, which is far
more mixed, men, women and children crowd together. They are either
in front of, or following the first group, taking part in the events by raising
their arms, shouting and giving the sign of V for victory, and sometimes
posing for the photographer. A third group, when there is a large gathering, is just as mixed as well, and stands in the background watching the
procession as it passes. Showing fewer emotions, this group observes
what is going on in an entirely passive way. If in general it is difficult to
make out the attitude of people standing to one side, they are nonetheless

also present. It is rare to find people who remain apart from what is going on, walking in the opposite direction or turning their back to it.

Photographs and films taken at the time provide invaluable information about those who took part in the shaving ceremonies and allow us to identify those carrying a weapon or wearing an armband. While after the war *la tondue* came to symbolize the Liberation – the sight of a shaved head being enough to evoke a whole period – it is not enough to take these documents merely as illustrations. Rather we should give them the importance of archival material and examine them critically.

The Role of the Photograph

Photographs of these events have the peculiar quality of being at once a contemporaneous record and part of them: they had an influence on the way the ceremony was conducted and on the attitude of those present.

There are plenty of photographs of women whose heads have been shaved. Some are the work of war photographers such as Capa and Lee Miller.[13] But on the whole they are the work of local photographers, professionals or amateurs, who wanted to capture this moment of national liberation. But by the fact that they are part of the event itself, these photographs cannot be considered just as records or testimonies. In many cases the photographer was actually taking part in the scene he was watching and by his very presence having an influence on the way things developed. In a letter which she sent to a friend, Lee Miller talks of the ease with which this shift could take place:

> I saw four girls who had been led through the streets and I rushed towards them to take a photograph. At once I found myself at the front of the procession and the local people thought I was the female soldier who had captured them, or something like that, and I was kissed and congratulated at the same time as slaps and spits rained down on the four unfortunate girls.[14]

Photography was an essential element of the whole process. In Craon (Mayenne), prints were sold by local photographers for the benefit of families who had had members deported;[15] other photographs were printed as picture postcards[16] and many more again were published in the papers.

These photographs have three principal and different themes. In the first place, the act of cutting the hair is what the photographer is concentrating on; the victim is in the middle of the picture and is not looking at the lens. According to how the photograph is framed we may also be able to see the person who is doing the shaving, hair on the ground, the crowd and the place where everything is happening. The second kind of photograph focuses on the victims as they are marched under escort through the streets. According to where he is placed the photographer has an effect on the attitude of those looking on. If he is at the front of the procession he causes arms to be raised in salute and he finds people smiling or looking directly at him. In this group of photographs we can also put those taken of the women as they are 'brought out' even if at this point their heads have not yet been shaved. In the third kind of photograph their attitude is determined by the presence of the camera – in other words they pose. Photographs of this kind are integral to the ceremony being as much a part of it as providing a mere record of events, and in many cases posing for the photographer followed on logically from the visit to the hairdresser.

Better than photography, films allow us to see how attitudes could change. Filmed by an American army cameraman, these five closeups last for 35 seconds and show how the arrival of a woman whose head has been shaved can be turned into a real sitting. In the first closeup, the woman is held by two men; the one on the right is in uniform, the one on the left is wheeling a bicycle. They are followed by four other men and two women in the background. This group is walking past some railings without there being anything significant in the way they behave. In the second closeup there are a lot more people, about thirteen, and their attitudes have changed. Most of them are looking at the camera. A man is waving a lock of hair above the victim's head and another is holding her by the ears. At the end of this sequence the man in uniform stops and pulls the woman by the arm towards the camera. The three following closeups are of poses in front of the camera – one face-on with her ears and chin held by two men; one taken at an angle, her head held by four different hands, and another with a man holding her by the back of the neck as another makes a pair of horns over her head with his fingers.

The number of photographs taken and the care with which they were posed ensured that the event would be recorded for posterity. It was also a way of being seen to be part of a collective action. In each town, as it was freed, events followed one another in a chronological pattern: the welcome of Allied forces, the march past of the FFI troops, speeches made by new authorities, the procession of German prisoners, the respectful gathering in front of the war memorials or the bodies of those who have been most recently tortured, the arrest of collaborators, open-air dances, the shaving of heads, sacking of premises that belonged to

Arrival of American troops in Paris, 25 August 1944. A selection of stills from a nine-minute silent, black and white film shot by an American. Vidéotheque de Paris. Original in the National Archives in Washington.

collaborationist organizations, the tearing down of notices and the names of streets, the reading of newspapers, erection of public decorations and the execution of collaborators. Although unpredictable, the ways these events took place depended at the same time on certain external factors and on the willingness of those in charge to organize them. There were some moments when there was more activity than others. All of them, however, had a common focus in the ceremony of the head shaving.

Resistance Fighters Out in the Open

For those who had fought in the Resistance the Liberation allowed them to come out of hiding and into the open. For those who had been in the *maquis*, among whom were a number who refused to participate in the STO scheme, it meant a return to their village or their town after a long absence. For others, it meant that their colleagues, those who were close to them, and their neighbours, only now learned of their activities during the Occupation. And beyond the individual circumstances in which pride, scorn, or surprise, or confirmation of suspicions were mixed, it also meant that groups that had been brought together by their underground struggle now confronted a population which, at least in part, had only ever heard words like 'bandits', 'terrorists', or 'assassins' being used about them. The ceremonies around the shaving of women's heads brought the many features of this confrontation out into the open.

In his study of the opinions held by French people, Pierre Laborie has shown how up to the month of August 1944 the *maquis* was generally viewed with disapproval. Nonetheless in Toulouse, as in Montpellier, fear of terrorism was only sixth or seventh in the list of concerns shared by the general public, and in any case was never registered by more than 5 per cent of the population. In general, though, the French did not have a favourable view of the Resistance. What those who fought in the Resistance thought about the rest of the population is far less known. So determined were they to convince others, so frequent were the calls to join the struggle against the enemy and so strong the appeal to patriotism, and subsequently the creation of the myth of the nation of resistance, that it is impossible to know what they thought of those who did not make the same choice. Those who belonged to the Resistance

> adapted themselves to their environment in order to take from it what suited them. They would even apply pressure, force, or persuasion, especially when, in order to impose the presence of the *maquis,* they found themselves in a real struggle with a reluctant local population.[17]

François Marcot has made clear the complex nature of the relationships between those who resisted and those who did not. Even if there was a shared sense of relief and joy, the experiences of the war meant that feelings on both sides at the time of the Liberation were ambiguous and uncertain. A photograph taken at Vesoul on 12 September 1944, the day the town was liberated by the seventh American Army, provides an excellent illustration of this. This photograph is an action shot. The fact

Vesoul, 12 September 1944 (J.-C. Grandhay Maé-erti Éditeur 94).

that nobody is looking into the lens, the presence in the foreground of someone with his back to the camera and the blurred image of someone else crossing the scene, all indicate that nothing has been set up. This photograph has been taken at the very end of the ceremony when a woman has had her head shaved, and when there is only one lock of hair remaining above her ear. We know nothing about what happened before or after. The picture as a whole provides an overview and is made more dramatic by the emptiness of the foreground and the presence of a huge building in the background. Nonetheless people standing to the side have been cut off and we can only suppose that the photographer was not alone but, like other people, was taking part in the ceremony.

Three individual scenes within the photograph on a line going from the bottom right-hand side to the top left attract the spectators attention just as they attract ours now. In the centre there is a woman dressed in a dark suit sitting on a chair. The man standing beside her is holding clippers in his right hand and he is getting ready to cut off the last lock of hair. Around them is space, and on the ground the locks of hair that have been cut off stand out.

Behind them are two men, one of whom appears to be a non-commissioned officer, and they are sitting at a table on which there are papers.

The one at the front appears to be holding something to write with. Behind them, several men are standing, looking over their shoulders. In front of the table it is possible to make out the silhouette of a woman (in a pale coloured dress, seen behind the person who is doing the shaving). Finally, crossing the empty space and going towards the right, there is a man wearing a beret; his sleeves are rolled up and he is stretching out his arm as though he were inviting someone to come forward.

These three scenes give a structure to the space. Around them there are forty or more people standing in a kind of arc and who can be divided into groups. Two-thirds of them on the left-hand side are men who, while not wearing identical uniforms, are all linked to the Resistance fighters. Some have armbands whereas others wear berets, or caps. Left and from behind, the first man has a revolver at his waist, the one following him a rifle slung around his shoulders. On the right-hand side the civilians can be made out – men, women and children.

It is difficult to know what the photographer wanted to capture and how subjective he was as he looked through his lens. Nonetheless it is probable that this particular photograph – and this is a point which is exceptional enough to be emphasized – offers us in one go three moments in the process of shaving a woman's head. The man on the right would appear to be looking at someone who is out of the picture, no doubt a woman who has been accused of collaboration so that she should present herself to the judges at the table. They in turn will question her and decide whether or not she should be punished. If she is sentenced to have her head shaved, all that remains is for her to sit down in the chair, the scaffold where the hairdresser will carry out the sentence. The way in which the events in the photograph are spatially arranged emphasizes the exclusively military role played by the soldiers present, and all the more so because the scene is taking place in a barracks. The table, the place where the leaders are sitting down represents power. The scene recalls thereafter the traditional military one, of officers grouped around a map before battle. The distance between fighters and civilians is underlined by the man who is walking across to the right and whose position when the photograph was taken is exactly at the point where the two groups can be divided. This feature is reinforced by the movement of his arm, which, if, as is likely, he is going to collect another women guilty of collaboration, also holds the group of civilians as a whole together, isolating it a little from the rest of those taking part. Three features in particular emerge: strength on account of various features associated with fighting men; order by the way the scene has been methodically organized; and vitality by the sense of the man's movement towards the right (the direction of reading too) and by his rolled up shirt sleeves. The cutting of the woman's hair is a real or symbolic extension of armed combat. The military nature of the operation dominates and gives it its legitimacy. By their presence, and while playing only a minor role, the civilians – few in number, but widely representative – lend this scene a national dimension.

The Assertion of Authority

As we have seen from what happened in Chablis or Vesoul, the FFI organized a number of head shavings and by adapting them, extended those that had already taken place during the period of the Occupation. Luc Capdevila is of the opinion that in Brittany in about 80 per cent of cases 'resistance fighters', and those who had been assimilated to them (FFI, CLL, Front national, and so forth) were responsible. In all this he sees 'an action whose task it was to establish the new power base and to impress the local people by an instant demonstration of strength'. However, to suggest that the ultimate point of the practice was to confirm the new authoritative order, is not without problems. If we take the few hours, or even days, which followed the establishment of the resistance fighters in positions of power, and in a context when 'the Vichy regime and its military support was disappearing',[18] then when 'a sense of patriotism carried everything before it – past weaknesses, present uncertainties and future disputes',[19] should the act of head shaving be interpreted as an expression of a battle of wills between those of the Resistance and the French generally? Certainly, when these ceremonies were organized, conflicts broke out but as often as not between members of the resistance groups as between the priest, the mayor, or the policemen in a particular commune and any of the local people. In fact the *tonte* was something that brought people together in a sense of patriotism, rather than simply a sign of strength.

In general the differences of opinion, opposition and conflict would only come later. Those that did arise were set to one side, such was the intensity of the moment. Whether or not it had already been practised by certain resistance groups during the Occupation the shaving of heads was known to the population at large, and became a hallmark of the Liberation. The recording of the numerous cases of the punishment having been carried out in answer to popular demand, is not the result of a reconstruction of events *a posteriori*. Members of the general population and those who had resisted both took part. If their respective roles were different on account of where they were, each group set about its task and by its attitude had an effect on the way events developed. Dialogue, rather than a battle of wills, became the norm.

At Romilly-sur-Seine, an official of the FFI reported

> the crowd is jubilant, shouting with enthusiasm outside the town hall calling for all bad French men and women to be punished, etc. The women, who were arrested the day before, have been held in the school in the Rue des Fontaines and put under guard by the FFI. The officer in charge and the delegate of the Liberation (the delegate of CDL), decided that the five most compromised women should have their hair cut off. The operation has been carried out. The officer in charge with the delegate at his side harangues the crowd and invites it to disperse, assuring people once and for all that justice will be done, that those who had been guilty, would not be handed over to, nor would they be made a spectacle of.[20]

How genuine the pressure exerted by the general population was is difficult to estimate. The decision taken was enough to satisfy at least some of those who had demonstrated and underlined the authority of those newly in power. More than conflict, what resulted was a compromise. The account given by the FFI official in his report more than a month later confirms that the two sides indeed came to a truce: 'The outburst passed. There was no looting, no brawling, no violence against anyone. Everything returned to order again. The local population showed themselves to be worthy, respectful and law abiding. They deserve to be congratulated.'

In Orly

> in spite of the request by the Committee which announced that no violence would be tolerated, a group of six women demanded that 'those who had befriended the Germans' should have their heads shaved. Six only were found and had this punishment carried out.[21]

Elsewhere it was sometimes the FFI by themselves who 'asked those people present whether women deserved to have their hair cut off. If the question met with applause and approval, the punishment was carried out'.[22] In this way, in most cases, it was not possible to know who was responsible for initiating the ceremony. At the beginning each group was distinct, but gradually copied the attitude of the other, thereby causing members of the local population and those who had taken part in the armed struggle to come together.

The frames of a black and white amateur film lasting 13 minutes shot in May 1944, at the moment when a commune in the Paris region was liberated, illustrates this dynamic. A scene that is twelve frames and forty seconds long shows us how the shaving of women's heads was carried out.

It is not a series of sequential shots. It seems that at the editing stage the film maker mixed different shots of two women having their heads shaved, and even reversed some. In the shots numbered 7 and 9 she still has hair on the back of her head, whereas, number 8, shows the back of her head to be completely shaved. The number of shots also offers variety from different perspectives: some are taken from above (numbers 3, 4 and 9), or below (numbers 8 and 12); some straight on (numbers 1, 2, 6, 7, 8, 9 and 10), some offer a general view (numbers 4, 11 and 12) and there is even a travelling shot (number 2); some are close ups (numbers 2, 6, 7, 9 and 11); another is a general view (number12).

The fourteen pictures taken in this film switch between shots of the crowd and shots of the town hall where the cutting takes place. This movement from the crowd to those doing the cutting, gives a dynamic quality to their relationship, which is more difficult to spot from stills. The actions are carried out by men only, most of them wearing an armband, whether this be at the moment of the arrest (shot number 1), at the moment when the head was being shaved (numbers 5, 6, 7 and 8), when the victim is shown to the crowd (number 12) or her departure (number 11). At the same time, the crowd (at least 120 people can be seen in shots 10 and 11) is far from being still. The main signs of the crowd's behaviour are the smiles on faces and the raised arms. There is only one schoolgirl dressed in white, probably lifted up on the shoulders of a parent, who seems to be watching the scene in a detached way, the expression on her face being totally at odds with the general atmosphere. It has to be noted that this good humour lasts for as long as it takes for the shaving to be completed. If the steps of the town hall and the armbands create a symbolic spacial gap between those who do the cutting and the general public, the attitude of the latter and the smiles of the faces of those doing the cutting show that they are at one. In shots 3 to 11 it is practically impossible to distinguish between them. Two images in shots 10 and 11 illustrate even better the way in which they come together. Once the head has been shaved, the woman turns around, a man in shirt sleeves by her side. This movement, filmed from above, captures all those taking part and the smiles on the faces of the onlookers push the woman out of the frame. The closeup (8), by virtue of the way it is framed, allows us to glimpse only a small part of the cutter's face. The clippers, held in his right hand, are a kind of extension of the emblem of the French Republic no

Head-shaving in the Paris suburbs (August 1944). Silent film, black and white, 13 minutes, shot by Maurice Krebs. Videothèque de Paris (Vdp 5693).

doubt recently restored to the town hall's balcony. The picture evokes the revolutionary symbolism of the armed strength of the Nation. Whether deliberate or not, this scene makes a number of allusions to the French Revolution which can be found generally at the time of the Liberation.

During the days of the Liberation, a number of demonstrations together form a sense of national unity. To carry out violence on the enemy represented a higher form of struggle and endowed the resistance fighter with a special identity that members of the general population could not share. The cases when the two sides could come together to rebel as one against the occupying forces were few. The *tonte* emerged then as the single act of violence that they could direct against the enemy together. It allowed those who had been involved in armed struggle for the liberation to be reunited with the majority, some of whom were fearful, others hopeful, who had been waiting for it to come. Whatever disagreements were to surface later, it was a moment when this fusion could be realized. The press at the time of the Liberation underlines this feeling. In *La Marseillaise* on 25 August 1944 it was 'our valiant FFI who have shaved heads'. In the Puy-de-Dôme, *La Nation* heralds, on 30 August, that after a number of women had had their heads shaved and after three militia men had been executed:

> Thiers demonstrated its joy in a particularly touching way: not only were there 150 meals supplied spontaneously by the local population, but the people of Thiers who were so grateful that they insisted that every member of the FTP should take away a souvenir of the town in the form of a razor or a knife!

Such objects were as much a statement of the identity of the town known for its cutlery industry as for that of those for whom they were intended. The knife and the razor were emblematic and contained the implicit promise that further *tontes* would be carried out in other places.

There is also the memory of the 'resounding *Marseillaise* sung by a choir made up of the general population and our worthy FTP'[23] at Tournon. Flattering descriptions, presents, the *Marseillaise*, the use of the first person plural – whatever form it took this was celebration of a rediscovered shared identity which had been hoped for during the Occupation and was now being confirmed.

Local and National Police and Allied Soldiers

While the act of shaving heads brought members of the general population and those who participated in the resistance together, other uniformed participants were often present. Members of the local and national police and of the allied forces appear in photographs and in accounts of what went on. However, the similarity does not go beyond the wearing of a uniform. If the involvement of the former was often ambiguous the latter were often critical.

An Ambiguous Involvement

For the local police, as for those of the national body, the situation at the Liberation was fairly confused. During the Occupation they had been active in their support of Vichy's policy of collaboration. On 10 January 1944 these two groups were brought under the authority of Joseph Darnand, who had been named general secretary for the maintenance of law and order, and when the Allies arrived in Normandy, there was a movement towards centralization. Many members of the national police force defected, a fact which is confirmed by the lack of reports made after the Liberation for the months of July and August 1944 on how various brigades conducted themselves. These defections were made easier by the attempt to bring the various brigades together in order to try to prevent people, or to stop the Resistance obtaining weapons.[24] As for the local police, its members' role in the Parisian uprising should not hide important differences to be noted in other towns, nor the repressive role they continued to play under Vichy. Simon Kitson underlines the difference between Paris and Marseille where the position of the police was 'more precarious and complicated . . . the police did not go along with Joseph Darnand's wishes to defend Vichy's institutions . . . nor did it unanimously rally to the Resistance, factors which, according to Raymond Aubrac, the first commissioner of the Republic, would explain its lack of authority after the Liberation'.[25] The question of authority is one of the clues which allow us to analyse the different ways in which the police were involved.

Like other public buildings, police stations and brigade premises, were often the first places where people were interned and where many women had their heads shaved. Chosen as much for their practical as their symbolic function, policemen mixed with members of the FFI, the latter bringing the necessary legitimacy to the actions of the body traditionally responsible for maintaining law and order. By virtue of their normal role and the fact that they were armed and wore uniforms, policemen played a dominant part in the way a *tonte* was carried out: they could be escorts, or guards, make arrests, and even share in the actual cutting of hair. Their participation could take the form expected, as was the case in a commune of the Haute Garonne where

> at the request of the person in charge at Blagnac, and in order to avoid a demonstration when five women from that town came to have their heads shaved for having had relationships with German soldiers, the armed members of the local police brigade formed a contingent to ensure that order would be maintained. The operation was carried out without incident.[26]

Whatever form the action took, there is no photograph or no record that allows us to see that police intervened in any autonomous way. The lack of authority that Raymond Aubrac talked about explains their need to go along with the majority and to take part in events bringing everyone together, even though their own role during the Occupation was far from forgotten. *Patriote*, the weekly paper the *FTP-Front national* in the department of Loir-et-Cher provides a reminder of this:

> As for the police who only last year would come during the night to wake up our young men and give them twenty minutes to go off to Germany, they have now tried to join ranks with those who have freed us by arming themselves with a pair of clippers; do they think their victims and the families of those who died will forgive them simply because they have shaved off the hair of a prostitute?[27]

Hostility of this kind can be seen expressed in a striking way towards the chief warrant officer of a police brigade in the Isère on account of the enthusiasm with which he had looked for men who refused to go to Germany to work and of his easygoing relationship with the *milice*. Arrested on the first occasion by the FFI on 22 August 1944, he was freed and then arrested again on 13 September 1944. Two days later

> the officer was led from the school where he was kept prisoner to the information services, and then to the police headquarters. He was taken back in the same fashion. He was dressed in a khaki shirt and combat trousers, bareheaded with his hair cut off to the skin. During the course of these two transfers he was escorted by three or four armed members of the FFI; several people, and in particular children, followed this procession. Jibes and offensive remarks were made at him as he went along. During the time I (the policeman making the report) was making my way. I noticed that the officer had in fact had his hair cut off and that his two eyes were circled in black.[28]

This is probably the sole case of a policeman who had his head shaved, reminding us that the police could be on both sides. But whatever individual or indeed group initiatives there may have been to join the Resistance at any time, the fact remains that the police had been active in supporting Vichy and the policy of collaboration.

The Attitude of the Allies

As part of the front line liberating the northern part of the country, as well as of a good part of the south-east, English and American soldiers often were present when women who had collaborated had their heads shaved.

A number of them have recalled these incidents in their memoirs published after the war.

Samuel Marshall tells of an intervention made by a sergeant against three women who had their heads shaved 'leave them in peace, let them be for God's sake. You are all collaborators!'[29] William Morgan remembers having 'had a skinful' so that he could forget the sight of a *tonte* carried out at Fresselines in the department of the Creuse.[30] For Alan Moorehead this feeling was a general one: 'Tommy and Sammy were sickened by the way the French treated women who had slept with Germans, dragging them into the public squares to shave their heads. It seems to them to be indecent and sadistic. They often intervened.'[31] At Saint Omer an officer stepped in to rescue three 'prostitutes' from the crowd.[32] On 29 August 1944 when Sables d'Olonne was liberated, a team from the *Jedburgh* stepped in to put an end to the looting of 'collaborators' shops' and to the shaving of the heads of women 'who had been friendly with Germans'.[33]

These few examples provide a partial picture in which Allied soldiers witnessed the shaving of women's heads, but if on the whole they all expressed a feeling of unease and even disgust, their interventions seem to be far less numerous than these accounts would lead us to believe. There is no French source that takes such incidents with the Allied troops into account. Always recalled on account of their arrival, or their passing through, the Allied troops are hardly mentioned at all in the context of women having their heads shaved. They may have been present, onlookers or photographers, but following orders, they did not allow themselves to get involved in the conflicts between French people.

What did the Authorities do?

Whether the representatives of central authority, namely prefects or commissioners of the Republic, local authorities, CDL, CLL and FFI, or major Resistance groups, no single, agreed line can be identified as coming from them. This can be explained by the fact that there were few explicit positions favourable or hostile whether about the practice of shaving heads, or about the lapse of time between the statements made about this – when they existed – and the actual way in which events developed. Given the importance of what would be said at the Liberation, however, such silence cannot be ignored. It is not attributable simply to missing sources.

Condemnation or *Laisser Faire?*

In the sometimes confused circumstances of the Liberation, concern for public order was expressed in similar ways by a number of Liberation committees. Appeals for people to remain calm, 'not to take justice into their own hands', or 'to forget individual revenge', can be found everywhere: in the departments of the Haute-Garonne, the Nord, the Seine-Inférieure, the Tarn,[34] and the list is far from being exhaustive. Most of them do not make explicit reference to the shaving of heads and there are many examples that suggest that this was not specifically targeted.

At Le Mans between 9 and 12 August 1944, appeals for calm were made daily in *Le Maine libre* by different authorities. On 9 August the prefect Costa and the local committee made statements in the local press and over loud speakers forbidding any arrests that were not legally sanctioned. The next day, a communiqué signed by the American authorities and by representatives of the Republican government, 'calling on the local people to remain dignified even in these days of celebration and not to give in to any rash actions towards people suspected of having collaborated with the enemy'. On 11 August it was the turn of the CGT to address the workers in Sarthe in the same way. Finally, on 12 August, the CDL renewed its call to people not to take justice into their own hands. Four successive calls for law and order, even though heads were being shaved in different parts of the town, and a 'march past of the women whose heads had been shaved' is recorded on 29 August 1944. Such repetition clearly signals the difficulties there were in maintaining order in a town that had not found itself in a particularly rebellious state and invites us to consider the extent to which the shaving of heads could be considered to be an irresponsible action.

In Clermont-Ferrand the general secretary of the local police indicated that 'during the week following the Liberation a committee looking into arrests was sitting in the central police station. After having had their heads shaved they ordered the release of seventy women.'[35] But Henry Ingrand, the republican commissioner for the same town, noted in the report he made when he arrived: 'at no time have we been overwhelmed. Severe tasks have been issued and carried out. It is true that actions based on revenge were to be feared.'[36] Is this a contradiction? Only apparently. In the capital town of the Auvergne, as elsewhere, the shaving of heads was hardly ever perceived as reflecting mere vengeance or the settling of scores.

Appeals quite explicitly condemning the practice as, for example, in the Nièvre, were less common:

Call to the general population: . . . the *épuration* must not appear to be victimization any more than it must be an opportunity for the satisfying of personal revenge. The carrying out of sentences issued by an over excited crowd on the town square can only be deplored. The masquerades of women of whose heads have been shaved must cease . . . the people of France . . . should know better than to lower themselves to those practices used by barbarians and Nazis. People of the Nièvre remain dignified![37]

This appeal was made by the local liberation committee from its headquarters in Nevers on 21 September 1944, or fifteen days after the town had been freed. A similar lapse of time can be found in the case of Paris on 4 September 1944. The newspapers, *Combat* and *Le Parisien libéré*, carried a decision made by Rol-Tanguy:

Colonel Rol, commander of the FFI troops in the Ile de France is sending this message to all of those in charge. It has been ascertained that women have been taken to police stations and town halls with their heads completely shaved and daubed with swastikas. All members of the Ile de France FFI are now ordered not to use such actions, anyone caught doing so will be liable to severe punishment.[38]

Whatever the reality of the punishments might have been, the date of this order is particularly late when we consider that the majority of women from the Paris area who had their heads shaved did so between 24 and 26 August 1944.

Does the fact that the positions – which were, to say the least, ambiguous – of a certain number of local committees and that a number of prefect's reports make no mention of these matters, suggest that there was a certain *laisser-faire* attitude on the part of the authorities?

On a national scale, most of the regional capitals throughout France witnessed this kind of violence immediately after they had been liberated; this is so for eighty out of the ninety *préfectures* that existed at the time. The case of the ten towns that constitute an exception deserves attention.

If Metz, Strasbourg and Colmar did not witness the shaving of heads at the time of their liberation in November and December 1944 and February 1945 respectively, there were women who had their heads shaved in the spring of 1945, even if some doubt remains about what happened in the *préfecture* of the Bas-Rhin.

The towns of Saint Lô and Caen were in large part destroyed and people evacuated. The shaving of heads took place in several villages in the departments of the Manche and of Calvados, but I have not been able to track down any record of any acts by people from these two *préfectures* – and this is also the case for Brest.

What happened precisely in Alençon, La Roche-sur-Yon and Mont-de-Marsan also remains unclear. There is no record of the practice either having been carried out or of not taking place at all. On the other hand, other areas in these departments certainly witnessed it, whether it was the Sables d'Olonne in the Vendée, Rémalard and Vire in the Orne, or Dax in the Landes.

The case of Épinal is different. Here the fact that there is no record may be interpreted as meaning that the punishment did not take place. Georges Savouirte, president of the local committee at the time of Liberation, confirms this:

> the Liberation took place with the order and the respect of the re-established republican traditions. A few people who emerged from safe hiding, or who had joined the Resistance at the last moment and who wanted now to play at being policemen, tried to demonstrate, but in vain. We quickly imposed order and decreed that the local committee that was installed in the prefect's offices would be in charge. There were not even any attempts to shave the heads of those poor creatures who had publicly demonstrated their affection for a German.[39]

The same was true of Tarbes. From the 24 August 1944, the *Nouvelle République des Pyrénées,* the official voice of the committee, published the following communiqué: 'no individual actions, no personal vengeance which would be shameful and which we would have to punish pitilessly. Anyone who tries to take justice into his own hands will be executed.' That there were no heads shaved is furthermore confirmed by the account of a visit made to the internment camp at Ger where 'all women – too bad for this picturesque description – have their hair intact'.[40] However, it is to be noted that at Lourdes the punishment was common, a fact which rather reduces the effectiveness of the position taken by the local committee.

Whatever form organization took, and in whatever way authority was shared out, it remains a fact that in eighty *préfectures* women had their heads shaved. If we adopt the typology proposed by Jacqueline Sainclivier concerning the distribution of authority in France at the time of the Liberation,[41] this is as true for those departments where the local liberation committee was subordinate to the prefects (in the departments of Aisne or Deux-Sèvres) as in those where, on the contrary, the committee challenged the authority of the prefect (in the Gard or Basses-

Pyrénées). The places where power was held were also those where the shaving of heads took place.

Without being able to provide an overall explanation for this attitude, there are a number of factors that have to be taken into account. The first is the expected nature of the punishment and the recognition by a large proportion of the population that it was appropriate. This is a point of view no doubt shared by those in positions of responsibility at the Liberation. The second is the speed with which the practice was carried out, in fact instantly and in some cases even before the new authorities were in place. Such authorities also had other urgent considerations to worry about and were probably concerned not to come into direct conflict with those who were carrying out the practice and who were supported by a large number of local people. What is more, women whose heads had been shaved became a visible proof of the beginnings of the *épuration* and of the first changes that were taking place. A desire to act as quickly as possible is also reflected, for example, by the number of local committees that were set up. And finally to shave women's heads could be seen as derisory and not worth taking any action over.

And yet if in some cases authorities showed little interest when it was something carried out during the first hours, or days of the Liberation, in others it was a practice that was in fact carefully organized.

Organization

The fact that a considerable number of women had their heads shaved in the same place already suggests there was an element of organization. To discover them, arrest them, escort, interrogate and judge them (even briefly) and finally to shave the heads of several dozen people, is not something to be carried out completely at random. This was the case, for example, in Beavais (eighty), Clermont-Ferrand (seventy), Creil (thirty-nine), Évreux (thirty). To carry out such acts requires numerous people; places for the punishment to be carried out or where the women can be held prisoner have to be selected and the time has to be fixed in order to forewarn local people. All of these decisions are taken by one or more people in charge. In a number of large towns throughout France therefore, what can only be described as a semi-official ceremony of head shaving can be found to have taken place.

In Romans (in the Drôme), a list of eight men accused of collaboration and being members of the *milice*, or PPF, and two women accused of 'intelligence with the *milice*' was published with the following comment:

'All these prisoners had their hair cut off on 6 September 1944.'[42] Given the fact that most of the people punished here were men, suggests that the practice was the result of an administrative decision applied to all those who had been collaborated and who had been interned.

In Grenoble, although women whose hair had been cut off were led through the streets on 22 August 1944, it did not mean that there were not other days following when other heads of hair were cut off inside the prison at Saint Joseph. On 25 August the daily paper *Les Allobroges* published a photograph with the following caption:

> on display yesterday afternoon outside the prison of Saint Joseph the good people of Grenoble could admire the aesthetics of the new wave in hair cutting much in favour amongst the high authorities of the Wehrmacht, in whose service these ladies had put their charm and their activities.

On 6 September in the same paper the last arrests were announced:

> A fine lot of traitors has been put under lock and key. Two more fine catches ... Two women have joined their associates in a prison which is already over full of detained people. The first of them was the mistress and accomplice of the sinister Max ... She would be very pretty if the prison hairdresser had not used his clippers in the fashionable way today for ladies ... Another wretched girl had a colonel as her lover who had her carry out activities against us. She too has had her head shaved and will very shortly have to reply to the judges for the crimes she has committed.

Once again inside the prison walls, the prison hairdresser continued the practice that had begun in public places.

Just about one case out of five occured in places where people were detained. In certain internment camps the mention 'to be shaved' or 'shaved' figures on the registers. In the Charente, the register by names of people in these camps includes a list of eighty-four people with the date when they entered the camp and the decision taken by the person in charge; there is also a file full of information:

> Mlle X spinster – entered the camp on 31 August. Decision taken by the committee: head shaved, eight days of detention in the camp. Released on 7 September 1944.

> Arrested by the officer in charge of the 6th Company, having been guilty of having a relationship with a German officer.

Mlle X admits that she was engaged to a German officer. She maintains that she should be excused on account of her youth (16 years). She recognizes nonetheless that she deserves to be punished.

Note made by the inspector: we propose the usual punishment – a few days of detention and the heads of both the mother and daughter to be shaved. Decision – heads to be shaved and eight days of detention for the daughter, eight days for the mother.[43]

Such examples illustrate the way the shaving of heads was methodically organized, at least in as much as it concerned a single prison or a single town. The decision could be the result of the initiative taken by an individual 'commander' of camp or prison without its having been approved by the liberation committee or the prefect. At a departmental level there is no trace of a decision having been taken by the authorities as a whole to organise the shaving of heads of women accused of collaboration. One region, however, is an exception – the Languedoc.

The Case of Languedoc

The liberation of Languedoc took a dozen or so days. On 21 August 1944 namely, four days after the beginning of the withdrawal of the remaining sections of the German army from the region, the garrison in Montpellier left the town. The following day the local committee, chaired by Jean Bène, who was the departmental representative of the MUR, the regional commissioner, Republican commissioner Jacques Bounin and the prefect of the Hérault, André Weiss, took over from the authorities representing Vichy just as the columns of the Wehrmacht crossed the town. This went on until 23 August. The FFI troops, who had among them most of the resistance fighters[44] from the hills above the town were still fighting with the Germans in the plain. The defence of Montpellier was assured by those few members of the *milice* who were patriotic, reinforced from 25 August by a few dozen men from the *maquis* of Valmy and Bir Hakeim. On 27 August, the FFI – about one thousand men – under the control of Gilbert de Chambrun entered the town. The next day the region as a whole was liberated completely and Emmanuel d'Astier de la Vigerie, commissioner for home affairs of the provisional government of the French Republic (GPRF), came to meet Jacques Bounin.

Immediately after the arrival of the FFI on 24 August 1944, a meeting was organized at the *préfecture* in order to 'define the role to be played by the *maquis* and the FFI.'[45] Twenty-one attended:

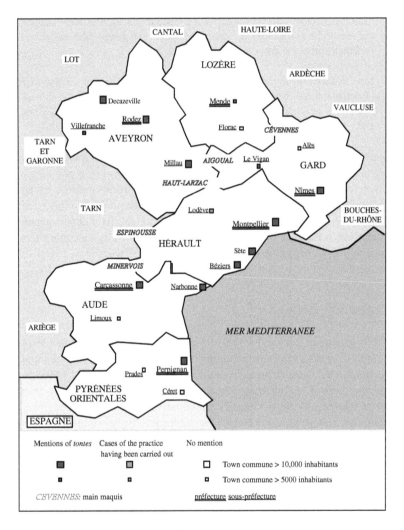

Map of the Languedoc region.

Chairman of the meeting, M. Maigret [J. Bounin], commissioner of the Republic. Present: M. Wallon [A. Weiss] prefect for the Hérault; M. Leveille member of the CRL; M. Hugon public prosecutor for the Republic; Gitard-Godin regional administrator for the local police; lieutenant-colonel Leroy in charge of armed forces; lieutenant-colonel Vernageau regional chief of the national police; colonel Carrel [G. de Chambrun] head of the FFI; lieutenant-colonel Mehar of the colonial infantry ; captain Benedict; commander Brugier;

captain Rabel; lieutenant Mene of the FTP; colonel Chauliac-Roland chief of the regional FFI headquarters; commander Arsac; lieutenant Michel; captain Granier, comrade Ollivet, MLN; comrade Planes, MLNPG; together with forty members of the patriotic *milice* and those from Rives.

The Republican commissioner underlined the difficulties which they had to face and those issues of immediate pressing importance: 'to re-establish law and order which had been undermined by certain "turbulent elements", who by their requisitioning, looting and unlawful arrests had gratuitously terrified the local population; to defend the town against any possible return of the Germans; to ensure that the town would be restocked with goods; and to organize the *épuration*.' The court martial was set up, but another decision was also taken: 'women who have slept with Germans will be sent off to work as prostitutes. They will have their heads shaved and be given cards.'[46]

In his memoirs, Jacques Bounin has no more to add by way of explanation to this decision and simply prefaces it by the simple comment 'it is proposed'. It is impossible to know who was behind this measure. Nonetheless it was taken by a group of people that, with the exception of the President of the CDL, represented almost all of the authoritative bodies in the region.

This decision had few echos. The *Bulletin officiel du CCR*, issued on 11 September 1944 makes no reference to it. The daily papers *La Voix de la Patrie* and *Le Midi libre* were published for the first time on the day the meeting took place. The last of these carries on 30 August a photograph of two women whose heads have been shaved with the following caption: 'This is the way that those sad creatures who compromised themselves with the Nazi soldiers are punished: their head shaved and plastered with a swastika is the mark of their shame.' Neither the place, nor the date when this took place are given, nor is the decision on 27 August mentioned. It is not until 13 September that *La Voix de la Patrie* carries a statement from the CDL of the Pyrénées-Orientales relating the decision taken at regional level: 'The CDL of the Pyrénées-Orientales region have just decided that with the exception of prostitutes working in brothels, women who had intimate relationships with Germans will have their heads shaved. In addition, like official prostitutes, they will be obliged to undergo a medical inspection twice a week.'

Contrary to what appears to be clear in other cases, the shaving of heads as a punishment was applied in the case of intimate relationships only. There was something paradoxical, it would seem, in the way these relationships were linked to prostitution, given that professional prostitutes themselves did not receive the same treatment. This confirms the scale on which 'horizontal collaboration' was viewed and the relative indulgence accorded to prostitutes. The further imposition of a twice-weekly visit to a doctor during a period of six months also reflects the way an administrative element was gradually being introduced as normality was restored.

According to the statistics for the *épuration* in this region, out of 802 people in total only thirty-two women were brought before the civic courts accused of having had 'intimate relationships'.[47] But it is clear that the *tonte* was not reserved exclusively for women guilty of 'horizontal collaboration'. For example, the daughter of a woman who had been interned complained to a friend about what happened to her mother: 'Mum was arrested and sent to the camp at Mérignac. And do you know what they did, those pigs? They cut off her hair in the way they cut off the hair of all those women who worked for the Boches.'[48]

From the files compiled on people interned in Béziers we have a better idea of the official policy about shaving heads in the Languedoc. The files of fifty-seven women arrested in Béziers between 25 August 1944, the date marking the liberation of the town, and the middle of November, were compiled by the committee responsible for the *épuration*. Forty of them lived in Béziers itself, the others came from fifteen other surrounding communes. In these files there is only confirmation of three cases of the punishment being carried out. Two women from Murviel had their heads shaved before they were arrested and there is a photograph of another with her name written on the back of it.

There are twenty-seven files indicating precisely what the women were accused of: fifteen of them were drawn up on account of their having had 'relationships with Germans'. A careful analysis would lead us to the conclusion that only three women in the town had their heads shaved, but other sources of information tend to suggest that there were more. It seems, in fact, that at least one other woman had her head shaved without the fact being recorded in her file. But above all, it is the committal order of a woman from Béziers which confounds the analysis. On this official document there is a hand written note which says: 'Madam X should not have her head shaved.'[49]

This note effects the way in which these files should be considered. It seems to have been normal that clippers should be used automatically, and whether they are mentioned or not in these documents seems to be a matter of chance. There is nothing which allows us to know what other

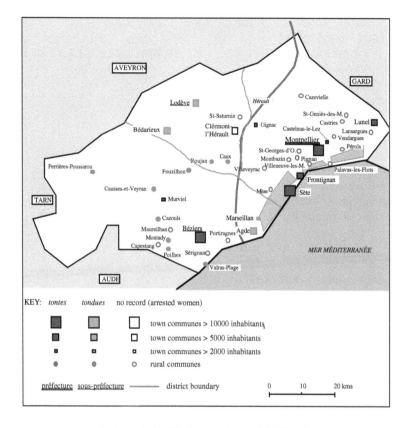

Tontes carried out in the department of the Hérault.

factors are at work (family links, personal knowledge, help given to the Resistance), or to know by what roundabout ways the order that a head should be shaved was given in other cases.

The reasons for the decision in the Languedoc remain unclear. There are no local or national circumstances that are sufficient to explain why the regional commissioner for the Republic in Languedoc chose to make this physical punishment an administrative matter.

As in other regions throughout France, women had their heads shaved before the Liberation. Four young men from Frontignan were even deported by the Germans because they had 'cut off a lock of hair' of a young woman during the Occupation.[50] By 27 August 1944, the day when the meeting took place in the prefecture, the shaving of women's heads had already been widely practised throughout the region, just as

SOUS-PREFECTURE
DE BEZIERS   REPUBLIQUE FRANCAISE
==========   ===========

MANDAT DE DEPOT

AU NOM DU PEUPLE FRANCAIS

Nous RAYNAUD, Sous-Préfet de l'Arrondissement
de Béziers, mandons et ordonnons à tous huissiers
ou agents de la force publique, de conduire à la
Maison d'Arrêt de Béziers, en se conformant à la
loi **la** nommée

X X X X X X X X X X Xxxxxxxxxx

demeurant à **BEZIERS**

Inculpé de relations avec un Allemand.

Enjoignons au gardien de la dite maison d'arrêt
de la recevoir et tenir en dépôt jusqu'à nouvel
ordre.

Requérons tous dépositaires de la force
publique de prêter main forte, en cas de nécessité
pour l'exécution du présent mandat.

En foi de quoi, le présent mandat a été signé
par nous Sous-Préfet et scellé.

Fait à BEZIERS, le **16 Novembre 1944**
Pour la Commission de Criblage
Le Sous-Préfet.

Reconstruction of a committal order. Béziers 16 November 1944.
Top left and over the stamp :MAISON D'ARRÊT BÉZIERS (Hérault), and a hand-written
note: No. 31 committed on 16 November 1944. Bottom left a round stamp: POLICE
MILTAIRE département de l'Hérault FFI (Croix de Lorraine) and a hand-written note
'Madame XXX should not have her head shaved. Lieutenant M.' followed by his
signature.

much as in the department of the Hérault. But the fact that it was carried out did not make it legal, any more than the claim that the medical visit was for prophylactic purposes hid the fact that it was a punitive measure. As elsewhere the decision was aimed quite precisely to punish women guilty of collaboration by a further humiliation – a kind of physical branding.

It is clear from work[51] that has been done on the liberation of Languedoc that this decision reflects the complicated relationship which existed between the FFI and the representatives of the GPRF. The FFI played a major part in the struggle against the Germans and in establishing the Liberation. For their local leader, Gilbert de Chambrun, otherwise known as 'Carrel', their task did not stop there. From then on it also had a judicial dimension with the establishment of the court martial from 29 August to 15 September 1944; one involving the police in the context of those patriotic members of the *milice*, which had been officially disbanded by the GPRF on 28 October 1944, who continued to carry out their duties in the region sometimes until January 1945; and a military one with the establishment of the 80th and 81st infantry regiments which included the first army. For his part, Jacques Bounin had two major considerations: to re-establish the authority of the state and to reassure the leading citizens of the area.[52] Aware of the situation he advised his prefects 'not to clash with the FFI'. In this way relationships between the FFI and the representatives of the Republic were based less on strength but rather on reciprocal confidence and compromise. Given this the setting up of 'administrative head shavings' can be considered to have been a way of putting an end to demonstrations which had got out of hand – the shaving of heads had taken place in Montpellier from the 21 August 1944 – to ensure that the FFI had the role of a police force and to make sure that all forms of purging were decided by the state. An incident related by the acting commissioner of police makes this clear:

> About four o'clock my attention was attracted by a noise coming from the theatre. Two women who had their heads completely shaved were being driven through the town in a car. I went down immediately to try and keep the crowd in check. I got four inspectors to help. I also sent an officer to the girls school to get further help, but before it could arrive, a car containing a group of FFI officers appeared. Quarante (a representative of the patriotic *milice*) took it upon himself to ensure that they would be protected, and took them by car to the 32nd DI.[53]

In this way police officers and members of the FFI worked together to bring this demonstration of 29 August 1944 to an end.

Was the main concern then 'to ensure as quickly as possible, if not immediately, the primacy of the civic authority of the state'[54] that persuaded Jacques Bounin to give quasi legal status to this sanction? The decision was a natural one and can only be seen to be something that had to be taken as a matter of urgency. At Narbonne (in the department of Aude), Béziers (Hérault), Rodez (Aveyron), women were still having their heads shaved in November 1944, nearly three months after the region had been liberated. And yet the authorities reacted only when such actions took place outside an agreed framework and when they were accompanied by public demonstrations.

This was the case of four women from Gignac, whose hair was completely shaved off by the FFI on 15 September 1944. Amongst the FFI troops, two were from the same community as the women, but the lieutenant in charge was unknown to those present. The president of the local committee was opposed to this action, which was carried out or initiated by four members of the Bir Hakeim group, but stated that 'in view of the way these men insisted, I had to give in'. Extreme pressure, even constraint, seems therefore to have been exerted. The father of one of the women, however, 'held the municipality responsible for not having prevented the punishment from being carried out'. He complained to Weiss the prefect of the Hérault, who transmitted his complaint to Colonel de Chambrun, head of the local FFI. The police finally carried out an inquest, but the result is not known.

More significant still is the correspondence from Weiss addressed to Raynaud, his deputy, based in Béziers:

> I have to inform you that my attention has been once more drawn to certain regrettable facts which have happened in Béziers. I have been informed that a certain Mme X, fifty years old, was arrested and led through the Allées Paul-Riquet, after having her head shaved. This woman's son had been shot a few days before. While repressive measures may be necessary, I consider it regrettable that there should be excesses of this nature, because they are contrary to the most basic humanity and are of a kind which will cause public opinion to turn against our government. I am asking you, therefore, to conduct an inquiry into these events and I am asking you to make sure with the mayor of Béziers that they do not occur again.[55]

This incident illustrates the high degree of tension that Béziers experienced. On 20 December 1944 two members of the *milice* and a married couple who had been agents of the Gestapo – the wife had already had her head shaved – were taken from prison and executed in the courtyard of the former *sous-préfecture*. Four other people were also killed between this date and 2 January 1945. From that moment on the prefect managed to restore order, Raynaud was suspended and the patriotic *milice*, which had been illegally kept in place since the end of October, was finally disbanded.

It is evident that for the regional or departmental authorities in Languedoc, head shaving should take place within agreed limits, in other words inside internment centres, without there being any showy demonstration and that it should be decided and executed by those in authority. While, therefore, the towns in Languedoc were no different from those in the rest of France during the days following their liberation, the establishment by the authorities of a paralegal organization meant that the shaving of women's heads would go on longer there than elsewhere.

However distinct the case of Languedoc should not be seen to be at odds with that of the rest of the country. The administrative nature of the *tontes* here, indicates a region where the influence of the FFI remained alongside that of local liberation committees. If, among others, the choice of this particular form of legal punishment made the region distinctive, it also shows how it was imposed in different, but general ways during the Liberation.

–5–

Head Shaving and Brutalities after the Liberation

The practice of shaving heads did not disappear once the Liberation was over, continuing for several weeks after that date. In one of the principal camps at Châteauroux, women had their heads shaved the day after their arrest, in other words up until mid-October 1944.[1] In other places like Cherbourg or Tulle, the first cases of heads being shaved date from two weeks (14 July 1944) and one month (11 September 1944) respectively after these two towns had been liberated. In Cherbourg this could have been the result of the intensity with which street fighting continued before the surrender of the German garrison, or to the strong, continuing presence of American forces. In the case of Tulle, it could have been due to the role played by the Committee of Martyrs, under the direction of Canon Espinasse, whose interventions put a check to the way the *épuration* was carried out in a town still traumatized by the savage nature of the repressive measures taken by the Germans in June 1944 (99 people hung, 144 deported). However, whatever the local circumstances, the practice became increasingly a fundamental part of the tense atmosphere which was created by the *épuration*.

The Épuration: First Signs of Discontent and the First Divisions

Work which has been done on the *épuration* puts on one side a period outside any judicial control and often defined as summary or even brutal and on the other a legal one once courts had been set up. The phenomenon of the *tontes* demands that this distinction should be qualified. While the consultative assembly in Algiers may have wanted to ensure there was a legal framework for the punishment of traitors, for many ordinary people the *épuration* was simply an extension of a fight that had begun during the Occupation and that was leading to the creation of a new France. As such, the desire to purge expressed a need not only for justice but also for a rediscovered purity. This political project in the widest sense of the term, meant that the *épuration* concerned everybody and was the foremost preoccupation of French people, at least until the end of 1944.[2] That this was so can be seen by the attitudes of people during the days of liberation when anyone could be involved in the arrest of a neighbour, in the shaving of the head of a local woman, or in the plundering of premises which had belonged to collaborators.

The movement towards a judicial *épuration* was not a simple linear one. The setting up of certain necessary structures – courts of justice, commissions to check up on internments – and the way in which prefects increasingly controlled how arrests and imprisonments were made, certainly meant that there were fewer illegal acts of violence even if they did not disappear altogether. Although it became less frequent, the practice of shaving heads – like executions or rebellious activities – continued during the last few months of 1944. It did so, however, in ways that were different from what happened at the Liberation and illustrated how French society was divided on the subject of the *épuration*. '[The *épuration* and repressive measures] have become the two vexing questions on which all discussions and critical remarks are focussed',[3] is what we can read in a general statement issued by the national police.

The way in which the courts worked, the way in which because of insufficient evidence people imprisoned at the Liberation were now released, appeared to many to be the result of the wish of the authorities to limit the effects of the *épuration* to a strict minimum. In February 1945 Yves Farge's description of the situation in the area around Lyon would soon be true of most of the country: 'The edge has gone from the sentences passed by the courts . . . and certain minority groups are taking this as an excuse to satisfy personal vendettas.'[4]

The press also had a large part to play in this debate and a number of articles castigated the way people were made scapegoats and the way in which the courts were becoming increasingly lenient. The fact that the *épuration* took a long time to take effect became a matter of public debate throughout the last months of 1944 and well into 1945. The court sessions often provoked demonstrations both inside and outside the buildings. Before the crisis of the winter of 1944–5 and much to the concern of the authorities attacks on prisons increased as did demonstrations during which women's heads were shaved. At Rodez on 19 November 1944, two had their heads shaved, were decked out with signs and led through the streets of the town by FFI soldiers and their captain. While there may have been general approval of this form of punishment in the same town at the moment it was liberated, opinions were now very divided. The local section of the Union of French women and the Committee of intellectuals condemned the practice quite firmly. Gaston Ferdière, president of the Committee of intellectuals, wrote in *Le Rouergue républicain* on 21 November 1944:

> On Sunday, around 12 o'clock I witnessed a dreadful scene for which those responsible should, in my view, be punished in an exemplary manner . . . I will protest using any methods I can, against such actions which degrade us, which drag us down to the level of a circus, which degrade us as they degrade the courageous troops of the FFI . . . A spineless group of people were following this scene and I have to say I am sorry that it included women and children. The first revolution to be undertaken is most definitely a moral revolution.

For the *épuration* to be revived, action was necessary, even if the prefecture did not respond.[5]

But any attempt to use the *tonte* symbolically for political ends no longer worked. Three months almost to the day after Rodez had been liberated, this procession provoked extremely angry reactions. The contrast with the position taken by the same paper on 23 August 1944 is quite clear: 'No signs of pity therefore for these women who have collaborated with the awful actions of the Boches, who have been brought forward now to answer for their misdeeds, a troop of women who prostituted their souls and devoted themselves to the enemy through their willingness to indulge in propaganda and denunciations.'

Failure to agree did not prevent those who feared that leniency was getting the better of severity from shaving the heads of women who acquitted and freed after several weeks of imprisonment, or who were given punishments by the courts which, in their view were, too slight. It was often in their homes that those who had been 'forgotten' were punished by those who zealously wielded hair clippers, sometimes against the advice of their leaders or of the local Liberation committee. These acts appear to have been carried out by small groups or even individuals.One supposed member of the FTP tells in a letter, which was intercepted by the authorities, that he took the initiative into his own hands: 'It's a woman who went along with the Gestapo and whom the court allowed to go free, but I was there and when she came out of prison I arrested her again and took her to our own prison where *I* cut off her hair completely on the pretext that she had lice and a whole lot of other things as well.'[6] The repeated use of 'I/me' as someone who would guarantee that the *épuration* would be carried out, gives us a sense of the increasing disillusion, which many shared. For them the gap between what they considered necessary and the incomprehensible decisions taken by the courts, simply grew wider. In most cases, however, those who disapproved of what they considered to be unjustified mercy – freedom, or the simple loss of rights – merely wrote letters of protest.

This attitude, even if it was not unanimous, was something the authorities had to take into account. In the Vaucluse, for example, to keep women in prison was sometimes a guarantee that they would be protected: 'In order to avoid future difficulties, it is better not to let them out of prison since this could provoke a dangerous reaction from the general public. If there remain in the prison of Saint Anne or the internment camp a few people against whom only a few charges can be made, it is in their interest, since they could be the object of continued bitterness and hence in danger.'[7] However tense and serious certain events might be, the practice of shaving heads became exceptional and gradually disappeared. While attacks on prisons in a number of towns took place during the winter, there is no record of them.[8] When attacks were made on prisons and were preceded by demonstrations,[9] the aim of those who were most determined was to do away with a person, whether man or woman, who had escaped being sentenced to death, or who could eventually expect to be pardoned.

The Second Wave: May–July 1945

The capitulation of Nazi Germany on 8 May 1945 marked the end of the war in Europe. In France this date was situated between the two rounds of municipal elections on 29 April and 13 May. That is to say the context in which the shaving of heads would continue to take place had nothing to do with the situation that the country had known nine months previously. The war was over, France was finding its way again, the fears of a civil war and then of revolution were fading. And yet there was a certain resurgence of violent acts intended to purge, which can be explained by the conjunction of a number of different events.

The weeks immediately before the end of the war were for many those when the world of the concentration camps[10] were first discovered. First of all there were photographs appearing in the press from the middle of April,[11] followed by films of what had actually happened, and then the return over a long period of time of those who had been deported. The shock was brutal and revealed the full horror of the Nazi plan.

Those who had been deported were not the only ones to come back from Germany. Nearly a million prisoners of war were repatriated after four years absence, as well as nearly 700,000 who had been taken off to work in Germany. Those who had voluntarily gone to Germany to work also returned, as did those who had fled with the Germans at the time of their retreat. The welcome they received was as varied as their numbers were mixed. There was the joy of reunion, the disappointment at not seeing the person who was expected, and the emotion or surprise when confronted with physical change; but there was also a desire for vengeance or justice and anger that became apparent on platforms in railway stations. The overview of events provided by the national police underlines this particular climate when in the confusion surrounding the arrival of each train 'it is not unusual to see members of the public taking care to sort out men and women who had left voluntarily to go to Germany from the prisoners and from those who were deported or conscripted'.[12] People were waiting for those who had collaborated and had remained unpunished; those who were deported wanted justice. For all of these people the *épuration* had not happened. What is more, a number of people who had been interned for having collaborated had, since the summer or autumn 1944, been released and were back home. This was an extra reason to want a wide-ranging *épuration* to be carried out against those who were guilty and who had been up to then spared, just as much as against those who were reappearing. All of these are reasons that may explain why there should be a return to the urgent practices of the *épuration* of which head shaving was one.

Although not as widespread as it had been at the time of the Liberation, violence erupted in nearly a quarter of the departments. First and foremost it was directed at those people who had not been living in France at the time of the Liberation. On the one hand, those voluntary workers amongst whom there were 40,000 women, who, unlike men, could not claim to have been conscripts for the workforce in Germany (STO). On the other hand those who had been deported and for whom experience made those who had sided with Vichy and the occupying forces unacceptable. In several places the part they played in the organization of violence was clear. The commissioner of the Republic in Dijon recorded for example that 'a number of incidents had taken place during the last fortnight . . . which showed the extent to which those who had been deported and had now returned intend to carry out justice'.[13] In the Dordogne the situation was similar where the prefect underlined the fact that 'when repatriation began, those who had been deported were particularly violent and showed a tendency to want to carry out purifying measures where, in their view, the judicial authorities had been too weak'.[14]

Whatever the role played by those who had been deported might have been, the scale of violence in the spring of 1945 went beyond their desire

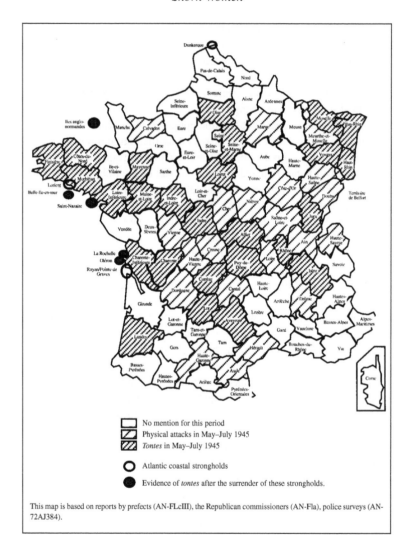

No mention for this period
Physical attacks in May–July 1945
Tontes in May–July 1945

O Atlantic coastal strongholds

● Evidence of *tontes* after the surrender of these strongholds.

This map is based on reports by prefects (AN-FLcIII), the Republican commissioners (AN-Fla), police surveys (AN-72AJ384).

Tontes and physical attacks (May–July 1945).

for justice or revenge. Such violence was rarely the work of just a handful, but rather of large and important groups. At Jarny (in the department of Meurthe-et Moselle) 200 people attacked an Italian family known for being fascist; as many inhabitants of Châlette-sur-Loing (in the Loiret) set about fifteen men and women who had been repatriated from Germany, shaved their heads and covered them with tar; at Cransac (in the Aveyron) as at Givors (in the Rhône) there were nearly 300 people who shaved the heads of those who had gone to work voluntarily in Germany; at Dives-sur-Mer at Cabourg (in Calvados), there were 500 people, 1,000 at Meaux (Seine-et-Marne), 1,500 at Annemasse (Haute-Savoie)[15] . . . The way in which crowds of people took part in this way shows how sensitive the issues of the *épuration* for many were.

Those who had gone to work voluntarily in German were not the sole targets. Sentences that were too clement, judgements that took too long to be realized, presidential pardons, all provoked reactions from parts of the general public that were at times violent. In Cahors on 26 June 1945 a crowd of people from Figeac went to hear the death sentence passed on a Gestapo agent responsible for rounding people up and for having deported 1,200. They tried to grab hold of him, but failed. After this moment of excitement, they decided to set about three women 'well known for their intimate relationships with German soldiers or officers, and who as a result had been imprisoned, but who were now released'. They had their heads shaved, were daubed with swastikas and then led through the streets of the town. This 'distraction' allowed the condemned man to be transferred to his prison and for calm to be gradually restored. He was eventually executed a few days later.[16]

The fact that information was more widely and more easily available than in the spring of 1945 nine months earlier, probably had an influence on the way in which the shaving of heads started again. The events in Cahors were reported the next day by *Le Patriote de l'Eure*. The Republican commissioner in Poitiers feared 'that recent demonstrations in Paris widely reported by the press and exploited by certain newspapers, would find an echo in the provinces.'[17] The wave of violence intended to purge during the months of May–July 1945, shows how much time was needed after the end of the war. Having been given up and condemned in the autumn of 1944, *tonte* returned and for a while was prominent. Had it lost all connection with the 'liberation' and simply become a form of sexist punishment or, on the contrary, did it allow those who had not had the experience of the Liberation to become part of the national community again and give proof of their presence and existence?

The Case of the Moselle

As an annexe of the Third Reich during the war, the department of the Moselle witnessed a situation that was very different from the rest of

France. The local context explains the unique way in which the shaving of heads took place; non-existent at the time of the Liberation, by June 1945, the practice was widespread.

Merged with the *Gau* of Sarre-Platinat,[18] the department had experienced a brutal policy of assimilation and Nazification. In July 1940 the first steps to expel those members of the population who were French speaking began; 20,000 people were forced to leave in that month, followed by 64,000 others during the following months until November. If to this number we add the 60,000 people who had left the department before the arrival of the Germans and who were forbidden to return, in all about 20 per cent of the population had been forced out of the Moselle. In certain areas in the south of the department, particularly around Château-Salins, there was hardly a living soul left.

The Germanization had various symbolic features: street names were changed, the wearing of berets was forbidden, books were burned in the town square of Saint Jean in Metz, on the war memorials the inscription 'To the children of Metz who died victims of the war' was replaced by 'Died for the Reich'.[19] But there was also a policy of Nazification which went much deeper. The school system was entirely changed. Nazi organisations – NSDAP, SS, NSKK, Hitler-Jugend, Bund Deutscher Mädchen, N.S. Frauenschaft – were gradually set up.[20] Finally, in 1942, German nationality was given to inhabitants of Alsace, Moselle and Luxembourg in order to draft men into the army. Among these there were 15,000 to 20,000 who came from Lorraine.[21]

In spite of repressive measures against any form of opposition to this policy, throughout this period there were demonstrations of hostility and more exceptionally of resistance. They could be the use of the French language, a refusal to give the obligatory Nazi salute, demonstrations at the time of incorporation into the Wehrmacht, desertions, and the organization of a few resistance networks such as the group known as 'Mario', most of whose members were deported.

The way in which the Liberation occurred in this region, made it different from the rest of the country. First of all it was late in coming and prolonged: American troops under the command of General Patton arrived on the left bank of the Moselle on 11 September 1944. Metz was not liberated, however, until 22 November 1944, Strasbourg on 23 November, and the area around Colmar not until the beginning of February. Before that the region experienced violent fighting and air raids and the liberation was more fragile there than elsewhere. The Ardennes offensive directly threatened the region and provoked a conflict between De Gaulle and Eisenhower on the subject of the defence of the Alsatian capital. Finally, and it is probably one of the most important features of the purging acts of violence in 1945, the Germans from September 1944 onwards sent numerous people from the Moselle[22] to Germany, amongst whom were those who were most favourably inclined towards them. Their return from the end of April 1945 onwards provoked a number of conflicts.

Contrary to what happened in neighbouring departments at the Liberation, in Alsace-Moselle there seems not to have been any shaving of women's heads. The first mention of the practice is dated 3 March 1945. The woman concerned was of German origin staying at Moyeuvre-Petite and who had fled to her native country with her three children on 30 August 1944. Repatriated by the Americans:

> She was welcomed by the female population of her town who took her to the town hall where she spent the night. In the morning she had her head shaved and had her face marked in red ink with the Swastika. About eight o'clock after having been led through Moyeuvre-Petite, the procession of more than fifty men and women went towards Moyeuvre-Grande. Here she was also led through the streets and then handed over to the police who shut her up in the local police station while waiting for her to be transferred to a detention centre at Queuleu. Already she was considered to be unworthy of being French even though she had been naturalised. She had received a number of German customs officers in her house and it was publicly rumoured that she had been responsible for denouncing a number of prisoners.[23]

Here we have a procedure similar to the one witnessed at the Liberation: the cutting of hair, the drawing of the swastika, the procession from the town hall, the active participation of the local population, but with the difference that what triggered it off was not the departure of the Germans, or the arrival of the liberating forces, but the return of people reputed to be in favour of the Nazis. It was the repatriation of these people that provoked lynchings and the shaving of heads in a number of towns and villages. There were also violent demonstrations carried out by many people, with blows being exchanged and stones thrown but which, in the department of the Moselle, do not seem to have caused any deaths.

The authorities were fully aware of the situation and increasingly appealed to Paris. Between mid-April and mid-June they insisted on the fact that violence was on the increase and that it was difficult to cope with it. On 1 May 1945 the prefect, who was already very aware of existing tensions, could foresee difficulties in the future ('those who were expelled will carry out justice in their own way') and regretted the fact that the government minister had failed to reply: 'I have already drawn your

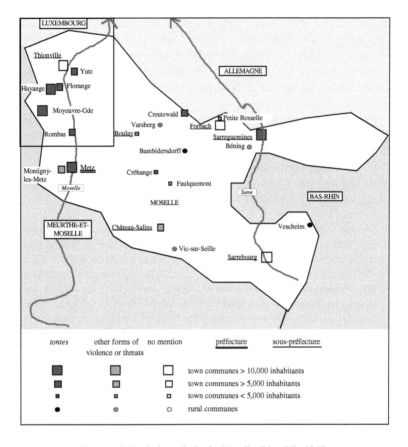

Tontes and physical attacks in the Moselle (May-July 1945).

attention on a number of occasions to this fact, but unfortunately my appeals have not been heard.' A fortnight later he would mention the first incident: 'Feelings towards those who showed a certain kindness towards the enemy during the Occupation are tense. During the days of celebration the crowd tore down a number of flags hanging at the windows of former collaborators. In the village of Kœnigsmacker, one of those who wanted to oppose the taking down of a flag slightly injured one of the demonstrators.' By the 1 June the situation had become markedly worse:

> the fears which I expressed as soon as I arrived in Moselle are being realised, and more than I imagined. When there is contact between those who had been expelled with those who remained here, there are always violent clashes . . .

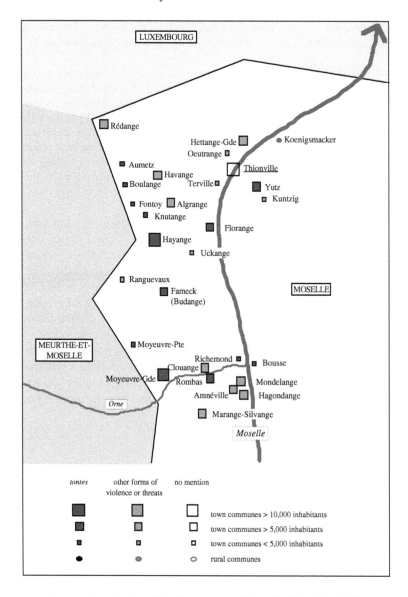

Tontes and physical attacks in the area around Thionville (May–July 1945).

When the end of the war was celebrated, many flags were torn down from the windows of those who had remained, swastikas were painted on walls, woman had their heads shaved.

Finally on 15 June the prefect made it clear that in spite of measures that had been taken, it was difficult to keep the situation under control:

> There have been incidents between those who were deported and those people from Lorraine who followed the German troops back home and who have now returned with the prisoners of war. I have been obliged to intervene and appeal for calm. I have ordered the imprisonment of certain local people with sympathy for the Germans. The crowd gathered outside the police station has tried to lynch the undesirable people who have returned and the local police can only protect them with very great difficulty. On 7 June last, by putting up notices and making announcements in the local press, I have called on the local population to show greater calm.[24]

In the Moselle, the shaving of heads was carried out at the same time as the judicial process of *épuration* and at break neck speed. On the one hand there was the local population who wanted to punish those persons reputedly in favour of the Nazis, and on the other were the authorities, concerned to carry out the *épuration* and the process of de-Nazification but also to maintain public order. The slowness of the judicial process was due to the very large number of files to be considered, and the desire to see justice done. In the Moselle there were 4,102 people to be judged,[25] or nearly 1 per cent of the population, a number of which with that of the Bas-Rhin, represents one of the highest percentages in the whole country.

In order to cope with this situation the authorities tried to introduce a system of rapid imprisonment for any persons who were threatened. On

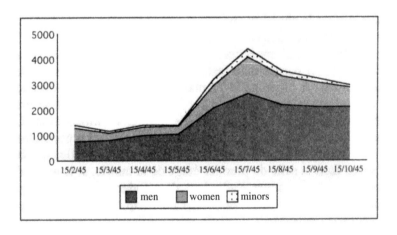

Evolution of the population imprisoned at the CSS in Queuleu (Metz).[26]

7 April 1945 the prefect took the decision to intern all those who had left of their own accord with the Germans in 1944.[27] In the supervised internment centre at Queuleu (Metz), numbers multiplied threefold between 15 May and 15 July 1945, and the proportion of women and children during the same period went from 24 per cent to 40 per cent. By 1 January 1946, 8,452 people had been arrested in the Moselle since the Liberation. The number is high, but most of them were only subject to provisional imprisonment; by the middle of July 1945 only 305 of them remained in captivity. Orders forbidding residence altogether were also used by the prefect in order to avoid incidents that would certainly have been provoked by the return home of a number of people who had been set free. In March 1946, 1,820 orders keeping people away from their homes were still in force. The court of justice, and in particular the civil court, also issued a number of orders (1,042) forbidding residence.

Such measures as these did not prevent national and local police forces from being overwhelmed by demonstrators who gathered whenever undesirable people arrived. At Florange on 22 May 1945, five women returned from Germany and, with their husbands who had been interned at Queuleu, went to the town hall to be given their ration cards. The mayor gave the following account of how events developed:

> The local population had gathered, intending to treat them badly and they were put into a room on the first floor of the town hall, and the person in charge of the police went to find his colleague from the national police force in Hayange to ask him to take them to the camp at Suzange, but this was not practical.
>
> Coming back from the factory at 18:30 I found a crowd of between 500–600 people in the courtyard of the town hall who were demonstrating, wanting the women to be handed over to them so that they could cut off their hair.
>
> After a series of ineffective attempts to restore calm, and still not having a telephone, I had to send the policeman in charge at 20:00 hrs with a letter asking for reinforcements.
>
> About 20:30 hrs five American soldiers came asking what was happening and saying that they wanted to see the women. In order to gain time, I let them go up to the first floor. Half an hour later, the crowd which had become overexcited, managed to get into the main corridor of the town hall, in spite of the resistance offered by our former guard, who was leaving the service that very day, as well as by the principal assistant mayor, and by myself. Three women were dragged into the courtyard and had their heads shaved, and the two others suffered the same fate. Around 21:30 hrs the officer from the national police headquarters arrived with seven or eight men. At that moment, some local people brought along two other women who had been taken from their homes. Finally at 22:00 hrs the seven women were brought together at the town hall could be taken to the camp at Suzange accompanied by policemen.[28]

For six hours, a section of the local population and the authorities confronted one another. Such highly tense moments were frequent, and illustrate the determination shown by part of the population in these places to shave women's heads. The same day, (22 May 1945) at Fontoy, the mayor managed to save an eighteen-year-old woman from having her head shaved by declaring 'that to cut off women's hair for reasons of reprisal, was forbidden in France, that the department of the Moselle was part of France, and that if notwithstanding his advice, they wished to carry on and cut off the hair of these women, they would be entirely responsible.'[29] That did not prevent a demonstration taking place that evening against others who had been repatriated and whose luggage had been burned in the public square. Such violence was only brought to an end by the intervention of members of the national police force. On 23 May 1945 another woman was taken aside and had her head shaved before the mayor could intervene. The next day it was the turn of a former SA to be beaten up after he had been let out of his internment camp.[30]

Nearly all the people against whom violence had been directed were those who had left the Moselle along with Germans, but that fact, was not the sole reason for their being accused.

Contrary to what could be observed in the rest of France, political collaboration was predominant here. To belong to a Nazi organization, to give the Hitler salute, to hang up a Nazi flag or the portrait of the Führer, were the most frequent reasons and were responsible for 84 per cent of all people before the courts during the *épuration*. For women, the principal organization to which they belonged was the Frauenschaft, and more rarely the NSDAP, but the accusations made against them were often directed at their entire family. Having come back from Germany together, couples, or families sympathetic to the Nazis – one of them was designated as 'bochophile'[32] – were a prime target. In Boulange, as in Bambiderstroff, men and women alike had their heads shaved.[33] The internment of whole families explains the number of women who were interned (34 per cent)[34] in the two supervised centres in the department, even though they only made up 17 per cent of the people who were condemned.

The figure of 12 per cent of women reproached for having had sexual relationships with Germans is the one which causes the biggest problem. François Rouquet has made the point that women who worked for the post office in Alsace-Moselle, 'were rarely pursued for having had amorous relationships with Germans'. He also has written: 'In Alsace-Lorraine, administrative sanctions were not handed out as they were elsewhere on the assumption that sexual relationships had taken place.'[35]

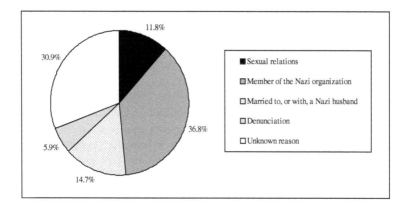

11.8%

30.9%

36.8%

5.9%

14.7%

■ Sexual relations

▣ Member of the Nazi organization

☐ Married to, or with, a Nazi husband

☐ Denunciation

☐ Unknown reason

Accusations made against women who had their heads shaved, or who were physically assaulted in the Moselle.[31]

Charles Hiegel, for his part, makes no mention of this kind of collaboration. Now if in other departments the proportionate number of women was lower, some were reproached for having had sexual relations, these being seen as the final evidence of an enthusiasm for Nazism. Even in the particular context of the Moselle, where women were concerned, sexuality was never totally seen as separate from general commitment. The accusations made against one woman who returned from Hettange-Grange illustrate this well:

Mme X has a reputation for being a 'modern', preferring to be a woman of leisure than one who looked after her house. Having gone to the local school in S, she remained there until her marriage. In the meantime she had spent a few months in Paris with her sister. She belonged to a number of local societies, liked to go to the theatre, liked camping, and regularly went to various performances. On one occasion, at a masked ball, she was awarded the first prize for being dressed up as 'Marianne'. During the Occupation no woman was noticed more for the way in which she dressed in a genuine German manner. With her authoritarian manner, minding everybody else's business, always being critical, she had everything about her which made her act as a *Frauenschaftsleiterin* . . . her greatest mistake was to have believed in a German victory, and above all to have dragged her husband into Hitler's schemes (NSDAP, SA). It seems that she had an intimate relationship with a German.[36]

This picture goes way beyond that of someone who was guilty of having an association with the Nazis; her way of life and her sexuality are equally condemned. In the eyes of her accusers she was guilty on two counts. Having as a French woman taken on the role of Marianne before the war, the change in her dress habits, once the region had been annexed by the Germans, was seen as a denial of the French nation; as woman she had dragged her husband into the German system. His weakness and submissiveness to his wife made him more a victim than an accomplice; a victim for having believed in the possibility of a German victory, and the victim also of the supposed adultery of his wife. What is more, the idle, bossy and extrovert behaviour of his wife was a negation of the woman's traditional role and its explicit 'modernity' was condemned.

Thus, whatever the particular circumstances of the Moselle, the imposition of head shaving as a punishment, followed the national trend. Here, as elsewhere, it would gradually disappear from the summer of 1945 onward.

The Practice of Head Shaving Comes to an End

After the resurgence during the months of May to July 1945, all indications – whether they be the reports by prefects, general statements provided by the police, or press accounts – show a clear and rapid reduction in the number of acts of violence intended to purge. Before disappearing completely, they lost their collective, ostentatious nature. As Luc Capdevila has already shown for Brittany, bomb attacks, the machine gunning of houses – in other words, actions of the underground military – continued for a few months although they reduced markedly less frequent from August 1945 onwards.[37] The growing hostility from local people, the systematic condemnation of different organizations that had emerged from the Resistance, interventions by national and local police when confronted by such violence, the determination of public authorities to maintain order by imposing exclusion orders more severely mark the end of a period that had begun with the arrival of Allied forces and the return to the normality of the Republic. The shaving of heads collectively, as something that confirmed how this change took place, was the first action to disappear. The last three cases of it took place at the beginning of 1946 and mark the end of it altogether.

In a village in the Savoie, 'on 23 February, five armed and masked individuals went into a house which was occupied by a widow and her nephew. Having molested them and cut off the woman's hair, they left without taking anything. Why this attack was carried out is not known'.[38] This reminds us of what happened during the Occupation. It took place in a secretive way, the motives were not established, the designation of those who carried it out by the term 'ill doers', classifies them under common law. The fact that the attackers did not appear to be claiming anything and that they needed to be masked, indicates a new context in which not only had the shaving of heads become illegal, but one in which those who carried it out were liable to be pursued in justice.

At Rombas in the Moselle a threat was made by a group of former resistance fighters who were expressing their anger and hostility at the return of a number of people who had previously been interned at Queuleu (Metz):

> We wish to state that we will oppose by all possible means, and by brute strength if necessary, the scandalous way that it is being claimed that people are being sent away. Questioned about what they meant by 'brute force', they replied that they would organise marches, mass demonstrations, and that women who had shown themselves to have pro-German feelings would have their heads shaved, and that men who had collaborated could be given a 'quick bath' in the Orne.[39]

The threat was sufficiently serious to make the *sous-préfet* decide to go ahead with twenty-nine orders for people to be sent away. A month later the threat was remade with the same result.

This incident is different, however, from anything that had happened when the shaving of heads was carried out in the region eight months earlier. In the period from May to July 1945, no warning was given before the punishment was carried out. There was a desire, on the contrary, for people to get hold of their victims when they returned from Germany before the authorities could intervene. The particular form the ultimatum took, the drawing up of a motion, and the appointment of a delegation, put this case in an institutional framework which was very different from anything that had existed previously. Only when the commissioner asked for an explanation of 'brute strength' was it clear that the forms of violence anticipated while slight, were nonetheless very evocative – procession, demonstration, enforced dips and head shaving. The aim of the group was more to have undesirable people sent away through exerting pressure in a very traditional way in a democratic society, than by indulging in violence. The juxtaposition of actions that drew on democratic traditions but at the same time recalled the kinds of violence used for purging purposes, make the Rombas incident a pivotal one between the two periods.

The last example does not contradict the movement towards a peaceful society, but it does show that there could be, whatever the general trend, differences continuing to exist because of local circumstances. The people of a village in the Gard were called together by the sound of their alarm bell on 14 March 1946 in order to 'give a woman and her son what they deserved'. They were molested, she had her head shaved and they were only saved 'thanks to the intervention by the police who had to invent an arrest warrant in order to keep them out of the hands of the crowd'.[40] Three days later, an attempt was made to blow up their house. The fact that this family had been deeply involved in collaboration explains the violence shown to them when they returned. The father had been president of the Special Delegation, the two sons members of the *milice*, and all three of them had caused serious problems for local people. The return, a year-and-a-half later, of two members of a family known to everybody, was sufficiently intolerable to provoke this immediate and collective reaction. However, this type of reaction disappeared as well and after this date there is no further mention of it. The beginnings of the Fourth Republic, the fact that the war belonged to the past and that there was a return to a society that was democratic and at peace, did not provide the opportunity for this kind of violence to be carried out.

Clearly stated, described and taking place within strict chronological limits, the practice of head shaving can be taken as a discrete event. It had an authentic character in the sense that the trend it set in motion differentiated it from other events in the same period. The practice cannot be understood as one single feature of the days when France was being liberated, as just one punishment among others. Even less was it a spontaneous manifestation of the emergence of some kind of ancestral practice taking advantage of the many chinks that open up in periods of crisis.

As such, a number of differences may be observed in the way it developed. There were moments of consensus, others when practices differed, which reflect changes in attitudes and perceptions. The most active periods – the days following the Liberation and, to a lesser degree, the end of spring 1945 – were those when people as a whole felt most strongly, people who had been deported or had been members of the Resistance, or belonged to a village or a particular neighbourhood. The fact that the practice of shaving heads was carried out by one or several groups cannot be understood without understanding what was at stake for individuals and what it meant for the nation as a whole. The practice was something common to the liberation of many different places at different times in a country that had been fragmented. Finally, by virtue of where it was carried out and of the intention behind it, it was a public act. Women having their heads shaved had to be seen. It was an act in which public and private issues overlapped completely. For it to be fully understood we have to take into account this pivotal role it played between private and public domains, between the individual and the collective, and between local and national interests.

Part III
Why?

Neighbourhood Violence

It is quite obvious that the shaving of heads fundamentally damages the physical and moral integrity of those people for whom it is intended. Legally such gestures or attitudes were qualified – and still are[1] – as 'blows, violence and assault', with those who carried it out being liable to conviction under Articles 309, 310 and 311 of the penal code. However, the law is not particularly helpful when it comes to understanding the phenomenon, given that 'the reality of violence varies according to how it is seen and how we wish to see it, or how it may even be seen'.[2] It is not enough therefore to estimate the 'degree of violence' that results from the practice – in the context of the Second World War, that would be derisory – but to investigate why there were differences in the ways it was carried out and the way in which it was perceived.

Unlike on a field of battle, we do not have two opposing forces acting violently towards one another at the same time. The acts of aggression carried out against men and women who had collaborated were done with constant reference to a past full of suffering, whether it was very recent or rather more remote. There was a gap between a period when violence had been experienced, and another when it was being handed out. As a result, people could share their experiences and could move from something they had lived through personally to a collective view of the enemy that the Germans' departure seemed in no way to modify.

'Peripheral' Brutality

In 1944, people reacted to the shaving of heads in different ways. Between a report in *La Marseillaise* on 3 September referring to 'the worst practices of the disgusting sadists belonging to the SA and SS' and *L'Écho de la Corrèze* on 21 September, which speaks of 'a treatment which after all was not very bad', it is clear that according to where the practice was carried out, and who was watching, judgements differed. At Brou (in the department of Eure-et-Loir) 'several women and young girls had their hair cut off, but without any violence'; at Pont-l'Évêque, 'there was no other violence'; at Aix-en-Provence, 'without there being any real violence exerted'; at Beaulieu (in the Indre-et-Loire), without 'any sign of serious violence'.[3] To characterize the shaving of heads as an act of brutality is just as unpredictable: in the Cantal, 'the only act of brutality ever committed was a sound spanking given to a young woman member of the *milice*',[4] even though the shaving of heads was taking place in Saint-Flour as well as in Aurillac. At Rodez, *Le Rouergue républicain* on 29 August 1944 spoke of 'slight acts of brutality'. In Nancy, 'there was no serious act of brutality', and in Bellegarde, there was nothing 'unfortunate'. On the other hand in Albi, cutting off hair and making women go bare, were qualified as 'odious and absurd acts of brutality' by Monsignor Saliège.[5] The differences in the way the practice was perceived already anticipated how it would gradually be rejected from the autumn of 1944. They also show the degree to which it became integral to events during the days of liberation, and how the violence associated with it could be temporarily overlooked.

This uncertainty plays a role too in any consideration of the extrinsic nature of the violence of the practice causing it to stand out from other forms of physical aggression. If we forget the evidence of a certain number of cases, it has to be acknowleged first of all that cutting hair off completely cannot itself be deemed a violent act. It can be the result of a decision taken voluntarily and prompted by motivations which could be religious, aesthetic, or social: it could be something necessitated for prophylactic reasons – we can think of children whose hair is cut off to make it grow more strongly, or to rid them of parasites – or again it can be part of a ritual, imposing, as in the case of those called up for military service, a standardization. A second characteristic is the absence of physical pain and the provisional nature of the physiological change that occurs (with one exception, the term 'ablation' is never used).[6] What we have, therefore, is an act whose violence can be measured by reference to the circumstances which surround it. The necessary use of force to carry it out, and the psychological suffering which it provokes, are what give it its specific meaning.

From all the acts of violence committed against women accused of collaboration, two different situations can be distinguished. There were cases where the cutting of hair is the only act which took place: 'At no moment was I insulted or brutalized by the men who carried out this punishment', 'Mademoiselle, the local people reproach you for your anti-French behaviour in 1940 . . . you are going to be punished, because the people in the crowd are insisting that you have your hair cut off. Off you go . . .'[7] Both the victim and the person who carried out the *tonte* offer an account of it as 'civilised' and as something carried out without passion. The physical (loss of hair) and moral damage (humiliation) were real and justified the complaint made by the woman concerned, but were not, as was often the case, worsened by other acts of violence. This is nothing like the description of a procession given by Mélinée Manouchian:

> Near to the métro stop Danube (19th *arrondissement* of Paris), a crowd was following a woman who was entirely naked. Her head had been completely shaved, and on her breasts two swastikas tattooed in Indian ink. I trembled at the idea that this woman would no longer be able to undress herself in front of a man without showing the shame that was on her body. On her back she also had tattooed a portrait of Hitler. The crowd which was out of control were throwing stones at her, pushing her and insulting her.[8]

In this case, the loss of hair and taking part in the ceremony, do not appear to have been enough for some people; gestures reflect the number of those taking part. The woman's body as a whole bears the marks of the blows from stones that had been thrown and the tattoos. In this case these more usual forms of aggression are mixed with what we might call symbolic ones. The damage to the integrity of the body is apparent as much from the physiological pain resulting from the blows, as from the psychological one caused by the humiliation of being tattooed.

Seen as one among all these brutalities, the shaving of the head assumes an extra specific quality. By its nature it is neither a substitute for, nor is it complementary to other forms of violence. Even if it is possible to have three general scenarios of the practice, the way it is accompanied by other forms of violence is individual to each case.

The Use of Force

The way the victim is arrested, is taken to the place of punishment and has it carried out depends on the number of people present. The amount of force used, also depends on the number of weapons there are, how menacingly they are used. Or there may simply be a brawl. But what matters is that those carrying out the cutting should be allowed to complete a task that in their view is legitimate and does not involve other forms of violence.

At Luzancy (in the department of the Seine-et-Marne), the accounts given by the mother of a girl whose head was shaved, and by those who carried out the task, are the same:

We heard noises in our courtyard. I got up to see what was happening. I noticed at that moment a number of young men who were armed, who shouted to me: 'IN THE NAME OF THE LAW, OPEN UP'. I was afraid of reprisals from these people, so I opened the door . . . They came into the house and called my daughters. They came down from their bedroom and the group asked them to follow them to the town hall to have their hair cut off. Given the threatening manner of these men, they complied at once and went to the town hall where their heads were shaved.

The same evening at nightfall, along with a number of FFI comrades, we went to the house of these women. After having had the door opened, we asked the young girls to follow us to the town hall, which they did, and they had their hair cut off in front of the main door. I insist on making it known that we were all armed, but that we were in no way brutal in the way that we dealt with these two young women.

Those involved agree on how matters took place, the verb 'to ask' is even used on both sides, and neither makes any mention of physical pressure. However, perceptions are different as far as the actual shaving of heads is concerned. The FFI maintained there had been no brutality. The shaving of heads had been carried out in the name of the law and was not, therefore, in any sense a brutal act. The family of the two victims complained against 'illegal entry' and 'assault', and refused to accept even the principle of the punishment which they considered to be unjust. One of the two sisters made it quite clear: 'It is true that I worked for the Germans as a cleaning woman, and I did that in order to earn my living and to bring up my child who is my responsibility.'[9]

But behaviour could become brutal if certain women resisted. It was a further way of restraining them and would stop once the victim had given in, as at Jaux in the Oise:

they (five local inhabitants) accused me of having collaborated and came to get me to cut off my hair. Hearing this, I replied that I should be judged by competent people. As I said this they brutally seized my wrists and twisted them. During this time 'Dupont' threatened my parents with his revolver. Seeing how events were developing, I stopped resisting, sat down on the chair, and let them cut off my hair. 'Martin' first of all cut my hair with scissors and then finished with clippers. The whole thing was carried out by these young men who left without saying a further word.

When we arrived, the father tried to escape, but I had all the doors shut. I was carrying a revolver that had been taken from his house on 1 September 1944, and since I was afraid he might have other weapons in the house I took this revolver just in case. Seeing that any form of resistance was useless, his daughter sat down on the chair of her own accord and let 'Martin' cut her hair off. After this had been carried out, I left without any words being exchanged.[10]

Given the points of view of both victims and those who carried out the punishment, it is clear that any differences relate to the practice itself and not to the way in which events took place. For those doing the cutting to shave the head of a woman who had collaborated was a legitimate punishment in which violence played absolutely no part. The degree of restraint exercised could vary according to each case, but it always remained subordinate to the ultimate objective. Violence was only seen therefore by the victims.

Cases of Extreme Violence

Accounts by those who wish to give a sombre picture of this period, and the fact that historians have not examined them sufficiently critically, means that rumours of extreme violence need to be studied carefully. In such accounts, atrocities are often evoked in the same way, but the sources are never referred to and contemporary reports make no mention of them. Thus, for example, there is the case of Arletty who, it is rumoured, had her breasts torn off in the camp at Drancy.[11] Luc Capdevila mentions similar cases in Britanny, but has not discovered any mention of them in the many archives he has consulted.[12] The same is true about the woman from Aigueperse, beaten up and then hung during the night of 7 and 8 June 1945. Six months later on 24 December, a journalist writing in *L'Époque* describes how a woman had to walk on sharp points 10 cm long until her feet had been completely pierced, then she was undressed and her tongue, eyes and breasts torn off. After that the battered body was stoned and then hung up. None of this is to be found in the reports made after this incident took place.[13] It is all the more difficult to conceive that there should be no known trace of such acts in any of the different reports made by national or local police, or by the prefect when mention can be found of other cases of extreme violence. In most cases this took place during interrogation.

In the barracks in the Rue Mousseau at Châteauroux in the middle of October 1944, several women underwent extremely brutal interrogations and were even tortured. One of them was threatened with having her hair cut off:

Not wanting to admit to certain things of which I was innocent, during the time I was being questioned, they threatened to cut off my hair, to cover me with tar and to lead me through the streets of the town. Each time I hesitated in replying they cut off a piece of hair. And it was then, thinking that the policemen were going to carry out their threats, I admitted everything they wanted, even those things that did not exist.

Two other women were undressed, forced to stand on one foot and were beaten with a belt throughout an interrogation which lasted for two hours. A fourth: 'was continually beaten with a rubber truncheon for two and a half hours. I eventually fell down and I was dragged along by the hair. It was then I was exhausted and not knowing what was happening to me that they made me make a confession which I unfortunately signed.'[14] While it could be used as a threat, or as a means of extracting a confession, the shaving of heads was no longer the main concern. Violence like this could be inflicted on women whose heads had already been shaved.

The way in which all this took place reveals a fundamentally violent society, one in which acts of brutality can be glimpsed through the gaps left by the absence of precise references. If it is not counterbalanced by a moral conscience, the feeling of impunity and of being all powerful can result in disorder on this scale. It was, however, the action of individuals, or small groups, and not something experienced on a large scale. In most cases it provoked conflict, so contrary was it to the ideals and ethics of true resistance. There was a particularly scabrous case that took place in the internment camp at Pouligny-Notre-Dame (in the Indre). A woman who had been arrested on 22 August 1944 at Châteauroux, was sent there after the Germans left. On the order of the captain in charge of the FFI she had her head shaved. A few days later

after a drinking session, three women were kicked and then handed over to some American officers. A police inspector tried to intervene and another, who had been warned about it, threatened the American officers with his revolver and prevented the worse from taking place. The Americans, having learned that the women did not voluntarily want to spend the night with them, called the guard and sent them back to their quarters.[15]

Here it was not the shaving of the women's heads as punishment for their having had sexual relations with a member of the Gestapo, but the threat of rape that caused a split to develop between those in charge of the camp. Two inspectors of the FFI police had to intervene to prevent rape from taking place, and only the threat of a weapon caused those who were intending it to refrain. The guard's intervention was necessary before peace could be restored.

In other cases, the higher authorities had to intervene in order to stop such practices. In Lyon, the Republican commissioner Yves Farge, had to take action against the group that had taken over the prison at Montluc:

> For several days on end, intolerable abuses had been committed. Three men and a woman had been taken out of prison and shot without trial. A number of others had been ill treated and even tortured. A distinction was being made between people who were well off, and from good society, amongst whom those who were most guilty could be found, but for whom all kinds of excuses could be made and the small fry, among whom there were hundreds of innocent people who had been arbitrarily arrested and made to suffer all kinds of hardships. With the agreement of Farge I had the person who was responsible for the FFI arrested and made members of the FFI leave prison.[16]

Unlike the Gestapo or the *milice* for whom torture was part and parcel of their fighting methods, it was in no way common among members of the Resistance.

Extreme acts of violence often carried out in cold blood are not simply the consequence of a state of disorder during a period of crisis and to understand them requires an extensive, psychological study of general behaviour. Dominique Julia has considered whether, when considering any collective violence historians can single out any particular inhuman quality. He has come to the conclusion that the historian's task is to 'unravel through his investigations the complex situation and to suggest an explanation for it, but one that will never be wholly satisfactory'.[17] The limits of such investigations are only too apparent when individual behaviour plays such an important role.

Collective Violence

The third scenario concerns those acts of violence that go way beyond the intentions of those few people responsible for arresting, interrogating and shaving the heads of these women. Such violence is carried out by all those present, who, to different degrees, want to make their mark. The acts of individuals are overtaken by collective violence – that of the crowd – with the result that individual responsibility for violence becomes absorbed. What is more, two opposing images emerge: 'that of the hysterical crowd', and 'that of legitimate popular anger'. Collective violence was very much in evidence during the days of liberation and for it to be fully understood, the image of the enemy has to be considered as well.

What Enemy?

Different from a war between two states in which there is a relatively uniform picture of the opposing country and its soldiers, the Second World War, because of its ideological and civil dimensions, produces images of an enemy in all kinds of guises. It could be on the one hand Anglo-American, Freemason, Jew, Gaullist or communist and on the other, German, Nazi, occupying forces, collaborator. At the Liberation, the use of the term 'enemy' was all embracing and the opposite side was focused around the central figure of the German or rather, to readopt the vocabulary of the time, the Bosch. Accusations made, and acts of violence carried out against those who had sympathy for the enemy were a natural extension of earlier hostility.

The fact that in most cases once the Germans left they did not return, that fighting generally disappeared from the country as a whole, that an official date for the liberation of each area was given, creates a picture of a country moving rapidly from war to peace. However, the days celebrating the Liberation were both the first of peace and the last of war, dragging in their wake a mass of fears, uncertainties, destruction and deaths. After an occupation which had lasted from twenty-one months to five years, according to the region, the enemy's 'presence' could still be sensed after his departure and especially during those first few days that belonged to war and peace at the same time.

The Departure of the Germans

Pierre Laborie has made the point that from June 1944 onwards fear became a major preoccupation.[18] Fear of air raids, fighting, or the outbreak of a real civil war, or of reprisals and the actions of an army beating its retreat. The names of Ascq, Tulle, Oradour, or Vercors were still there as a sign of Nazi barbarities and would remain for the future. It should not be forgotten that massacres in these places took place before the Liberation of France, namely on 2 April, 9 June, 10 June and 23 July 1944. In several towns Liberation brought with it the discovery of the bodies of prisoners or hostages who had been shot the day before the Germans departed: in the Bois de Boulogne in Paris, in the prisons at Caen or Montluc, or at Sainte-Radegonde at Rodez. The list of villages that had been martyred grew in the press daily, accompanied by photographs of open graves discovered in many places. If in the long run fear gave way to relief, the change was less brutal and less irreversible than the train of events might allow us to believe.

Many private diaries published subsequently would recount day after day how there were moments of uncertainty. In Le Mans, Doctor Delaunay recalls the events of mid-August 1944:

> 8 August. We heard that Americans had advanced towards the Place de la République. German soldiers holding grenades and accompanied by two women, crossed the Botannical Gardens without being challenged. Around half past five American tanks arrived in the square . . . The Germans, at a loss as to what to do, fired on passers by . . . On 9 August . . . other armed individuals brought in three unfortunate women who had had their heads shaved for having had dealings with the occupying forces . . . On the 10, . . . even though Le Mans had resisted, 1,200 bombers would have blown the town to pieces . . . On 14 August, American convoys continue to pass through . . . We heard that in the night of 14–15 German tanks had attempted a counter offensive against Le Mans.[19]

The anticipation of the Germans' departure, the retrospective fear of massive destruction and the fear of their possible return, did not prevent several women from Le Mans having their heads shaved, nor did it stop the local population from celebrating their freedom. Such an attitude, which was often considered as one that put people needlessly at risk, may also be seen as the demonstration of a will to underline what was happening, making it impossible to turn back.

In many towns the departure of the Germans was the key moment in a period full of indecision. Nearly 1,200,000 German soldiers were stationed in France in 1944.[20] If nearly half of them were put out of action during the battle of Normandy, hundreds of thousands remained travelling across the country. In many places their withdrawal marked the beginning of the Liberation. Then the relief at having avoided armed conflict, or atrocities, and at the same time fear of what might yet come, began to be seen. This feeling was accentuated by the fact that withdrawals took place at night after several days of intense activity that had left local populations full of expectation. This was a time of suspense between the departure of the occupying forces and the arrival of the Allies or the FFI, a time when the hours ticked past without people knowing whether or not they were free. And yet this interlude was not without activity; material which had been removed or left by the German army revealed a number of old or new conflicts. There was an increase in the number of complaints made to the police about bicycles, or horses, or any other means of transport having been stolen. Thefts, whether or not they had been carried out by soldiers in retreat, fuelled new bitterness. At Bussac-Forêt (in the Charente-Inférieure), one female smallholder accused one of her neighbours: 'it's the Bosche's prostitute, it's she who is behind what they looted from my place on their way out, saying at the same time that I had been a collaborator and that I ought to be shot by the *maquis* within the next forty-eight hours'.[21] She was not shot and lodged a complaint for slander.

It was not just the Germans in retreat who were guilty of looting; there were many who tried to get all kinds of material for themselves. After years of frustration, the different ways of salvaging material that the Germans had left behind, caused conflicts to break out between the local people and the new authorities. Attention was drawn to some in investigations carried out during the *épuration*. Thus, one woman who had been employed at the German base at La Martinerie near Châteauroux and who had her head shaved after the Liberation, was also convicted of looting. A women from Feuquières in the Oise, suffered the same fate and was accused of 'collaboration, looting (a bicycle), and stealing a radio'.[22]

Beyond their anecdotal nature, these examples give us the opportunity to see an extra dimension to the conflicts that developed at the time of the Liberation; a clutch of motives and accusations, each one bringing with it a further explanation, however unimportant it might have been. Any object, whether it was a present from Germans, or something left behind, or on the contrary something taken by soldiers as they withdrew, anchors these events a little more firmly in a daily way of life that did not come to an end with the last days of the Occupation.

The Departure of the 'Collaborators'

The Germans were not alone in leaving and many were the French who followed them. The departure of those extreme collaborationists has often been talked about, as have the conditions under which Pétain, Laval and a number of others were transferred towards Belfort and then Sigmaringen. Philippe Burrin has estimated that between 10,000 and 15,000 collaborators left for Germany, many of them accompanied by their wives and children,[23] and to these should we not add the thousands who left Alsace and Moselle at the same time? And how many were those who, without managing to get quite as far as Germany, left their homes for fear of reprisals? Amongst them women known for having had relationships with

Germans left their homes in the hope of escaping the punishment of having their hair shaved off.

Women were questioned as they travelled in German convoys. At Senlis, two young girls aged eighteen and nineteen respectively were arrested: 'Soldiers' women, they were making the journey from Paris to Avilly in an SS convoy going to Germany'.[24] After their heads were shaved, they were then interned for five months. Still in the Oise, but at Beauvais, two Parisien prostitutes who were accompanying an armoured division of the Wehrmacht, also had their heads shaved, but were freed a week later. At Béziers, a woman of German origin was stopped in a convoy of the enemy army coming from Perpignan; probably having had her head shaved; she was freed six weeks later. In the Indre, a linen-keeper was discovered by the FFI in a German lorry at Écueillé; she was not let out of the CSS until 22 January 1945.

Not all these women appear to have followed the Germans of their own choice. Some of them, as part of their defence when they came back, maintained that they had been threatened. However, even without having been stopped along with Germans, the simple fact that they had gone away and were not known locally, caused suspicion. In the lists of those people who were interned are the names of many people who were travelling. The 10 per cent of women interned in the department of the Indre, came from other departments.[25] At Montpellier, the proportion was as high as 15 per cent, with a mixture of people coming from other departments near and far.[26] The frequency of the reports of searches undertaken by policemen at the request of their colleagues in other departments, confirms the importance of these attempted escapes; other reports made later of arrests and enquiries also inform us about what happened to these women. All of them refer to the fear of reprisals as something which explains their reason for leaving. Real threats, or mere rumours, forced a large number of them to leave their homes. One housewife held for trial in the Oise, questioned in Paris, but who worked in Rheims, said precisely: 'I took my meals in a restaurant in Rheims, and it was after open threats made by other customers that I became frightened and decided to leave for Germany by any means possible.'[27]

The threats were sometimes so precise, that a women from Barbery (in the Oise) knew in advance who was going to have the job of cutting off her hair. She told her lover, a non-commissioned German officer about it:

> I said to him that I had to leave Barbery the same day to go to my parents' house. He asked me why I was leaving, I said to him that I didn't want to stay

any longer in that area because I had been threatened with having my hair cut off . . . I pointed out Marcel to the German officer because I knew that with others he was going to cut my hair off as soon as the Allied forces arrived. His wife was telling everybody who wanted to listen to her about it in the shops in Barbery.[28]

For others warnings were unnecessary as the atmosphere alone was sufficiently threatening to cause them to take flight. At Soubise, in the Charente-Inférieure, two friends left the town after having warned one of their friends that 'they were leaving because they were afraid they were going to have their hair cut off, having heard that this was going to happen to any women who had worked for the Germans'.[29] Sometimes the departure could be catastrophic, as at Betz in the Oise: 'In the month of August 1944, before the arrival of the American troops, Charlotte came for her mother in the middle of the night; they left for an unknown destination. I [the president of the local liberation committee] had them looked for and learned that they were hiding in Paris in the 16th *arrondissement*. The Paris police were informed.'[30] They were finally arrested on 6 December 1944, but like many others, they were able to avoid the humiliation of having their hair shaved off.

Those women who did not leave with the Germans tried to hide with their families. Some did not hesitate before undertaking a long journey. One woman from Guer, in the Morbihan, left to stay with a cousin in the department of Lot-et-Garonne. Others only went a few kilometres: one young girl from Grisy-Suisnes, in the department of Seine-et-Marne, fled to her parents' home at Chevry-Cossigny about six kilometres away. In this case, that was not enough: the local FFI went to find her and cut off her hair on the spot.

The Enemy Remains

During the confused weeks of the summer of 1944 despite the departure of their troops the German presence did not disappear altogether. The Germans' importance is shown in two diametrically opposed ways by the following observations. At Berlaimont, in the department of the Nord, an FFI commander is reported as having said: 'there is no exception to the rule, they must have their hair cut off, the Bosch are no longer there to defend them and we are in charge'. Opposed to this, members of a family in the Oise that had collaborated threatened: 'just wait until the Germans come back and then we'll teach you.'[31] Even after their departure the Germans could cause opposing positions to harden and continue to be a negative point of reference. Immediately after the Liberation, the fear that they might return, that their agents would continue to work for them, revealing those who had betrayed, made it certain that the image of the enemy remained present.

The advance of the military front made it easier to return to a state of relative security. Daily accounts of operations also show how the war was moving further away. Allied soldiers stationed or passing through, numerous unexploded mines[32] or shells, and the explosion of several V1 rockets in the autumn of 1944, accidents caused by the large number of weapons, an urban landscape still scarred by ruins – all of these features, different from one location to another, were enough to remind people of a daily life scarred by war and left them with the fear of a possible reversal of the situation. The German counter-offensive in the Ardennes in December 1944, made this fear particularly acute.

The consequences of the attack carried out by Von Rundstedt on the region around Compiègne have been recounted in a very personal way by A. de Passillé a *sous-préfet*:

> After the panic from 1940 to the end of 1944, people have not had time to reflect and come to any decisions. They act only by reflex. In September they were shouting victory, in December they thought only of trying to flee. People have suffered too fundamentally to be able to control themselves. We should always be wary of the animal side of a population which has been set out to grass for too long, and those who try to stir up trouble know that only too well and make their speeches accordingly. Therefore, we should encourage the rational side of people in order to get them to go forward in a straight line. The military advance of Von Rushtedt [sic] will have done more to bring us back to have a healthy and logical view of what actually is happening, than all the speeches about democracy which everyone has been dishing out for the last four months.[33]

No matter how many stereotypes were trotted out and no matter how much local populations tended to sneer, the real anxiety in a department which was only 250 km from Bastogne, could not remain hidden and there were plenty of people who thought only of fleeing. In the south of the country the threat appeared to be further away, and yet it had an effect and provoked other kinds of reactions:

> The news of military activity that has caused many to be less optimistic and reckless, has been compounded by the increasing number of enemy planes flying over the region . . . These circumstances, and the news that there are enemy agents around still, have prompted town councils and local liberation

committees to adopt certain security measures. In La Ciotat, for example, there has been an increase in the number of arrests of collaborators, or those suspected of collaboration . . . In no case have these arrests remained in force.[34]

Reactions like these illustrate not only how a population still bearing the scars of the war was sensitive, but also how the influence of military events relatively far off, affected matters politically at a local level. It is then sometimes easier to spot the combative side of the *épuration*, which in more cases than not was obscured by its punitive one. But it was not simply the result of reaction to enemy counter-offensives; it also included the determination to pursue those who had collaborated and who remained potential spies, or members of a threatening fifth column.

Used for the first time by Franco during the Spanish Civil War,[35] the expression 'fifth column' has since become famous. For some it 'summed up the Second World War'.[36] This way of defining the enemy on the inside further illustrates the confusion between combatants and non-combatants, nationals and trans-nationals, which can be found in the description of collaborators. Drancy, where several thousand men and women accused of collaboration from the region were interned, was nicknamed a 'holiday camp for the "fifth column" where semi-fashionable women with neither scruples or homeland could meet.'[37] In its guidelines for the *épuration* the local liberation committee for the Moselle, stressed: 'We must purge. We must vaccinate the country in order to immunise it against the evil of collaboration and the virus of the fifth column.'[38] This is no longer just a military matter, but rather something approaching fantasy. Members of the *maquis* are mentioned in various regions, as if they were French agents parachuted into the country from Germany; official notices[39] continued with the theme that had existed since the beginning of the war, reminding people that even though the Germans had left, there could still be spies around in 1944 and 1945. This created a situation in which the *épuration* had a military element as well as a way of getting rid of the threat of a fifth column. The term German or Gestapo agent, which appears quite frequently in the files on women who collaborated, here assumes its full significance. It is no longer simply a matter of circumstances, of irresponsibility or naivety, or of sorting things out, but rather of an organized system of betrayal, of being part of the enemy forces.

The Memory of the Occupier

Representations of the German are based, at the same time, on a rejection of an hereditary enemy and, more recently on Nazi barbarity. In the first place there are different terms to designate the people who lived beyond the Rhein in earlier centuries. *Allemand* is the most recent, but there is equally *Prussien,* which sends us back to the 1870 war, and *Teuton* and *Germain.* Most of the slang vocabulary used during the First World War reappears. *Boche* remains, as in 1914–18, the most frequent. In use since 1916 according to the *Dictionnaire des termes militaires et de l'argot poilu,* it originates in the second-half of the nineteenth century, though how precisely it evolved remains unclear. It either comes from a translation of the word *Allemoche,* which, in 19th-century Lorraine slang meant Germans, or with the loss of the first phoneme and the suffix 'boche' which comes from *caboche,* resulted in *Alboche,* meaning the head of a German. We may also note that *Italboche* was used to describe Italians. The second term which was used frequently was 'Fritz', with a number of words associated with it: *frisé, fridolin, fritzou.* Used from 1914 onwards, 'Fritz' is merely the diminutive regularly used of Friedrich and had nothing to do with hairstyles. As for *Vert-de-Gris,* it designated German soldiers simply by reference to the colour of their uniforms. *Chleuh* (Gerry), *doryphore* (Collorado beetle) only appear during the Second World War, the second indicating an insect that fed mainly on potato leaves. The 1946 edition of the *Larousse illustré* states: 'When it appeared in Europe at the beginning of the twentieth century, the Collarado beetle caused a great deal of damage.' Whether it was because there were so many of them, or because of the way they fed, the word was widely used to describe the occupying forces from 1941 onwards. Finally *Chleuh* (or *Schleu)* is probably the most enigmatic. The name of Berber tribes from the Upper-Atlas mountains in Morocco, it became a slang term used by soldiers who had fought in Morocco, and designated colonial troops. It would not appear in France until 1933. In 1936 it was used to describe those non-French speaking people who lived on the borders of Alsace, or Franche-Comté. In 1939 it described Germans and from May 1940 onwards, German soldiers.[40]

Taken as a whole, the vocabulary used to describe the enemy with its references to the First World War, to the war of 1870 and still more to the Tutons, suggests centuries of confrontation between the two countries. The description of the enemy is always national before it is ideological. Army troops, soldiers and garrisons are always referred to as German and not Nazi. National and political features become confused when it is a matter of describing the actions of the occupying forces and those who were responsible for them. Methods, practices, barbarity, savagery, can be qualified as Nazi, Hitlerite, or German. More surprising, but evocative of how the enemy could be seen in two ways, is the description of the German language and music as Nazi, thereby having the national description gradually tainted with an ideological one.

The ultimate purpose of all this language was to denounce the collaborator as German, thereby underlining his commitment. The evocation of German is in itself sufficient and does not require any further comment on German or Nazi methods. It alone constitutes proof of betrayal. The Gestapo is a significant example as well. Often used to accuse men and women of collaboration it assumed the value almost of an adjective. The horror and terror that the word evoked underlined in the most serious way possible the actions of those with whom it was associated.

In descriptions of the intimate relationships between French women and Germans, the latter are regularly described as officers or non-commissioned officers. Nearly 13 per cent of women who had their heads shaved on account of their 'horizontal collaboration' had, or were accused of having, a German officer as a lover.[41] Unlike the army as a whole, German officers were more easily described as Nazi. Their grade, in as much as it indicated power and authority, was then to be associated with the regime. In this way the political dimension of an intimate relationship, a link between feelings and commitment could be established more easily.

The German plays a fundamental, but not exclusive part in the way the enemy is represented. The idea of collaboration is developed around him and while with the Liberation his role became less significant, his accomplices remained. A study first of rumour and then the importance given to the names of women whose heads were shaved, will indicate more clearly how these shifts occurred.

The Weight of Rumour

In a period when information, letters, the spoken word were constantly watched, when propaganda and counter-propaganda gave rise to all kinds of contradictory information, other means of communication, amongst which there was rumour, assumed new importance. The police, the FF1, the office of general information and the prefects, all indicate public rumour as a source of information. Above all it was a way of transmitting a piece of news at a time when there was a dearth of general information, and ensured a huge audience. Rumours could be about provisions, new military or political decisions, measures taken to do with the *épuration* on a national scale, or on a local one. They had direct influence on the way events developed. When they were to do with the actions of someone suspected of collaboration, they brought people together, allowed them to share information and incited action against the person rumoured to be guilty.[42]

As they often bring together related pieces of evidence to do with the activities of women who collaborated, police reports throw an important light on how rumour worked. However, they offer evidence in the light of what has already been made public by a punishment having been carried out. Compiled after this had taken place, they allow us to see a clear distinction between a general public rumour and the statements provided by individuals. 'I have never seen these young women with Germans, but I have often heard it said that they had been seen with them',[43] states a bank employee from Bucquoy (in the Pas-de-Calais) about a young woman who had her hair cut off on 1 September 1944. This cautious position could be explained by the nature of the person to whom the comment was addressed, namely the police. The eventual consequences of the acts committed become apparent, even if they have not been envisaged before. Fear of the police, even reduced given the circumstances, causes those involved to modify their accounts, but there is nothing to prevent rumour from growing. 'I know because I heard people say so that this woman was the mistress of a German . . . Each time he went to see her he had a heavy bag, no doubt full of provisions.'[44] This witness is using information that is based on supposition – his knowledge comes from what he has heard others say – and then it is given extra weight by what he says about the bag. In this way, having become valid, the rumour is transformed into a certainty. Each person participates in creating a knowledge, which becomes a collective shared knowledge, and thereby further helps to bring people together.

Above all, rumour could lead to an offence appearing worse than it was. In a scheme where, as we have seen, collaboration is more a question of betrayal, than something based on precise activities, one form of it can frequently shade off into another. In the case of one young woman from Blanc (in the Indre), pieces of evidence and rumours became confused that the picture of her is worsened. Witness No. 1: 'Early in 1943, Madame X was sitting at a table with some German civilians.' Witness No. 2: 'I saw Madame X with some German soldiers in the streets of Blanc. They were walking together in a particularly friendly way.' Witness No. 3: 'I heard Madame X say: If my husband would let me, I would go and work voluntarily in Germany.' Witness No. 4: 'I heard Madame X say at her ticket office at the end of 1942: I am very pleased with the damage that the Germans have inflicted on the English.' Witness No. 5: 'According to public opinion, this woman was a collaborator. She took pleasure in German victories and was very fond of those German soldiers who went to fight for the German army on the eastern front.'[45] Socializing, going for walks, making anti-Allied and pro-German comments, but it was finally for a denunciation not mentioned by any of these witnesses, but nonetheless admitted by this woman when she was interrogated, that the courts condemned her to ten years hard labour. For many, denunciations would have been the natural outcome for relationships of this kind with Germans: 'After drinking sessions like that it's not surprising that there will be easy confessions following on the couch.'[46] This is the point that those people carrying out the enquiry would try to clarify. But the creation of the portrait of this woman who had been guilty of collaboration was more influenced by rumour than by hard facts; less by the seriousness of the crime, as by the supposed degree of immorality and perversion.

If rumour alone was not always enough to have a woman accused of collaboration condemned by the courts, it was often enough to encourage those to see her as someone whose head should be shaved. Such a woman who had become 'notorious' and whose crime was a public one, was already considered by most people as someone who should be punished in this way. At Luzancy in the Seine-et-Marne, the local FFI group justified applying this punishment in the following way: 'If we have cut off the hair of the girls called X, it is because they had the reputation of having had close relationships with Germans.'[47] The confirmation, or otherwise of the acts for which they were reproached came later, but at the time their heads were shaved, local people had an image that events then turned into a truth. Rumour provoked the event, and this in turn validated in the accusation. A shaved head 'was the proof beyond all doubt that people had been correct'.[48]

An account of events in a neighbourhood in the eighteenth *arrondissement* of Paris at the time of the Liberation, allows us to see how a rumour could develop and how it could lead to action being taken. We know this from the accounts given by two headteachers, and by a primary-school teacher from a local educational establishment who were directly involved in the events that were taking place.[49] The incident occurred on 26 August 1944. During the previous days local people had witnessed moments of violent conflict with German troops. Since 23 August barricades had been constructed more or less everywhere in order to stop the Germans fleeing towards the north. On the morning of 26 August fighting stopped and the first tanks of the Leclerc division, the day before they entered central Paris, were making their way towards Saint-Denis on the north side of the city. In the afternoon, firing seemed to come from the school buildings. Three members of the FFI accompanied by two local people, went and discovered in the head master's office gunpowder, a cartridge case and four cartridges for a Mauser gun. These bullets which had been left behind by other rebels the day before, were then at the root of a whole succession of events. A careful search of the premises was carried out and nothing was discovered, but the head teacher and one of his colleagues were suspected, threatened, and then arrested to be taken off to the town hall where a second company of FFI were stationed.[50] Once they were in the car taking them, a dense crowd surrounded it crying 'He's the one who was shooting! Death! Kill him! Kill him at once!' Finally, taking advantage of the diversion caused by the unexpected passage of French troops, the car was able to start up and reach its destination. The head-teacher was interrogated and then freed by the commander of the FFI. During this time, and according to the testimony of a teacher who had stayed behind 'there was a woman whose head had been shaved who was jeered at by the crowd as she passed by' the school premises. It was probably the caretaker of the kindergarten whose son had been a member of the PPF and who, according to another witness, had been arrested more or less at the same time and badly treated.

The following night, silhouettes continued to be seen on the roofs of the school, even though it was empty, the people who had been there having decided for the sake of safety to spend the night elsewhere. After further enquiry it was revealed that the FFI soldiers who had carried out the arrest were part of a group that had not been properly checked. No other event subsequently disturbed the school, but rumours continued to circulate in the area. Far from being proved innocent, the headmaster found himself at the centre of all kinds of accusations: 'The school held an arsenal of weapons'; 'The headteacher and his son [he was fourteen years old and had been in the Allier since the beginning of July] fired on passers by'; 'The headmaster's wife has had her head shaved (when in fact she had been killed in 1940 after a German air raid) . . . In the market, a woman stated that she had seen the headmaster in his pyjamas, firing from his window, with a machine gun under each arm; two complained to the newspapers: 'Just think that we are giving our children in the hands of such a dreadful person!' Finally, the rumour extended to the rest of the capital. In the Rue de Varennes where there was a service for refugees, it was heard said: 'The headmaster and his wife, his son and his servants!!!

had fired on the crowd!' According to the headmaster himself, all that could be seen to be part of a vengeance campaign on the part of certain local people, because he had been opposed to the looting of another group of school buildings whose objects had afterwards to be restored.

The situation in which these events took place was extremely tense. It is true that the Germans had surrendered, or had left Paris, but the obsession with the 'shooters on the roof' continued. Moreover, the neighbourhood had known several violent clashes during the days before, when at least one person had been killed and several injured from the ranks of the FFI. On 26 August, when the headmaster was in the town hall, there was a rumour that the Germans were returning to Paris. Once the gunpowder had been discovered, and once the headmaster had been taken outside, all kinds of rumours began to spread. The scene as a whole became proof of guilt in the eyes of those people who witnessed the arrest. The few cartridges became an 'arsenal' and the other accusations added substance to this feeling.

The rumour was based on an accumulation of facts in characteristic fashion spiced up by a number of details – here the headmaster's pyjamas – which gave it the appearance of truth. It also takes as a whole those people who were in the school premises, which then becomes a den of collaborators. Four of the five people who lived there were all worried. As in the case of relationships with Germans, a simple contact with the enemy was enough to arouse suspicion. The two women mentioned in the account have their head shaved. One literally in front of the school, and the other simply in the minds of people in the neighbourhood who seemed not to know anything about what had happened to her in June 1940. The imagined punishment carried out on her became a further proof of the guilt of her husband. Finally, once the rumour had grown in the crowd that had gathered in from of the school on 26 August, it would then be passed on through the traditional places of town conviviality, such as the market and the newspaper shop. Only the cafes are missing and, given the circumstances, the school, the other place where meetings tradition-ally took place, but here evoked by the two mothers as the place where the headmaster in charge of their children had become 'a dreadful person'. When in mid-September the three reports on this event were issued, they concluded by underlining the seriousness of it all: 'Rumours are still circulating'; 'People are spreading all kinds of fantastic ideas about the headmaster, about the female head teachers, and about me, throughout the neighbourhood'; 'As a result of all these slanders . . . the school became discredited.' Without there being any heads shaved, internment, or trial, the indication of the guilty person, even without any physical consequences, could also be one of the reasons that caused him to be excluded from his local community.

At the House of the Shorn Woman

The target of numerous rumours, collaborators' houses were often where events started. The 'house of the woman with the shorn head' appears twice in the geography of the Liberation. First of all it is the place where the crime has been committed, a place where German soldiers have been, and secondly somewhere that has to be freed, that is to say occupied and then purged.

The house where 'pillow talk' took place is seen to be one of collaboration. Women guilty of it were reproached for having used all the techniques of seduction in order to attract the enemy to them: 'This extremely sensual woman also knew how to look after her customers well, and could attract to her house Germans who were likely to put some pretty good benefits in her way';[51] noted the commissioner for the *épuration* of the Oise in his report. Here again, between reality and fantasy, witnesses can be multiplied to designate the homes of these women. Comings and goings, music, noises, shouts at every hour of the day or night, nothing seems to have been missed by anybody in the neighbourhood. The mayor of La Garde, in the Charente-Inférieure, stated to the policeman who came to carry out an inquest on the 'conduct and morality' of one of the local women, that 'real orgies took place in her house at night and the neighbours could not sleep on account of the racket made by the Germans'.

As accounts grew, so the home 'of the Germans' female friend' became more a public issue: neighbours, caretakers, local people, did not have words strong enough to denounce what was taking place. It could be a German soldier kissing his mistress in one of the corridors of a building, another seen at six o'clock in the morning clambering out of a window, a teacher who complained about a woman 'whose debauchery was a real scandal . . . since I had a lot of children in my place, I was strongly against all the gestures and conversations that she had with Germans, which I could hear through the open windows. It was a real brothel . . . it was a lesson in immorality for the children'.[52]

Windows, shutters, walls would disappear, making the homes of these women the target for everyone around them. But given the close network of any neighbourhood, to know what the other person was doing could bring something else in its wake. Where these 'female collaborators lived' was not only the scene of betrayal, but the place real or imagined, from which the enemy could spy on the local area. The whole neighbourhood would be under threat. On the 13 September 1944, an article in *Les Allobroges* tells how the neighbours of two young girls, one of whom was the mistress of a Gestapo agent from Lyon, left their homes because they were so afraid. And so, as the Occupation went on, the homes of these women could be picked out in the local community. Some of these women, more cautious than others, would meet their lovers in other places. Hotels could be used for these meetings. But they were not necessarily a guarantee of anonymity, as one woman from Castelroux explained when she was arrested by the local FFI police: 'I had sex with this German in my house and not at a hotel, because chamber maids too often notice women who frequent Germans, and also so that I did not have to fill out a registration form.'[53] Others would go to the German camps where the walls and sentries allowed them to escape the eyes of others, but also accentuated the element of fantasy in what was taking place. This did not prevent such women eventually from being spotted when they returned home. Anyone returning to their home after the curfew was immediately a suspect.

The Occupation and Purging of these Places

After the withdrawal of the Germans, bolted doors no longer offered any protection. The editorial in the *La Dépêche de l'Aisne* on 27 September 1944, imagined 'those women who listened, shut up in their bedrooms, to footsteps in the street, fearful of the terrifying squad coming for them'. The homes of these women who had collaborated became primary targets in the repossession of the locality. Their arrest often took place in their homes. The crowd would gather in front of the building, whether or not they had been marked before with a swastika did not matter: they were known. First of all there would be shouts and insults and then the buildings would be occupied by the most determined. The shaving of heads would be carried out in such cases with a ritual that took away the identity of the people living there. This is the statement of Mlle X, twenty-four years old:

> Thursday evening on 31 August 1944, towards 19:00 hrs, when throughout the area decorations had been put up to celebrate the Liberation, like every-body else, we had put a blue, white and red flag in the window of our house. About a quarter of an hour later, three men from the neighbouring town of Jallais came and took it down saying: 'You are not French, you don't have

the right to put a flag up at your window.' Towards 20:00 hrs three young men unknown to us came to knock at our door and said: 'Open up. It is the *maquis* police.' Having opened the door they then said: 'You are more Bosche than French. We've known your house for a long time. Tomorrow at first light you will know what it's all cost you', and then they left. They came back at 21:20 hrs accompanied by three men and many other people from the town. When they arrived they attacked me first. B and someone I didn't know held me by the arms, while another I also did not know, cut my hair off with scissors. When they had finished cutting off my hair, A and B took a paintbrush and plastered my face with coal tar. After that these men set about cutting off my mother's hair and didn't do anything else to me. As a result my arms and legs are covered with marks from their blows. I have been checked by the doctor from Jallais who has given me a medical certificate which I am handing over to you. I am making a complaint against these individuals for blows and injury. This is the version I am sticking to.

Mme X, a widow born in Y, fifty-seven years old and without a profession:

before leaving they dropped and broke my oil lamp, tore off the back of my radio and broke the glass in the main house door. Once outside with what remained of the coal tar, they put three swastikas on the wall, one of the shutters and the garage door. After that they left and I didn't see them again. I have been accused of collaboration, but I can assure you I have never belonged to any group indulging in this. It has happened that I had Germans in my house and that I even fed them, but on each occasion they were accompanied by M. D de Chamillé. I can swear to you that I have never had any political dealings with Germans and that I have nothing to reproach myself for.[54]

The home of these two women was somewhere that had to be liberated. First of all it was singled out, it was then occupied and purged. By hanging up the French flag they had hoped they would blend into the whole liberated area. It is not possible to know whether by this they hoped to forget that Germans had been in their house during the Occupation, or whether they really did not understand what they were being reproached for and completely disassociated personal relationships from political convictions. Whatever the case, the fact that they hung up the French flag had no influence whatsoever on local people. Not to have put it there would have indicated what they had done; the fact that it was there was a provocation. On the scale of somewhere like Jallais, their house was known 'for a long time' as a place where the enemy gathered. It embodied the presence of the occupying forces, however slight, and made Liberation, if not impossible, then incomplete. The action taken against the women had three stages. The initiative came from the three local men who were responsible for law. An hour later there was the demonstration of force by the three members of the FFI who had come to assess the situation. Finally, the FFI and local people took possession of the house so as, in some way, to purge it of the enemy presence. This purification took place first of all inside with the shaving of the heads of the mother and her daughter, and then by the use of coal tar,[55] probably because it is so dirty, but also, we should not forget, because of its antiseptic quality. In this case there was no looting, but objects were broken. The breaking of the lamp seems accidental, but the damage to the radio may have been deliberate if its music could be heard across the neighbourhood when these women received Germans in the house. The purification process continued outside, as if people had wanted to scrub the house from the community of Jallais by making it transparent to everyone. With its broken door and open shutters, people could see the women with shaved heads, or with them shut, the swastikas. In the neighbouring department of Mayenne, at Château-Gontier, hair was collected and stuck on the doors of houses.[56]

Crossing the Threshold

Whether they were made to leave their homes before or after their heads had been shaved, when they did they had to face another and more unpleasant form of punishment. First of all it was clear that they had been arrested. It was not clear how long things were going to last but once they emerged from their houses these women who had collaborated were welcomed by jeers, spits and even blows.

The accompanying photograph was taken on 6 July 1944 in Cotentin near Sainte-Mère-L'Eglise.

Inhabited by only a few dozen people, there were at least three women who had their heads shaved, among them this school teacher who is coming out of her school house in the village. The photograph is framed in such a way that we do not know whether there are other people waiting for her; all we know is that there was a photographer present.[57] The woman has just crossed the threshold of the building. She was pushed out of her home and pulled towards the outside by two French patriots who can be identified by the French badge sewn on their jackets. These two men who can be seen on four other photographs taken in the same village, seem to be the ones who had been made responsible for shaving

Cotentin, 6 July 1944. The original caption: The teacher called X, 28 years old. When the allied troops liberated the community the French patriots dragged her from the town hall and cut off her hair, just as they had the intention of doing to all women who had collaborated. Imperial War Museum.

of heads of women who had collaborated. The fact that they are smoking suggests that there is something almost routine about this operation. The teacher is getting ready to go down the steps she goes up and down every day. However many other people there are around her, this woman can now see her daily world transformed into a hostile environment. With her head down she is warding off the moment of humiliation when 'her crime' will pass from being a private matter to something publicly known, from obscurity into light.

It is rare that authors and victims of violence confront one another individually. What relationship can there be between a bomber pilot and a civilian who is several thousands of metres below him; between an American soldier who puts his foot on a Normandy beach and a German soldier who fires at him; between the general secretary of a prefecture and a Jew who has been deported? The ritual shaving of heads is special in the way that it puts two opposing sides directly in contact with one other, but with one adversary who has changed. The person who is the cause of the suffering, namely the German, is not the one to whom violence is carried out. Suffering makes for a division therefore; the victim is more guilty for not having suffered, than for having been an accomplice to the acts of violence carried out by the Germans.

The relationship between those who carried out the practice and those who were the victims of it often predated the particular moment of violence. They are a feature of people being neighbours, and explain why those taking part could indicate others by name. The circumstances also raise questions about the relationship between an individual and the violence being perpetrated. So complex were such relationships that the political nature of the practice was lost, becoming instead a way of settling accounts. At a local level it could express revenge, hatred and jealousy and was quite different, therefore, from the political struggle against collaboration, attributed to the Resistance, and to the military one against Nazi Germany that was carried out by the Allied armed forces.

Personal Revenge?

The highlighting of personal motives quite separate from any political ones, needs to be examined. This is not in order to take a certain pleasure in bringing together anecdotes of a more-or-less sordid nature, and which in the end seems, according to those who tell them, to illustrate a certain baseness in human nature, or with a more ideological dimension, to discredit the idea of resistance by reference to some of the excesses that were carried out. Rather it is to throw light on the complex relationships between the individual and collective, the intimate and the public. Jealousy and hatred, like revenge, crop up sufficiently frequently to indicate the role they play and the way violence was carried out. There are examples of those responsible for shaving heads whose initiative seems to have been motivated only by personal considerations. A lover, or a suitor who had been rejected, a professional rivalry, a financial difference between two people could be motive enough. Nonetheless in addition to actions taken by individuals which were rare enough, these motives do not explain how a number of people could become involved in what was basically a dispute between two people.

Aggression at La Mure

The case of the assault at La Mure in the Isère on 27 May 1945 on three people, two of whom were women who had gone as voluntary workers to Germany, allows us to have a better look, at the relationship between individual and collective violence, for it is rare to find the testimonies of several people who recognize that they have been involved. The day after this incident, the police drew up three reports on the arrests made. All of them begin with a general presentation of the facts:

At our headquarters it came to our attention that three voluntary workers had just returned from Germany and were at the railway station at La Mure where the crowd was going to assault them and beat them up. We went into town where we saw a crowd of about two thousand leading a young man [woman and a girl] and were hitting them. We intervened and took them back to our squad.[58]

Five months later, after a complaint made by one of the women, eight witnesses were heard.

Madame A, a widow, twenty-five years old:

Near the Hotel de Ville square, seeing that everyone was hitting these voluntary workers, I went over and slapped the girl X to take revenge for my husband who had been shot by the Bosch before the Liberation. I certify that I only hit her once.

Madame B, a widow, twenty-eight years old:

I was near the town hail and having had my husband shot by the Germans in August 1944, I could not prevent myself from slapping the girl X. What is more, almost the entire population of La Mure had been hitting these voluntary workers.

Madame C, widow, thirty-one years old:

It so happens, that on 27 May I went to a reunion of war widows. Around 16:00 hrs the train arrived from Grenoble and I saw a crowd going towards the station. I saw the girl X, the son Y and another girl, who had left as voluntary workers in Germany, come out. My husband had died in captivity in Stalag VII and I could not prevent myself from slapping the girl X. What is more, I was not the only one to do so, but I didn't recognize any of the others who were hitting her with me.

M. D., twenty years old:

I followed the group to the town hall where the crowd hit these two individuals. I deny having struck them myself and I also deny having taken the wallet from the girl X as she accuses me of having done. I cannot give you the names of the other people who were beating these two voluntary workers.

M. E., thirty-one years old, hairdresser:

On 27 May, around 16:30 hrs, some young people came to fetch me to cut off the hair of some voluntary workers who were coming back from Germany. I went to the town hall square with my clippers where I simply ran them over the girl's head. I should mention that this voluntary worker's hair had already been cut off.

Madame F., thirty-five years old:

I was at the railway station at La Mure with my horse and cart to fetch some fruit and vegetables for my sister, who has a shop. There were people waiting for voluntary workers who had been in Germany and without my agreeing they took my horse and cart and put three prisoners in it and then led them to the square by the town hall where, after they had unloaded them, I was allowed to have my horse and cart back.

M. G., thirty-one years old, repatriated prisoner of war:

I was near the railway station where I saw a crowd. I went up and saw that there were voluntary workers who were returning from Germany. There were three of them and they were put into a cart and led from the railway station to the town hall. Seeing that they had had enough, I intervened with some other prisoners. The one who was hitting them most of all was the cousin of the girl X, whose name is H, who then kicked her after she had fallen to the ground. The girls' possessions had scattered all over the ground and it was I who collected them and gave them to the police. Her wallet was not taken.

M. H., twenty-four years old:

On 27 May I was in various cafes in town with friends. At that moment someone came into the bar and said that the girl X (my cousin) was arriving from Germany. I went to meet her and when I arrived at the town hall square I saw a crowd of people who were hitting the three voluntary workers. Seeing that everyone was doing it, I punched Y a few times as well as my cousin X. I was overexcited and it may be that I gave her a kick when she was on the ground. I also went to Germany under the following circumstances. I worked at the sanctuary of the Salette à Corps (in the Isère). After a spot of trouble with the priests about the people who worked there, I left. I went to Grenoble, but did not have a work permit or identity card and was arrested by the Gestapo who took me to their headquarters in the Hotel Terminus. Threatened, I was obliged to sign a contract to go to Germany. I did not go voluntarily.

The police report finishes by the summing up: 'H is an individual of bad character, who went to Germany after committing a theft in the sanctuary where he worked. He certainly went to Germany voluntarily, but has always persisted in saying that he was obliged to do so. As for the other persons, they are all of good conduct and moral standing.'

Eight testimonies, and almost as many different accounts. All the people were present. Five acknowledge having hit the voluntary workers, two deny having taken part in any active way, a third states that he intervened against the violence taking place. The testimonies of the three women have a number of similarities. Their husbands were shot or died in a Stalag. They acknowledged that they hit the workers, in each case by slapping them, all the while putting themselves into a collective frame ('everyone was hitting'). What we have here is a group which probably was made up, as is mentioned, of 'war widows' two hours before the train arrived. The similarity between these testimonies allows us to suppose that the contacts between these women continued during the five months after the incident took place.

Two other people were present by virtue of their profession, a hairdresser and a market gardener whose cart was 'borrowed'. The first cannot deny that he took part, but defends himself by saying that people came for him, that he did not go on his own initiative and that he only finished off the shaving that had already been done. The attitude of the market gardener is even clearer. Her cart, necessary for work, is at the centre of her testimony and is her main concern. The three voluntary workers are 'loaded' and 'unloaded', just like any other merchandise.

The role of M.D. is more ambiguous. He follows the group to the town hall and when he is interrogated, like the group of widows, does not mention any other name. He puts himself in a position where he is on one side. Whether he does this out of conviction or from fear of being prosecuted afterwards is not clear and he 'denies having hit' when 'the crowd was hitting them'. M.H. is the classic example of the 'September member of the Resistance'. Political motivation gives way completely before the combined effects of alcohol (various cafes) and the effect of belonging to a group ('seeing that everybody was hitting them') making him 'over excited' as far as the one who seemed to be more his cousin than a voluntary worker. He is the most violent of them all (kicks when the victims are on the ground), but above all, even if he tries to defend himself, also seems to have been a voluntary worker who went to Germany. Depending on the account of this event we accept it is easy to see it as being either 'the sordid settlement of accounts' or the expression of a 'legitimate, popular anger'.

The testimony of M.G. throws a slightly different light on the events. He has authority on two accounts: by virtue of his experience as a prisoner of war and by virtue of the fact that he is a town counsellor. He has known suffering in the past and will be part of the suffering that is now taking place and is still to come. He puts himself between the crowd and the prisoners, intervening once 'they had enough', and ensures that the punishment they were being given was not accompanied by theft. He situates each person in context, the suffering and legitimate violence of the widows, the treachery and guilt of the voluntary workers and the uncertainty surrounding H. By recognizing the fact that H had volunteered to go to Germany, risks casting a slur on the action taken by the local people as a whole and having the women seen as victims if they are successful in obtaining compensation as a result of their complaint. To deny it is to embrace someone whose profile in no way corresponds to the image of a person belonging to a liberated people. This ambiguity already contains within it the contradictions that will be seen in the way that the Liberation is represented in the future.

As Marie Moscovici has written, 'here hatred appears or reappears, a hatred which the psychoanalyst knows from experience exists in the subconcious, but which war causes to come to the surface and find expression.'[59] In a situation of crisis, when private and public, individual and collective vengeance and justice become confused, the historian finds himself confronted with things he is not used to. Antoine Prost has already shown how in the newspapers which circulated in the trenches in the First World War, the term 'brother of misery'[60] revealed that the enemy was considered to be simply another man, even if there was hostility expressed towards him. How should we interpret the ever present use of the word 'hatred'? How should we consider the phrase 'hatred of the enemy' which, during a period of war has nothing exceptional about it? Is it a way of underpinning propaganda by appealing to basic sentiments such as 'love of the homeland' and 'hatred of the enemy' which are two opposing features of the same discourse?[61] It is a stylistic phrase that shows more how a particular discourse can take hold, rather than the depth of feelings involved. And yet when the object of hatred is there –

not just the enemy but a neighbour, a colleague, or a relation – how influential is it?

In considering this I will limit myself to a few observations and questions. In terms of individual testimonies, the verb 'to hate' is not conjugated in the first person. What we have is simply hatred of the other. It is through the accounts of victims, or witnesses that hatred is expressed. 'The people overwhelmed me by their hatred' a young woman who had escaped having her hair cut off says in her statement to the police. 'Madame X attracted the hatred of the people of Clouange by the work she did for the Nazi regime, and for her personal safety she should not return home', stated a local policeman. According to a typist questioned in Châteauroux when she was arrested and had her head shaved, the 'fierce hatred' and 'a disgusting plot' dreamed up by her boss accounts for what happened to her.[62] How should we address the problem of putting feelings into words? Can they be spoken by other people? What actions, or what words have to be taken into account as expressions of hatred? When a young seventeen-year old man justifies himself for having taken part in a ritual of drenching a woman, stripping her bare and then having her head shaved states: 'if I behaved in that way it was because I was overexcited and sickened by the way this girl and her sisters had informed against good French people', and equally when three widows in La Mure say 'I could not stop myself from slapping her', is this a kind of defensive reaction, or can such actions be considered as a legitimate expression of their hatred?

The difficulty of using the term 'hatred' when it is an individual matter is not raised when it is a collective one. Then it has a completely different value, that of being a violence that enables people to be free. Raised to the level of a national feeling, it becomes more noble and its archaic and ambivalent nature disappears. When they are appropriated by the Nation, hatred and violence become legitimate because they become used for the purpose of setting people free. 'French citizens, when you slowly burn the vile flag bearing the Swastika on the steps of the public buildings in Biney, that hatred which is roaring inside you is holy. Therefore, no show of pity whatsoever for those who have collaborated with the vile acts carried out by the Boche.'[63] From a symbolic point of view to endow an impulse which is normally considered negative with a sacred quality is sufficiently strong for it not to be taken simply as something which is written about. Oppression, suffering and silence, all imposed during the Occupation, can only be got rid of, it would seem, by the explosion of those who had to suffer them. On 6 September 1944 the editorial in *La Voix de Nord* said: 'That there should be an instinctive reaction from the people faced with what is despicable, is no bad thing'. An unusual reference to instinctive behaviour and the way of showing how deep this experience was.

Hatred provokes hatred, violence violence. Why should people be surprised if a few things get out of hand after an orgy of violence unleashed by a barbaric regime based on spying, torture and even death. If we are to finish with violence, we have to have recourse to violence. There is no other way of going about it. Christ himself – gentleness in the form of man – used a whip to chase the dealers out the temple. Violence is not our aim. In order to root out hatred and violence from the souls of men, there must be no more oppressed and oppressors, or those who are exploited and their exploiters. A better distribution of goods, a life that is less hard and less uncertain, social conditions which are more humane can do more for a struggle against violence than a thousand calls for fraternity. Let us then use our strength, our minds, and everything we have at our disposal to arrive at a little more justice in the areas of the economy, politics and society and we will have achieved a lot in order to bring men together and to realize their true brotherhood.[64]

This period was split three ways; a past full of suffering and frustration, a future of 'mornings which sing' and between them the fractured present. Violence did not come simply to put an end to a painful and immediate past, it was also there and seen by many as a necessary condition for the construction of a better future.

Mélinée Manouchian gives an account of a procession in which she took part in the following terms: 'The eyes of those taking part showed a suffering stored up over five years, five years of suffering and struggle. The scene was hardly bearable, but I could not criticise these people who had been disfigured by war. Through their own cruel behaviour they tried to recover the honour which had been snatched from them: they needed to take revenge on what Nazism had done to them.'[65] This is a feeling expressed thirty years after the events, but which gives a good picture of things at the time. The Liberation was an outburst of tales of suffering that had been experienced: letters from soldiers who had been shot, accounts of interrogations by the Gestapo, photographs of open graves, revelations of massacres committed by the Germans and by the *milice*, this long list of martyrdoms could finally be made public. It shows how during the Occupation there were no limits to the cruelties carried out by the occupiers and by the Vichy authorities. The death of a few members of the *milice*, the beating up of collaborators and *a fortiori* the shaving of women's heads seem as derisory as they were necessary. For people as a whole to become involved was not just the result of a group dynamic, of an 'intoxicated' crowd unaware of what it was doing. These actions grew out of the real suffering of individuals and were legitimized by them. Excesses contravene normal social behaviour during the time of peace, but war causes them to explode. 'Our sense of being civilized was revolted by the spectacular degree of repression we formerly suffered and which belonged to another time. Would our sensitivity have been dulled to this point by the barbaric acts of the Teutons? I do not think so. But our indignation was such during these four years that today our anger has exploded.' The writer of these lines in *L'Écho de la Corrèze* on 14 September 1944 sets two periods against one another – one civilized, the other barbaric. He is also more than aware of the break with normality caused by the war. Such is the pressure exerted by the context that violent practices can be authorized and the way hatred can be directed against an individual or a whole group of people can be explained.

In a Village Somewhere in France[66]

In *Histoire des femmes,* Hélène Eck underlines the 'degree to which the Liberation revealed what had taken place during the Occupation, and how that had blurred the division between private and public life.'[67] Is not such an effect a feature of total war? Was the deep impression which these events made not also worsened by four years of silence and did it not come to light much more strongly once freedom and democracy had been restored? The case history of a village gives us an insight into the practice of shaving heads carried out under the influence of public and private interests alike.

The events took place in the south of Picardie. The village in question was liberated on Wednesday 30 August 1944 by the arrival, late in the day, of the American troops of the 19th division under General Corlett (1st US army). In the evening, the mayor and two of his deputies, one of whom we will call Martin,[68] met to organize on the following day a distribution of meat from two German horses that had been shot that very day. Martin, a rich smallholder, had paid for several rounds of champagne to celebrate the Liberation. During this time the second person, Dupont, with his partner[69] and daughter, spread insults about Martin in the only cafe in the village. The scandal spread quickly. A farm worker heard it said that the Dupont family was insulting Martin, and warned him.

The next day some young FFI troops arrived from the neighbouring community about ten kilometres away and that had the reputation of being 'red'. They had just got hold of some German weapons that had been gathered together by Martin and were looking for German soldiers who were fleeing. During this time the local people were out along the main street to welcome a new convoy of American forces. The two Dupont women stayed in their house, but from their window opposite the church they could see the Americans going by. From this moment on the two versions differ. Apparently the FFI went past the Dupont house with Martin and a couple of others. The crowd then called to them asking them to punish the women who had collaborated. According to some of the testimonies it was Martin who first gave the order to break through the garden gate and to fetch the Dupont family; others maintain that he played no particular role in this at all, which is what he himself said in his statement. Two members of the FFI climbed over the gate and threatening the members of the family with their weapons brought them out. One of the FFI standing on top of the gate, asked whether the women's hair should be shaved off. The vigorous response was positive. The shaving of their heads was begun, whether by the FFI, or by men from the village – testimonies differ on this particular point – but each one seemed afterwards to come in turn to cut off a lock of hair. Dupont asked the mayor to help him, but got the reply 'Everyone is against you.' With insults coming from all sides they were led through the village streets. One young man brought a bucket of tar, but Dupont was taken back to his house and there is no account of how events finished. In the afternoon the search for German soldiers continued. The account stops there.

The choice of this incident is justified for two reasons. First of all the quality of the sources. Twelve days after the events, namely on 12 September 1944, Dupont made an official complaint for 'breaking and entering, threats of death, violence and theft'. He accused Martin for having been responsible for starting the *tonte* and, moreover, for having been a collaborator. The procurer of the Republic in Beauvais on 20 September asked for an inquiry to be carried out. This was done between 3–21 October 1944 by the national police. Twenty persons were heard, amongst whom were one of the women whose heads were shaved, numerous people who had been present, the FFI, the mayor and, on two occasions each, Martin and Dupont. The records were completed by a file from the *épuration* commission against Martin who had been a former member of the special delegation under the Vichy regime. The other interest of this account concerns the village itself. With four hundred inhabitants it had not experienced any extraordinary events to distinguish it from numerous other villages in France. Without being an entirely closed community, it was sufficiently withdrawn from what was happening on a national scale for local events to come to the fore more easily.

This village had not known fighting or air raids, nor had it suffered from any atrocities carried out by the German army or the *milice*, and yet the war was everywhere. Not just as a distant event whose development could be followed through the newspapers or on the radio, but as something that was part of everyday life. First of all by those features that have already been referred to: the rout of the Wermacht, the arrival of the American army, that of the FFI and the requisition of German weapons. But its presence is also marked by a number of expressions used in the accounts that evoke hunger (horse meat to be divided up, stolen carrots) or the fear of air raids that had been experienced by the neighbouring industrial town from which a number of people had come as refugees. What the women who had collaborated were being reproached for by the crowd that demanded that they should be punished, may appear derisory: dips in the local pond, music and meals shared with Germans. The contrast between pleasures flaunted for all to see and the depravation or the suffering of others, was enough to bring the larger stakes of war down to the scale of this village. The shaving of heads assumed a political quality that any number of private and professional antagonisms and affairs together could not disguise. The adversaries, here two women and a man, were not simply seen as three individuals, but as part of a group and moreover as belonging to the oppressor who had now been con-quered. In the eyes of many over and beyond the advantages they had enjoyed, they were part of the collective responsibility of which Germans and the collaborators were guilty. Here we have a micro society with its own dynamic that reflects events on a much larger scale.

All the way through the testimonies, the disputes opposing the different protagonists are evoked. Martin rejects the accusation of four witnesses that point him out as the person who had been responsible for starting the *tonte*. According to him, each one had a reason for bearing him a grudge. The first had stolen rabbits, carrots and potatoes from him and as a result had been condemned to a fortnight in prison; he was also furious that a German radio that he badly wanted had slipped through his fingers. The second was bitter in that, as deputy mayor, Martin had refused to give financial help to his partner. The third reproached him for having bought the house in which he was living in order to provide accommodation for his workers. The fourth was in his debt. As for Dupont and Martin, the dispute between them seems to have gone back sometime and had already occasioned insults, court cases and apologies. A professional difference might also be at the root of the rivalry between them, one being a rich market gardener and another a grain dealer.

It is also possible to see how the private and public overlap in the description of where events took place. The gate separating the Dupont's house from the street is referred to on nineteen occasions in the testimonies and becomes one of the main issues of the enquiry. From a legal point of view, the fact that it was crossed constitutes breaking and entry, for which an official complaint was lodged. From a symbolic point of view, climbing onto it allowed the FFI to have more warlike body language in front of the people who were there. It was from the top of it that he spoke to them, and in jumping over the gate the FFI broke down the barrier between private life and public life and put the women and the relationships that they had with the occupiers into the public domain. Dupont was pursued as far as the bathroom, the daughter and her mother into their bedroom; then 'they made us go down and dragged us into the street' the latter stated. The street is also more than just the road taken by the American troops; it is the square by the church and the cafe. All these places where village people would meet were also those in which Germans could be seen daily going to the Duponts' house where a gramophone could be heard playing for their pleasure.

From the twenty testimonies collected by the police and with the exception of M. and Mme Dupont, it appears that seventeen people witnessed the shaving of the women's heads. All of them talk about the part played by the crowd by referring to it in the third person. It was the crowd that asked the FFI to punish the women who had collaborated; it was the crowd which applauded and replied positively to the question: 'Should they have their hair cut off, yes or no?' It was the crowd that threw insults at Dupont as he went by; and it was in a certain way the crowd that cut off their hair. The crowd has therefore become the principal actor in this ceremony, each individual person who took part withdrawing once the event was over. Some people maintained that they were outside their houses, or their shops at the time when the shaving of heads took place. Others say that they only arrived once it had been started. As for the FFI soldiers, they simply attribute to themselves the job of carrying out the will of the local population. The representation of a 'menacing', 'stormy' and 'clamouring' crowd or better still one which according to two witnesses could say: 'Since you are there, you must cut their hair off', can be discovered as well in the testimony of one of the victims. Dupont spoke in fact of 'the foreign rabble that was insulting him and shouting out: 'Shoot him''. The term 'foreigner' seems to have been applied here to people who had come from a village less than ten kilometres away, but in the way Dupont refers to things, the crowd essentially is probably both the 'rabble' and 'foreign'. Mme Dupont (her daughter who also had her head shaved, did not give a testimony) is the only person who did not use at any moment the term 'crowd'; she designated by name those people who cut off her hair and accused Martin of having given the order.

The *épuration* commissioner cleared Martin of the accusations made against him in his report of 30 December 1944 stating:

> Martin has provided all the useful explanations relative to the accusations made against him by the group of the most suspect individuals. His statements carry the stamp of the most complete frankness and the information gathered from the surrounding region about him are very favourable. There is no act which can be held against him allowing him to be accused of collaboration. As for those who accuse him, alas they have little to recommend them. Dupont who has taken to drink has just been fined 500 francs with interest for having insulted Martin and his family. Dupont and his wife and daughter who live with him, and who had their heads shaved on account of their scandalous conduct with the occupiers have had to leave the region. At this moment (December 1944) the Dupont family lives in the Parisien suburbs.

Victory, Punishment and Reconstruction

In a village where nothing dramatic and spectacular seems to have happened during the Occupation, the Liberation was something that arrived from outside and everyone watched and noted as it developed. The glasses of champagne both celebrate and mark the end of this period, of the time which now belongs to the past. Offered by the richest market gardener, the rounds of drinks belong to the quality of life in the village and are a token of the respect for village worthies, which nothing could upset. It was, moreover, as part of this state of affairs that the unexpected but welcome distribution of meat was made. Liberation was here observed on 30 August 1994 rather than experienced, but the next day the village was overcome by the event we have heard of. The upheaval was provoked by the arrival of the FFI from a neighbouring village. Did they give expression to a sense of frustration that the community felt and that only needed a pretext to show itself, or on account of their prestige, mixed the fear they inspired, did the FFI drag the rest of the village into this action with them – we should not forget they were 'red', young and armed.

As in a classical tragedy, the local population is caught up in the unities of place, time and action and the most pressing aims are to win, punish and reconstruct. The garden gate, which quite clearly none of the parishioners in front of the church dared go through, is like the front line of a battle inside the village, and is removed. A victory without a struggle allows the local population to seize three prisoners, to re-enact the fight from which it was absent and to become the craftsmen of its own freedom. There is a question of punishment. Even if it had been premeditated – as the victims indicated – it is something that everyone was involved in, from the sentence until its execution, when anyone could take the clippers to the heads of those who had been defeated. As for the procession, it is a model for the expulsion that would become a reality for the Dupont family two months later, and is one of the conditions for reconstruction, for the rebirth of a community cleansed of its traitors and acting out its own future. As a ceremony, the shaving of heads allows the local population to come together and to rediscover its place within the French nation. In this way we have a picture of the village community acting together and in this way, too, by having events meet with general approval, the responsibility of individuals is lessened. Such violence, unacceptable if it is seen as the settlement of a personal matter, is legitimized by a collective decision, and beyond that, by a national one.

Did the Shaving of Heads Channel Violence?

The fact that it was as a lesser or minor form of violence when measured against others has prompted a number of writers to see the practice as a kind of vector for it. Peter Novick imagines that 'girls whose heads were shaved were, in large measure (unbeknown to them and unbeknown to their executioners) being used to save those members of the Milice and collaborators who without them ought to have died to appease the wrath of their fellow citizens.'[70] Many other testimonies bear this out. In his memoirs the priest Roger More writes: 'This business of the horses was to cut our losses. What was essential was to avoid any bloodshed. There had already been enough of that! For a long time these girls who are now wearing turbans won't say 'bonjour M. Le Curé' to me anymore, but there was no blood.'[71] the way in which other *tontes* were carried out supports this feeling.

In Cahors on 27 June 1945, the crowd outside the court rooms demanded that a Gestapo agent who had been responsible for the deportation of 1,200 people from that part of Figeac in May 1944 and who had just been condemned to death, should be handed over to them before he was taken to Figeac to be executed. By their interventions, the prefect and a number of responsible people managed to restore calm, but in the evening the unrest broke out again:

After they had been shaved and had the Swastika drawn on them in pencil three women were taken on a lorry through the main streets of the town and shown like this to the large part of the local population who found in this a distraction from their overexcited state which had grown from their wish to carry out the judge's sentence themselves at the end of the court proceedings. While the crowd was preoccupied by what was going on, L was taken back to the station in Cahors since it was feared that had the official instructions been followed ordering that condemned prisoners should be taken to a central prison to await execution, the public, if it had known this and misinterpreted it to mean that the prisoner had been let off execution, would have resorted to much greater violence.[72]

Can the prefect's decision that three women should have had their heads shaved in order to cause a diversion and allow a delicate operation to take place, be considered an alternative to execution when L was shot a few days later? It is true that had the demonstration organized at the time L was tried not taken place, the three women would probably have escaped their punishment. Quite often, however, the way in which the head-shaving ceremonies were carried out did not avoid more serious violence taking place.

In Mulhouse during the night of 31 May to 1 June 1945, the fact that three young women had their heads shaved as they left the cinema, did not prevent a man reputed to have been a Nazi from being shot a few hours later.[73] In Vichy on 6 June 1945, the fact that four women and a man had their heads shaved at seven o'clock in the evening, did not prevent a member of the *milice* from being hanged fifty minutes later.[74] During the Liberation certain towns where courts ordered executions experienced just as many head shavings as others. At Nîmes the two punishments took place in the same place, in the Roman amphitheatre. On 21 August 1944 at Gap, the local Gestapo Chief and two of his assistants were executed and a dozen women who had collaborated had their heads shaved. In Guéret the courts condemned a woman to a year in prison for having had relationships with Germans; in return a woman member of the *milice* was condemned to death and shot on 24 September 1944.[75]

Any link between the shaving of heads and executions is difficult to establish. If we chart the distribution of the former across the country, it is not possible to say whether this practice was more widespread in some regions than in others. As for the map showing the number of executions that took place, it is even more unclear. Nevertheless a comparison of departments where the number of executions carried out differs widely weakens any hypothesis of a correlation between these and the number

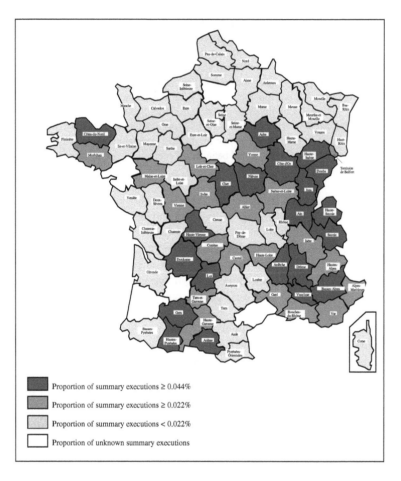

Summary executions as a proportion of the total population in each department.[1]

of incidents of head shaving. In departments where there was a significant number of summary executions, the shaving of heads was known in the principal towns. In the Dordogne where an enquiry carried out by the CHOLF on the repressive measures taken at the Liberation accounts for at least 375 executions, or as a percentage nearly five times the national average, women had their heads shaved at Périgueux as well as at Bergerac. In the Drôme where the proportion is the same, the practice was carried out at Valence, Montélimar, Die and at Romans. In Savoie, Haute-Savoie and the Ardèche, where the rate of executions was near 1 per cent, hair fell in the principal towns. Against this there were just as many occurrences of head shaving in departments where no executions took place. This was the case at Cherbourg, Villedieu, Avranches, Granville and in several villages in the department of the Manche which had the reputation for being the most peaceful of them all. In the department of Ille-et-Vilaine, with 578,000 inhabitants, only eleven executions (0.02 per cent) were carried out, but the shaving of heads took place nonetheless in at least ten communes among which were Rennes and Redon. Such situations as these do not constitute proof, but without the precise mapping of the two phenomena studied they do not put the theory of using women as scapegoats seriously in doubt. The violence with which the shaving of heads was carried out reflected a desire for freedom and purification in any district, and varied considerably according to the local state of affairs.

The shaving of heads was a violent statement made by people who had been freed. However much the perception of them and the practice varied, it allowed everyone at any social level – personal, local and national – to make a statement. At the time of the Liberation in the widest sense of the term it converged with all the other things that took place during these days, but it alone, by its violence, was an outlet for fear and suffering. Its uncertain nature also explains why an episode that was limited in time should reflect a much longer period. The practice was rooted in the immediate past of the Occupation, but also reflects the upheavals of any community life. It anticipated a better future and offered an indispensable opportunity to 'turn over a new leaf'. The role played by violence in bringing whole groups together does not in itself allow us fully to understand why heads were shaved. The fact that violence took other forms, that the public was present and that a procession formed part of the proceedings also had a direct influence, but the distinctive feature was the cutting off of hair. The designation of the guilty women and their ensuing punishment was made easier by the closeness of a community, but the full significance of the *tonte* only becomes apparent in the fact that the victims were women.

A Punishment for Women

In the majority of cases the shaving of heads was carried out on women and the fact that only a few men suffered the same fate is really irrelevant. But which women? Did they come from a particular social group? Were they all more or less of the same age? What is clear is that situations differed widely to the point where the problem can be examined in a different way and the question whether or not there is a sexual dimension to it has to be asked. Punished because they were accused of collaboration, is it not that *as women* these people had their heads shaved? And if it is not simply a question of an act of violence against women, but against these specific women, what does that signify? As we shall see the shaving of heads is symptomatic of a deep crisis existing between men and women that was brought into the open by wars – world and civil – throughout the continent of Europe.

Is there a Profile of *La Tondue*?

Female and accused of collaboration – these are the two principal characteristics of women whose heads were shaved. Let us try to refine this portrait by looking more closely at age and at their matrimonial and professional situations.

Out of the 586 women whose heads were shaved and whose name we know, the ages of 290 of them is also known. The first thing to notice is the wide difference: three young girls only fifteen years old had their heads shaved, 20 per cent were minors less than twenty-one years old; at the other end of the scale the oldest woman was sixty-nine and if there were only two of them who were more than sixty, nearly 10 per cent were over fifty.

Furthermore we should also notice the importance of the age range of the younger ones, particularly those between twenty and twenty-five. Their youth was all the more underlined by the many descriptions of them as 'young girls' or 'young women', rather than simply 'women'.

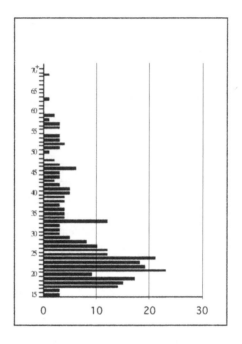

Age of women whose heads were shaved, throughout France (a sample of 290 individuals).

Nonetheless the young age of these has then to be balanced by the average age, which is marginally above twenty-nine years.

As far as their civil status is concerned, the number of married women among those who had their heads shaved is appreciably lower than for the population of France as a whole: 35.5 per cent against 55.2 per cent. It is true that the available documents do not always allow us to be certain and sometimes it becomes clear from their files that although they may appear under their family name, they were married to a collaborator, a prisoner of war, or even to someone who had voluntarily gone to work in Germany.

Nonetheless, on the scale of departments such as the Oise or the Hérault the same relationship can be observed: women who had their heads shaved were on the whole young and usually single.

Finally 35.7 per cent of these women had a trade. This figure corresponds to the national average,[1] but the absence of details for more than half of them means that we have to be careful. Most of the women for whom there is no indication of any profession were probably without one,

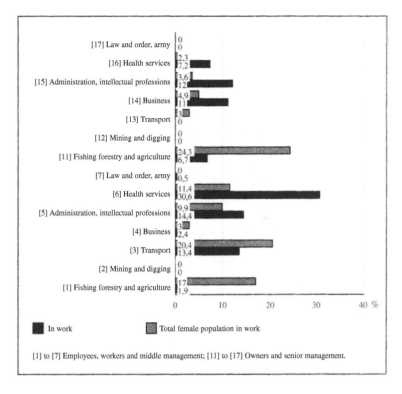

[17] Law and order, army — 0 / 0
[16] Health services — 2.3 / 7.2
[15] Administration, intellectual professions — 3.6 / 12
[14] Business — 4.9 / 11
[13] Transport — 3 / 0
[12] Mining and digging — 0 / 0
[11] Fishing forestry and agriculture — 24.3 / 6.7
[7] Law and order, army — 0 / 0.5
[6] Health services — 11.4 / 30.6
[5] Administration, intellectual professions — 9.9 / 14.4
[4] Business — 3 / 2.4
[3] Transport — 20.4 / 13.4
[2] Mining and digging — 0 / 0
[1] Fishing forestry and agriculture — 17 / 1.9

0   10   20   30   40 %

■ In work   ▧ Total female population in work

[1] to [7] Employees, workers and middle management; [11] to [17] Owners and senior management.

Professional activities of women whose heads had been shaved by comparison with the number of women in France as a whole.

although nearly a tenth of them had proceedings brought against them for 'having worked for the Germans' or 'willingly gone to Germany'. The rate of professional activity then rises to 41 per cent or a proportion that is appreciably higher than among other French women. An identical state of affairs can be seen when the case of all women who have been interned is analysed: 50 per cent in the Hérault, 53.2 per cent in the Oise and 57 per cent in the Indre.

The difference is also one of professional activity. Set against the census figures for 1946 and the groupings by profession in place at the time, a comparison reveals significant differences in certain ones. The majority of women whose heads were shaved were those employed in public and health services in administration and in intellectual professions.

Against this workers in industry and agriculture are distinctly less represented: respectively 13.4 per cent against a working female population as a whole of 23.4 per cent and 8.6 per cent against 41.3 per cent. In the most industrial region, the department of the Oise, workers who had their hair cut off only represented 12.8 per cent of all women who suffered that fate and yet made up 25.9 per cent of the overall female population in work, compared with 28.7 per cent of women in middle management jobs.

A more detailed analysis of the occupation of women whose heads had been shaved reveals the most vulnerable professions. In the first place, those in demand, and indispensable for the good running of the German military administration, were cleaning ladies, laundresses and dish-washers in the service sector; shorthand typists, interpreters or secretaries in administration. Next were women who, without actually working for the enemy, by their profession came into contact with it. Such was the case of shopkeepers or women working in business, but also those who were barmaids, waitresses, hairdressers, or again among the owners and upper management those who had restaurants, hotels or bars. By virtue of their activities these women were close to the occupiers. Suspected of giving favours to the 'German customer' at a time of hardship and of benefiting from his money, as well as from his protection, it is logical to find that these women should appear among those who had their heads shaved. Finally in the management class of the administrative and intellectual professions the situation of the teacher stands out. Given the closeness of their school premises and those requisitioned by the occupy-ing forces, they were investigated on several occasions.

Women who had contact with the enemy whether he was their employer, customer, or someone who was simply given accommodation, were at risk even though their activities as such did not automatically condemn them to having their heads shaved. Differences between activities of professions were also important. What mattered was how close they were to the enemy and not a social distinction between 'poor girls' who were victims of an implacable justice and those who were better off and were spared. Taking all professional activities into account the percentage of those women in senior management jobs whose heads were shaved was more or less the same as others: 36.9 per cent to 38.1 per cent.[2] Even if among these women who had their heads shaved we can trace those who regularly went to receptions in the German Embassy in Paris, or were the wives of collaborationist leaders, we know that at a local level, such women would include the owner of a town's main hotel-restaurant, the headmistress of a school, the wife of a rich farmer or of an industrialist. An examination of statistics based on age, marital status or profession produces complementary but contradictory information. There is no dominant one, but certain features can nonetheless be noted. Those women who were relatively young, mostly unmarried, and had a more important if insecure professional activity, and one where the social control exerted by the group was not the same as it would be in the factory or in the fields, could more easily escape attention. And yet it is not possible to talk of a single profile. Women who had their heads shaved came from every section of French society and were no more all guilty of having sexual relations with the enemy than they were all 'young', 'manless' and 'skivvies'. Any attempt to create a uniform picture – of a 'poor girl' who then became the scapegoat – is to say the least imprecise. Amongst these women we find girls living with their mother, the wives of prisoners of war and of collaborators who were all punished in the same way, as were divorced women and others who were simply unmarried.

Violence in Contempt of Women

The head of hair is the focal point of punishment but not a punishment that is intended to destroy or neutralize an adversary. Unlike killing or wounding an enemy, the shaving of a head cannot be considered to be a normal act of violence in a time of war. Its symbolic character is more important than the reality, but the acknowledgement of the fact that the hair is feminine, and the memory of similar practices carried out in the past are not in themselves a sufficient explanation. It is as difficult to establish a link between a practice that has gone on unchanged throughout history and its huge deployment in 1944–5, as it is to ignore it. It would be dangerous and even wrong to want to reconstruct direct causal links with practices that are so distant, but it would be equally risky to reject them on the pretext that it was not possible to establish any positive influence they might have had.

Why should hair be cut off? As a symbol of femininity the head of hair is reason enough and questions could stop there. But beyond this apparently neat equation, the place hair holds when we are dealing with body language is more complicated. From a physiological point of view the hair on a head forms part of body hair in general. Among European populations it makes a physical distinction between the two sexes, but in itself – unlike a beard – does not make one between men and women. The ambiguity arising from the implied reference to pubic hair and to the genital distinction between the sexes, makes hair on the head a vital element in the question of appearance. When, in his Epistle to the

Corinthians, Paul asserts that what reflects cultural practice is 'natural', he underlines the sexual distinction revealed by hair quite categorically:

> And every woman who prays or prophesies with her head uncovered dishonours her head – it is just as though her head were shaved. If a woman does not cover her head, she should have her hair cut off; and it is a disgrace for a woman to have her hair cut or shaved off, she should cover her head. . . . Does not the very nature of things teach you that if a man has long hair, it is a disgrace to him, but that if a woman has long hair, it is her glory? (1 Corinthians 11: 5–6, 14–15).[3]

The use of this quotation from the New Testament is not an attempt to give a date to the time when sexual difference was signified by a head of hair, but to recall the cultural reference to the fact that to have one's head shaved was a disgrace. Shaving of the hair as a punishment against women based on sex can be found equally in a number of different societies. Tacitus records in *La Germanie* that:

> In this highly populated country adulterous women are few; punishment is immediate and it is up to the husband to carry it out. The guilty woman who is stripped bare and whose hair is shaved off is chased from the house in the presence of relatives by the husband, who then leads her through the streets of the town and beats her. [*abscisis crinibus nudutam coram propinquis expellit domo maritus ac per omnem uicum uerbere agit*][4]

The barbaric origin of this practice is equally confirmed by its use in Visigoth law. Reference to it is also found recorded in the Carolingien period in 805,[5] but there it was used for punishing men who had been robbers or conspirators, the humiliation associated with it being due to the loss of hair as a sign of male honour. The shaving of heads as a punishment for adultery during the thirteenth and fourteenth centuries is attested to in a number of stories,[6] but the best known example is that of Marguerite de Bourgogne who, on the orders of her husband Louis X in 1314, had her head shaved and was then strangled on account of her adultery. In the south of France, according to customary law, the punishment was directed against the adulterous woman and her lover by having them cross the town naked followed by the shouts and blows of the local population. According to Jean-Marie Carbasse, such dramatic punishment disappeared from the end of the sixteenth century. Then the adulterous woman was 'authenticated', that is to say she was shut up in a convent.[7] For two years her husband could forgive her and take her back, but if he refused she would then be 'shaved, given a veil, clad in religious habits and made a recluse for life'. In a very different context the practice is mentioned by Michelet in the account he gives of 5 October 1789: 'On the road [from Versailles] women were dragging along all those they could find, threatening those who would not go with them to cut off their hair.'[8]

To conclude from these random examples that this punishment was reserved for adulterous women and had been the norm for centuries, would be mistaken. Not only did many societies practise other forms of punishment (rejection, stoning, putting to death), but the cutting off of hair could have other significance (religious,[9] sacrificial,[10] or prophylactic[11]); to acknowledge this reveals the sexual dimension associated with women's hair, something also recognized through the actions of displaying it, hiding it, or cutting it off.

It is difficult to know how we should judge the fact that this punishment based on sex keeps recurring. It shows that in no way is it something invented with the Liberation of France. Even if it could not be considered part of a tradition, it draws on a common cultural heritage, and the symbolic significance of hair is strong enough for the practice of this punishment to be highly evocative for modern people. In accounts of the Liberation we find a number of allusions to the middle ages: Jean-Paul Sartre railed against this mediaeval sadism in the newspaper *Combat*;[12] in *Voies Nouvelles* on 8 September 1944, the writer of a brief note entitled 'The Ballad of the Shaven Women' rather seems to regret 'processions like these which the same streets during the middle ages had witnessed in a passionate period when adulterous women would be lead naked through the street, sprawling and facing backwards on a donkey.'

To make a causal link between the punishment of adultery as it was practised during the mediaeval period and that of the Liberation in 1944 would be risky. Its eventual re-emergence has to be explained and to consider it simply as a matter of similarity cannot take the place of analysis, particularly as other elements have to be taken into account. What importance should we give to the renewed interest in the body in the twentieth century?[13] During the First World War nurses discovered mutilated bodies of soldiers who had been wounded. A slow but growing concern for the body is evidenced by the fact that a room is increasingly reserved for personal washing; it can also be seen in the growth of sporting activities through the century. If these changes relate principally to the private domain, evidence of public awareness of the body's value is even more noticeable. Given greater value by the totalitarian aesthetic of Fascism, Stalinism and Nazism, the body becomes an ideological vector and the proof of the benefits of the proposed political system. And finally, different fashions of which the public becomes increasingly aware through films and photography are bodily manifestations of a new language dealing with appearance. The shaving of heads that radically modifies the way people look, is also related to fundamental changes in the relationship between the individual and society as a whole.

Appearance Matters: from Urchin Cut to Hep

In the years following the First World War a new fashion caused a scandal. Many women adopted a hairstyle known as an 'urchin cut' inspired by a novel of the same title by Victor Margueritte.[14] One woman quoted in the daily paper *Le Temps*[15] laid claim to this new attitude: 'Our long hair is the symbol of our past slavery; having it cut off puts an end to our humiliation.' Against this the review *La Coiffure de Paris* considers that this was an act of violence that women were carrying out against their own nature. 'Slavery', 'female nature': twenty years before the liberation a hairstyle is at the centre of a debate intimately bound up with the relationship between the sexes. A single allusion to it can be found in August 1944 in Agen, where a popular song of the 1920s *They've All had their Hair Cut Off*[16] became popular. It is difficult to know what role this episode from the inter-war period played in the imaginations of French people at the time of the Liberation. Let us consider it as a marker in the development of relationships between men and women and a further example of the growing importance of the body as a vector for identity. Whether we are talking of those who adopted the urchin cut in the 1920s, the hep cats during the war and more recently of pop fans and punks, the wilful choice of a different hairstyle is a sign of dissent. With each generation the century has known a new style that has caused a scandal and provided a brutal reaction. The hep cats were the targets of the clippers wielded by the Jeunesses populaires françaises in 1942,[17] as they were as well by certain members of the Resistance at the time of the Liberation:

> War has been declared against the hep cats. Alas we know that the swing style persists and the hep cats are many in number. These young people with their strange behaviour still dare to look down on those people who fought in the Resistance all the while smoothing down their wavy hair with their effeminate hands. Men of the Verneuil regiment do not hesitate to put these young people in their place, and if they persist in behaving the way they do, just take a bit of their hair off. We don't need hep cats anymore.[18]

Without wishing to put the shaving of the heads of women accused of collaboration in the same context as these reactions against different fashions, we can nonetheless see one in which hair is given a political dimension – the choice of a different cut was seen as a gesture of refusal. Hair became eloquent. We could even offer the hypothesis that it was hardly surprising that for most people an idea (in this case the condemnation of collaboration) should have been expressed by a hairstyle, even if it was not deliberate.

Hair as a 'Murder Weapon'

In the summer of 1944 the 'ancestral sign of femininity' to quote Philippe Perrot,[19] was one of the targets of those wielding the clippers. The symbolic value attributed to collaboration was often greater than the reality. The punishment defines the crime *a posteriori* and the length of hair becomes the measure of guilt. A woman who protested against the lenient treatment which her neighbour had received and who was spared having her hair shaved off said: 'She would come out even more arrogant and aggressive than ever with her hair as long as anybody's and longer even than mine. Nothing wrong with anything she had done then.'[20]

But a head of hair is not only an *a temporal* symbol of femininity, a tribute to be paid by those who had collaborated, it is also an incarnation of 'the weapon used in horizontal collaboration': 'Experience has shown us that around the age of forty a woman's beauty, however great it may be, cannot prevent scissors from having an effect. Samson lost his strength when he had his hair cut off; you madame, if by any chance that should happen to you, you would loose your sex appeal.'[21] To shave the head is a way of showing women to be entirely responsible for their guilt, of having them act out their betrayal. The usual roles are forgotten in the game of seduction. Hair becomes a vector for bodily collaboration; ideology takes second place and feelings, when they exist, are lost. In some accounts hair is of central importance. In the department of the Yonne, for example, references are made to hair that has still not been touched: 'Words fly off but hair remains behind . . . but yes! Mesdemoiselles and Mesdames, there are still those among you whose pretty and silky heads of hair, often coloured in the most original way, run the risk of receiving the attention of our FFI hair artists';[22] in the department of the Oise, what remained of 'opulent heads of feminine hair have been sacrificed to the avenging scissors. A plentiful harvest of brown and blonde curls has been the ransom paid for the emotional and rational weaknesses of a few shameful individuals . . .'[23]

Here we have descriptions both of hair before the clippers have done their job and a fleeting glimpse of curls strewn upon the ground left by the woman whose head has been shaved. In other words the description of a physical action has taken the place of one denouncing collaboration. Moreover to focus on the act of cutting reduces the harshness of the punishment. Little by little the hairdresser takes the place of someone who is carrying out the purging process, and with language becoming deliberately more humorous, the stigmatization associated with collaboration is lessened. The language describing the women whose heads have been shaved opens the way for reflections on their flirtatious nature. The political gives way to the bawdy, the punishment becomes less severe, and collaboration itself becomes a secondary issue.

The Reappropriation of the Body

The sight of a shaved head, the way an appearance is modified, causes the practice to become a focal point in a system involving the whole body. Hair is not only the adornment of a body which has betrayed: it is that of a woman. The way in which the practice of shaving takes place can be analysed in two stages. First a foregrounding of sexuality that accompanies a shift of emphasis from the idea of women as collaborators to the role played specifically by their bodies. Second branding as a symbolic destruction of the body. With the body having been desexualized in this way, the local population can reappropriate it and forbid the victim to recover those features contributing to a certain idea of femininity. All sexuality is henceforth forbidden.

Insults and Placards: the Focus on Sexuality

Whenever the shaving of heads was carried out, there were words offered or written down whose function was twofold. On the one hand they designated the guilty person and indicated her crime; on the other they were part of the way the ritual was carried out and expressed collective approval. This language shouted, repeated, most frequently chanted by everyone together – became an integral part of the punishment itself.

Newspapers at the Liberation did not resort to deliberately vulgar vocabulary when they described the shaving of heads.[24] But expressions such as 'hetaera' or 'frivolous tarts' were probably not part of the language used by a shouting crowd. The insults mentioned in the reports made by the police are in fact of a quite different register: 'bitch' and 'prostitute' are the most frequent. They are accompanied by calls for punishment by 'death' and with slogans like 'off with their hair'. The sexual connotations and the constant likening of these women to prostitutes do not mean that accusations of a political nature are missing and the word 'Boche' appears regularly in these insults.

Sometimes when the ritual was performed, the victim carried or had displayed alongside her a notice. The dozen notices which have been found all link collaboration and sexuality. Several inscriptions are made in the first person, whether singular or plural, and the confession written on them both explains and justifies the punishment: 'We are sorry our Germans are gone', 'I slept with the Boche!', 'I slept with the Germans', 'I [illegible] with Gerries on the beach in Mâcon'.[25] In the two cases of men whose heads were shaved at Saint-Étienne, the text is similarly composed even if the nature of the crime is different: 'I handed over two patriots to the Gestapo for 5000 francs', 'Looter – I carried it out pretending to be a member of the FFI police'.[26] With the exception of one woman whose notice bears the inscription 'Had her husband shot',[27] in general when the first person is not used, the slogans are directed more at the women or at their punishment than at the 'crime' committed: 'Shame on these women who are in love with the mark', 'Sold to the enemy', 'A prostitute bearing the swastika', 'The collaborationist's cart', 'Hair set in the Nazi style'.[28] Apart from the fact that they require a certain foresight on the part of the individual, these notices are not different from other forms of description. The enemy and women's sexuality are linked, but first and foremost it is the body of the woman who had collaborated that personifies betrayal.

Showing the Body

The shaving of heads only has a sense if it is recognized in the way that branding was under the *Ancien Régime*. Punishment and branding together allow everybody to identify the guilty woman. If in the cases where the practice is carried out secretly or in prison, the public only comes to know about it later, in the case of others the presence of the crowd is part of the punishment. The attack on the body is made ten times worse by the humiliation of the punishment being carried out in front of the woman's own people. Pushed onto a balcony, hoisted up onto a stage, or put onto a flight of steps, the woman whose head is to be shaved has to be seen. In Vierzon:

> on the premises of the prison that had been used by the Germans, a number of people of all ages and from different social conditions were shut up waiting more or less without causing trouble for the time when the hairdresser would make them beautiful. The latter eventually arrived and set about his business in a regular way inside the premises. Considering where he was to be rather uncomfortable, he had the bright idea of going outside and setting himself up in the middle of the square. People, curious, quickly gathered around. One can judge the embarrassment of the customers who were not expecting to be honoured quite like this. We say honoured because the crowd, eager to know who the women were, demanded that those whose heads had already been shaved should be brought out. These women did not appear to share fully the view of all the others present, and they were far from being amused by publicity like this. The Boche were much more gallant weren't they? But what do you expect, there is always another side to the coin.[29]

The punishment is a show and the population is invited to witness its production. The word 'show' is found in a number of articles describing the processions of women whose heads are to be shaved. The daily paper of the Resistance movements in the Var (MUR) *Résistance* informs its readers on 27 August 1944 of the following programme:

> Permanent wave Gestapo style. On Sunday at 17:00 hrs outside the prison gates a public demonstration of this permanent wave, carried out with clippers no. 0 will be given. The customers will be chosen from women who have collaborated intimately with members of the Gestapo. This demonstration will be followed by an exhibition in the band stand in the Allées.[30]

The following morning the newspaper confirmed that eight women 'had the honour of being on stage and of having had their heads shaved'.

Sometimes a session that had been planned had to be cancelled. This was the case in Pommerit-le-Vicomte where eleven women had been arrested on the order of the CLL and were to have their heads shaved on Sunday 3 September 1944, at a time when celebrations were being organized by the local community. Only by order of the chief of the local Resistance movement were they finally set free.[31]

The setting up of a stage, or the choice of a place that was a bit higher, the presentation of women once their heads had been shaved, the taking of photographs, the shaking of fistfuls of hair, all of this puts emphasis primarily on the body. With a shaved head, lead through the streets bearing a notice, naked and marked with the swastika, the body of the woman who has collaborated bears the sign of the crime committed and takes part in its own condemnation.

The body which arrives on the scene where the shaving is to be carried out is the one that seduced the enemy: 'sweet pretty little faces', 'smiles which were reserved no doubt for the gentlemen of the Wehrmacht', 'beautiful little mouth'.[32] The clippers or the scissors are going to destroy the seductive body and many commentaries refer to the dexterity of makeshift hairdressers who, as their victim's skull appeared, made their femininity disappear. Articles praise 'experienced hairdressers who showed a real virtuosity in their handling of clippers', others spoke of 'unpaid and often inexperienced hairdressers'. Whether a tuft, a plait, or several locks remained, or whether on the contrary the skull was as smooth as a billiard ball,[33] the imagination came up with all kinds of descriptions for the same result, namely that of an image of ugliness. Ugliness that was not horrible but acceptable and presentable, and about which it was possible to make jokes. Smiles and laughter or applause would endorse the change in appearance. The body simply became something bearing evidence of betrayal with the shaved head the most flagrant sign.

Taken to extreme, the insistence on physical sexuality is reflected in the partial or complete stripping of these women. For a society that was still modest and in which the body remained hidden, processions of naked women constituted a clear break with tradition. Before rape, which we will consider later, these processions were the final expression of the way in which women's bodies had been reappropriated by those who had recently won the war.

Practised in fifty or so towns amongst which the most important are: Paris, Marseille, Lyon, Toulouse, Bordeaux, Avignon, Albi, Mulhouse, Rheims, Agen, Valenciennes, Versailles, Rodez, Troyes, Colmar, Périgueux, Aix-en-Provence, Angers and Le Mans, the stripping of women was the result of individual initiatives in which voyeurism and sadism, encouraged by the way in which the sexuality of the women was emphasised, were combined.

On 30 August 1944 once the allied troops arrived, the members of the Resistance divided themselves into two groups. The first lead by M. Pierre, head of the FFI, set about pursuing the Boche, the second with Jacques at its head started to look for women who had been singled out as having been guilty of relationships with Germans. This group had its headquarters in the local château. While Pierre was looking for Germans in the surrounding countryside, Jacques played at being head of a court in the château's tower. Here people suspected of collaboration and women of having had amorous relationships with Germans were brought before him. On 30 August 1944 R and B, two market gardeners claiming they belonged to the FFI, went to the home of Miss M. where in the presence of her invalid mother they stripped her and tore her clothes into pieces and then led her naked to Jacques who had her hair cut off. This woman had to remain entirely naked in front of children and young girls for several hours and then return home only half dressed. The same day, around 16:00 hrs the two same individuals went to the house of Mrs V. and made her undress completely in front of her little girl aged three. They then lead her completely naked to the château where she was shown to Jacques who, after having her hair cut off, set her free. This woman had to make the journey back to her home (about 2 km) completely naked. A reading of the statement made by Mrs. L. is more instructive for an understanding of Jacques' thinking. It is the same if we read that of R.M . . . the behaviour of the men R., B. and Jacques disgusted the majority of people in the area. R had on various occasions made advances towards the young girl on whom he had so odiously taken his revenge. This individual is entirely responsible for his behaviour. This is not true of B, father of seven children, who is weak minded and easily allows himself to be dragged along. As for Jacques, his behaviour is just as reprehensible. Since he was playing the role of judge, it was up to him to give orders so that these women should not be put on public display and he should have given them clothes instead of insulting them. He voluntarily joined in with R and B and sent these women to the hairdresser in the public square.[34]

In this case we have a telling example of people whose motivations were a long way removed from any political activity and who were allowed to play the role of little tyrants in the area by the prevailing circumstances. It is obvious that Jacques profited from the absence of the leader of the local resistance who went off to look for Germans so as to set himself up in the local château from which he could have his two accomplices carry out his orders. If we are to believe the report on these two people, one was weak minded and the other a rejected suitor. As for Jacques himself, he was known by the vice squad as the manager of a 'special house' in Paris. We need, however, to question the attitude of the local population which according to the report is said to be revolted, but nonetheless very present during the 'several hours' when Miss M. and Mrs V. were being shown off.

Faced with scenes such as these, disgust is expressed much more clearly than it is over the shaving of heads, and the presence of children here, as elsewhere, shocks those present. On 3 September 1944 a journalist in *La Marseillaise* speaks out about such practices:

Danger! On Friday afternoon people living in the district of Endoume were involuntary witnesses of an unworthy and sickening sight. A group of young men, fortunately few in number, went to get from her home a woman known to have intimately frequented Germans and, what is more serious, to have denounced patriotic defaulters to them. They made her run through the streets completely naked in front of innocent children playing outside their houses and who looked on in alarm. If the actions of this woman (whose husband is a prisoner) are proved correct, once she had been judged she certainly deserves an exemplary punishment. But there is nothing which excuses in our country, freed from the savagery of the Germans, the use of methods which recalls very precisely the worst ones used by the sadistic SA and SS. We are crying danger! We should not have our victory, our fine popular victory sullied in this way.

The accusation made here is particularly strong and the author makes it as much on a moral level as a political one.

Stripping, although more often condemned and less frequent than the shaving of heads, nonetheless became customary. At Troyes women had their heads shaved, were stripped and covered with tar. They were led to the town hall where they were photographed with policemen, Resistance fighters and in front of a crowd of men, women and children. This scene took place on Sunday 27 August 1944, two days after Troyes had been liberated, and when the new authorities were in place. These activities were reported as such by the new prefect who, let us remember, stated in his report: 'The working-class people of Troyes have behaved irreproachably. Very few cases of looting. There have been very few cases too of women who have been stripped and had their heads shaved and people in general have listened to the advice and orders of the authorities.' The CDL whose official leaflet was published a little later in celebration of the Liberation of the town also recalled:

> The following day, early in the morning, there was a noisy disturbance outside the gates of the town hall where there was a crowd gathering. Without any sentence having been passed, the FFI brought into the courtyard of the town hall on foot or by truck, collaborators who had gone into hiding and women who for a few marks had not feared to dishonour themselves. With hardly any clothes on, branded with the sign of the swastika and smeared with a particularly sticky tar, after having received cutting jibes, they would go and have their heads shaved in the regular way and would then look like so many strange convicts. Begun on the evening before, this merciless hunt would go on throughout the day, much to the great pleasure of the local people who would form ranks in the streets to watch these women walk past wearing Wehrmacht caps.[35] This extract is all the more remarkable given that the leaflets published immediately afterwards and in which the events of the

Liberation are retold, generally failed to include 'the episode' describing the shaving of women's heads.

Examples can be found too of similar treatment handed out to men arrested on account of collaboration; they could be beaten, partly or completely stripped and have a swastika daubed on them. The masculine body can just as easily bear signs of betrayal as the female one. In Escoussens in the department of the Tarn, two men, having had their hair and beards shaved off were undressed and taken to stand outside the church as people came out of the mass.[36] In Saint-Girons German prisoners were undressed in public.[37] And in Paris, a photograph taken by Roger-Viollet shows a procession of women whose heads have been shaved, accompanied by four men on whose bodies the swastika has been drawn.

The similarity in the way in which men and women were treated is marginal, however. Even though both sexes carried the marks of their betrayal and of their condemnation, it was only in the case of women that sexuality became a particular issue. It was only the woman's body that became of particular importance in being reappropriated by the community as a whole. For men, not only was stripping rarer, but in most cases, only partial, limited to the removal of trousers or shirt and without the exposure of the sexual parts of the body – quite contrary to the case with women.

Corporal punishment is also very fundamentally based on sex and spanking is an illustration of it; if both sexes could be victims of blows, spanking was reserved particularly for women. By the removal of their hair, by drawing the sign of the swastika on their breasts and by giving them a good spanking, what is really being targeted is the sexual difference between women and men. In 1944 *Le Gaullois*, an organ for the 'smiling Resistance', published advice given to 'occupied people' already written by Jean Texcier[38] in July 1940. A reporter for the *Cantal libre* wrote on 23 September 1944 that 'the only brutality [sic] ever was a fine spanking given to a young woman who had belonged to the militia'. The journalist then asked the questions: 'Are there requests for voluntary executioners?' If by using a punishment usually administered to children, it is possible to see that the irresponsibility and immaturity of the guilty person is being underlined, there is no doubt either about its sexual dimension. There are only a few scattered references to spankings having been given, but how many behinds must have been subject to slaps and pinches which were in effect a banal way of indicating domination?

A spanking is somewhere between an unfortunate and banal example of harassment and real bodily violence. The person nominated by the CDL in the department of the Hérault to be present at interrogations, made known the violence to which one interned woman guilty of collaboration was subjected: 'No brutality was carried out on S. She was simply stripped and her backside slapped.'[39] The sexual nature of the violence from which women could suffer often reduced its true significance for those who carried it out and for whom it was mixed up with bawdiness, pleasure, misogyny and male chauvinism.

Rape

In a process in which female sex and the reappropriation of the female body are of prime importance, should rape, the height of sexual violence be seen to be the logical outcome of events? The hypothesis can be justified by the sequential way actions are linked – the shaving of heads, stripping and blows.

From recorded accounts it seems that rape was never an extension of the shaving of heads in public and essentially was something suffered by women who had been interned and occurred during the time they were held or just after their arrest. In the department of the Indre the officer in charge of the local national police force indicates that reports contain a number of complaints about brutality. For example he quotes the case of a woman and her daughter: 'They were arrested on 22 August last and the daughter was raped a dozen times in the same night by those who had arrested her.'[40] The three other cases of rape committed in the department were not collective and two of them were committed by the same person who was finally arrested by the police. In the Charente the newspaper *La Liberté en armes* reports on rape having been committed by two individuals on the pretext that it was part of an interrogation. Arrested, they were condemned to five years' hard labour.

There were also cases of rape taking place when the houses of collaborators were raided by masked individuals. The Republican Commissioner for the region around Toulouse stated that on 18 December 1944: 'a group of a dozen or so masked people went to Moissac (in the department of Tarn) and to the homes of two women who had recently been set free. They shaved their heads and tried to rape the younger one.'[41]

There is no way in which a definitive analysis of cases of rape committed against women accused of collaboration can be carried out.

The extent of this sexual crime is in fact completely unknown and deserves a study that would open up the whole question of the incidents of rape during the months following the Liberation of France. There were, after all other cases of rape. First of all those carried out by the soldiers of a retreating German army. Carried out against the women of the enemy, they are more like the rapes of war defined by Stéphan Audoin-Rouzeau which took place in the First World War, but with the significant difference that they were part of a retreat and not an invasion. In these cases we have 'the wish to impose by force, total humiliation on a woman by reducing her personal integrity to nothing'.[42] On the other hand it is difficult to see in them the 'action of a conqueror'[43] for whom the taking of a body by force would be the sign of a victory that is already in his grasp.

Rape was carried out as well by other soldiers, those of the allied forces. The general reports of the national police recalled them as having been 'every bit as numerous',[44] particularly in the department of the Manche. Police reports record cases of rape attributed to members of the Allied forces amongst whom several of those accused were black soldiers. Whether they were American or belonged to the French colonial forces, fear and racism caused these soldiers to become the focus of attention and it is probable that rape carried out by black soldiers was more easily tracked down and punished. Cases of rape committed by soldiers of the Allied armies have the particular characteristic that they are not carried out on women belonging to the enemy. The cases of rape that took place at the Liberation cannot, unlike the shaving of heads and rapes that took place in ex-Yugoslavia,[45] be attributed to a practice which, since it was not planned, had the appearance of being systematic. Nonetheless rapes committed by Frenchmen against women accused of collaboration, whether they were the act of an individual or a group, were carried out against women who were perceived as enemies. They took place in a context during which sexuality was absorbed completely by political issues and in which women suffered other punishments based on sex. And yet rape cannot be seen as an extension of the *tonte*. There are two reasons to explain this apparent paradox. On the one hand, unlike the case for enemy or Allied troops, those taking part in the arrest of women who had collaborated and in the shaving of their heads, were rarely people who were passing through. Their past and their future remains in their locality, or at least in the region. The eventual legal impunity for the person guilty of the rape does not mean that it will be forgotten by neighbours, parents or spouse. What is more, the victim cannot disappear once the crime has been committed, unlike the soldier whose passage through a region is a matter of a few hours only and for whom social impunity is practically guaranteed. The other reason has to do with the symbolic nature of the practice of shaving heads. This is a kind of execution but is a more acceptable form of violence allowing everybody to share in it. With rape there is a change in the nature of the violence that most people find quite unacceptable.

Desexualization

Taken as a whole any practices directed at the body are intended to degrade its image rather than to destroy it completely. The body has to reflect an interior moral ugliness, which is thereby denounced. Logically, therefore, in the case of women, we witness their disfigurement. Articles and testimonies confirm this result, evoking as at Tulle 'the hideousness of a loss',[46] namely of hair. But hair was not the only symbol of seduction targeted by those who were trying to purge these women. Lipstick also had its function changed. It is used in Paris where 'the woman's face had swastikas drawn all over it in lipstick';[47] at Moulins (in the department of the Allier), the balcony, the privileged place for amorous couples is transformed into a scaffold. Such a slippage would not in itself be particularly surprising were it not to be accompanied by a complete inversion of Nazi symbols as they form part of this degrading process. Swastikas became 'magnificent' when they were daubed across the foreheads of women whose heads had been shaved in Albi.[48] In this there is a way of taking over the emblems used by the enemy to change the meaning of them, and even by deriding them to get rid of them completely. How can we otherwise interpret the fact that the swastika would be regularly painted on the bodies of collaborators, men and women alike, in the same way as in some cases they would be made to carry the Nazi flag or a portrait of Hitler, to make the Nazi salute, to shout 'heil Hitler', to dance to the tune of *Deutschland über Alles*, or to march with the goose step.[49] Through this matching of a moral state with the physical one, these women's heads were shaved to assume a kind of beauty. External ugliness does not get rid of unworthiness, but it is a way of excluding women who had collaborated from society, which can then set about rediscovering its own beauty: 'and so as the storm disappears French people are faced with the huge task – that of recreating the image of our beautiful France which the Nazis have sullied by their presence.'[50]

The branding of women's bodies meant that they were secluded from the nation both as citizens and as women. Their bodies remain emblems of betrayal until such time as they are reabsorbed into their community.

The presence of women with shaved heads goes well beyond the ceremony itself and remains a visible symbol of the way the crime is being expiated. Measures were sometimes taken, as at Angoulême, to forbid women to wear anything which would hide their skull;[51] elsewhere there were incidents over a wig or a scarf. At Saintes, for example, a woman who had her head shaved and who had 'covered her head with an ingenious kind of turban decorated with bits of hair' was unmasked by an FFI member who took her wig away;[52] in the same department during the showing of a film, a young girl had her turban taken by someone sitting next to her who threw it to another woman was there. When the latter refused to give it back to her the young girl had to return home bare headed.[53] Such incidents as these were only part of what these women, who had been profoundly traumatized, had to put up with as their lives went on, lives that, after punishment had taken place, were marked by four things: suicide, flight, reclusion and resignation.

The loss of hair was experienced as an intolerable humilation. A letter sent to the *Écho de la Corrèze* records the reaction of a number of people who witnessed shavings: 'I heard women and girls around me exclaiming: I would rather be dead than have that happen to me.'[54] In *Combat* Jean-Paul Sartre records the case of several women who committed suicide.[55] I have only personally been able to find one reference to suicide, the account of which appeared in *La Marseillaise* on 4 September 1944. After having deplored the fact that a woman had had her head shaved and been made to go naked in one of the areas of Marseilles, the author goes on:

> Epilogue. Yesterday we cried out: danger! when we informed our readers of how a certain number of young people had decided to punish a woman in a way that was quite unworthy of a civilized people. Today we are obliged to tell our readers that unfortunately at the end of this sad story the woman in question committed suicide by throwing herself off the gangway of the St Maurice onto the quayside of the careening dock. You may ask: did she recognize that she was guilty then? Perhaps. Unless quite simply she had not been able to live with the shame. Not so much in front of those who had punished her, nor even the peaceful population of her area which had been unanimous in condemning what had happened to her, as in the innocent eyes of her little boy who will now have to wait for his father who has been a prisoner to come home alone.

Women would leave places where they had been humiliated and would try to escape from the hostile environment of their neighbourhood and try to rebuild their lives elsewhere. Others seemed to be pushed at the whim of events: after several months of being interned as well as being forbidden to live locally thereafter, they would finish by moving. Taken together search warrants as well as orders forbidding women to stay in their area indicate a certain mobility, but it is not always easy to know the precise reasons. At Fontainebleau a shop worker whose head was shaved when the Americans arrived on 25 August 1944, 'No longer dared to go to her employer's shop and from the 16 October left the town, probably to rejoin her family.'[56] As in the case of Madame Dupont and her daughter, both of whom had their heads shaved, we have already seen that three months after having had this done to them they left their community in the south of the department of the Oise and went to live in a Parisian suburb.

The number of incidents of head shaving in 1945 is also proof of the difficulty women experienced in returning home after having been in prison for collaboration for several months. Very often the time of their punishment went beyond that which it took for their hair to regrow. The case of the 'recluse of Saint-Flour', who was discovered by the police in September 1983, in other words thirty-nine years after she had her head shaved at the Liberation in the sub-préfecture of the Cantal, is an example of how this could happen whether it was voluntary or imposed by those near to her. However, such an extreme example does not allow us to know how many and for how long women like this remained cloistered in their homes. Withdrawal, silence and forgetfulness leave the historian with few clues and beyond the number of extraordinary situations it is only a collective local memory that retains the faded picture of the 'invisible woman with the shaven head'.

For all the others the time it took for their hair to regrow determined the moment when they would eventually be reintegrated into the local community. Wigs, scarves, hats or turbans made it easier for them to bear others looking at them. They became a kind of accessory of the post-Liberation period and articles and testimonies, often humorous, tell of strategies used to try to hide the sign of their dishonour. A woman who described herself as 'a general help' put in a complaint about those who had cut off her hair and who had been guilty of doing something 'which gave me no pleasure, and moreover cost me money. I have been obliged, in order to start work again, to buy a wig which has cost me 1500 francs'.[57] A man from Berlaimont also lodged a complaint against those who had carried out shaving: 'so they could have a head which seemed normal, my wife and daughter have had to have themselves made a wig each, costing 4,000 francs'.[58] A mother took her daughter 'who was wearing a scarf with a certain elegance' into a hairdressers in Grenoble:

Do you want to try something Miss? Mother and daughter are both extremely embarrassed. She had some of her hair shaved off but she is quite innocent! In the well-stocked shop there was some quiet humour as wigs were tried on. It's a bit too blonde. Wouldn't you rather have something browner? We don't have too much stock left, there is a lot of demand for wigs at the moment. Ah! That did it and the mother took a pile of notes from her bag, pushed her daughter out advising: at least watch out for the gusts of wind now.[59]

Such examples only reveal life as it went on in a very superficial way after heads had been shaved. They are part of a daily routine in which there is little room for private moments to be recorded. The main preoccupation was the possibility of taking up activities or work again. The fact of having had a head shaved and the consequences that followed were an ordeal to be overcome and something to be forgotten. Yet thanks to a handful of testimonies we know something of the shock it caused. At Bernay (in the department of the Eure) a laundry worker was, according to the Head of the hospital, 'in a state of constant nervousness'. During her trial four months later she 'sobbed without stopping and convulsions shook the whole of her thin body'.[60] At Blanc (in the Indre) a shopkeeper also had to be taken to hospital after she had been shaved, stripped bare, tarred and feathered and led through the streets of the town. At the hospital she was in a 'state of complete nervous depression'.[61] At Luzancy (in the Seine-et-Marne), two sisters who had their heads shaved at the same time and in the same circumstances, without there being any other violence, reacted quite differently. The older one who was twenty-three lodged a complaint for assault and battery and justified having worked for Germans as a housekeeper 'so that she could earn her living and bring up her child'. Her sister remained in the hospital at Villejuif to receive treatment.[62]

The violence of the punishment, the character of each victim, and the feeling of injustice – these are just three of many elements that are difficult to identify precisely and that explain the differences in the way people reacted. A letter sent by a woman to one of her friends illustrates the consequent ambiguous feelings – the need to carry on with daily life on the one hand, and on the other a deep, increasing trauma:

I was very happy to hear from you since I have not had the pleasure of seeing you for such a long time – I can say that I am very well, as is my family and my daughter – in spite of all the troubles I have had, but happily all that is past because I do not think I could put up with it anymore. Let me tell you dear Jeanne that my hair was cut off, but it has regrown well and is even more beautiful; Alphonse's fiancée, you will remember Paulette the dressmaker who lived with her mother with the ~~Germ~~, she had her hair cut off and had to spent three months in prison, and how many others have also, alas, had to suffer in the same way, anyway everything is over but we've really suffered.[63]

This type of document is as precious as it is exceptional since it allows us a real insight into the way people experienced these events in their private lives. Here the testimony has not been reworked by the police, nor been shaped by questions put during interrogation. The syntax reflects the ambivalence of the feelings. Each phrase which expresses the desire to break with the past is counterbalanced by one recalling the suffering experienced. Once she has re-established contact with her friend, the writer of the letter hesitates between the past and the present tenses: 'I am very well . . . in spite of all the troubles . . . it's in the past . . . I wouldn't be able to put up with that again', up to the point where she refers to the fact that her head was shaved, expressed in the same style: 'my hair was cut off . . . it has regrown well.' The desire to get over the experience conflicts with what has happened in the past and the degree of suffering is confirmed by the spontaneous use of the word 'Germans', which is instantly crossed out. (At the time of writing this letter her mother could no longer live with the Germans.)

Punishment of Women, or Punishment of Sexuality?

Despite its powerful sexual connotation, we should not forget that the punishment of having the head shaved was not solely used for 'horizontal collaboration'. If sexual relations with the enemy seem in particular to have caught the imagination, the shaving of heads was above all a specific form of punishment directed at women.

Its violence does not have the same sense if we consider it to be something that allowed women to escape a more permanent fate, or on the contrary, a kind of supplementary punishment directed at them alone. There lies the interest of putting this particular punishment in perspective with all other forms used to repress collaboration. In the first place it has to be noted that not all women whose heads were shaved were treated in the same way. Some of them were set free with nothing further happening to them. In general there are a few traces of them in the archives but the numbers are certainly underestimated. Nearly half of the women were interned for periods of time going from a few days to several months. A third of these again were subsequently condemned by the courts. Finally, a few of them were executed with or without a trial. Nevertheless, so varied were the situations that it remains a fact that the *tonte* was a punishment that by definition was neither a substitute for, nor complimentary to others.

The case of several women who were arrested in the department of the Oise at the time of the Liberation illustrates how treatment could vary. First a postmistress had her hair cut off and was immediately set free. Six months later, however, in the context of an administrative enquiry the Post Office head in the department contacted the commission responsible for the *épuration* in order to know whether a file had been established about her, which in fact it had not. An enquiry was begun. Brought before the courts, the woman was condemned on 21 August 1945 as being unworthy of French nationality for life and was banned from returning to the departments of the Oise, of the Seine-et-Oise and of the Seine[64] for four to five years. In contrast the file on a young woman from Amblainville was rejected on the grounds that her family could be considered 'scapegoats' (written in red) and 'that she has had her hair cut off' (underlined).[65] At Chambly twelve women had their heads shaved on 31 August 1944 and on the following day five more suffered the same fate; their names appear in the documents of the local administrative commission, but none of them are traceable in the departmental lists of persons who had been interned or handed over to the courts.

At Guéret (in the Creuse), a woman who had been a prisoner of war was judged by a court martial for having had relationships with Germans. The account of the hearing held on 30 September 1944 by the local FFI paper *L'Embuscade* records the two punishments she received: 'FFI punishment already carried out: hair shaved off. Punishment issued by the court: one year in prison.' The fact that one punishment affected the other in this case is obvious, unlike that in the Oise where the *tontes* carried out at the moment of the Liberation spared the victim from further punishment.

In the Charente two young girls had their heads shaved and were then imprisoned for having had relationships with Germans and for having denounced people to them. The enquiry showed that the charge of denunciation could not be proved. The inspector concluded his report: 'Since they have already had their heads shaved, we think they have been punished enough. Proposal: have had their heads shaved, to be released.' However the *épuration* committee took a different view and the two young girls were finally brought before the court. The youngest, aged fifteen, was acquitted when she produced a certificate attesting to her virginity. By contrast the older one was condemned to two years' imprisonment.[66]

The Punishment of Martial Unrest

Women who had their heads shaved were above all reproached for their collaboration, but it was also a moral issue that went beyond the simple matter of relationships with the occupiers. The misogynous nature of the punishment and of the way it was discussed is quite obvious.

The references to marital conflict recorded in the files on women whose heads were shaved highlight the way in which the sexual and the political were closely related. Adultery, violence within marriage, divorce, alcoholism, desertion – reading the files produced by the committees and courts soon reveals the importance of conflicts of a private nature. The interaction between crises in private life and the intervention of a powerful external authority helped extend what had already occurred during the Occupation to well after the Liberation. The Feldgendarmerie and the Gestapo were first drawn into matters of private disagreements, but on the pretence that the reasons were political. By appealing to a stronger body women who were victimized by their husbands could turn the balance of power around. By denouncing their husband for hiding weapons, listening to the English radio, belonging to the Resistance or refusing to go to work in Germany, some women briefly protected themselves against marital violence; others, either on their own initiative or with the help of their lovers, got rid of a jealous husband. Whatever the rights and wrongs within the marital crisis, by allowing the occupier to intervene in private matters amongst the French it meant that these conflicts had a political dimension.[67]

In the same way, besides being a collective punishment for collaboration, the shaving of heads could be the way an individual could take revenge for the behaviour of his partner. On 31 August 1944 at Coye-la-Forêt (in the Oise), a rejected lover took advantage of the fact that several women were having their heads shaved to revenge himself on his former partner. According to the mayor:

> around 21:00 hrs when the cutting of the women's hair was nearly finished, an FFI car from Chantilly arrived. Two FFI soldiers, one of whom was a fireman. The latter went to fetch Mademoiselle from her home. He forced her to go to the public square and then proceeded to cut off her hair himself, all the while making abusive remarks about her. This fireman was the ex-fiancé of the young woman who had broken off their relationship. It was a personal revenge carried out like a hold-up in a disgusting way. The other FFI soldier even fired his machine gun in the courtyard of the town hall. As far as I am aware Mademoiselle was never guilty of any bad behaviour with German soldiers and does not merit the punishment which has been inflicted upon her.[68]

The disapproval of the mayor is not directed at the practice itself but at this particular case of a personal and entirely private act of revenge. Contact with the Germans was enough to hide the private nature of marital disputes which would then become public. The fate of a young woman in the Pas-de-Calais shows how a conjugal dispute lead to an act of betrayal:

A mother who had denounced her husband is condemned to fifteen years' hard labour. Renée, the daughter of an ex-prisoner, was married when she was eighteen to a worker, Robert, who already had seven children. She has had three children of whom two have died. Therefore eight children remain for her to look after. Renée indulged in scandalous and debauched behaviour with the Germans. One day her husband discovered her and gave her a good hiding. To take her revenge, the woman denounced her husband as someone who had a hunting gun hidden and who was part of a group of patriots . . . At the Liberation Renée was led to the main town in the area where her hair was cut off. With the exception of her husband who forgave her and showed himself very kindly disposed towards her, everyone at her trial accused her. The government commissioner demands that this woman 'who is still in the early years of her life, but whose debauchery has lead to the most serious of crimes' to be sentenced to fifteen years' hard labour.[69]

Reconciliation between a married couple does not prevent a condemnation being made in the name of French people as a whole. The way in which this collective factor can intervene is even more clearly seen when we look at the case of women who were wives of prisoners of war.

Wives of Prisoners of War

Out of 1,600,000, French prisoners of war in Germany, nearly half were married and a quarter of them fathers. Most of them, namely a million, would not return to France until April 1945. The same number of women found themselves alone with or without children during five long years. Several studies have underlined the difficulty and sometimes the impossibility of readapting to married life. Christophe Lewin[70] and Sarah Fishman,[71] to mention the most recent pieces of work, put at around 10 per cent the divorce rate of those who returned to France, in other words there were nearly 50,000 couples who separated during the period 1945–8. While the contribution of ex-prisoners to the general increase in the divorce rate after the war has to be relative, they were involved in a quarter of all divorces between1945–8. It is also the case that from 1942, unlike the preceding period, divorce settlements in favour of husbands outnumbered those in favour of wives. Adultery by women also became the chief reason for divorce whereas, before, men and women were more or less equally responsible. Nonetheless at the end of the day, as Sarah Fishman reminds us, 'we can say that 90 per cent of couples who were separated during the war managed to continue to live together afterwards'.[72]

The way in which the marital situation with couples in which the husband was a prisoner of war evolved was as sensitive an issue during the Vichy regime as it was at the Liberation. During the Occupation the wives of prisoners constituted a group in themselves and were identifiable by the situation in which they found themselves. Most of them were obliged to work in order to make ends meet and did so in complete contradiction with the kinds of patriarchal statements which came out of Vichy. Sarah Fishman points to the fact that as a result they were

considered as real heroines by some since they had worked hard and suffered a good deal in order to keep their family together in the absence of their husbands. At other times they were also considered to be vamps, sexually liberated, unworthy of being trusted and likely to succumb to the slightest temptation. Some people also saw them as children who were quite incapable of assuming their new responsibilities on their own and needed to be guided and protected.

But contrary to what Fishman claims, the image of the 'prisoner's wife whose head had been shaved' is not a figment of a collective imagination, but in fact a reality. Thirty-three of the women who had their heads shaved and whom we have been able to trace can be identified as wives of prisoners; in other words 15.8 per cent of those who were married. This proportion is higher than the average. The fact that they can be identified and named also tells us something about how they were regarded by others. Their being alone resulted in their being almost automatically suspected of adultery, whether it was with a French man or a German.

The fact that the husband was away resulted in two attitudes that were quite different from one another. The first was to respect the husband's authority, or at least not to increase his difficulties when he returned. An FTP lieutenant from the department of the Isère recalls his decision to have a woman spared from having her head shaved:

around the 20 July 1944 having learned that the woman Agnès had collaborated with German officers, we carried out an enquiry which confirmed what we had heard and we decided to arrest her. This person is the mother of a child. We kept her for three hours. During that time she admitted she had lived it up with the Germans and we learned that it was not the first time that she had slept with German officers. She had guilty relationships with Germans. The punishment which I decided to carry out was to cut off her hair, all the while waiting for other decisions to be made about her, but in deciding this I had to consider that this French woman, however evil she had been, had a child and a husband who was a prisoner. It was simply for that reason that we decided to leave her alone, all the while keeping her under surveillance. I learned later that this woman was on bad terms with her husband and that in any case he had been freed.[73]

The initiative which this member of the Resistance fighters took was not isolated. On 4 November 1944 in Poitiers, the newspaper *Hebdo Poitou* announced the official decision which had been taken not to shave the heads of the wives of some prisoners, even though they had been guilty of having relationships with Germans. The committees decided 'that the husband, when he returned from imprisonment, would be the sole judge of this matter'. Such an attitude was unusual, however. Since 23 December 1942, the minister for public affairs had reserved the right to prosecute for adultery 'people who had been kept away from their homes by the circumstances of the war'. This particular detail depends on the fact that the concubine was considered to be the most likely guilty party. Nonetheless, as Michèle Bordeaux has pointed out 'the husband retains the patriarchal right to pardon under Article 337 paragraph 2, even if he does not have the right to decide whether or not to prosecute. Family order is an affair of the State which cannot be a matter for the husband alone; the public prosecutor's office takes the place of the head of the family'.[74] By punishing prisoners' wives who had been guilty of having had relationships with Germans the local population not only took over the role of the husband while he was away, but also after he came back.

There is the case of a primary-school teacher from the region of the Seine-Inférieure who 'carried on in a scandalous way with German officers. Since the return of her husband (in 1942) she has led a quiet life, but she nonetheless had her head shaved in 1944'.[75] The confusion between marital life and public action is clear in the attitude of husbands. Adultery and the political context were often closely associated. In a case brought by a former prisoner of war against his wife on the grounds of her loose living, the husband stated:

I returned from captivity on 5 February 1941. The next day my wife left home. I learned that my wife was arrested on 14 February 1941 by the French police because she was suffering from venereal disease. On 12 March 1941 she left to go and work voluntarily in Germany. I subsequently learned from what people told me that my wife had slept around during the Occupation and that she had compromised herself with German soldiers. Having suffered as a prisoner of war for eight months in Germany, I now demand that my wife be severely punished.[76]

Another more unusual case is that of a woman who brought charges against her husband whose mother even witnessed on her behalf:

> my son left the family home on 13 September 1944. His wife is actually ill, stricken with pneumonia and is living in absolute poverty. He is living with the woman of bad habits whose husband is a prisoner of war. This woman had her hair cut off the day after the arrival of the American forces on 30 August 1944.[77]

To be the wife of a prisoner could be a further aggravating factor that witnesses did not fail to mention. To the unworthiness of having had relationships with the enemy was added the failure to remain faithful within marriage. These cases illustrate the way in which the political can intrude into the intimate as far as women were concerned. Against this, it has to be noted that affairs between prisoners of war and German women are completely blotted out. Facts about this still remain completely unknown and impossible to estimate, even though a number of clues tell us that such affairs were real enough.

A large number of the prisoners spent much of their time in *Kommandos* which were spread throughout Germany. There they met German women and shared the war years with them. When this daily cohabitation turned into real intimate relationships the greatest discretion was necessary because the risk taken was as great for the German women as it was for the prisoners. A decree issued by Himmler on 31 January 1940 is quite unambiguous:

> German women and German girls who have relationships with prisoners of war and thereby crudely undermine what should be a healthy racial awareness must henceforth be placed under house arrest and then taken to a concentration camp for at least a year. If the women and girls from the local community decide to pillary a guilty women, or to cut off her hair before she is taken to a concentration camp, there is no reason why police measures should be taken to oppose such action.[78]

For the prisoners themselves the risk they ran was that of being executed (a confidential circular drawn up by Reinhard Heydrich, Chief of Security

Services for the SS on 8 January 1940). This measure was applied to Russian, Polish and Serb prisoners; Belgian, British or French prisoners seemed to escape it, even though a decree issued by Hitler on 5 August 1940 anticipated that they should suffer the same punishment.

German women therefore could also have their heads shaved. This is confirmed by a report dated March 1941 issued by the Security Services Offices of the town of Ebern in Franconia: 'The innkeeper in D from Bramberg has had illegal dealings with a French prisoner . . . when Madame D was summoned to appear before the authorities a few of the local people shaved her head and then hung a notice around her head which read: "I have sullied the honour of German women", and they then marched her through the town.'[79]

The photograph of a public *tonte* in the Neckar[80] shows, contrary to the report above or to the decree issued by Himmler, that it was neither the 'fellow citizens' nor the 'women or girls from the local community' who organized or carried out the punishment. The obsession which the Nazis had over race and the way in which they were truly haunted by the idea of sexual relationships taking place between German women and foreigners explains why the authorities of the Reich should intervene and take charge of the shaving of heads. We can only guess as to why there should have been a need to hide such a punishment under the guise of a popular reaction by the female population. Was it a form of popular punishment, whose violence was controlled and acceptable to the great majority, or was it a practice already in vogue at the time of the occupation of the Ruhr and the Rhinelands during the 1920s? Whatever, it seems that the public shaving of heads was abandoned and that German women who had relationships with prisoners of war were sent to concentration camps.

In France a report dated 15 September 1945 tells of another feature of the relationships that existed between French prisoners and German women. The Commissioner for the Republic in Nancy reports that amongst women held in the camp of Écrouves (in the department of Meurthe-et-Moselle) were 'German women who for the most part were brought back to France by prisoners of war and who begged to be sent back to the other side of the Rhine'.[81] Some German women, therefore, followed their partners back to France. Those in the camp of Écrouves had probably been intercepted like all citizens of a foreign enemy power, but how many in all managed to slip through the net, or were arrested elsewhere?

To compare the fate of the wives of prisoners suspected of having had relationships with the enemy, with that of prisoners of war – like those requisitioned for voluntary work in Germany – who carried on in the same way with German women, highlights the differences in the treatment and perception of feminine and masculine sexuality. To notice the difference in the way a sexual issue was taken over by political considerations, forces us to consider what, beyond collaboration, was actually being punished.

An Independence Refused

As we have seen, the denunciation of women who collaborated was closely tied to their sexuality. I now propose to disassociate for the time being these two aspects of the problem in order to isolate those elements that relate specifically to the behaviour of these women from the point of view of the relationship between sexes. If we forget for the time being a relationship with someone who is an enemy, we see a certain number of reproaches being made that concern the women's private lives. If we put aside the accusation of 'bad French woman', we find those of a bad mother, a bad wife, a bad daughter and more generally of a bad woman. The traditional roles of women are underlined and condemned at the same time.

In most cases the picture of children 'left to their own devices', of abortion, of cohabitation, or of an unmarried mother, would serve to worsen the image of a women already in trouble for having collaborated. The file of a woman tried for having gone to work voluntarily in Germany contains a complaint against her for the ill treatment of her child. Writing about a woman condemned by the courts[82] in the department of the Hérault to hard labour for life, the author of the report issued by the court session regrets that once 'she had served her sentence (three months in prison for an abortion carried out at the beginning of 1944) she changed her address and her name, but not her life, alas'.[83] Elsewhere we find the case of a woman who on the advice of her lawyer, threw her lot in with the Germans in order to avoid a punishment of a year in prison for having had an abortion. At the Liberation she was arrested and had her head shaved.[84] Finally in the department of the Yonne, a woman was charged with denunciation and a month later with having had an abortion.[85]

The question of immorality occurs frequently in accusations made against women, even though the enemy is in no way involved. The report of the house arrest of a woman who had been a voluntary worker in Germany, lists how one after the other, she had given birth to a daughter on 29 March 1943, had only married in September of 1943, had then denounced a man from Lorraine and threatened people with reprisals. She had her head shaved, was imprisoned at the Liberation and was set free on 17 January 1945.[86] To have had her child before marriage was something for which a woman called X was also reproached: 'She is a woman of loose morals (she had one child before her marriage and a second with a lover in 1943, her husband having been a prisoner of war since 1940), is said to have been the mistress of the Boche at Angoulême where she used to go regularly, but she denies this last accusation which it has not been possible to check'.[87] The uncertainty about her relationships with the Germans means that all that remains in this report are the facts concerning her married life. In a good number of cases it becomes clear that the nature of the relationships takes precedence over the partner's nationality; it is equally true though that in others the issue of collaboration is almost completely overtaken by accusations of morality.

At Glanville (in the department of Calvados) the local FFI group decided to summon several women from the neighbouring community 'whose behaviour towards the Germans had been an offence to morality'. Amongst them was a woman 'who had had two children since her husband had been in prison. At the same time she was a bad mother and it was that which justified her being summoned in order to make her have a better attitude towards her children.'[88] There is no mention of collaboration, nor of anti-patriotic behaviour; the only things brought against her are her duties as a mother.

Virginity, or venereal disease also then become factors in the way French women and collaborators were treated.

Virginity as Proof of Patriotism

Some of the women who had their head shaved protested against the fate which had been reserved for them. Some attacked the punishment itself: complaints were lodged for 'blows and injury' or 'assult and battery'; others did not reject the kind of punishment they received, but protested their innocence. Thus in certain files it is possible to find certificates of virginity that had been established to prove that it was impossible for there to have been sexual relationships with someone from the enemy. Rejecting the accusation made against her daughter for having danced naked in front of German soldiers, one woman from Saint-Paul in the Oise, provided a medical certificate proving that her daughter was still a virgin after the Germans had left.[89] A woman from Hergnies in the Nord, lodged a complaint for defamation against a neighbour who had accused her of sleeping with Germans and had demanded she have her head shaved: 'she produced two certificates of virginity which had been obtained from two different doctors'.[90] In Saint-Clément a female interpreter worked with the Germans, denied having had any sexual relations with them and took it upon herself to 'be examined by a doctor'.[91] For those carrying out enquiries, attention was focused on the presence of the hymen. In the case of the young girl from Saint-Paul, the *épuration* committee concluded that she was innocent because 'it would be extraordinary that soldiers would respect the virtue of women who were dancing naked in front of them'. Against this, we have the case several months later of a young cleaning woman, seventeen years old, imprisoned in the camp at Jayat (in the Charente), who could not manage to convince those holding the enquiry of her good faith. The inspector noted that 'all appearances suggest that Mlle B has had sexual relationships, even though she declares that she is no longer a virgin due to the fact that the German doctor who examined her when she was ill (with gonorrhoea in 1943) performed a vaginal examination using a speculum. However, she appears to be sincere in what she is saying.' Noted in red pencil on the papers is: 'to have her head shaved'.

The cases of two other women who had their heads shaved and were imprisoned in the same camp illustrate the importance the certificate had. The first, X, was only fifteen years old, the second, Y, was thirty-three. They were arrested on 4 September by the CLL in their village, situated to the north-west of the department. Their heads were shaved and they were interned because they were suspected of having had 'constant links with the Bosch, for having given information to the occupying soldiers, to have denounced to the Bosch the FFI group in the village'. The reports of the enquiry which took place three weeks later only took into account the first of these accusations. X and Y denied having given information to the Germans, pointing out that no arrest had taken place in the village. The enquiry then went on about their sexual relationships which the two women equally denied. The young one did so on account of her age, the other because she claimed she had 'a prolapsed womb, a state that made all sexual relationships with a man impossible.' A certificate issued by the medical services of the FFI indicated that 'the prolapsed womb which this woman claimed to have did in fact exist, but that it in no way prevented her from having sexual relationships and consequently could not constitute sufficient proof for her to be acquitted'. However that may have been, the inspector proposed that the two women should be freed and considered that they had already undergone sufficient punishment by having their heads shaved. Freed, they nonetheless found themselves called to the courts in the Charente at the end of December, the lawyer representing X presented a certificate of virginity. Given her age as well, the court acquited her; in contrast Y was sentenced to two years' imprisonment. These examples illustrate once more how sexual relationships became a focal point. But how should we assess this inquisitorial concern about the intimate lives of accused women? The certificate proved *in extenso* that no sexual relationships with a German could have taken place; but the absence of a hymen in no way indicates the lover's nationality. These medical checks are then a further proof that men wish to continue to control female sexuality.

Purging and Prophylaxis

Consideration of venereal disease was as important that of virginity. We have already noted the decision taken by the liberation committee in the department of the Pyrénées-Orientales to force women guilty of sexual relations with the enemy to be checked for venereal disease over a period of six months. Similar measures can be found to have been taken in other regions. Women had to carry a card, to undergo examination for venereal disease, or could be sent to hospital. At Noyon (in the Oise) two women were arrested. One of them had 'led a debauched life with the German troops which had meant she was hospitalized in a clinic for venereal disease', the other was 'arrested because she had venereal disease which was the result of her loose behaviour.'[92] Purging and prophylaxis were confused with one another. At Creutzwald (in the Moselle), women had their heads shaved as a result of a decision taken by the camp commander for the following reasons: '1) Loose behaviour by these women during the occupation with German soldiers. 2) For having given bread and cigarettes to prisoners of war. 3) For having helped one of the prisoners to escape. 4) For having become infected with a transmissable disease.' The report goes on:

> The women were subsequently made to follow the horse-drawn cart, in which there were musicians, through the streets of la Houve, la Croix, Du Nassau and around the railway station, much to the satisfaction of the working-class population of Creutzwald. On 8 June a police enquiry made it clear that they had in fact been made responsible for the escape of a prisoner and were infected with a transmissable disease.[93]

If an intact hymen could be proof of innocence, venereal disease became one of 'horizontal collaboration'.

Gradually a situation emerged in which the condemnation for immoral behaviour by certain women could be seen to be more important than their love for Germany. It is revealing to find that very quickly after the arrival of the Allied forces there are explicit references to relationships which women who had had their heads shaved, had with the new conquerers, whether they were American, British or French. That they associated first with the occupying forces and then with the soldiers of the liberating armies is made clear by various testimonies. The verb 'to continue' reappears regularly in all the statements that were made; women continued their 'scandalous behaviour with the officers of the Allied armies', 'to have a good time with the Americans, if that seemed the thing to do', to lead a 'debauched life with the Americans'.[94]

The sight of an American soldier leaving at two o'clock in the morning the home of a young girl suspected of having had relationships with Germans, like the fact of working for the Americans, were equally reasons for her to be reproached. 'She flaunted herself scandalously with the Germans, and today she is after the English. She's depraved. I have even heard say recently that she has got a venereal disease and that a young man from Hardivillers has been infected after having had sexual relations with her. She's thrown herself into complete debauchery, putting a large number of young men at risk.'[95] The way in which the nationalities of the lovers of this eighteen-year old farm girl changed shows that the scandal continued after the Germans had left. After denunciation comes the danger of contamination.

The absence of any distinction between the relationships with the Germans or a member of the Allied forces may appear surprising but it illustrates the anger that was felt over the fact that these women, who had already been punished, refused to conform. This feeling is illustrated by an article in the *Patriote de l'Oise* on 28 October 1944:

Suzanne loves uniforms: it is useless to introduce her to the people of Gouvieux; she has been known to them for a long time. No one was surprised to see her in July 1940 having a good time with the Bosch, and that was no less than after having lived it up for nearly a year with the officers of the French army (1939–1940). Suzanne now has designs on the Chief of the Kommandantur. But events change. The 30 August, Liberation! Horror! Suzanne has her head shaved, what an injustice! Finished the good life: here she is relegated to her kitchen without any immediate hope of being able to walk about on the arm of an American. But fate is watching and after an arrest, here she is again free and with French officers. Suzanne puts herself under their protection and the whole scene starts again. They take her around by car and are proud to be seen with her, without worrying about the scandalized attitude of the local people. A little decency! Is this scene ever going to finish because nobody finds it funny.

The hope of seeing Suzanne, once she had her hair cut, conform to the dominant feminine model, is destroyed by the associaton with the French officers. The car ride and the advantages she would get from her relationships, already spotted during the Occupation, are highlighted once again. Similarly at Amblainville (in the department of Oise), the local *épuration* committee sent a letter to the prefect's office underlining the ineffectiveness of the *tonte* as a punishment for a local woman:

> The committee requests the punishment to be made against the woman Dupont, whose husband is a prisoner. This person lives with her parents at Laudricourt, which is a commune of Amblainville. This woman behaved scandalously during the Occupation to the point where her husband's family was obliged to tell him. Having had her hair cut off (underlined in red) she still said to a person in Amblainville: 'I couldn't care less about having had my hair cut off, I don't write to my husband anymore and that won't stop me enjoying myself with the Americans if I feel like it'. These words had been heard by President of the liberation committee.[96]

In such a refusal to conform we can see the temptation of the chance to escape from the fate of most and to benefit from the advantages offered by the allied troops, but even more it gives the appearance of a life centered on pleasure. Sexual relationships no longer have anything to do with betrayal, but they nonetheless remain shocking for society as a whole and are condemned. Women were forbidden to have their own sexuality; if it was something doubly condemned during the Occupation, it was certainly no more accepted after the Germans had left. The expressions of delight made by French women as they welcomed the Allied forces are noted in nearly all of the records. At the same time they are condemned on numerous occasions by various authorities who saw in them an immodesty and an image that degraded French women as a whole.

A European Practice

As we have seen, to cut off a woman's hair is an affirmation of male domination. One final element sharply illustrates this crisis in the relationships between the sexes. During the first half of the twentieth century the shaving of heads can be found practised in a number of European countries. With the exception of Denmark – and now of France – no other European country has been subjected to an in-depth study. A few articles and books write in a more or less detailed way about this practice, but it is not possible yet to know whether it was carried out as widely as it was in France and under what precise conditions. In each case the practice concerned women and took place in situations when the country in question was in a state of crisis.

In Belgium women had their heads shaved at the end of the First World War after the Germans left in November 1918. This is in contrast to France when no case seems to have taken place in areas occupied by the Germans.[97] Thus a British officer notes in his diary that 'women have had their heads shaved in the market square at Renaix (Ronse) in Flanders on 11 November 1918'.[98] Georges Simenon, in an autobiographical novel *Pedigree* published in 1947, describes how a woman had her head shaved in the streets of Liège the day after the armistice.[99] According to Francis Balance, 'the news reports for November and December 1918 describe how in a number of our towns and villages in Belgium which had been liberated, the same kind of punishment was accompanied by women being forced to strip and be publicly spanked.'[100]

Concerning the liberation of Belgium in September 1944, the author refers to at least twenty towns across the country where women, and sometimes men, as at Wervicq, had their head shaved. For him

on the one hand studies of local regions and oral enquiries carried out in a very precise way as part of university research seminars allow part of the scale of the phenomenon to be measured . . . and on the other, the fact that this popular stigma was not applied simply to those considered guilty of horizontal or sentimental collaboration, but for all types of relationships with the occupying forces.[101]

Martin Conway also refers to numerous cases of women's heads being shaved in September 1944 creating for him a carnival atmosphere at the time and revealing the way in which the population generally actively participated in purging those who had shown themselves to be weak in the face of the occupier.[102] Finally, as is the case for France, there are many photographs of women whose heads had been shaved.[103] At least until the precise count can be made, the practice seems to have been just as important in Belgium as in France. There is evidence for it in the different provinces of the country and in the main towns, as well as in the tiniest communities.

In Germany before the war, women who opposed it also had their heads shaved by the Nazis. Claudia Koonz quotes the case of a young German woman who was a Jew and a Socialist, arrested with eighteen of her work colleagues; she had her head shaved and was then released after a brutal interrogation.[104] Unfortunately the episode is not dated, but it probably took place at the beginning of the Nazi regime when the repression fell essentially on communist or social democrat militants or their sympathizers. There are also traces of the practice during the Republic of Weimar. After the occupation of the Ruhr in July 1924, the *Scherenclubs* (clubs where the practice took place) went for women accused of having relationships with French soldiers.[105] The phenomenon is identical in the Rhine land. In this region where the military presence of Americans, Belgians, British and the French lasted for twelve years (from 1918–30), the question of relationships between local women and the occupying forces also became a matter of considerable importance. From 1919 campaigns conducted by the nationalist German press under the heading of the 'black shame', violently attacked colonial troops who, according to the nationalists, were responsible for all the attrocities carried out against German women, including those guilty of shameful behaviour.[106] According to the statistics that have been established for that period on the French side, the total number of illigitimate births which could be attributed to soldiers in the Allied forces, was 3,841, of which only fifteen could be attributed to 'coloured men'.[107] It was in July 1930 after the final evacuation of the Rhine lands, that numerous incidents took place against people who were in sympathy with France: shops and appartments were ransacked, women had their heads shaved.[108]

During the Second World War several tens of thousands of Danish women had relationships with the soldiers of the Wehrmacht during the Occupation of Denmark, and more than 5,500 children were born from these unions. The scale of these relationships in a country with less than four million people, caused women to be particularly targeted by the Resistance. The shaving of heads was carried out essentially during two distinct periods. In August 1943, a widespread strike developed in opposition to the curfew imposed by the Germans. At the same time the underground press lead a campaign against the *tyskerpiger*, who had been very unpopular since the beginning of the German occupation. This campaign also contributed to the population's general demand that women should be made redundant. In various parts of the country the shaving of heads took place. The practice was particularly widespread at the Liberation, thereby completing an official *épuration* in which the law concerning treason did not include 'sexual help given to the enemy'.[109]

As far as Italy is concerned there is no study on the *donne rapate*.[110] A few writers have mentioned the practice of shaving heads, which was carried out during the civil war opposing the partisans against the Nazi fascists of the Salò Republic up to April 1945, as well as at the time of the liberation of several Italian towns. For Marco Dondi[111] they were the way in which the general population showed its disapproval of those women who had collaborated and befriended Germans. As in France, the practice went on after the Liberation. A report was drawn up by the police of Pisa on 18 September 1945 concerning an attack made by a crowd of 500 people some on police barracks in order to shave the heads of two women who were detained there.[112] In Italy, as elsewhere, photographs[113] enable us to see that the practice was carried out in several large Italian towns like Milan or Bologne.[114]

In Jersey, affairs between girls from the island and German soldiers were well and truly noticed. After the island was liberated the *Daily Mail* spoke of 3,000 children born from these unions, or 1,000 more than all births in the island during the five years of the Occupation.[115] Quite obviously this number is a long way from the truth, but it shows how these matters could be represented once sexuality was involved. Against the *jerrybags*, the nickname given to those women who went with Germans, Madeleine Bunting mentions the appearance in 1944 of an underground network in the island of Guernsey, which took on the name of the Underground Barbers, but without being able to be precise either about what it was or how widespread its activities were.[116] After the surrender of the German garrison on 9 May 1945, British soldiers intervened on a number of occasions to prevent punitive actions being made against these *jerrybags*. Not all of them were able to escape, and there are a few testimonies which talk of women being thrown into the port at Saint-Hélier, having had their heads shaved, having been stripped and sometimes covered with pitch.[117]

For the sake of completeness reference should be made to other countries for which we have only found an occasional mention of the practice. In Norway, according to the Paris paper *Ce Soir* at the end of 1944, and therefore nearly nine months after the liberation of that country, there was a practice of publicly denouncing women who had relationships with Germans: 'The Norwegians put the knickers of the woman concerned, marked with a swastika, on a pole on the top above her house.'[118] There were women as well who had their heads shaved after the country had been liberated in May 1945.[119] Finally, in the Netherlands, the practice of shaving heads was carried out at Maastricht in that part of the country that was freed in 1944, and at Amsterdam which was liberated six months later on 7 May 1945.[120]

From all those examples the *tonte* appears to be a recurring form of punishment of women, sometimes during the Occupation and always at the time when the Germans leave. Like those carried out in Belgium, or the Ruhr, or the Rhineland at the time of the First World War, they are a consequence of foreign occupation. However, during the civil wars in Spain or Greece, women also had their heads shaved. In Greece after those women who had been accused of collaboration with the occupying Nazis, it was the turn for those who fought for the EAM/KKE (National Liberation Front/ Communist Party) who had their heads shaved during the civil war of 1945 to 1949. Tassoulla Vervenioti has shown how condemnation for sexuality is associated no longer with collaboration, but with the fact that these women could be armed.[121] Propaganda issued by the government in fact likened these fighting women to those of little virtue, and military judges defined them as prostitutes and when they were arrested made them undergo an examination for virginity.

The case of Spain offers us another situation arising during the civil war, when the ideological divide involved that between sexes. Yannick Ripa[122] has enabled us to understand better a practice relatively unknown until now, except through a reference in Ernest Hemingway's novel, *For Whom the Bell Tolls*, and above all by the shaven head of Ingrid Bergman in the film adapted from the novel. There are no indications of the precise time when each took place, but thanks to a prolonged oral enquiry he has been able to highlight this *vieja costumbre fascista*[123] carried out against women on the Republican side from 1936 onwards. Used in a systematic way by the nationalists, the removal of hair was intended to be both purifying and punitive. It was carried out on women guilty of having given birth to Republican children, as well as to those women fighting for the Republican side who were likened to prostitutes. The practice was part of a Francist crusade for 'a total re-education of women'.

Our aim here is not to produce a history of this form of punishment in Europe, nor to track down the way it spread from one country to another,[124] nor to establish causal links between the practices. All hypotheses are possible and we can ask how many women among the thousands of Republican refugees in Spain who crossed the Pyrénées in 1939 had their heads shaved by the supporters of Franco, and how many men knew a friend, a mother, or a sister who had suffered the same fate? What influence could that number of refugees or their role in the Resistance have had in France?[125]

The same applies for the countries beyond the Rhine. Does the appearance of this practice over a period of time, in 1919, 1924, 1930 and 1940, allow us to refer to it as a 'German' one? Certainly a number of articles that were published at the Liberation suggest that this was so. *La IVe République* on 30 August 1944 speaks of a vexatious measure 'applied in all French towns; copied from the Germans themselves unfortunately, and which amounts to shaving heads!'; against this *Le Patriote de l'Eure* on 28 July 1945 simply notes a similarity: 'It seems that in the Reich, German women who have fraternized with Allied soldiers, have their hair cut off. Well, well! So the Tutons also have a form of popular punishment.' With regard to the only case of the practice being carried out by Germans in France at Fontainebleau in August 1944, the author of an article which appeared on 26 September 1944 in *La Marseillaise de Seine-et-Marne* notes that a certain number of girls who refused to leave for Germany had their heads shaved by the Germans. The initiative for this came from the occupiers and there was no sense of punishment associated with it.

The similarity between all these events, or the fact that they had existed in the past, is not enough to allow us to establish any causal links between them. Uncertainty prevails and is preferable to any risky conclusions. But in different contexts, women did have their hair cut off: because they were German and had relationships with 'non-Aryans' during the Third Reich or with the occupiers during the Weimar Republic; because they were 'red' in Spain or in Greece; because they were accused of having had sexual relations with German soldiers in the majority of occupied countries during the Second World War. In each of these periods of crisis a very special violence is carried out against women who are perceived not simply as enemies, but as women. Their body and their sexuality become a way in which national and ideological identity can be expressed. The other person is punished and part of the collective self is recovered and purified through the practice of bodily markings. During times of major crisis, fathers and husbands seem to loose control over women's bodies. For that control and domination to be recovered necessitated political struggle.

–8–

Virile France

Sudden and total, the defeat in May – June 1940 traumatized French society, smashing completely those individual and collective features that had hitherto served to cement it together. It accelerated a crisis in national identity, already present in the 1930s, which the contradiction resulting from submission to the enemy on the one hand, and acknowledgement of the patriotic propaganda pushed out by the Vichy regime on the other, could not resolve. From this point of view the Liberation allowed France to recast herself; it allowed French people to 'rediscover their true identity in an image of their country which had become ill defined and elusive'.[1]

The Liberation was a time of self-affirmation and of coming together as each individual took part in the reconstruction at local and national level of a state of affairs which affected everybody and which embraced past, present and future. The events of the Liberation, among which was the practice of shaving heads, constituted a moment when a republican past, a return of a fighting heroism, an identity with suffering, a rediscovered virility, were brought into common focus, but from which certain features of French society such as racism and male domination, which had been given even greater value by the Vichy regime, would not completely disappear. So frequent and so widespread was it that the practice of head shaving was an element in this reconstruction of an identity. We have seen how it was embedded in the life of a community, how it brought private and public together both by its violence and the way it reflected relationships between the sexes. Consideration of this practice should be extended by looking at it in the wider perspective of all events relating to the Liberation and by asking how in particular it contributed to a national identity still in the stage of being reconstructed, and by asking questions about the meaning to be attributed to its disappearance.

Participation in the events of the Liberation allowed the individual to be associated with the collective. Any action therefore, however derisory it might have seemed, had a significance and contributed like others to the Liberation at a national level. Taking place at different times and in different places, unlike the arrival of the Allied forces, it functioned as a common denominator. It was one of the features by which communities rediscovered the rhythms and sounds of their way of life and their memories; a rediscovery which allowed everyone once again to be in charge of their own life.

The End of the Night

In representations of the Second World War references to the night appear inexhaustible. For different authors the period can be assimilated to a 'long night', to 'black or dark years'.[2] The metaphors used to evoke a period of full of suffering and horror also echo the actual black out of the Occupation. Out of fear of air raids, lighting in public places was done away with and windows were fully covered; because of shortages and to save energy, the strength of lamps was reduced as low as possible, the illumination of signs and shop windows forbidden.[3] Moreover by imposing German time, dusk was brought forward and therefore the curfew with people being forbidden to leave their homes once night had fallen. And finally one of the most fashionable pleasures of the time, namely films, were shown in darkened cinemas – paradoxically lit up during the news reels in order to avoid demonstrations of hostility. But as in the matter of food, or dress, the rigours of the time were not suffered by everyone. While the 'forbidden night' caused many to suffer, certain men and women managed to avoid it. The curfew did not apply to women who were taken back home by their German friends, or who were in possession of an *Ausweiss* granted by the German authorities. In an article in *La Libération de l'Aunis et de la Saintonge*, which on 27 September 1944 celebrated the reappearance of public lighting in the main street in Saintes, the author reproaches the 'female friends of the Germans' for not having to have put up with the restraints imposed by the curfew and to benefit from darkness in order to meet their lovers: 'The night was necessary for this Prussian officer to go to the unworthy assignation with his "woman who would subsequently have her head shaved".'

The days of freedom also brought with them nights during which collaborators were arrested, women had their heads shaved and dances were organized. Even fifty years after the event, the account of a *tonte* at Puteaux illustrates the end of the night of the Occupation:

I saw a woman whose head had been shaved sprawled across the shoulders of men who held her prisoner in the middle of an excited crowd. She was carried towards a lamp outside a shop, which at that time was shut, but with nightfall the light was all the more weak since the bulb was one of the regulation blue ones of the Passive Defence. The crowd could no longer enjoy this terrible spectacle and showed its disappointment. It was then that the shop owner who lived just above and at the same height as the street lamp, appeared at his window and shone the beam of an electric torch onto the shaved head and scared face of the woman . . . much to everyone's pleasure. That was in 1944. On one of those fine days of the Liberation.[4]

Some *tontes* were continued and even began with nightfall. Those who took part in them did not, as during the Occupation, hope to benefit from the discretion afforded by darkness, but could take advantage of a new space, or rather a new time enabling them to extend as long as possible the pleasure of being together. At Laval on the evening of 7 August, the day the town was liberated, several women had their heads shaved outside the town hall. On 24 September 1944, the writer of a column in *Les Nouvelles Mayennaises*, sees this as a kind of festive demonstration: 'People needed to do something unusual to express their pleasure in an original way. Since it was not possible to have fireworks, they cut off the hair of some women who had sinned with the Germans.' The wording here, which underlines the originality of what took place, modifies the specific nature of the *tonte*, which became simply one way amongst others of escaping from German time.

Like the curfew, dances which had been forbidden by Vichy mark a break between those who had continued to dance during the Occupation and those who rediscovered this pleasure with the Liberation. The Liberation Committee at Angy (in the department of Oise) reproaches two of its local citizens for having 'gone with German officers and soldiers to cafes and dances where they would drink and smoke in their company; they would walk through the streets holding on to their arms and would have themselves taken back home by the Germans by bicycle and even by car.'[5] The people of Céret could not understand how a woman could be acquitted by the courts of the Pyrénées-Orientales and reproached her for having been 'in permanent contact with German officers with whom she would flaunt herself in the streets of Céret. She would go to their dances and all their fun and games.'[6] The dances held at the Liberation became one of the emblematic images of these days and like the shaving of heads, were another way of recreating a new public space, both during the day and night.

But woe betide any women who, having taken part in the fun and games organized by the occupying forces, wanted then to take part in those of the Liberation! The FFI of Crèvecœur-le-Grand (in the depart-ment of Oise) prevented women from going into a dance organized by the British army. Incidents like these were repeated up to May 1945 during the time when dances celebrating victory were taking place. As an expression of happiness and of the joy of being together again, these dances were connected with the Republican tradition of 14 July and were not possible unless they were fully part of the process of liberation. In the same way as the FFI processions, services held before the war memorials, and the shaving of heads, dances allowed people to recapture some urban space for a few days. For these moments at dusk, or at twilight, also those marked the shift from war to peace. If regaining control of the night was a way of emerging from the war, the latter was still not over. At Marmande, in order to avoid any excesses, the head of the local Resistance decided to maintain the curfew and threatened to fire 'without warning at anyone found in the streets after it had begun'.[7] Once again dances were forbidden by order of the Prefects, for with war continuing and day to day problems and men being caught up in it, no demonstrations of happiness or pleasure could be allowed if they were not directly related to the priorities of the moment. In fact German time remained in place at the request of the Allied command until October 1944.[8]

Recaptured Sounds

In the middle of the twentieth century sounds rarely provide source material for the historian. Such were the conditions for recording, so cumbersome was the equipment at the time, that only a few sounds were captured live.[9] Nonetheless a few sound images of the Liberation do exist: swing imported from the other side of the Atlantic, the cheers of crowds, shots fired by rooftop fighters, De Gaulle's speech at Notre-Dame are among the most famous. As it is not possible to reproduce the sound world of the days of Liberation, we can, thanks to other sources, nonetheless sketch in what noises the French heard and produced in the streets.

In Versailles on 26 August 1944, gunfire could still be heard as several women had their heads shaved outside the town hall.[10] An increase in the noise of fighting gradually drowned the sounds of marching boots, of the Wehrmacht bands and the German language, all of which had become symbols of oppression. By the fear they inspired, the whistling of shells, the explosion of grenades, bursts of sten gunfire, brought together in a few extremely intense moments the concentrated sound of warfare and a sense of the proximity of death. At once the Liberation marked the end of this morbid symphony, a break from the period of occupation and the hope for a world in which there were neither sirens, nor whistles, nor bomb explosions. In a moment of crowning and sonorous glory, bells rang out to celebrate the return of peace. Except in communities where they had been destroyed,[11] bells accompanied the people's repossession of the streets, and celebrated the marriage between ordinary citizens and those who had fought. But if they glorified the moment, their sound also recalled the messages they carried in previous centuries. Just as they could draw the public's attention to an important event, church bells or the Republican drum announced that an expiatory shaving was to take place. 'At Liancourt it is well known to the general public that during the Occupation the girl X made a point of going about with Germans. The day after the liberation of the town by the American troops I had the following notice published, accompanied by the sound of the bells: "Now that the German vermin has disappeared, the Mayor invites people to disinfect the places which they occupied." The following day the girl X was apprehended and her hair cut off.'[12] In Cherbourg on 14 July, the cart containing women who had collaborated passed by accompanied by the sound of the drum. At Creutzwald on 6 June 1945, a full orchestra was installed in a horse-drawn cart and went in front of the procession of women whose heads had been shaved.[13]

On these days the sirens did not sound, it seems. There are probably two reasons for this. The first explanation is military and reflects the need to retain some way of sounding an alert: the enemy was still near and if air space was under the control of the Allies planes, an attack by the Luftwaffe could not be excluded; 224 people died in the attack on Paris on the night of 26 and 27 August 1944. The second reason is to do with the fact that they had too long been used to sound a warning of air raids. The fear and anguish of an air raid were still very much alive and to use a noise that had previously anticipated destruction was not possible for festive purposes. This was especially so because since the spring of 1943, sirens had warned of the approach of Allied bombers and these same forces were now being fêted. Even if this seemed paradoxical it was no less painful.

Bells and drums were not the only instruments to form part of a return to lost sounds. Yet while they were heard, they were not played by everyone. Only the human voice could make up its own part. What happened in Méry-la-Bataille, in the Oise, is a perfect example of how feelings of relief, joy or revenge, could be expressed through sound. In

Cherbourg, 14 July 1944.[14]

the evening, when the American troops passed through, a local woman – whom we will call Madame Dupont – was threatened by local people. She recorded the experience in a letter of protest sent to the Prefect of the Department:

> At eleven o'clock in the evening, the Mayor, his new assistant and the secretary, lead a raving crowd of about fifty people into the courtyard. They were shouting 'Down with Dupont the traitor and his sister the collaborator' then they kicked the doors of the house where I had taken refuge with Mme Durand and her terrified children. When Mme Durand opened the shutters she was immediately insulted and then a stone broke one of the panes of glass and fell onto the bed. The Mayor took good care not to placate the people, or make them keep quiet and they started to sing *L'Internationale* and *La Marseillaise*, after which there was dancing in the square until two hours in the morning. Bricks and stones were constantly thrown against the windows of my bedroom and then suddenly there were shots fired under the window.[15]

Sounds accompanying the shaving of heads, are widely reported. A mixture of happiness and joy on the one hand, and on the other of hatred and anger, they express the ambiguity of the moment.

From the vocabulary used by witnesses, it is difficult to reproduce the precise words that were uttered. The choice of a word to transcribe a sound says as much about the feelings of the person who used it as about the noise itself. To talk of 'uproar' or of 'din', to prefer 'cheers' to 'yelling', illustrates not only the variety of the sounds but as the way they were heard. The degrees of the intensity of the sounds causes a second problem. The intensity that results from words uttered by individuals and those uttered by groups of people together is impossible to define. Here again to judge when the sound went beyond a barrier, say 60–80 decibels, is impossible, just as it is to estimate the kinds of sound which, in any case, would be registered differently according to whether it was the persons making them, or hearing them.

Nonetheless, distinctions can be made between three kinds. Non-verbal sounds, such as jeering or jibes, but also applause, cheering and laughter. Whether these were signs of hostility or approval, depends directly on the context. Jeering would accompany the arrival of the woman whose hair was to be cut off. Applause would accompany her being led through the streets. There were also cries that, without forming part of anything specific, were quite explicit. On the one hand shouts proclaiming victory and cheers, and on the other cries of vengeance and insults, coupled with calls for punishment. And finally, there were songs and slogans sung and chanted by everyone. Few accounts of Liberation fail to evoke the singing of the national anthem. Often 'vigorous', 'rousing', or 'sung with great gusto', *La Marseillaise* had a front-line role on days of liberation, bringing together all those who had taken part. In a few moments it caused the differences between those who had fought and those who had not, between civilians and soldiers to disappear. Struck up as an accompaniment to the *tontes*, it shows that those who sang it were part of a national community. Only rarely in accounts of these days are words chanted in common recorded. They are noted rather by the women whose heads were shaved when they subsequently lodged complaints. It is logical that the words that were directly aimed at them and that contributed in large measure to their fear, should be the ones recalled. 'Do her to death', 'Hair, hair, hair', or 'Cut them off! Cut them off! Cut them off!' are the only traces we have of slogans that were chanted collectively by those who witnessed the *tontes*.[16]

The part played by noise is significant as it fills out and rounds off the role of the spectators. Their voices accompanied, gave support to and had an influence on the whole procedure. The contrast between jeers and applause, between insults and cheers, directly reflected the ambiguity of people's feelings. Joy and anger came together as traitors were castigated and liberators encouraged. To be able to sing *La Marseillaise*, to shout out one's hatred of 'collabos', or one's support for De Gaulle without risking being arrested, was proof of a rediscovered freedom.

A Territory Reconquered

H. R. Kedward reminds us that 'The Liberation of France is first and foremost about territory, specific territory. It is about the fight for territory, and the reclaiming of territory.'[17] In each area, there could have been any number of places where *tontes* were carried out, each one retaining its original character, but all of them joining together to form a shared patriotic space.

The Town Hall – Seat of Power and Local Centre

During the Liberation the town hall, guarantor of a region's history and the administrative and geographical centre for the local community, became a seat of power. Throughout France in the summer of 1944, the French flag claiming Liberation, was hung over the front door of the town hall. Here the new authorities emerging from the Resistance, established themselves once the Vichy representatives had been removed from office; it was here too that the first prisoners were held and interrogated; and it was on the steps that raised the town hall above the general area where the women who had been accused of collaboration had their heads shaved and were exposed for all to see. After fifty years of having been the traditional administrative centre for towns and villages,[18] the town hall briefly became the victorious symbol of the Republic, which had been eclipsed during the Occupation by the German presence.

This was a building the entire population could identify with and where women accused of collaboration could be taken. The town halls were familiar with each stage in the ritual. In Compiègne, a woman who had a child with a German 'went to the town hall herself suspecting she would be arrested'. Unlike others 'she was set free the same evening and did not have her hair cut off.'[19] At Pont-sur-Yonne, on 25 August 1944, the first accusations were being made by the crowd outside the town hall:

> As our region was being liberated, and as local people started to talk of men and women who had collaborated, the woman named X shouted out in the street that my two daughters A and B, aged 21 and 17, as well as myself, should be taken to the town hall to have our hair cut off. I did not personally

hear these words being spoken, but they were told to me by another of my daughters C, who is 23 years old, who heard the chemist's wife talking on the town hall square.[20]

The town hall acted as a nerve centre for the community. People would gather there to obtain information and to share their relief and happiness, and also to see what was happening. Having been one of the targets of the Liberation, the town hall conferred a legitimacy on its occupiers, as it did on the practice of shaving heads. With its facade decked out with flags and the symbols of the Republic back in place, the town hall and its square provided everyone with a climate of patriotism, the opportunity to remake links with the nation. On 22 August 1944, in the 17th *arrondissement* of Paris, people went so far as to hang locks of hair, taken from women who had collaborated, on the railings around the town hall.[21]

Inside, resistance fighters, rebels and collaborators, mixed together in utter confusion. In a Parisian town hall, Sacha Guitry found one of his women friends, whose hair had been shaved off.[22] In the main town hall in Paris, Jacques Debû-Bridel, a member of the CNR under the pseudonym of Octave Duval, tells how a dinner on 24 August 1944 was served by women whose hair had been shaved off under the supervision of members of the FFI. But according to the author, they had been arrested to allow them to escape from the 'savage vengeance of some mad groups of people brought together by neighbours'. If many town halls witnessed the shaving of heads, they also offered protection against agressive threats uttered by people who had gathered outside places of temporary imprisonment.

Throughout the Town

In three hundred and twenty-two communes,[23] the practice was a public one, or was followed by showing the women whose heads had been shaved to the crowd. In 42 per cent of cases, leading the women 'through the streets of the town' and the presence of 'the crowd', are merely recorded without there being any more precise details. This does not *a priori* exclude in any way the passage in front of the town hall, or a central square, or a detention centre. In fact references to these three other places are more or less equal. Women were held mainly in prisons. They could be transferred there after their heads had been shaved, as in the prison of Saint-Michel at Toulouse, where as *Le Patriote du Sud-Ouest* recalls on 26 August 1944, 'one of them arrived sheepishly, her hair having been shaved off – the punishment inflicted out of anger by the

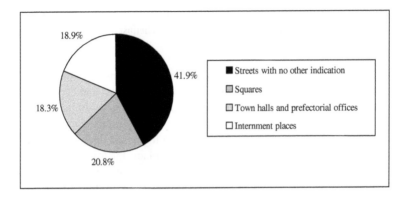

18.9%

41.9%

18.3%

20.8%

■ Streets with no other indication

☐ Squares

☐ Town halls and prefectorial offices

☐ Internment places

Places where the shaving of heads was carried out in public.

people of the area where she lived, because, of course, no other punishment would be carried out while she was in prison'. In Grenoble, it was 'the prison hairdresser who used his clippers on his women according to the style and taste of the day', but that did not necessarily prevent some of them being publicly humiliated: 'Outside the doors of Saint-Joseph prison, the people of Grenoble could admire the beauty of the new wave in favour in the headquarters of the Wehrmacht.'[24]

The situation was the same in a number of other detention centres provisionally set up in schools (six cases), barracks (six cases), police stations (eight cases) and police headquarters (five cases) and even in stadiums (four cases). People would go there to see those who had collaborated, to insist on their being punished and to make quite sure they had been arrested.

But above all the place where people gathered first and foremost was the square. The square occupied a central position and it was there that most people could congregate. Some of them are well known: Oeuf at Montpellier, Saint-Sulpice in Paris, the Place d'Armes in Poitiers, the Horloge in Avignon, the Terreaux in Lyon and Saint-Jacques in Metz. The processions of women whose heads had been shaved in Moulins and Saintes took place respectively on the banks of the Allier and of the Charente. Elsewhere they took place, for example, outside the cathedral in Autun, on the Cours Saint-Louis in Aix-en-Provence, in the Jardin du Mail in Angers and in the middle of the Roman amphitheatres at Nîmes and Lunel. Many more examples are easy to come by.

Beyond the strictly political character of any single one of these places, what is important is the variety of them which turns the town or village as a whole into the scene of punishment. Nor are outskirts excluded. At Le Mans, for example, *tontes* occurred in the Place Thiers outside the prefectorial offices, but also in the area of Pontlieu to the north-east. In Marseille, in addition to the Canebière and the prefect's offices in the centre of town, they took place in the suburbs of Le Prado, Endoume, La Pomme and the La Rose. At Montauban there was a only one place where the practice was carried out, but the procession went through all the different districts: it came from the north by way of the avenue of Gambetta, and then passed in front of the Prefecture, the cathedral and the town hall, crossed the town and then went along the left bank before coming back by the Pont Neuf.[25] The number of places used and the various processions allowed everyone to have a sight of the women whose heads had been shaved.

From the spring of 1945 and the second wave of the practice, war memorials and railway stations became the new places where this punishment was carried out. There is no doubt that the ceremonies that took place at war memorials were moments of high tension that punctuated the days when freedom was being celebrated and in some cases, even more tragic than that, when people stood to reflect and meditate in front of the remains of those who had been the last victims of Nazism. But if these two ceremonies could take place on the same day, the places where they were practised remained quite separate. That tributes to the dead and the punishment of those who had betrayed should overlap was forbidden by the fact that death had been so recent. Several months later, however, between May and September 1945, women did have their hair cut off in front of the war memorials in at least five towns.[26] More than being simply a place for reflection, the war memorials then witnessed the way in which past suffering and the memories of the occupation and the war on a much larger scale, could come together. To take those women whose heads were to be shaved there was a way of preserving a link with the suffering of the past that was gradually being forgotten.

For very different reasons the practice of shaving heads and other forms of aggression also occurred outside railway stations. During May and June 1945 stations took on a new life with the return not only of those who had been deported, or had been prisoners, or had been taken for work in Germany, but also of those who had gone there voluntarily. Collaborators, of whom people had been without any news for a very long time, were awaited by the police who came to arrest them. But there was also a number of people who wanted at any price to ensure that the collaborators who were known and identified should not escape their anger. In Cransac (in the Aveyron) on the 31 May and 2 June 1945, a Polish man and a Polish woman returned from Germany had their heads shaved by nearly 300 people who were waiting for them and were then led through the streets of the town.[27] The railway stations of Limoges, Poitiers, Guéret, Châteauroux, Épinal, Belfort, La Mure and in many communes of the departments of Moselle, Bas-Rhin and Saône-et-Loire, the Centre d'accueil in Toulouse, were also places where people were attacked. The symbolic role of the act of shaving heads was modified by this new location. At Hagondange (in the Moselle) the local people would gather at the railway station to wait for the trains to arrive. Until now the local police had managed to take any collaborator who was returning from Germany to the police prison.[28] The railway station became, therefore, a place that allowed people to get hold of these undesirable persons before the local or national police were able to do so.

We can attribute four different levels of significance to local populations' reappropriation of their living space: political (town halls and prefectures), repressive (detention centres), patrimonial (traditional places forming an urban identity), local (individual streets and areas), or collaborators' houses. In this way, the whole of the living area, whether in town or village, was completely covered by the local population, rather as if by walking everywhere those who had been newly liberated were obliterating the traces of Nazi boots.

Large gatherings that took place on the days of liberation recalled others in the recent or distant past, related to local history. They prompted people to look into the collective memory of their towns in which places, events, traditions and the daily pattern of life were mixed.

The Ceremony as Part of History

Like speeches, the way the practice was carried out contained references to a past specific to each locality. In Tours, women who had their heads shaved were thrown into the fountain outside the town hall; at Nogent-le-Rotrou, they were made to sit down in a trough of water and then showered; in Angers they were made to process as far as the Jardin du Mail, where they were also thrown into the ornamental lake. According to Jean-Marie Carbasse, in the Middle Ages, this water treatment was frequently practised and was intended to be a therapeutic punishment in which cold water was intended to 'calm down excessive sexual passions'.[29] There is evidence that this practice was carried out at Rouen, at Toulouse and in a number of towns in the south of France. Another form of punishment from the same period carried out at Autun, was that women who had their heads shaved were made to run through the town wearing a donkey's collar;[30] at Melun a red tongue was attached to the women's back as a symbol of scandal mongering.[31] In an article published on 14 September 1944 in *L'Écho de la Corrèze*, about women who had their heads shaved, there is a reference to the 'colourful processions on Maundy Thursday which gave so much pleasure to us as children'. The author then goes on: 'surrounded by butchers in their immaculate starched smocks, a number of fat bulls covered with flowers and ribbons would run through the streets of the town with a noisy crowd of children all around them.' And the writer finishes by asking why there should be this connection between the two ceremonies: 'I would have pity for the poor beasts who are doomed to be sacrificed. I cannot have any, however, for the herd which was produced the other evening under the curious gaze of the local people.'[32] And finally, in Périgueux, the author of *Ballade des tondues* evokes the 'processions which were like those which the same streets had witnessed in the Middle Ages in a passionate carefree period when adulterous women were lead naked through the streets of the town, perched looking backwards on a donkey'.[33]

Tontes – Just a Lot of Noise?

When he considers that 'more than anything else the ceremony resembled a "fools' feast" which provoked popular laughter, having its origins in the depths of the past', Alain Brossat[34] turns it into an 'ugly carnival' dominated by noise and tradition. There is no doubt that with their showy, festive and collective nature, and with the foregrounding of sexuality, this ceremony becomes a punishment that justifies such a comparison with the noisy riotous ones of the past. References to periods of history that we find there confirm this. However, no causal link can be established by virtue of any earlier similarity, or even of recent examples. Several reservations have to be made. The first, which is fundamental, relates to the objects which we can compare. There is no single model for the practice, and I have shown on several occasions that those features which recur, are related more to the nature of the punishment – corporal and based on sex – and to the definition of the victims – women accused of collaboration – than to the way the punishment was carried out. The festive nature of the *tonte*, to which attention is often drawn in order to underline a similarity with carnival, should not cause us to overlook either the shaving of heads that took place in detention centres, or the lists of the names of women who were to be punished in this way and then set free. There is nothing light-hearted about detention centres or public places, when the seriousness of the crime committed or the sanctioning of the guilty woman are what matter. There are no smiles to be seen on the faces of the women who had their heads shaved in Vesoul.

Nonetheless a comparison is sustainable when we are dealing with the *tontes* as a public event, even if a number of fundamental differences can still be noted. The *charivari* was a way of punishing, outside the law, any deviant act. It has a long history and has appeared regularly in the way people who infringed regular sexual practice were dealt with. For example, it could be provoked by the remarriage of a widower or by adultery, and gave a kind of authority to those who intervened. The shaving of a head is the punishment for sexual deviancy, but unlike what happened in a charivari, it is not intended to exclude the women who are the victims. Seen through the prism of the Occupation, to have sexual relations with the enemy was more than an infringement of a communal law and order; it was a betrayal and was infinitely more serious. Not only did a woman who had been punished in this manner remain a 'shorn woman' long after her hair had regrown, but she would be excluded from society either by imprisonment, by being forbidden to remain in her locality, or by being executed. But if the settling of social tension was one of the functions of the charivari, it was not one of the *tontes* which were less a way of channelling violence at the Liberation than a distinctive feature of it.

One final difference bears on the relationship between charivari and authority. Those ceremonies of head shaving carried out during the summer of 1944 were no way at odds with the new authorities; they were part and parcel of their very being. Unlike the charivari, to which, specialists remind us, Church and state were hostile, the practice of shaving heads was part of the cleansing process urgently sought by everyone.[35]

How then should we interpret the archaic features of this practice? Do we have here the resurgence of a past, whose descriptive features are still latent, in spite of the intrusions of modern society? The urbanization of society has not succeeded in erasing the traditions associated with village society, instead they have come back at a time of real crisis. If we consider them as ancient practices, do we not in fact diminish their full significance simply by not allowing any influence of the contemporary world?[36] To see in the practice of head shaving a punishment which is always subject to masculine directives, is not enough to explain the importance it had at the Liberation. In this period it was distinguished by its systematic and wholesale nature, something that we do not find associated with *charivari*, or during the wars and periods of occupation that France previously underwent. If we analyse them simply as something emerging from the past, these practices can no longer be be explained either by the Liberation itself, or by the circumstances of the Second World War in general.

Moments of Patriotism

More than being a reappropriation of the past, the practice of head shaving belongs very much to the present, to a time of a shared patriotism experienced by all. As Luc Capdevila explains, in a France that had been broken into small pieces, 'very powerful centrifugal forces immediately acted so as to reaffirm the sense of national unity and the restoration of Republican values'.[37] Amongst these forces 'the cleansing of local communities exacerbated the feeling of national unity'. The point of reference was above all the Republic and for a certain period of time, the practice of shaving heads contributed to the re-establishment of national identity.

As we have seen, town halls became the focal point for many of these ceremonies and *La Marseillaise* was strongly represented in any singing which accompanied them. The picture would also be incomplete without the *tricolore*:

> Moulins freed. Wednesday 6 September 1944, Resistance forces came into Moulins and into Yzeure at five o'clock in the morning. The noise of motorcycles and cars woke people early who feared yet another battle. But everything remained calm and soon from every corner came shouts and flags were draped over all the memorials and hung at all the windows. Delirium was everywhere. People were crying. Those who were late getting there and who had not prepared anything, hurried to see whether they could still find a *tricolore* ribbon and soon everyone had his or her ribbon and rosette and flag. Never before has the national flag been so honoured.[38]

The evocations of the extraordinary proliferation of the French flag at the Liberation were too many to be recorded. Rosettes, ribbons, flags, the blue-white-and-red was everywhere. Used as much by Vichy as by the Resistance, the national symbol became the object of a 'real conflict in which each person sought to have the flag for himself.'[39] At the Liberation the French flag was the patriotic symbol above all others.

Two other examples during the uprising in the Paris area show how during the course of the week flags appeared or disappeared at windows as the fighting progressed. They were the signs of the first moments of the Liberation and marked those areas that had been gradually freed. At Aubervilliers on 19 August at ten o'clock, the FFI occupied the town hall and put up the French flag. Something peculiar there was that the Russian flag did not remain and it was finally the Belgian one that was put up alongside the French one. In the 18th *arrondissement* the town hall was decked out with flags half an hour after the one in Aubervilliers, and soon after that so were several schools in that part of town. The next day the flags were taken down at the request of the FFI and did not reappear until 25 and 26 August. Despite FFI advice about being careful, other flags appeared in windows and attracted gunfire from Germans for whom their meaning was quite unambiguous.[40] Outside the Parisien region, in other towns that were in a state of insurrection, the practice, as in the town of Moulins, was even more widespread.

The national flag was proof of a rediscovered honour and a confirmation that people belonged once more to the nation. It was, therefore, at odds with all that was represented by women whose heads had been shaved. The presence of a flag in houses of people who had been accused of collaboration, or the fact that some of these houses displayed a rosette, gave rise to a number of incidents. At Hergniers, in the Nord, in the middle of a crowd which had come to welcome the Allied forces in front of the town hall, one woman turned on another: 'I told her that she was the one [whose hair was going to be cut off] because she had been singing at the châteaux where the Germans were. I told her that she didn't have the right to wear earrings in national colours, nor the national rosette, and I tore everything off her.'[41] In Jallais,[42] the event which set off the *tonte* was an intervention by the neighbours of two girls making it clear that they had to take down the flag that was hung up at their window. In his report of 31 May 1945, the Republican Commissioner for Nancy made it clear that

> the renewal of contact between people who had been sent away in 1940 and those who had remained could not take place without violence, not only verbal violence, but also physical. Acts of violence have taken place. When war ended, *many flags were torn down from the windows of the houses of those who had stayed behind* and the swastika was painted on walls and women had their heads shaved, etc.[43]

The local population decided whether or not people had the right to put up flags.

Against this, there were cases when the lack of a flag could be considered a proof of collaboration. In Agnetz a woman and her two daughters were reproached in the following way:

I am certain that the woman Martin and her daughter were in favour of the Germans. This is even more noticeable now that we have been liberated. All the local people were happy and were decorating their doors and windows with French and allied flags, but the Martin women chose not to do this. They were not happy to see those who were freeing us.[44]

In the aftermath of the *tontes* the *tricolore* soon replaced the Nazi flag and was a powerful indicator of people having rediscovered their national identity. The woman from Basse-Yutz told the police about a family during the Occupation. According to her 'The family had always shown itself to be pro-Nazi during the Occupation, her husband would only greet people with the *Heil Hitler* salute. The woman had hung up the Nazi flag which she had made from the material of a French one'.[45] Even if we put on one side the simple practical difficulty of such a transformation, this constitutes nonetheless an outstanding example of betrayal. The *tricolore*, which was hung up all over many towns, could often be found in the background when a woman's head was being shaved, though without being directly associated with the punishment. It never figured at the head of a procession, or where the punishment was taking place, nor was it carried by anyone who was close to the woman in question. Only the Nazi flag was allowed to be close to her.

While a woman would be degraded by having her head shaved, the hair itself, once cut off, could become another symbol of Liberation. On 12 August 1944, at Nantes, the former General Secretary of the town hall described an unusual scene: 'In the afternoon two girls accused of having given in to the insistence of the German army, were dragged into the street. One of them was a brunette and the other blonde, at least as far as their hair, which was carried around on the top of a pole which had been used for the French flag, told us.'[46] Without being always quite as explicit as this, there were many actions of a similar nature carried out at the Liberation. People would underline their patriotism by carrying a national flag, by singing *La Marseillaise* and by taking part in shaving the head of a *kollabo*.

The practice was also part of a more general evolution of demonstrations that, according to Danielle Tartakowsky, reached their peak in this affirmation of nationalism.[47] This political dimension, according to her, had its origins in certain provincial demonstrations that, from July 1935, were centered on local political and cultural struggles. Tartakowsky also tells us that, during the Occupation, certain central and symbolic places became the focal point of demonstrations of a commemorative, or similar nature. And during the Liberation, the same phenomenon can be observed;

Shorn woman in Paris. *Libération, de R. Seguin et R. Legrand.* Vidéothèque de Paris.

all fragments of local history, or geography, could only be understood if they could be seen to be part of the nation.

The period of the Liberation is both a break with the past and a renewal. There is no question that the huge patriotic explosion drew on the events and values of the 1789 Revolution, but for those setting about the creation of a new Republic, what mattered above all was the future. A future that would break away as much from Vichy as with the period before that. More than providing the link with the past, the practice of shaving women's heads was an essential part of the image of the new and a pure future.

The Reconstruction of Identity

The dynamics set in motion in the aftermath of the *tontes* affected individuals as much as groups. The variety of approaches proposed and the multiple explanations offered and the refusal to create any order in the reasons for the practice, mean that any single view is impossible other than an acceptance of something that was extraordinarily complex. At the same time the practice did not simply reflect other features of the time; it also crystallized movements that could be contradictory, and in so doing helped to give shape to the identity that was being reconstructed.

Anyone who took part in the *tontes* could reassert himself individually, simply by being present. And this assertion could be affirmed by sharing those feelings experienced by everyone – fear, hatred, jealousy, humiliation, guilt. There was also a sense of once more becoming part of a group hitherto fragmented by war, and of being able to rediscover an individual identity which had been pretty well unsettled by circumstances. A new self image could be forged, that of the 'good Frenchman' whose principal characteristics, according to Luc Capdevila, were a sense of belonging to 'a group whose fate it had been to suffer during the Occupation, but had never lost hope in victory'.[48] The *tontes* allowed everyone to share in the action and they could confirm their patriotism by working for freedom. They also allowed a new found virility to be expressed.

All of these things were features of individual and collective experience alike. A rediscovery of a national identity that allowed individual citizens to 'recognize themselves and feel recognised by the community to which they belonged'[49] also necessitated getting rid of the blemishes of the past if a new, virile and regenerated France were to emerge. The practice of the *tontes* was at the heart of this process.

Masculine Failure, Feminine Betrayal

To trace features based on sexual difference in accounts of the period is vital if we are to understand how people related to it.

To talk of masculine versus feminine in descriptions of the enemy is not specific to France, or to the period of the Second World War,[50] even if during the Occupation and at the Liberation such a contrast assumed a particularly strong meaning. The shaving of women's heads put the relationship between men and women under the spotlight, highlighting the disorder that prevailed at the time. The practice did not confirm any archetypal relationship between the sexes, but rather showed French society in which traditional features and the disruptive elements of the time where intertwined.

How could a woman, who is the mother of nine children, take up arms? This was a question put by the president of the military tribunal in Lyon, and to which Marguerite Gonnet, the head of the Libération-Sud movement in the department of the Isère replied: 'Quite simply Colonel, because men had dropped them.'[51] In addition to the exceptional character of the person concerned, this stinging reply was also in condemnation of men whose failure to carry out their traditional role had lead to the present disaster. The most obvious evidence of the failure by men to prevent defeat were the Occupation, surrender, the exodus and the departure of prisoners to Germany. Even though they were called up to serve under the French flag, men had not prevented the country from being invaded. As prisoners they were not able to help their families struggle through the years of the Occupation. But the scale of the tragedy in 1940 should not hide deeper features of a crisis of masculinity. Well before the defeat, the myth of the warrior no longer had any status; during the period of the *drôle de guerre* there were many ways in which soldiers were represented which were a long way from those of traditional warriors.[52] Work which examines the question of masculine identity is still in its early stages, but a few points need to be looked at if we are going to understand the extraordinary resurgence of virility in France at the time of the Liberation.

For Michael Kelly there are two elements to the crisis of masculinity. Men were humiliated both in their role as fighters and in their failure to protect the country, which can be seen as feminine. According to him the fact that women became economically active and also participated in the Resistance, only served to make the problem worse.[53] Yet the debacle did not stop at a defeat for men. French society as a whole was traumatized by it and the military failure was above all one of leadership. As Jean-Pierre Azéma has stressed 'for political reasons the Vichy government chose to make a comment about the atmosphere of rejoicing when it exonerated its army officers from all responsibility for the defeat.'[54] Political reasons? To an extent there were some, but it should not obscure other cultural ones to do with men's perceptions of Vichy, of their head of state, and of the men and women who made up French society. The language of national revolution suggested that women were quite specifically responsible for a climate of rejoicing and consequently for the defeat of France. Francine Muel-Dreyfus has shown how the 'close association of women with a general *mea culpa* was an essential part of Vichy's attitude to them.'[55]

According to the values asserted by Vichy, women should be mothers looking after their homes, and whose existence depended on their families and on their male opposite numbers. It is also to be noted that from the three symbols of national and republican identity, *La Marseillaise*,[56] the *tricolore* and Marianne, it was only the last that was rejected by the Vichy government, which from March 1941 replaced all feminine busts by others of Pétain.[57]

Yet if the Republic – or the 'slut' as the extreme right liked to call it – was considered to be female, so was Vichy and the whole policy of collaboration. After the war, Jean-Paul Sartre noted in the collaborationist press 'curious images which presented the relationship between France and Germany in which France was always playing the part of the woman'.[58] Among all texts probably the most celebrated sentence was one written by Robert Brasillach: 'We belong to those few French people who, having thought about it, slept with Germany and the memory of it is sweet.'[59] Because it relates to stereotypes of submission and to fantasies of domination, because in reality there was a German presence, almost entirely male, in a country where more than two million of its men folk were absent (prisoners or workers in Germany), collaboration was seen entirely in sexual terms.

At the end of the first chapter I made a point about the split that resulted from women having sexual relationships with the enemy and consequently their being accused of collaboration. 'Horizontal collaboration' became one of the most unbearable types of collaboration, not on account of its immediate effect, which was negligible, but because it represented the absolute defeat of France. It went beyond both private relationships and even perhaps beyond collaboration in general. As Pierre Laborie has observed

> everything that makes reference to a submissive France, to a France which is sleeping with . . . has become intolerable. In a country in which symbols of verticality are numerous and which makes a point of exalting its strength, horizontal collaboration – did it happen by chance – can only unleash all kinds of fantasies.[60]

Indeed it is possible to find references everywhere to the way the body in France was stained by the enemy, to the loss of national identity, to the dangers of cultural assimilation and even more virulently, to the fear that the French nation would disappear altogether.

A *Virile France*

'Action alone is virile. Struggle is fertile.'[61] References to verticality[62] in any discussion of the Liberation are not just a figure of speech. The idea of virility is completely tied up with that of national liberation. It is part not only of any description of victory against the enemy, and in the expression of the need to 'remove the stain', but features in any representation of a future in which the uncertainty of waiting would have disappeared.

When in 1940 Pétain visited Marseille, the *Petit Journal* had as its headlines: 'With all the generosity of its soul , Marseille has given itself to Maréchal Pétain, the living symbol of a renewed France.'[63] Four years later De Gaulle evoked 'the virile cheers of our towns and villages, finally purged of the enemy'.[64] The comparison is perhaps a facile one, but the difference between them is no less deep. The struggle against the occupier followed by the Liberation allowed a new masculine posture to emerge, the return of the warrior, thereby re-establishing the links between traditional roles in times of war. The link to be made between fighting, victory and virility, banal in as much as it corresponds to intangible schemas to do with the difference between sexes, is nonetheless to be found in many other places and in many other periods. At the same time the stress on virility, which we can see at the Liberation, has three dimensions: it is not simply the development of the stereotype in relation to a particular event, but a rediscovery of a virile identity that had been completely demolished; it is not limited either simply to the battlefield, but embraces society as a whole; and finally it finds expression through a massive demonstration of sexual violence.

Luc Capdevila has written: 'Whereas before the struggle was above all a matter for civilians at best acting underground and with few arms, with the result that the social differences between the sexes began to disappear, now by having the final phases of the Resistance become the preserve of men, the sexual division has been reintroduced.'[65] At the Liberation the difference was accentuated and if women were present during the events of these days, it was the figure of the FFI fighter which dominated. 'Valiant', 'courageous', or 'magnificent', the FFI fighters were glorified for the way they had carried out an underground campaign. They were to be found everywhere in those areas that had been freed, their processions were greeted with cheers and they often formed the first row of people around a woman whose head was being shaved. Their presence was a sign of a new legitimacy that allowed everyone to take part in the action and to have a tiny share in the struggle and with the new authority.

In Bucquoy (in the Pas-de-Calais), a group of men looking for help questioned a young agricultural worker, asking him whether he was 'French' and 'whether he would chicken out' at the idea of shaving the heads of two young women from the commune. The worker agreed to go with them. The *tontes* provided many opportunities for people to become involved in a collective action, or to associate themselves with those who had fought and to participate in what was going on. They also provided the means to act and this is an essential element if we are to understand the way in which those who gathered around the woman whose head was being shaved behaved. The derisory nature of an act in the course of which clippers took the place of a rifle and the victim represented the enemy, should not obscure the fundamental issue of identity.

In the Var, a primary school teacher and head of the FFI group, made a declaration to the administrative committee of the *épuration* about the shaving of the heads of three of his colleagues in which he had taken part. He finished what he had to say by declaring:

> On the day of the Liberation I behaved as a FRENCHMAN and no more; it was simply my being FRENCH which dictated my attitude towards them. At the Liberation I no longer behaved as a primary school teacher, but as a patriot and a soldier. My attitude towards these colleagues was not dictated by any prejudice, by any rivalry, or need for revenge. Except as far as their relationships with the enemy was concerned I had nothing to hold against them.[66]

Once more the *tonte* is seen as a duty, the national and combative dimension of it excludes all other. To punish those women who had collaborated reflects the absolute need to wash away the 'stain' left by the occupying forces. Whether the metaphors used are taken from the realms of pornography, medicine, or morality matters little. Sexual betrayal is always the same and the shame of it could only be got rid of by the removal of hair. The threat to national unity, of which a number of collaborators were accused, was not enough as a definition of 'stain'. This is an image which only works if and when the bodies of the women accused are symbolically interchangeable with the nation. Unlike during the First World War when the word 'stain' was used with reference to rape by German soldiers, it was now a case of ongoing relationships between French women and the occupiers. This was all the more painful for men who were themselves suffering:

This anger was justified, it was a cruel but necessary way people had to express themselves, a people who had for too long been ridiculed by their own daughters: girls who had forgotten that their brothers, their fathers, their fiancés and their parents had been shamelessly mollested by the self same Germans they were themself frequenting, that these Germans had kept them prisoners in their camps far from France. *Dura lex sed lex.*[67]

The obsession with cleansing can only be understood in the perspective of a better future. To shave heads simply as a form of punishment is not a sufficient explanation; it was merely one of several methods used to purify the country thoroughly as a whole. 'Purity' is not only etymo-logically linked to 'purification', but also reflects the necessity to break with the past in order for reconstruction to take place. As the periodical *14 juillet* proclaimed in Lyon in May 1944, purification was 'the first step towards our future'.

The ambition expressed at the Liberation was every bit equal to the drama which the country had lived through during the four previous years. It was for a country that had been on its back, now to be upright again, to have recovered its strength at the same time as its blood and to be purified for having rediscovered its honour. On 30 August 1944 *La Renaissance républicaine du Gard* published an article entitled 'The virile law', which argued for the necessary harshness of the measures used at the *épuration* and the need as well to continue the war. It concluded with the sentence: 'France will be virile or dead.' Once again the alternative here expresses the absolute need for the country and for its men to rediscover their power.

Rejection of the *Tonte* and the Re-entry of Women into Public Life

In April 1944, when the right to vote was given to women by a law passed by the consultative Assembly in Algiers, the practice of shaving heads had already taken place all over France.

Many people expected a liberation in which those women who had collaborated with the occupying forces in one way or another would be punished. Between the two rounds of municipal elections in the spring of 1945, the first at which women had the right to vote, the practice of shaving heads had again taken place in more than a quarter of the departments in France. Between these two dates, several thousands of women had been punished in this way creating a paradox between a political equality that had finally been obtained and a real equality when it was a question of punishing men and women for their collaboration.

Disapproval

From the autumn of 1944, disapproval of the practice was heard more widely. As we know, the rejection of it did not mean that it had dis-appeared: on the one hand, hostility to it was not unanimous, and on the other opinion could vary and the uncertainties of any local situation left open the possibility of its being renewed. Disapproval has to be examined

carefully, not simply as something which helped explain its disappearance, but also as the sign of an increasing rejection of violence. We have
to distinguish between condemnation dictacted by political reasons and
condemnation based on strictly moral grounds. As the state began to be restored, the fact that there were still incidents
of the practice caused the authorities problems. From being a legitimate
para-legal practice, it was gradually rejected to the point where it became
illegal. Only a renewal of legitimacy, as for example when prisoners and
those who had been deported returned home, allowed acts of violence
used for purposes of *épuration,* to have a momentary resurgence. The
tonte was one of them.

The way in which the press in the department of the Oise described
the practice of shaving heads at the Liberation is significant. Let us recall
that almost eighty women had their heads shaved in the courtyards of the
préfecture and the prison on 30 August 1944. The twice weekly paper
L'Oise Libérée, which was the official publication of the CDL, carried
the following report on 2 September 1944: 'In the region around Beau-
vaisis the cleaning up process continues. The clippers have cut off the hair
of eighty women whose conduct with the occupying troops was by far
too flagrant and scandalous. Forty-five of these *hetaeras* had their curls
cut off completely in the courtyard of the town hall and thirty-five others
suffered the same fate at the prison and all for the moral health of our
country.' On 30 September the same publication carried the account of a
CDL meeting dealing with complaints made by women who had been
aggressed:

Certain repressive measures (notably the cutting off of hair) authorized by the
leaders of FFI groups and carried out on women who were guilty of collaboration, or unbecoming behaviour, will be endorsed and those who carried them
out protected, but cases of violence carried out as an individual initiative and
without authorization will eventually be referred to the courts who will judge
them quite independently.

The punishment itself is not condemned. There is clear distinction
made between those who carried it out and the reasons. The CDL's
declaration is in no way a formal one. A woman from Amblainville, who
had her head shaved, made it clear that a member of the FFI had come to
undertake an enquiry about those who had cut women's hair off and that
'the person responsible for such acts would be shot if it was the case that
he had acted out of personal revenge'.[68] Still on the subject of the shaving
of heads, on the same day the official departmental publication of the

Front national, talked of orders which had been given and carried out by 'kids with no responsibility'. A week later, the editorial of the same publication, discussing the *épuration* 'expected it to be demonstrated by ways other than that of shaving heads'.[69] Finally on 10 January 1945, *L'Oise républicaine* recalled 'that during the first days of the Liberation popular justice was seen in the most unexpected way: luxurious heads of hair were sacrificed to the avenging scissors . . . never was a punishment inflicted with such justification.'

The gradual slippage in the way those who carried out the practice are designated reveals a change in perception. From being something carried out by the FFI with the approval of their leaders and with the agreement of the CDL, the practice becomes one of popular justice, but even if it can still be called legitimate, it is no longer claimed as such and remains something which belongs strictly to the past.

From the autumn of 1944, the appearance of complaints made by women whose heads had been shaved, or by their families, must equally be interpreted as a sign that attitudes were changing.

Sometimes the first complaints made by women who had their heads shaved were reported not without irony. The two daily Parisien papers *Aube* and *Combat* in an article called 'Un comble' report that on 20 October 1944 in Buzenval (in the Seine-et-Oise) two women whose heads had been shaved at the Liberation lodged a complaint against the local 'Resistance leader'. On 10 October 1944, *La Marseillaise de Seine-et-Marne* displayed even more vehemently its disapproval at the proceedings taken out against 'patriots':

> Is this a joke? Representing the Republican prosecutor from Melun, police from the Châtelet came on Friday, 29 September to the Chapelle-Gauthier to investigate a strange business. This extraordinary affair was set up as the result of complaints made by 'ladies' of easy virtue, whose activities during the Occupation had been doubtful. Their sensitivity did not take having their heads shaved easily, but the practice was quite properly carried out by indignant patriots. This punishment, lenient enough, ought to have prompted these 'muses of the Colorado beetles' to be more modest if they were to avoid complications later. It also has to be asked whether in the present circumstances the courts have so little to do that they can investigate affairs like this and to get upset about patriotic people who were revolted by the way in which such 'ladies' behaved.

Whatever kinds of reactions to these complaints made by women whose heads had been shaved, sometimes even by their mother, or by their husband, the number of them seems to have increased despite of pressures exerted and threats. I have tracked down about fifty of them, a number that is large enough to give a sense of the injustice experienced by certain victims. It shows, above all, that by the introduction of judicial procedures, there was a willingness on the part of the authorities to put an end to the practice. It would be particularly instructive to know what the outcome of such complaints was; the archives that I have been able to consult have only exceptionally followed the matter through to the end. At Évreux, in July 1945, a baker was fined five hundred francs for having been 'the voluntary and unpaid hairdresser' at a *tonte* organised by a local commune.[70] In the majority of cases it seems that those responsible for cutting off hair were not bothered beyond being asked a few questions by the police, and yet the change in the context was noticed by those responsible for carrying out the practice. Public shaving became rarer and the cutting off of hair once again took part in the homes of those women accused of collaboration and were quite often accompanied by threats to ensure the victim's silence.

The last example of the gradual rejection of the practice was the publication on 2 December 1944 in *Les Lettres françaises* of a poem by Paul Éluard entitled *Comprenne qui voudra*:

> Let them understand who will
> Me, my remorse was that young girl
> Left on the cobbles
> The victim of reason
> Her dress torn
> Her lost child's eyes
> Disfigured, her head shaved
> Like those who have died
> For being loved
> A girl fit for a bouquet
> Covered
> With the spit of darkness
> A girl fresh
> Like a May-day dawn
> The most loveable of creatures
> Stained but who does not understand
> That she is
> An animal caught in the trap
> Set by lovers of beauty
> And my mother, woman,
> Wants no more than to pamper
> This ideal image
> Of her suffering on earth.[71]

Written by one of the foremost intellectuals of the Resistance, the poem clearly shows that the *tonte* is rejected, but contains a double sense. The first records remorse which is translated by the silence surrounding the *tonte*, or the incomprehension of what the it was; the second is the reader's understanding which is not necessarily shared by the poet. Does the first line of the poem not underline the poet's uncertainty? Furthermore, its ambiguity would meet twenty-five years later with an unexpected reaction. Quoted by Georges Pompidou in reply to a journalist's question about the Gabrielle Russier affair,[72] it gave rise to a number of commentaries and interpretations. Even though he disassociates himself from the practice, Paul Éluard nonetheless sees the symbolic dimension, namely a betrayal reflected by the stain, but whose significance is modified by the lack of awareness on the part of the girl who has caused it. 'Stained and who does not understand/that she is stained.'

While the *tontes* are seen and described as a spontaneous phenomenon, their disappearance does not require an explanation. The practice was a huge but brief explosion of violence by a disorientated population, torn between feelings of joy, relief and guilt. When we properly examine what happened, the analysis is quite different; this was a reaction which, whatever the different forms it may have taken, was deeply felt, and generally accepted and confirmed at least during the summer of 1944. The disappearance of the practice was neither the result of a linear process, nor something that happened suddenly and without warning. It was different and irregular according to the places where it was carried out; furthermore its rejection did not mean that acts carried out at the time of the country's liberation were to be condemned.

The reason for the practice ceasing can be explained by a series of factors relating to the way the period developed. First it was part of a general sense of emerging from a war and a desire to break with the period of that war. If, to adopt Pierre Laborie's expression 'the intensity of the Liberation struck people's imaginations', as time went by so there was an increasing wish to turn away from the war years. Any remaining signs of violence associated with war, that formed part of the *épuration* came in for increasing criticism as they blocked the way forward into a post-war period.

As the state gradually reassumed control, there were fewer opportunities for those who wanted to challenge the authorites to do so. The changes occurred more quickly in the more highly populated regions where conflicts were provoked by commuted sentences, or by people who had been imprisoned being freed. Sensitivities could be high. Suffering was so recent that violence was considered to be legitimate when official justice was seen to be too lenient. This was not a case of a knee-jerk reaction by people desiring revenge but the expression of a real need to punish those whose collaboration had stained the country. The acts of violence intended to purge, which lasted through 1945 and the first months of 1946, gradually disappeared – certain public ones, those directed at individuals (brutalities, head shaving and executions), or at property (machine gun and bomb attacks). As war disappeared and democracy was restored, the armed struggle carried on by a few became out of line. Yet the difference between the two periods does not mean there was antagonism between the Resistance and the provisional government, the population as a whole, or the FFI. It was simply that peace was being restored at different speeds.

The rejection and then the disappearance of the *tonte* did not simply result from the way matters were evolving generally. The specific sexual nature of the punishment has also to be considered and this leads us back to what appears to be a basic paradox – the fact that the practice continued as women's right to vote was introduced. This is not then just a question of a law and a punishment, but of two opposing images of women – those who had their heads shaved and those who were French citizens.

French Woman

Whether it was Maurice Schumann who, in December 1943, paid glorious tribute on the radio from London to 'the hundreds of thousands of women who fought for France',[73] or of Rol-Tanguy who, on 31 August 1944 declared in *L'Humanité*: 'Women? Without them half of our work will have been impossible', examples abound of statements praising the virtues of French women. At the Liberation then, we find two contradictory representations of women. On the one hand 'the French citizen' whose faith in the future had remained, who had courageously overcome the trials of war and had shared in the victory; and on the other 'the collaborator' who had remained indifferent to the fate of France and whose egoism had resulted in all kinds of compromise and whose betrayal was now there to be seen by everyone. It is common to see the two types opposed to one another, with the condemnation of women who had collaborated made worse by accounts of an alternative behaviour: 'The acts of these miserable and vile creatures who were dishonoured and corrupted by the enemy, were an insult to those French women who had sacrificed themselves.'[74] Paula Schwartz has emphasized that 'in many cases women were seen to be exemplary by virtue of the fact they were like men. They were in charge of key posts at the heart of their organisations, they were partizans who fought with weapons just like their soldier "brothers".'[75] Apart from a few exceptions such as these, the qualities of 'the true women of France' were no different from those traditionally attributed to women in French society. The editorial of the *Travailleur alpin* on 15 September 1944 is quite clear about the role they played: 'Honour be to you Women of France . . . French women have maintained behind the lines that honourable place which is theirs, that is to say they have been good mothers, good sisters and good wives.' To have shared in the Resistance and to have experienced the suffering of those years does not significantly modify the way women are represented.

The activities of women who had resisted impinge as well on the roles traditionally attributed to them: care for the wounded, the preparation of meals, the concealing of papers or weapons under a fake pregnant stomach, or in a child's pram. Some became partners, thereby creating 'couples' in order to provide more discreet means of using the escape network. François Rouquet has pointed out in this regard that 'in spite of a good deal of progressive thinking about women at the heart of the Resistance, there was still a kind of opposition between the image of the woman at home and at war. So much was it considered to be a guarantee of efficiency, that virility was still demanded when it came to fighting'.[76] The responsibilities of all women were increased by the war. They had to take care of the home when their husbands had been taken prisoner, they had to be nurses during periods of hardship and protectors at a time of uncertainty,[77] and above all they had to be faithful to their husband as well as to their country.

Their commitment to the Resistance, their sharing in the celebratory days of freedom and their carrying out of their duties as citizens constitute the most conspicuous expression of the break with the period of the Vichy regime and the Occupation. But that must in no way hide the degree to which the language used to promote the national revolution was deeply sexist. According to it women had no role to play other than that of wife and mother; they should only exist within the family and live at home.

In all of this language hammered out during the period of four years to the French population, we find any idea of autonomous sexuality condemned and the need for society to regain control of women's bodies, although it is impossible to measure what influence it had. We can, however, see what is implied by an observation made by Paula Schwartz about the Resistance: 'Is there anything surprising about the fact that the form women's efforts took and the struggle they shared, should be seen in a sexist way when that was a principal feature of the whole social and political world of which they were part?'[78] Over and above the specific image of the 'eternal woman' promoted by Vichy, we have to consider the ideological intentions of the *tontes*: were they intended, together with the idea of 'horizontal collaboration' associated with Vichy policy, to destroy the image of the woman associated the National Revolution, so as to recreate the Republican ideal?

Such a hypothesis allows us to understand the limited duration of the *tontes* better for was there not a danger that, if it became too prominent, the image of 'horizontal collaboration' would destroy that of the new 'French woman'? The article from the *Travailleur alpin* quoted earlier goes on in the following way:

> So what then! Are women who had their heads shaved French women? We were wrong perhaps to have their photographs in our newspapers. They played the same role as a killer, a hired assassin. And when they sold their bodies to the men of the Gestapo and of the militia, they sold the blood of their French brothers, because there was nothing left in them that was representative of true French woman. And so let us banish the pictures of these dreadful creatures from the pages of our daily papers and show rather on the first page a photograph of those who have fallen for France. Let us have a picture soon of our beloved Danièle Casanova, who died deep inside Germany because she symbolized everything that was most youthful and vital in French women.

Behind the explicit and immediate meaning of the *tonte*, namely a way of punishing women accused of collaboration, there was a deeply misogynistic element as there was in the language used to describe it and which highlights a number of contradictions – the difference between a language that promoted equality and a practice that was sexist, a break with Vichy and yet the continued impact made by the language used. The coexistence of these two different images of women impeded recovery. The betrayal by those who had collaborated was symbolically too strong not to dominate any images of women and, in the long run, damage them. The role women played during the war had to be seen as a kind of sacred duty. In his indictment of a woman accused of intelligence with the enemy, the prosecutor in the court of justice in Arras evoked the ideal young French woman in the following terms: 'She is youth, purity and grace, and the future wife and future mother of the French family. Just as the vestal virgins were devoted to looking after the sacred flame, so young French women are the guardians of the flame of patriotism.'[79] Virginity and patriotism are closely associated in an ideal image of women which was intended to get rid of and even shut away for ever that of those who had committed sacrilege.

The Right to be a Citizen

Women whose heads had been shaved were ostracized in various ways. There were, of course, all kinds of ways, some of them tragic, in which they could live out their individual lives, but within society as a whole they were also excluded legally and politically.

The question of the right to vote and of collaboration was at the very heart of the order issued on 26 August 1944, dealing with the removal of citizens rights: 'Clearly those who had collaborated could not retain the same rights as those French citizens who had not given in. It was in this way that the idea of the loss of citizenship and all that went with it was conceived.'[80] The removal of citizenship was a way of excluding from society as a whole those, both men and women, who had shown themselves to be unworthy. This law applied only to those persons who had been brought before the courts, however – something that had not been the case for many women who had their heads shaved, but who were not legally prosecuted. The difference between the punishment imposed on someone at a local level and the uncertainty of what it meant when issued 'in the name of the French people' was something about which people were permanently preoccupied. During the last months of 1944 and in 1945 various demonstrations which were more or less violent, was one of the signs of changes that were registered and sometimes painfully. Various positions that were adopted at an individual or collective level, bear witness to the concern for a consensus.

At a time when the civic courts had barely come into operation, an article in *L'Indépendant d'Eure-et-Loir* on 27 October 1944 maintained that only by removing citizenship would a definitive exclusion be guaranteed: 'The punishment I am talking about is the loss of civil rights. In a way, this removes the hair from those guilty women, but with the difference that the hair would not grow back unless there were to be an amnesty which is most unlikely.' A report on the judicial services makes it quite clear that there was a perceived link between sexual relationships and perceived citizenship: 'In some regions it is clear that action has been limited to the shaving of heads and to imprisonment. In our view a general instruction should be given with regard to those French women who gave their bodies to the enemy, so that they should be deprived of the vote [underlined in the text] which has been given to them and of which they have shown themselves to be completely unworthy.'[81] In its issue on 10 February 1945, *Le Patriote de l'Eure* made a sharp comparison between French women and those who had collaborated, so that the latter should be excluded from the new emergent French nation: 'Very shortly we are going to see those women at the ballot box alongside valiant French women, mothers of families and wives of prisoners. In no way should those who sneered, who sometimes threatened us and who swooned in the arms of the Boche be allowed to have a say in the future of the renaissant France. We demand that they have their rights of citizenship taken away.' Finally on the 9 March 1945, the prefect of the Vosges expressed the indignation of a part of the local population about the right to vote given to those women who had no sense of duty: 'The wholesome members of the area are indignant when they see that no action has been taken against those women and that they have not even lost the right to vote, even though they have more than fully demonstrated that the sense of duty a true French woman should have towards the nation and homeland, was quite absent.'[82]

That women should have full rights of citizenship granted to them, was something that caused a significant proportion of the male population to be anxious. All talk of women's right to vote, or of 'the duty of French women', made this anxiety clear and it was generally felt that the franchise should be removed from anyone who had collaborated, men and women alike. In the long run, however, between those women whose heads were shorn, but who had not been prosecuted further, and those whose punishments were annulled, or came to an end (for example the loss of citizens' rights for a year),[83] few had the right to vote removed. Contrary to what the journalist of *L'Indépendant d'Eure-et-Loir* imagined in October 1944, the loss of civil rights at a local level was not, after an initial brief period, extended to a national one. Even if it is possible to suppose that many women who had their heads shaved did not take the opportunity to vote at the first elections through fear either of incidents, or because they were imposing some kind of personal censure or wanted to marginalize themselves, nothing allows us to be certain, and in the many articles relating to the first vote given to women, namely in the municipal elections of April/May 1945, there is no mention of any incidents to support this.

The physical punishment driven by sexist attitudes and suffered by thousands of women accused of collaboration, did not result in their being totally excluded. Any traceable links between the removal of hair and subsequent judicial sanctions can, in most cases, be found in the first months of the Liberation. Any anxiety that men had that the thought of the electoral body might double, was quickly nullified by their continuing dominance in civil matters and as well, probably, by the way they exerted renewed control over women's bodies. Without being excluded from national life, women whose heads had been shaved, nonetheless disappeared from view. This disappearance was not planned, but was due almost certainly to the way in which the difference between private and public lives was gradually reestablished. But while the women themselves may now have been relegated to private memory, the moment of their punishment will never completely be forgotten.

Notes

Introduction

1. Henry Rousso, 'L'épuration en France, une historie inachevée', *Vingtième siécle,* Vol. 33, January–March 1992, pp. 78–105.
2. Pierre Laborie, 'Violence politique et imaginaire collectif: l'exemple de l'épuration', in Bertrand Michel, Laurent Natacha, Taillefer Michel (eds), *Violences et pouvoirs politiques,* Toulouse, PUM, 1996, pp. 205–16.
3. See Luc Capdevila, *Les Bretons au lendemain de l'Occupation. Imaginaire et comportement d'une sortie de guerre 1944–1945,* Rennes, PUR, 1999.
4. 'La tondue' sung by Georges Brassens may be recalled. The best known films are: Alain Resnais, *Hiroshima mon amour,* 1958, screenplay by de Marguerite Duras. Claude Berri, *Le Vieil homme et l'enfant,* 1966, or again but in Italy, Bernado Bertolucci, *Norecento,* 1976. Novels containing scenes of a *tonte* are many. For each decade since the war we could refer to: Simone de Beauvoir, *Les Mandarins,* Paris, Gallimard, 1954; Violette Leduc, *La Bâtarde,* Paris, Gallimard, 1964; Joseph Joffo, *Un Sac de bille,* Paris, J.-C. Lattes, 1973; Régine Desforges, *Le Diable en rit encore,* Paris, Ramsay, 1985; Robert Sabatier, *La Souris verte,* Paris, Albin Michel, 1990.
5. The earliest known example is that of the Emperor Napoleon, nicknamed 'the little bald one' by his soldiers.
6. The use of the noun to describe someone whose head has been shaved is not new, but since the Liberation in its feminine form (*tondue*) it has become associated with women punished for having collaborated with the Germans.
7. Peter Novick, *L'Épuration française 1944–1949,* Paris, Balland, 1985; re-published in the collection 'Points', Paris, Seuil, 1991, p. 128.
8. Herbert Lottman, *L'Épuration 1943–1953,* Paris, Fayard, 1986, p. 105.
9. Pierre Laborie, *L'Opinion française sous Vichy,* Paris, Seuil, 1990.

Chapter 1 Sexual Collaboration?

1. Olivier Wieviorka, 'Épuration', in Jean-Pierre Azéma and François Bédarida (eds), *1938–1948. Les Années de tourmente de Munich à Prague. Dictionnaire critique*, Paris, Flammarion, 1995, pp. 933–43.
2. This is the case of most historians. Robert O. Paxton writes in his introduction to the new edition of *La France de Vichy*, Paris, Seuil, 1997, p. 16: 'At the risk of what is perhaps an over simplification let us say that archival evidence proves that Vichy sought to go beyond the armistice and to establish a voluntary, but military neutral collaboration with Germany.'
3. 'La Répression des faits de collaboration', *Notes documentaires et études*, No.245, Paris, 1946. Articles 75 and beyond of the Penal Code specifically sanction crimes of treason in time of war.
4. *Ibid.*
5. Courts of justice: between 55, 331 and 55,532: civic courts between 69,282 and 77,296. The first figures are taken from those published in *Les Cahiers français d'information* (31 December 1948); the second from the official figures issued on 31 January 1951. See Henry Rousso 'L'épuration en France: une histoire inachevée', *Vingtième siècle,* No. 33, January–March 1992, pp. 78–105.
6. François Rouquet, *L'Épuration dans l'administration française,* Paris, CNRS, 1993.
7. The information collected for each one refers as much to her civil status, profession and the accusation made against her as to the punishment inflicted. Geographical distribution is not significant since there is only the original source to go on. Fifty-two per cent of the sample comes from only six departments (Charente, Côtes-du-Nord, Hérault, Indre, Moselle and Oise) and only sixty departments have been mentioned. The only criteria taken into account in drawing up this list have been the fact of having had the head shaved and of being identifiable by name in order to avoid appearing twice. Even sources found in the files established at the time of the *épuration* are equally vague.
8. File of the Court of Justice, 12 April and 3 May 1945. Departmental Archives, Oise, 998 W 47198-47195.
9. Philippe Burrin, *La France à l'heure allemande*, Paris, Seuil, 1995, p. 215.
10. Statistics obtained from the files kept on women who had been interned.

11. François Rouquet, *L'Épuration dans l'administration française, op.cit.,* p. 90.
12. Individual file from those of interned administrative workers and police reports, 1 November 1944. Archive Deparment, Indre, 1279 W 2.
13. Pay-rolls, 1 July 1943–14 April 1945. National Police Archives.
14. Individual file taken from the police reports made by administrative employees, December 1944. Departmental Archives, Indre, 1279 W 16.
15. Police report from Coubert, 16 November 1945. National Police Archives, 29 D 1 (Seine-et-Marne).
16. Report of the prefect, 24 December 1944. National Archives, FlcIII 1208.
17. See the testimony of Dora Schaul, a German woman opposed to fascism and a member of the resistance. Her account was ratified by the Front National. Gilbert Badia, *Exilés en France. Souvenirs d'antifascistes allemands émigrés (1933–1945)*, Paris, François Maspero, 1982.
18. See Denis Peschanski and Pierre Milza (eds), *Italiens et Espagnols en France 1938–1946*, CEDEI-FNSP, pre-publication of the transactions of an international conference, 1992.
19. 42 per cent of the total involved.
20. Peter Novick, *op. cit.,* p. 123; Henri Michel, *La Libération de Paris,* Bruxelles, Complexe, 1980, p. 87; François Bédarida, in *Dictionnaire critique, op. cit.,* p. 616; Olivier Wieviorka, in *ibid.,* p. 936; Philippe Buton, 'L'État restauré', in J.-P. Azéma and F. Bédarida, *La France des années noires,* t.2, Paris, Seuil, 1993, p. 423.
21. Commission centrale d'épuration, Ministère des Communications. National Archives, F 90 20739.
22. Information proviced by Jean-Marc Berlière.
23. For the Hérault and Oise which have not been examined in this way I have relied on my own data. In both cases it is not a question of people who were punished but simply harassed.
24. Errors can be found as much in the collecting as in the recording of information. The number of people punished at the Liberation is, in certain cases, underestimated. Equally the inquiry numbers at 71,507 those who were punished, which gives a percentage of 0.21 per cent of the population of the seventy-seven departments under consideration (34,288,000). This is markedly lower than two other figures. According to Peter Novick quoting from statistics provided by *Le Cahier français d'information* of 15 March 1949 it is 0.25 per cent.

A figure of 0.235 per cent based on statistics published on 31 January 1951 is given by Emile Garçon (ed.) in *Code pénal annoté*, new edition by Rosselet, Patin and Ancel, Paris, Sitey, 1952, articles 1–294.

25. On this subject see Luc Capdevila and Fabrice Virgili, 'Épuration et Tonte des collaboratrices: un antiféminisme?', in Christine Bard (ed.), *Un Siècle d'antiféminisme*, Paris, Fayard, 1999, pp. 255–68.

26. Cécile Dauphin and Arlette Farge (eds), *De la violence et des femmes*, Paris, Albin Michel, 1997, and Robert Cario, *Les Femmes résistent au crime*, Paris, L'Harmattan, 1997.

27. Renée Martinage, 'Les Collaborateurs devant les cours d'assises du Nord après la très Grande Guerre', in *La Revue du Nord*, Vol. 309, 1995, pp. 95–115.

28. Map established from information obtained from the CH2GM inquiry and from the 1946 census. The rate of 0.21 per cent has been calculated for seventy-six departments or 85 per cent of the national population (34,288,000 inhabitants).

29. The six cases envisaged are: 1) to have been a member of the government after 16 June 1940; 2) to have belonged to the governments propaganda service; 3) to have been a member of the commission investigating Jews; 4) to have belonged, after 1 January 1941, to certain collaborationist groups; 5) to have organized artistic, economic or political demonstrations in favour of the Germans or of collaboration; 6) to have written or spoken in favour of collaboration.

30. Émile Garçon (ed.), *Code pénal annoté, op. cit.,* articles 1–294.

31. Public Prosecutor, Besançon, 28 February 1944; General Inspection of the judicial services, 1 May 1945; Report by the Commissioner of the Republic, 20 February 1945. National Archives, BB18/7133 and F1a 4021.

32. Correspondence: prefecture of Vosges, Minister of Justice, 9 March and 10 April 1945. National Archives, BB18/7133.

33. Extract of the clerk of court's minutes, Court of Appeal, Angers, 10 March 1945. National Archives, BB18/7133.

34. Civic Chamber, 4 December 1945. Departmental Archives, Ile-et-Vilaine, 213W.

35. Correspondence: Ministry of Justice, prefect of Vosges, 10 April 1945. National Archives, BB18/7133.

36. Appendix IV, Henri Noguères, *Histoire de la Résistance en France*, Paris, Robert Laffont, 1967, t.1, pp. 468–71.

37. Document of the Court of Justice 19 January, 3 May 1945, 29 December 1944; Document of the Civic chamber, 23 March 1945. Departmental Archives, Oise, 998 W 47189-47195-47188-47220.

38. Philippe Burrin, *La France à l'heure allemande, op. cit.,* p. 211.

39. Police report, Lacroix-Saint-Ouen, 23 October 1944. National Police Archives, 69 D 3 (Oise).

40. *Dix commandements*, 10 September 1941. National library, Rés. G. 1476(II-4).

41. Xavier Scarbonchi, 'Corses en avant!', resistance chant of the movement 'Combat corse' in 1942. National Archives, 72 AJ 113.

42. *Le Patriote de l'Oise*, 1 November 1943; *Le Patriote de Saône-et-Loire*, 1 October 1943; *Femmes françaises*, January 1944; *Bir Hakeim*, 1 June 1943.

43. Anette Warring, *Tyskerpiger. Under besaeltelse og retsopger*, Gyldendal, København, 1994.

44. Figures quoted by Philippe Burrin, *La France à l'heure allemande, op. cit.,* p. 211, Franz Seidler, *Prostitution, Homosexualität, Selbstverstümmelung. Probleme der deutschen Sanitätsführung 1939–1945*, Neckardgemünd, Vowinkel Verlag, 1977.

45. Details drawn from German documents: AOK 7-1c Abwehrroff, reports for the period 1 November 1941 and 31 January 1942. Bob 116 fl 1., Tours, 12 January 1942; ArmeeOberKommando 7 – Ic ABWEHROFFizier No. 30/43 of 31 December 1942, Lorient, 8 December 1942; 338 Infantry division, 11 March 1943, Deutsche Waffen Stills Tands Kommission KontrollAB. Teillung, Bourges, 3 January 1943. National Archives, 72 AJ 135; 164; 104.

46. Letter from the judge at Beauvais to the prefect of the Oise, 3 March 1945. Departmental Archives, Oise, 116 W 11.837.

47. Report of the prefect of Rhône, 15 April 1945. National Archives, FlcIII/1225.

48. Out of 728 women investigated at the Liberation.

49. Report of the commissioner of the Republic of Poitiers, 15 February 1945. National Archives, F1a 4026.

50. *Rouergue Républicain*, Rodez, 29 August 1944.

51. Security Branch papers: MLN tract distributed at Montpellier, 21 June 1945. Departmental Archives, Hérault, 137, W5. The so-called Dr Kollaborateur was the leader of a collaboration group and a member of the PPF. He had his citizenship withdrawn for ten years.

52. *Voix de la Patrie*, 13 September 1944.

53. Police reports and inquiries concerning persons arrested and accused of collaboration. Register of those in the 'concentration camp'. No date but probably August 1944, National Archives, 72 AJ 108 (AVIII).

54. Police report Sens, 28 October 1944. Archives of the National Police, 239 I 2 (Yonne).

55. Policy reports and inquiries about persons arrested and accused of collaboration. Register of names of internal people, 5 September 1944. National Archives, 72 AJ 108 (AVIII).

56. Luc Capdevila, 'La collaboration sentimentale: Lorient, mai 1945', in François Rouquet and Danièle Voldman (eds), *Les Cahiers de l'IHTP*, No. 31, 1995, pp. 67–82.

57. *L'Appel de la Haute-Loire*, 28 August 1944.

58. *Épuration* committee file, 20 November 1944. Departmental Archives, Oise, 34 W 847bis.

59. *Épuration* committee file, Béziers, 11 September 1944. Departmental Archives, Hérault, 506 W 317.

60. Louis Hugueney, 'Crimes et délits contre la chose publique', *Revue de Science criminelle*, 1947, p. 225.

61. *Midi libre*, 27 October 1944. My italics.

62. Sous-préfecture of Thionville: individual *épuration* files classified by commune: Security Branch papers, 25 May 1945. Departmental Archives, Moselle, 76 W 492.

63. Court of Justice, 18 May 1945, report issued by local *épuration* committee, 10 October 1944. Departmental Archives, Oise, 998 W 47191.

64. Carcassonne, Security Branch papers, 11 June 1945. Departmental Archives, Hérault, 137 W 27.

65. Susanna Barrows finds in metaphors based on crowds, women and drunks a new and revealing insight into French society at the end of the nineteenth century. For the last decade of that century she has counted 372 works about women of which 149 deal with 'their illnesses and hygiene'. Susanna Barrows, *Miroirs déformants. Réflexions sur la foule en France à la fin du XIXe siècle,* Paris, Aubier, 1990, p. 45 onwards.

66. *Midi libre*, Montpellier, on account of the court of justice session, 28 October 1944.

67. 1 French franc = 0.05 Deutschmark.

68. Police Report, Méru, 20 September 1944. National Police Archives, 68 A 6 (Oise).

69. See the photography by Lapi-Viollet in Alain Brossat's, *Les Tondues.
Un carnaval moche*, Levallois-Perret, Manya, 1992.
70. Police report, Grenoble, 12 February 1945. National Police Archives,
189 H 1 (Isère).
71. CDL, *La Libération de Troyes*, Troyes, 27 August 1944.
72. *L'Eure libérée*, 16 December 1944.
73. 'France doesn't belong to French people but to 200 families. France
doesn't belong to the French.' Words taken from the film *La Vie est
à nous*, directed for the Communist Party by Jean Renoir, Jacques
Bedeer and Jean-Paul Le Chanois. This film highlights the opposition between the wealth of a few and the nation as a whole.
74. Dominique Veillon, *Vivre et survivre en France 1939–1947*, Paris,
Payot, 1995.
75. *Quarante-quatre*, 21 August 1944.
76. Reports and inquiries made of persons arrested and accused of
collaboration. Register of names (199 in all), Charente, Police report,
7 August 1944. National Archives, 72 AJ 108 (AVIII).
77. *Patriote*, 18 October 1944.
78. Pierre-Henri Teitgen, *Les Cours de Justice*, talk given on 5 April
1946, Paris, Le Mail, 1946, quoted by Henry Rousso, 'L'Épuration
en France: Une histoire inachevée', op. cit, p. 86.
79. See for example Jean-Marie Flonneau and Dominique Veillon (eds),
'Le temps des restrictions en France 1939–1949', *Les Cahiers de
l'IHTP*, Nos. 32–33, May 1996.
80. *Assaut*, Privas, 25 September 1944.
81. *République de Franche-Comté*, Besançon, 9 October 1944.
82. Police report, Luchon. 13 September 1944. National Police Archives,
109 F 1 (Haute-Garonne).
83. Police report, Ligny-le-Châtel, 3 July 1945. National Police Archives,
289 G 1 (Yonne).
84. *L'Appel de la Haute-Loire*, Le Puy-en-Velay, 21 August 1944.
85. Police report, Ligny-le Châtel, 3 July 1945. National Police Archives,
239 G 1 (Yonne).
86. Quoted by François Rouquet, *L'Épuration dans l'administration
française, op. cit.*, p. 131.
87. Police report, Crèvecoeur-le-Grand, 3 November 1944. Departmental Archives, Oise, 34 W 8466.
88. Prefect's office, police report, Crèvecoeur, 9 December 1944.
Departmental Achives, Oise, 34 W 8467.
89. *Le Patriote de l'Eure*, 10 February 1945. My italics.

90. Luc Capdevila, *L'Imaginaire social de la Libération en Bretagne*, thesis, Université de Rennes 2, 1997, p. 585.

Chapter 2 Where and How Many?

1. Among the 624 communes I have tracked down where *tontes* were carried out, 228 were rural and 396 urban. (At that time a commune was considered urban if its main centre had a population of 2,000. Today the number is 2,500.) The exception to this was the department of the Seine where all eighty-one communes were considered urban whatever their population. Of the communes I have recorded, 183 had a population of over 10,000. The more important the town the easier it is to find records. Given the difficulty of moving about and communication generally at the time, as well as the absence of local editions of regional newspapers, events in main towns tended to be known about but described in the major publications only. Similarly any report giving an overview could easily leave out incidents if they were considered to be of little importance and too local. In the absence of registered complaints it is also possible to imagine that violence occurred in some of the villages without the authorities being informed.

2. Report of a first hearing, Court of Justice, 29 March 1945. Departmental archives, Oise, 998W47192.

3. According to the census of 1946, 128 562 inhabitants or 32.4% of the department's population.

4. Jean-Pierre Besse, 'The example of the psychiatric hospital at Clermont in the Oise', in Dominique Veillon and Jean-Marie Flonneau (eds), 'Le Temps des restrictions en France (1939–1949)', *Les Cahiers de l'IHTP*, Nos 32–33, May 1996, pp. 433–6.

5. Jean-Pierre Besse, 'L'Oise', in Philippe Buton and Jean-Marie Guillon (eds), *Les Pouvoirs en France à la Libération*, Paris, Belin, 1994, pp. 183–92.

6. In his work on the Liberation of Brittany, Luc Capdevila has shown how heavily involved the military (the FFI and the FTP) and political resistance (the Front national) were. See Luc Capdevila, *Les Bretons au lendemain de l'Occupation. Imaginaire et comportement d'une sortie de guerre, 1944–1945*, Rennes, Presses Universitaires de Rennes, 1999. See as well Christian Bougeard, *Le Choc de la guerre dans les Côtes-du-Nord, 1939–1945*, Paris, J-P Gisserot, 1995.

7. Saint-Amand-Montrond in the Cher was liberated for the first time on 7 June 1944 but then reoccupied by the Germans and the *milice*. See Tzvetan Todorov, *Une tragédie française,* Paris, Seuil, 1994.

8. Only the centres at Le Douadic and Saint-Hilaire were officially recognized as supervised from October 1944. Like other places of internment, Saint-Hilaire has no administrative status.

9. Individual files on persons working for the administration, 31 October, 3 November and 1 December 1944. Departmental Archives, Indre, 1279 W 2 and 1279 W 4.

10. Exhibition of the departmental archives of the Indre, *Indre 1940–1944*, 1994. The commune of Graçay is in the Cher but was considered to be in that part of the Indre where the FFI intervened.

11. Individual files on persons working for the administration. Letter from the National Liberation Committee, the CDL, 7 February 1945. Departmental archives, Indre, 1279 W 10.

12. Paris, Marseille, Lyon, Toulouse, Bordeaux, Nice, Nantes, Lille, Saint-Étienne, Strasbourg, Toulon, Rennes, Nancy, Reims, Clermont-Ferrand, Limoges, Rouen, Le Havre, Grenoble, Roubaix, Dijon, Le Mans.

13. Report by the Commissioner of the Republic for Strasbourg, 15 May 1945. National archives, F1a 4028.

14. General report of the National Police, 15 May 1945. National Archives, 72 AJ 384.

15. Prefect's report for the Haut-Rhin, 4 June 1945. National Archives, F1a 3334.

16. *La Liberté du Pas-de-Calais*, Arras, 26 January 1945.

17. *La Croix du Nord*, Lille, 12 September 1944.

18. File of the Teaching Authorities for the Seine, September 1944, National Archives, 72 AJ 62.

19. Two files from civic courts (Department of the Oise Archives, 998 W 47225 and 47226), and one on the *épuration* committee (Department of the Oise Archives, 34 W 8465bis).

20. Fonds Madeleine Baudoin, 1984, library in the Institut d'histoire du temps présent.

21. Gertrude Stein, *Les Guerres que j'ai vues*, Paris, Christian Bourgois, 1980.

22. Marcel Basseville, *Ouf . . . les lilas ont refleuri*, Nancy, 1945.

23. Journal of vetinary doctor E. Lecomte, which ended on 13 September 1944. National Archives, 72 AJ 191. Theuse of the word *rasement* to describe the shaving of a head was already not much used at the time. This use is the only one I have discovered in all the documents I have examined.

24. *La Libération de l'Aunis et de la Saintonge*, Saintes, 14 October 1944.

25. An inquiry carried out by the police for the period 1946–8 considers there to have been 9,673 summary executions. In 1952 the Security Branch came up with the figure of 10,822. See National Assembly debates, *Journal* Officiel, 7 January 1954, p. 35.
26. Georgette Elgey, *La Fenêtre ouverte*, Paris, Fayard, 1973.
27. Rhône prefect's report, 1 October 1944. National Archives, FlcIII 1225.
28. Daily police reports, Sète, 31 August 1944. Department Archives, Hérault, 161 W 92.
29. Police reports from Méru, 12 October, 20 and 28 November, 27 and 28 December 1944. National Police Archives, 68 A 6 (Oise).
30. Albi: *Le Tarn libre*, 21 August 1944. Annecy: memoirs of M. Depollier 28 July 1943–11 November 1944. National Archives, 72 AJ 189 CI, 3. Clermont-Ferrand: Department of Puy-de-Dôme Archives, MO 7268, 24 April 1945, Regional Secretary for the Police. Report of the activity of the regional secretariat for the period 27 August–27 September 1944, cited by John Sweets, *Choices in Vichy France,* Oxford University Press, 1986. Creil: private collection of photographs. Évreux: AN, 72 AJ 122, testimony of M. Louis Hermier, Commissioner of Police at the Liberation. *Paris Normandie*, August 1974. Montélimar: testimony of Elsa Triolet, *La Drôme en Armes*, 5 September 1944. Sète: Department of the Hérault Archives, 161 W 92, reports of police journals of Sète, 31 August 1944.
31. This figure has been obtained from the surveys carried out by the Committee on how collaboration was repressed in 73 departments. In some cases (Brittany, Eure) they have been brought up to date, elsewhere (Moselle, Oise, Hérault) they have been completed.
32. Charles Hiegel, 'La Répression de la collaboration et l'épuration en Moselle. Bilan statistique', in François-Yves Le Moigne (ed.), *Moselle et Mosellans dans la Seconde Guerre modiale*, Metz, Editions Serpenoises, 1983, p. 394.
33. Report of the principal commissioner of Vichy, 5 June 1945, and 6 June 1945; report of Procurator General, 8 June 1945; report of the Commissioner of the Republic, 6 June 1945. National Archives, F1ª3334.
34. This range is based on 2,148 to 4,449 persons who had their heads shaved; 98.65 per cent refers to the first of these numbers, 98.9 per cent to the second.
35. Monique Luirard, *La Région stéphanoise dans la guerre et dans la paix, 1936–1951*, Saint-Étienne, Centre d'Études Foreziennes, 1980.

36. General report of the CCR,Toulouse, 31 December 1944. National Archives, F1a/4028.

37. Individual file on persons interned from the administration, 16 September 1944, Departmental Archives, Indre, 1279 W 2.

Chapter 3 During the Occupation

1. In other words all those incidents of it taking place more or less continuously and in the same place. The number of persons therefore is not taken into account here and where the *tontes* took place over a period of a few days only the earliest date is recorded. In forty-seven cases it is not possible to give the precise date, hence the difference between the 591 locations and the 638 communes where it is known the practice was carried out.

2. The 25 August 1944, with the capitulation of Von Choltiz, is the official date of the liberation of Paris, but the period generally extends from 19 August (the outbreak of the Paris uprising) to the 26 August when Allied troops marched down the Champs-Elysées.

3. Still more if the liberation of Corsica in October 1943 is taken into account.

4. Marcel Baudot, 'L' Épuration, bilan chiffré', *Bulletin de l'IHTP,* Vol. 25, September 1986, pp. 37–53.

5. Peter Novick, *L'Épuration française 1944–1949*, Paris, Balland, 1985.

6. In fact the courts of justice would continue to be held until 31 January 1951.

7. Individual files of the *épuration* committee held in the sous-préfecture of Béziers, 16 November 1944. Departmental archives of the Hérault, 506 W 320.

8. The beginnings of the *tontes* are not easy to trace. There is no 'date of inauguration', no voting of a law, no unchallenged call for action or decisive struggle; rather they were dictated by events as difficult to track as it is to date their beginning.

9. *Défense de la France*, No.11, 15 February 1942. In 1942 30,000 copies of *Défense de la France* were printed. See Olivier Wieviorka, *Une Certaine idée de la résistance. Défense de la France, 1940–1949*, Paris, Seuil, 1995, pp. 104–5.

10. To these examples we could add a song entitled *The Cows' Waltz* (*Valse des vaches*), but since there is no indication of author, place or date it is better left out. 'After the rain the fine weather will come.

And then revenge. We'll see these all these sluts again. No pardon for them. They can keep their charm. No French person will want it. The swastika on their faces and their hair cut right off.' BN Rés. G.1476 (II-2), p. 33.

11. Philippe Burrin, *La France à l'heure allemande,* Paris, Seuil, 1995, p. 213.

12. Summary of facts concerning resistance in German documents: LXVI AK-1a (66e corps d'armée, section des opérations) October 1943. National Archives, 72 AJ 141.

13. *Le Pilori,* published by the movement France d'abord, 1 December 1943, aproved by Louis-Frédéric Ducros, *Montagnes ardéchoises dans la guerre,* II, Valence, L'Auteur,1977, annexes VI and IX.

14. Yves Martin, *L'Ain dans la guerre, 1939–1945,* Le Coteau, Horvath, 1989.

15. Files of the *épuration* committee, the Italian Question . National Archives, F1a 3813.

16. Paul Silvani, *Et la Corse fut libérée,* Ajaccio, La Marge, 1993; *La Corse des années ardentes: 1939–1976,* Paris, Albatros, 1976.

17. Pierre Laborie, *L'Opinion française sous Vichy,* Paris, Seuil, 1990, p. 386.

18. *Femmes Françaises,* No.1, newspaper of the Union des femmes françaises, January 1944.

19. *La Marseillaise,* publication of the MUR of Sud-Est, No.1, February 1944.

20. Reproduced by Jean-Pierre Perrin, *L'Honneur perdu d'un résistant. Un épisode trouble de l'épuration,* Besançon, La Lanterne, 1987.

21. Pierre Laborie, 'L'Idée de Résistance, entre définition et sens: retour sur un questionnement', in 'La Résistance et les Française. Nouvelles approaches', *Les Cahiers de l'IHTP,* Vol. 37, December 1997, pp. 15–27.

22. Insa Meinen, 'Wehrmacht und Prostitution – Zur reglementierung der Geschlechterbeziehungen durch die deutsche Militärverwaltung im besetzten Frankreich 1940–1944', in *1999 Zeitschrift für Geschichte des 20 und 21 Jahrhunderts,* Vol. 2, 1999, pp. 35–55.

Chapter 4 The Explosion of the Liberation

1. André Devaux, *Bapaume pendant la Deuxième Guerre mondiale,* Paris, EPA, 1987.

2. Reports submitted by primary school teachers to the education authorities on the liberation of the department of the Seine, September 1944. National Archives, 72 AJ62.

3. Respectively: Chablis 1,796; Bapaume 2,748; Boulogne-Billancourt 79,410 (1946 census).

4. From a speech given 6 June 1944, quoted by Jean-Pierre Azéma, *De Munich à la Libération, 1938–1944*, Paris, Seuil, 1980, p. 327.

5. Philippe Buton and Jean-Marie Guillon (eds), *Les Pouvoirs en France à la Libération*, Paris, Berlin, 1994, p. 15.

6. Jean-Pierre Azéma, *De Munich à la Libération, op. cit.*

7. Jean-Pierre Rioux, *La France de la Quatrième République. L'ardeur et la nécessité 1944–1952*, Paris, Seuil, 1980.

8. *L'Ardennais*, 14 September 1944.

9. Charles d'Aragon, *La Résistance sans héroïsme*, Paris, Seuil, 1977, p. 209.

10. Serge Ravanel, *L'Esprit de résistance*, Paris, Seuil, 1995, p.444.

11. CCR report, 19 September 1944. National Archives, F1a 4022.

12. A recent example throughout France was that of the massive expressions of joy in July 1998 when France won the World Cup.

13. Capa took the best known photograph at Chartres on 18 August 1944. Lee Miller photographed women at Rennes. See Anthony Penrose, *Lee Miller; photographe et correspondante de guerre*, Paris, Du May, 1994.

14. Anthony Penrose, *Lee Miller; photographe et correspondante de guerre, op. cit.*, p. 65.

15. Security Branch report. National Archives, 72 AJ 164. Hostile acts carried out against collaborators, 21 September 1945, Departmental Archives, Mayenne, I.W.1121.

16. I happened to see one of these photographs on sale in 1995 for 1000F. Published at the Liberation these cards were not intended to be posted but to be kept as souvenirs.

17. François Marcot, 'La résistance dans ses lieux et milieux: des relations d'interdépendance', and 'La Résistance et les Français. Nouvelles approaches', *Les Cahiers de l'IHTP*, No. 37, December 1997, pp. 129–46.

18. Jacqueline Sainclivier, 'Le pouvoir résistant (été 1944)', and Philippe Buton and Jean-Marie Guillon (eds), *Les Pouvoirs en France à la Libération, op. cit.* pp. 20–37.

19. Philippe Buton, Jean-Marie Guillon, 'Introduction', *ibid*. P.15.

20. Report by Cdt Bourgeois (group captain) on the activities of the Resistance around Romilly-sur-Seine and in the liberation of the town, 30 September 1944. National Archives, 72 AJ 101.
21. Report by the headmistress of the local girls' school in Orly, 19 September 1944. National Archives, 72 AJ 62.
22. Police report, Méru, 21 October 1944. National Police Archives, 68 A 6 (Oise).
23. *Assaut*, 25 September 1944.
24. See Marc-Olivier Baruch, *Servir l'État français*, Paris, Fayard, 1997, p. 568.
25. Simon Kitson, 'La Reconstitution de la police à Marseille (August 1944–February 1945)', in *Provence Historique*, fascicule 178, October 1994, pp. 497–509.
26. General police report in Register 'R4' from Blagnac, 12 November 1944. National Police Archives, 109 F1 (Haute-Garonne).
27. Weekly FTP-FN paper, *Patriote*, Loir-et-Cher, 18 August 1944.
28. Police register '2', Isère, 15 September 1944. National Police Archives, 138H3 (Isère).
29. Samuel Marshall, *Bringing up the Rear*, San Rafael, Presidio Press, 1979.
30. William J. Morgan, *The OSS and I*, New York, Norton, 1957.
31. Alan Moorehead, *L'Éclipse*, Paris, Le Sagittaire, 1947.
32. Raymond Dufay, *1940-1944. La Vie dans l'Audomarois sous l'Occupation*, Longuenesse, EPA, 1990.
33. The eighty-seven Jedburgh teams were part of the American and British secret service and were to support the FFI by giving them weapons and instructions. Each team was made up of an English or American officer, a French officer and a radio operator. They entered France from June 1944 on. *OSS équipes Jedburgh en France*, June-November 1944. Sheet 87, 'Jedburgh team Tony' – M2 – Area: VENDÉE: 'The inhabitants started to celebrate the liberation though trouble started when collaborators' shops were ransacked and the hair of women who had been friendly with Germans was shaved off. The Team set out with forty men under Lt. P. To try to establish order.'
34. *La République du Sud-Ouest*, Toulouse, 21 August 1944. *La Liberté*, Lille, 6 September 1944. *La Normandie*, Rouen, 1st September 1944. *Le Tarn libre*, Albi, 21 August 1944.
35. Report on the activities of the regional police secretariat during the period 27 August–27 September 1944. Departmental archives, Puy-de-Dôme, MO7268, quoted by John Sweets in *Clermont-Ferrand à l'heure allemande*, Paris, Plon, 1996.

36. Report on the installation of the regional Commissioner for the Republic, Clermont-Ferrand, 6 October 1944. National Archives, F1a 4021.
37. *Le Patriote*, Nevers, 21 September 1944.
38. *Combat*, Paris, 4 September 1944. It should be noted that this was not published by other daily papers in Paris such as *L'Humanité, Ce Soir, Libération, Le Figaro, Défense de la France*.
39. Quoted by Pierre Rothiot, *Cent cinquante ans au service du peuple*, Vol. 2: 'Pour la France et la Liberté', Vittel, EPA, 1979.
40. *Victoire*, Tarbes, 18 September 1944.
41. Jacqueline Sainclivier, 'Le Pouvoir résistant (été 1944)', in Philippe Buton and Jean-Marie Guillon (eds), *Les Pouvoirs en France à la Libération, op. cit.*, pp. 20–37.
42. *Le Patriote romanais*, 8 September 1944.
43. Police reports and inquests on named persons arrested and accused of collaboration. National Archives, 72 AJ 108 (AVIII). The precise name of the camp and its situation are not given. It would be the one at Jayat set up before the Liberation by AS in an area under his control to the north-east of the department. This camp was shut on 11 September 1944 and those held there were either freed or transfered to Angoulême.
44. In particular the *maquis* groups from Aigoual, the Cévennes, Espinousse, the Minervois and Haut-Larzac.
45. Jacques Bounin, *Beaucoup d'imprudences*, Paris, Stock, 1974. p. 156.
46. Report from the court, 27 August 1944. Departmental Archives, Hérault, 136 W5.
47. Jean Larrieu, 'L'Épuration judiciaire dans les Pyrénées-Orientales', in *Recherches historiques sur la Seconde Guerre mondiale*, No. 112, 1978, pp. 29–35.
48. Technical report carried out for the Montpellier region (October–November 1944). Departmental Archives, Hérault, 137 W 14.
49. Individual files established by the *épuration* committee at the *sous-préfecture* of Béziers, 16 November 1944. Departmental Archives, Hérault, 506W320.
50. *Voix de la Patrie*, 20 October 1945.
51. Hélène Chaubin 'L'Hérault', in Philippe Buton and Jean-Marie Guillon (eds), *Les Pouvoirs en France à la Libération, op. cit*, pp. 508–17. Roger Bourderon, 'Jacques Bounin et la restauration de l'État', in *Lendemains de Libération dans le Midi*, Actes du colloque de Montpellier, 1986, université Paul-Valery-Montpellier-3, 1997,

pp. 67–80. Jacques Bailly, *Aspects de la Libération dans le Langue-doc méditerranéen 1944–1945*, university thesis from Montpellier.

Roger Bourderon, *La Libération du Languedoc méditerranéen*, Paris, Hachette, 1974.

52. Roger Bourderon, 'Jacques Bounin et la restauration de l'État', *op. cit.* p. 68.
53. Daily police report, police headquarters, Montpellier, 29 August 1944. Departmental Archives, Hérault, 161W92.
54. Roger Bourderon, 'Jacques Bounin et la restauration de l'État', *op. cit.*, p. 68.
55. Letter from the prefect to his deputy in Béziers, 18 October 1944. Departmental Archives, Hérault, 506 W 316. A handwritten note probably from the *sous-préfecture*'s records that this woman was 'taken for interrogation' and that the information about her son was incorrect.

Chapter 5 Head Shaving and Brutalities After the Liberation

1. Individual files on prisoners. Departmental Archives, Indre, 1279 W 27.
2. Pierre Laborie, 'L'Opinion et l'épuration', in *Lendemains de Libéra-tion dans le Midi*, Actes du colloque de Montpellier, 1986, université Paul-Valery-Montpellier-3, 1997, pp. 47–61.
3. General police report, National Archives, 72 AJ 384.
4. Two-monthly report issued by the commissioner for the Republic in Lyon, 15 February 1945. National Archives, Fla 4022.
5. Josian Albinet, *Le Pouvoir en Aveyron à la Libération*, mémoire de maîtrise, université Toulouse-Le-Mirail, 1989.
6. Letter dated 12 September 1944 from Carcassone contained in a technical report, Montpellier. Departmental Archives, Hérault, 137 W 14.
7. Report made by the Commissioner for the Republic in Marseille, 31 December 1944. National Archives. Fla 4023. On the original the word 'détenus' (indicating those retained) was written with an 'e' (détenues) before being corrected: the 'e' being crossed out.
8. One woman who was executed could well have had her hair cut off at the Liberation, however. This was the case in the former *sous-préfecture* of Beziers where four members of the *milice* were shot. One of them was a woman. Report from the general police secretary to the Minister of the Interior concerning illegal executions carried out

Notes

at Béziers, Montpellier, Alès and Rodez, 26 January 1945. Departmental Archives, Hérault, 136, W6.

9. On 9 January at Gap a woman was forced from her escort outside the courtroom and severely assaulted. She later died from her injuries. General police report, National Archives 72 AJ 384.

10. Olga Wormser-Migot, *Le Retour des déportés. Quand les Alliés ouvrirent les portes*, Bruxelles, Complexe, 1985.

11. Barbie Zelinger, 'La Photo de presse et la libération des camps', in *Vingtième siècle*, No. 54, April–June 1997, pp. 61–78.

12. General police report, 15 June 1945. National Archives, 72 AJ 384.

13. Monthly report from the Commissioner of the Republic, Dijon, 30 June 1945. National Archives, Fla 4021.

14. Monthly report from the Prefect of the Dordogne, 15 July 1945. National Archives, FlcIII/1217.

15. Monthly report of the Commissioner of the République of Nancy, 30 May 1945, Fla 4024: General police report, Châlette, 16 May 1945, 72 AJ 384; letter from the prefect of the Aveyron to the Minister of the Interior, 5 June 1945, Fla 3334; General police reports, 72 AJ 384, National Archives; Police Register '4' from Givors (Rhône), 4 June 1945. National Police Archives, 129 C3.

16. Letter from the prefect of the Lot to the Minister of the Interior, 26 June 1945. National Archives, Fla 3334.

17. Monthly report by the commissioner for the Republic, Poitiers, 5 June 1945. National Archives, Fla 4026.

18. From 30 November 1940 it will be in the German province of westmark. The departments of the Bas-Rhin and Haut-Rhin were attached to the *Gau* of Bade.

19. Monique Sary, 'La Vie à Metz sous l'Occupation nazie', in François-Yves Le Moigne (ed.), *Moselle et Mosellans dans la Seconde Guerre mondiale*, Metz, Éditions Serpenoises, 1983, pp. 143–72.

20. NSKK: motorized sections; *Hitler-Jugend*: Hitler youth (boys); *Bund Deutscher Mädchen*: young girls' association; *N.S. Frauenschaft*: women's association.

21. According to Pierre Barral, 30 thousand 'L'Alsace-Lorraine: trois départements sous la botte', in Jean-Pierre Azéma and François Bédarida (eds.), *La France des années noires*, Vol. 1, Paris, Seuil, 1993, pp. 233–50; 15 thousand according to Bernard Meddahi: 'L'Immédiat après-guerre en Moselle', in François-Yves Le Moigne (ed.), *Moselle et Mosellans dans la Seconde Guerre mondiale, op. cit.*, pp. 143–72. Such a difference is due to the difficulty of being able to work out from German statistics how many were forced to join.

22. They were also accompanied by Germans who settled in this region to accelerate the process of Germanization; 160,000 hectares were appropriated for this purpose and put under the control of the Ostland.
23. *Sous-préfecture* at Thionville. Files established at the *épuration* on individual persons by commune. Security Branch file, Thionville, 12 May 1945. Departmental Archives, Moselle, 76 W 507.
24. Prefect's fortnightly report for the period 15 April–15 June 1945. National Archives, Flc III/1222.
25. Unless otherwise indicated statistical information on the judicial *épuration* in the Moselle is taken from the extremely thorough survey carried out by Charles Hiegel.
26. *Épuration* files; arrival and departure lists of the camp at Queuleu, 15 July 1945. Departmental Archives, Moselle, 151 W 365-1 and 2.
27. Note from the sub-prefect at Thionville to the CLL president at Florange, 18 June 1945. Departmental Archives, Moselle.
28. Letter from the mayor of Florange to the sub-prefect at Thionville, 31 May 1945. Departmental Archives, Moselle, 76 W 513.
29. Sub-prefecture of Thionville: individual persons dossiers established at the *épuration* by commune, 6 September 1945. Departmental Archives, Moselle, 76 W 508.
30. Police register '2', Thionville. National Police Archives, 210 J 4 (Moselle).
31. Figures are based on the cases of named persions I have been able to trace for the department of the Moselle.
32. Individual files of the administrative *épuration*. Departmental Archives, Moselle, 151 W 212.
33. Police registers '4' (Moselle) and '2' (Faulquemont) 23 May and 8 September 1945. National Police Archives, 210 J 4 and 210 J 6.
34. For the same reason we find nearly 105 adolescents less than seventeen years of age in these two camps.
35. François Rouquet, *L'Épuration dans l'administration française, op. cit.,* p. 162.
36. Files on individual persons by commune held by the Security Branch, 28 May 1945. Departmental Archives, Moselle, 76 W 476.
37. Luc Capdevila, *L'Imaginaire social de la Libération en Bretagne*, thesis, université de Rennes-2, Rennes, 1997. p.284.
38. Police report, 23 February 1946. National Archives, 72 AJ 384 and *La Savoie française*, 2 March 1946, Albertville.
39. Letter from the Chief of Police at Hagondange to the sub-prefect, 25 February 1946. Departmental Archives, Moselle, 77 W 298.

40. Police report, 20 March 2946. Departmental Archives, Gard, 1 W 711.

Chapter 6 Neighbourhood Violence

1. In 1981 a man was condemned to six months in prison for having shaved off his wife's hair after a quarrel. *Le Matin*, 3 April 1981. Quoted by Madeleine Baudoin.
2. Yves Michaud, *Violence et politique*, Paris, Gallimard, 1978, p. 12.
3. Georges Brédier, *Brou pendant la guerre*, Chartres, impr. De Durand, 1945. *La Libération du Calvados, 6/6-31/12/44*, Caen, conseil général du Calvados, 1994, p. 146. La Libération d'Aix par le Président de la délégation municipale. Archives Nationales, 72 AJ 104. Registre 2, section de Loches, 17 juillet 1945. Archives de la Gendarmerie Nationale, 41 A 2 (Indre-et-Loire).
4. *Le Cantal libre*, 23 September 1944.
5. Nancy: rapport du CCR, 15 October 1944. Archives nationales, Fla4024. Bellegarde: *La Renaissance républicaine du Gard*, 28 August 1944. Albi: Charles d'Aragon, *La Résistance sans héroïsme*, Paris, Seuil, 1977, p. 209.
6. *Le Patriote de l'Eure*, 16 December 1944.
7. Police Report from Lacroix-Saint-Ouen, 23 October 1944. National Police Archives, 69 D 3 (Oise).
8. Mélinée Manouchian, *Manouchian*, Paris, Les Éditeurs Français Réunis, 1974, p. 73.
9. Police report, La Ferté-sous-Jouarre, 30 October 1944. National Police Archives, 30 A 4 (Seine-et-Marne).
10. Police report, Lacroix-Saiont-Ouen, 17 October 1944. This account given by one of the group confirms how the events took place. National Police Archives, 69 D 3 (Oise).
11. *La Marseillaise de Seine-et-Marne*, 3 October 1944.
12. Luc Capdevila, *L'Imaginaire social de la Libération en Bretagne*, université de Rennes-2, Rennes, 1997, p. 194.
13. Report of events taking place 8 June 1945 at Aigueperse. National Archives, F1a 3334.
14. Individual files 9, 12, 18 October, 30 November and 2 December 1944. Departmental Archives of the Indre, 1279 W 14-18-16-27.
15. Individual files, 9 October 1944. Departmental Archives (the Indre), 1279 W 21.

16. Unsigned report on the situation at Lyon at the Liberation, 19 September 1944 made by the regional police headquarters. National Archives, F1a 4022.
17. Dominique Julia, 'La Violence des foules: peut-on élucider l'inhumain?' in Jean Boutier and Dominique Julia (eds), *Passés recomposés. Champs et chantiers de l'Histoire*, Paris, Autrement, 1995, pp. 208–23.
18. Pierre Laborie, *L'Opinion française sous Vichy*, Paris, Seuil, 1990, p. 312.
19. Delaunay and Pioger, 'La Libération du Mans', in *La Province du Maine*, 4e série, 1977, pp. 464–7.
20. One million troops and two hundred thousand in the security services as well as those employed by the German administration in France and the Todt organization.
21. Police report, Montlieu-la-Garde, 20 September 1944. National Police Archives, 100 H 3 (Charente-Inférieure).
22. Civic court hearing, 16 February 1945. Departmental archives (Oise), 998 W 47219.
23. Philippe Burrin, *La France à l'heure allemande*, Paris, Seuil, 1995, p. 461.
24. *Épuration* committee report, 6 October 1944. Departmental archives (Oise), 34 W 8472-1.
25. Cher, Creuse, Dordogne, Gironde, Loire, Loire-Inférieure, Morbihan, Moselle, Seine, Seine-et-Oise, Haute-Vienne.
26. Ain, Ariège, Aude, Aveyron, Bouches-du-Rhône, Gard, Haute-Garonne, Lot-et-Garonne, Lozère, Pyrénées-Orientales, Seine, Tarn, Tarn-et-Garonne, Var.
27. Account of a police interrogation in Paris, 29 May 1945. Hearing in the Civic Court, 20 July 1945, Departmental archives (Oise) 998 W 47224.
28. Courts of Justice hearing, 29 March 2945. Departmental Archives (Oise), 998 W 47192.
29. Police report on Rochefort-sur-Mer, 21 December 1944. National Police Archives, 100 K 3 (Charente-Inférieure).
30. Police report, Betz, 6 December 1944. National Police Archives, 68 f 1 (Oise).
31. Police report, Berlaimont, 31 October 1944. National Police archives, 54 C 4 (Nord). File from civic courts, 20 April 1945. Departmental archives (Oise), 998 W 47221.
32. Danièle Voldman has put the number of mines dug up in France between 1945 and 1948 especially in the fifty-two most affected

departments at 13 million. She sees this operation as being a 'necessary first move in establishing peace' and shows too how the passage from war to peace is a difficult one. Danièle Voldman, *Le Déminage de la France après 1945*, Paris, Odile Jacob, coll. 'Opus', 1998.

33. *Sous-prefet*'s monthly report, Compiègne, 15 January 1945. Departmental Archives (Oise), 33 W 8270.

34. Monthly CCR report, Marseille, 31 December 1944. National Archives, F1a 4023.

35. During the attack on Madrid by nationalist troops organized in four columns, Franco talked of the support provided by a fifth column, already established in the city.

36. Alexandre Koyré, *La Cinquième Colonne,* Paris, Allia, 1997, article first published in *Renaissance*, New York, Nos. II-III, 1945.

37. *L'Humanité*, Paris, 28 September 1944.

38. CDL directives dealing with the *épuration,* 15 February 1945. Departmental archives (Moselle), 73 W 75.

39. Two posters with the captions 'Taisez vous! L'Allemand a fui . . . L'espion reste' ('Be quiet! The Germans may have gone . . . but spies are still here') in Laurent Gervereau andDenis Peschanski (eds), *La Propagande sous Vichy 1940–1944*, Paris, La Découverte, 1990, pp. 89 and 125.

40. See *Le Trésor de la langue française. Dictionnaire de la langue du XIXe et du XXe siècle*, Paris, CNRS-Gallimard, 1971–1994, 16 volumes; *Le Grand Robert de la langue française,* Paris, Éditions Le Robert, nine volumes.

41. Calculated on the basis of 586 named women whose heads were shaved.

42. Maurice Olender, 'La Rumour' in *Le Genre humain*, Special issue, 5, 1982.

43. Post office *épuration* files. National Archives, F90 20739.

44. Police report, Bagnères-de-Luchon, 13 September 1944. National Police Archives, 109 F1 (Haute-Garonne).

45. Individual files on persons interned from the administration, 12 October 1944. Departmental Archives, Indre, 1279 W 16.

46. Post-office *épuration* committee report.

47. Police report, La Ferté-sous-Jouarre, 30 October 1944. National Police Archives, 30A4 (Seine-et-Marne).

48. Police report, Marseille-de-Beauvaisis, 3 November 1944. Departmental Archives, Oise, 34 W 8466.

49. Teaching authorities' reports on the Liberation, 13, 15 and 19 September. National Archives, 72 AJ 62 (c.iv).

50. The district was divided into two sectors each with its own company. On 15 August 1944 there were in all 600 men there.

51. *Épuration* committee report, 5 January 1945. Departmental Archives, Oise, 34W 8453.

52. Police reports of 5 October, 24 and 30 November, Montlieu-la-Garde and Rochefort-sur-Mer. National Police Archives, 100 H3 (Charente-inférieure).

53. Files on individual persons interned from the administration, 3 January 1945. Departmental Archives, Indre, 1279 W23.

54. Police report, Chemillé, 5 September 1944. Departmental Archives, Maine-et-Loire, 95W.

55. Obtained by distillling coal. Used for treating wood and as an antiseptic disinfectant.

56. Marc Valée, *Cinq années de vie et de guerre en pays mayennais*, Château-Gontier, IENA, 1962.

57. Probably taken by an American photographer. The original caption is in English and Cotentin was in the area where the First American army was operating.

58. Police report, La Mure-en-Isère, 28 May 1945. National Police Archives, 140 A 3 (Isère).

59. Marie Moscovici, 'Tuer', in 'Guerres', *L'Inactuel*, No. 1, Calmann-Lévy, 1994, pp. 111–17.

60. Antoine Prost, 'La Représentation de la guerre en France', in *Vingtième siècle*, special issues: 'La guerre de 1914–1918. Essais d'histoire culturelle', No. 41, January–March 1994, pp. 23–31.

61. Stéphane Audoin-Rouzeau, *La Guerre des enfants 1914–1918. Essai d'histoire culturelle*, Paris, Armand Colin, 1993.

62. *Épuration* committee file in the Oise; police report, Moyeuvre-Grande (Moselle), 15 June 1945; individual files on persons interned from the administration in the Indre, 12 October 1944. Departmental Archives, oise, 34 W 8471-1; Moselle, 76 W 522; Indre, 1279 W 16.

63. *Le Rouergue républicain*, Rodez, 23 August 1944.

64. *L'Appel de la Haute-Loire*, Le Puy-en-Velay, 28 August 1944.

65. Mélinée Manouchian, *Manouchian, op. cit.*, p. 73.

66. The subject was treated in a talk given at a conference held in Brighton, 4–6 July 1996: *After the War was Over. Reconstructing the Family, Society, and the Law in Southern Europe, 1944–1950*.

67. Hélène Eck, 'Les Françaises sous Vichy', in Françoise Thébaud (ed.), *Histoire des femmes en Occident. Tome 5: Le xxe siècle*, Paris, Plon, 1992, pp. 185–211.

68. All the names have been changed.

69. For ease of reading we will call them Dupont as well as his daughter even though they were not married.
70. Peter Novick, *L'Épuration française 1944–1949*, Paris, Balland, 1985, p. 123.
71. Abbé Roger More, *Totor chez les FTP ou la Résistance vécue*, Paris, 1947.
72. Report by the prefect of the Lot sent to the Minister of the Interior, Cahors, 27 June 1945. National Archives FLa 3334.
73. Security Branch report, 6 June 1945. National Archives, Fla 3334.
74. Vichy police Commissioner's report sent to the Criminal Investigation Department, 5 June 1945. National Archives, Fla 3334.
75. FFI paper *L'Embuscade*, Creuse, 30 September 1944.
76. 0.022 per cent: average calculated from the statistics of eighty-four departments by the Comité d'histoire de la Seconde Guerre mondiale in its study of the repression of collaboration at the Liberation. (Departments not included are: Hérault, Landes, Loire-Atlantique, Loiret, Lot-et-Garonne, Oise.) Statistics for Bretagne, Eure and Moselle have been brought up to date by more recent studies.

Chapter 7 Women as Scapegoats

1. During the first half of the twentieth century women constituted 36.6 per cent to 37.9 per cent of the active population in France. See Anne-Marie Sohn, 'Entre deux guerres', in Françoise Thébaud, *Histoire des femmes*, Vol. 5, *Le xxe siècle*, Paris, Plon, 1992, p. 95.
2. This relatively important figure can be explained by the number of primary school teachers, agricultural workers and shop keepers who were not excluded from this category on account of their modest income.
3. Saint Paul's Epistle to the Corinthians 11. There are also numerous passages in the Old Testament referring to the symbolic significance of hair. In particular we might think of those dealing with Samson in *Judges* and with Job in *Job*.
4. Tacitus, *Germanicus* XIX, translated by J. Perret, Paris, Les Belles Lettres, 1949, p. 82. Since the reign of Augustus, adultery committed in Rome was punished by public rejection and deportation to an island.
5. See Jean-Marie Carbasse, *Introduction au droit pénal*, Paris, PUF, 1990.
6. Anatole de Montagion and Gaston Raynaud, *Recueil général et complet des fabliaux des XIIe et XIVe siècles*, Paris, Librairie des

Bibliophiles, 6 volumes, 1872-1890; republished in facsimile repro-
duction Genève, Slatkine, 1973.

7. Jean-Marie Carbasse, '"Currant nudi". La répression de l'adultère
dans le Midi médiéval (XIIe-XVe siècle)', in Jacques Poumarède,
Jean-Pierre Royer (eds), *Droit, histoire et sexualité*, Paris, L'Espace
Juridique, 1987.

8. Jules Michelet, *Les Femmes de la Révolution française*, Paris,
Éditions Carrère, 1988. p. 73.

9. Carried out on the final taking of vows.

10. In ancient Greece young girls had their heads shaved before being
sacrificed.

11. Amin Maalouf quotes a *Chronique arabe des Croisades d'Ousama*,
of Ousama in which a frankish doctor proposed cutting off the hair
of a woman who was dying. He said: 'She has a devil in her head
who is in love with her. Cut off her hair!' Amin Maalouf, *Les
Croisades vues du côte des Arabes*, Paris, J'ai Lu, 1995.

12. Jean-Paul Sartre, 'Un Promeneur dans Paris insurgé', *Combat*, 2
September 1944.

13. Antoine Prost 'Frontières et espaces du privé' in Philippe Ariès and
Georges Duby (eds), *Histoire de la vie privée*, Paris, Seuil, Vol. 5,
1987, p. 94.

14. See Christine Bard, *Les Garçonnes*, Paris, Flammarion, 1998; Mary-
Louise Roberts, *Civilisation without Sexes. Reconstructing Gender
in Post-War France 1917–1927*, Chicago, University Press of
Chicago, 1994.

15. Quoted by Steven Zdatny, 'La mode à la garçonne, 1900–1925; une
histoire sociale des coupes de cheveaux', in *Le Mouvement social*,
No. 174, 1996, pp. 23–56.

16. *Quarante-quatre*, Agen, 21 August 1944.

17. Jean-Claude Loiseau, *Les Zazous*, Paris, Editions du Sagittaire, 1977.

18. *Le Maquis, organe officiel de la brigade Verneuil* (FFI), Yonne, 19
October 1944.

19. Philippe Perrot, *Le Travail des apparences. Le corps féminin,
XVIIIe–XIXe siècle*, Paris, Seuil, 1984, p. 203.

20. File of the Court of Justice, 1 June 1945. Departmental Archives
(Oise), 998 W 47196. This concerns a woman accused of having run
an illegal brothel frequented by Germans, and where there were
pictures of Hitler and Pétain.

21. *Le Renouveau*, 22 September 1944.

22. *L'Yonne libre*, Auxerre, 24 October 1944.

23. *L'Oise républicaine*, Beauvais, 10 January 1945.

24. Fabrice Virgili, *Tontes et tondues à travers la presse de la Libération*, DEA dissertation, Paris I-Sorbonne, 1992, p. 99.
25. *Nation*, Thiers, 30 August 1944; *Assaut*, Privas, 4 September 1944; Musée Résistance, Montauban, 20 August 1944; André Jeannet and Marie-Hélène Velu, *Le Saône-et-Loire dans la guerre 1930–1945*, Le Coteau, Horvath, 1984, Mâcon, 5 September 1944.
26. *L'Espoir*, Saint Étienne: 14 and 20 October 1944.
27. *Le Parisien Libéré*, 26 August 1944; *L'Humanité*, 27 August 1944: Paris, 25 August 1944.
28. Photo by Roger-Viollet in Alain Brossat's *Les Tondues. Un carnaval moche*, Levallois-Perret, Manya, 1992, (date and place unknown); *Défense de la France*, No. 11, 15 February 1942; police report, Ligny-le-Châtel, 16 February 1945, National Police Archives (Yonne); Documentation française, OFIC, Cherbourg, 14 July 1944; *Le Midi Libre*, Montpellier, 30 August 1944.
29. *Le Berry républicain*, 23 September 1944.
30. The band stand at Castelnaudary was also used. See Paul Tirand, *Castelnaudary: d'Auguste Fourès à Jean Mistler 1870–1945*, Castelnaudary, EPA, 1991, p. 221.
31. Pommerit-le-Vicomte, 31 August 1944. Departmental archives (Côtes-d'Armor), 2 W 97.
32. *L'Yonne libre*, Auxerre, 24 October 1944; *La Nation*, Clermont-Ferrand, 30 August 1944; 'Star and Stripes' translated in *La Gazette de Lausanne*, 3 October 1944.
33. *Le Tarn libre*, Albi, 29 August 1944; P.L. Petitjean, *Reims et la Champagne dans la tourmente de 1939–1945*, typed monograph, 1959, p. 81; *La Quatrième République*, Pau, 23 September 1944; H.J. Gros, *Août et septembre à Tonnay-Charente et Surgères*, Angoulême, EPA, 1985, pp. 76–8; *Lyon libre*, 21 September 1944.
34. Complaint lodged for indecent assault to the *épuration* committee, 5 December 1944. Departmental Archives (Oise), 34 W 8453.
35. CDL, *La Libération de Troyes*, 25, 26, 27 August 1944, Troyes, impr. Paton, 1944.
36. Data resulting from a regional inspection at Montpellier, 10 September 1944. Departmental Archives (Hérault), 137 W 14.
37. Report on the Resistance M. Gardelle produced in 1945 (Chief AS of the Ariège II network. Cdt. FFI at the Liberation). National Archives, 72 AJ 100.
38. *Le Gaullois, organe de la Résistance souriante*, No. 4, Lyon, 1944. 'Don't forget that with all her goings-on this so-called honest woman would be publicly spanked on the other side of the Rhine. So when

you're looking at her pick your spot and savour your pleasure in advance.'

39. Report by the general secretary of the Police, 4 November 1944. Departmental Archives (Hérault), 19 W 3.

40. Report by the leader in charge of the Police in the Indre, 20 October 1944. National Police Archives, 39 A 6.

41. General survey prepared by the regional commissioner for the Republic, (Toulouse), 31 December 1944. National Archives, F1a 4028.

42. Stéphane Audoin-Rouzeau, *La Guerre des enfants 1914–1918. Essai d'histoire culturelle*, Paris, Armand Colin, 1993, p. 33.

43. See Susan Brownmiller, *Le Viol*, Paris, Stock, 1976, p. 71.

44. General police report, 15 October and 15 November 1944. National Archives, 72 AJ 384.

45. Véronique Nahoum-Grappe, 'Guerre et différence des sexes: les viols systématiques (ex-Yugoslavie, 1991–1995)', in Christine Dauphin and Arlette Farge (eds), *De la violence et des femmes*, Paris, Albin Michel, 1997, pp. 159–84.

46. *Voies Nouvelles*, Périgueux, 8 September 1944.

47. *Ce Soir*, Paris, 25 August 1944.

48. *Le Tarn libre*, Albi, 29 August 1944.

49. *Libération*, R. Seguin and R. Legrand, 8 mm silent, black and white film lasting for 16 minutes, 1944, Vidéothèque of Paris; photo Lapi-Viollet 60 944, in Alain Brossat, *Les Tondues, op. cit., Sud-Ouest*, Toulouse, 29 August 1944; police report, Souppes-sur-Loing, 15 September 1944. National Police Archives, 31 C 5; individual files by commune of 22 May 1945. Departmental Archives (Moselle) 76 W 513; Henri-Jacques Gros, *Août et septembre à Tonnay-Charente et Surgères*, Angoulême, EPA, 1985, pp. 76–8.

50. *Le Travailleur de l'Oise, organe du PCF de l'Oise*, 7 October 1944.

51. *La Charente libre*, Angoulême, 15 September 1944.

52. *Libération d'Aunis et de la Saintonge*, Saintes, 20 September 1944.

53. Police report, Montlieu-la-Garde, 12 November 1944. National Police Archives, 100 H 3 (Charente-Inférieure).

54. *L'Echo de la Corrèze*, 18 September 1944.

55. *Combat*, 2 September 1944.

56. Register '2' of the Fontainebleau brigade, 19 October 1944. National Police Archives, 30 F 5 (Seine-et-Marne).

57. Police report, Coubert, 11 October 1944. National Police Archives, 29 D 1 (Seine-et-Marne).

58. Police report, Berlaimont, 31 October 1944. National Police Archives, 54 C 4 (Nord).
59. *Les Allobroges*, Grenoble, 14 September 1944.
60. *L'Eure libérée*, Évreux, 16 December 1944.
61. *Pages d'un carnet. Souvenirs d'un sous-préfet dans une ville du Berry*, National archives, 72 AJ 134.
62. Police report, Ferté-sous-Jouarre, 30 October 1944, National Police Archives, 30 A 4 (Seine-et-Marne).
63. Civil court hearing, 6 July 1945. Departmental Archives (Oise), 998 W 47224. The writing and crossings out in the original have been respected.
64. File of the *épuration* commission, 16 February 1945. Departmental Archives (Oise), 34 W 8467bis.
65. File of the *épuration* commission, 28 December 1944. Departmental Archives (Oise), 34 W 8466.
66. Police reports and inquiries dealing with individual persons arrested and accused of collaboration, National Archives, 72 AJ 108 (AVIII); *La Charente libre*, Angoulême, 21 December 1944.
67. While we are talking here about women and marriage the same situation can be discovered in professional conflicts involving men.
68. *Épuration* committee files, police report, 29 September 1944. Departmental Archives (Oise), 34 W 8472-2.
69. *Liberté du Pas-de-Calais*, 6 January 1945.
70. Christophe Lewin, *Le Retour des prisonniers français,* Paris, Universitaires de la Sorbonne Press, 1986.
71. Sarah Fishman, *Femmes de prisonniers de guerre 1940–1945*, Paris, L'Harmattan, 1996.
72. *Ibid.*, p. 209.
73. Police report Pontcharra, 4 October 1944. National Police Archives (Isère), 140 D 1. My italics.
74. Michèle Bordeaux, 'Sept ans de réflexion, divorce et ordre social (1940–1945)', in Jacques Poumarede and Jean-Pierre Royer, *Droit, histoire et sexualité*, Paris, L'Espace Juridique, 1987, pp. 229–47.
75. Report submitted to the Council responsible for inquiring into education during the Occupation. Hearing of 20 April 1945. National Archives, F17 16705.
76. Police report Lacroix-Saint-Ouen, 4 December 1944. National Police Archives (Oise), 69 D 3.
77. Police report Méru, 12 December 1944. National Police Archives (Oise), 68 A 6.

78. Decree [Côte: B Nr. IV 98/40] quoted by Rolf Hochhuth's *Un Amour en Allemagne*, Paris, Ramsay, 1983.

79. Report of the Security Services in Ebern, part of Main-Franconia, 14 March 1941, reproduced by Rolf Hochhuth, *op. cit.*

80. *Chroniques en images de la Deuxième Guerre mondiale*, Paris, Éditions du Griot, 1995, p. 274.

81. Report by the commissioner for the Republic, Nancy, 15 September 1945. National Archives, F1a 4025.

82. File from the Court of Justice, 19 January 1945. Departmental Archives (Oise), 998 W 47189.

83. *Le Midi libre*, Montpellier, 27 October 1944.

84. Reports and inquiries dealing with individual persons arrested and accused of collaboration, 27 August 1944, National Archives 72 AJ 108 (AVIII).

85. Police reports, Saint-Florentin, 25 May and 30 June 1945. National Police Archives (Yonne), 239 J 3.

86. Reported house arrest, date unknown. Departmental Archives (Charente).

87. Reports and inquiries dealing with individual persons arrested and accused of collaboration, 7 August 1944. National Archives, 72 AJ 108 (AVIII). The original typing has been retained.

88. Report of the Glanville FFI group's activities, 30 August 1944. National Archives, 72 AJ 105 – AII.3.

89. *Épuration* committee, 21 November 1944. Departmental Archives (Oise), 34 W 8453.

90. Police report, Condé-sur-l'Escaut, 21 September 1944. National Police Archives (Nord), 54 C 7.

91. Police report, Sens, 15 October 1944. National Police Archives (Yonne), 239 I 2.

92. File of the Court of Justice, 4 January 1945; file of the Civil Court, 21 February 1945. Departmental Archives (Oise), 998 w 47190 and 34 W 8467bis.

93. Register '2' of the Creutzwald brigade, 6 June 1945. National Police Archives (Moselle), 210 J 6.

94. Police report, Méru, 28 December 1944; *épuration* committee, 5 January 1945 and 3 February 1945. National Police Archives (Oise), 68 A 6; Departmental Archives (Oise), 34 W 8453 and 8470.

95. *Épuration* committee, 29 October 1944. Departmental Archives (Oise), 34 W 8468-2.

96. Prefect's office, 28 December 1944. Departmental Archives (Oise), 34 W 8466.

97. Annette Becker, Stéphane Audoin-Rouzeau, Françoise Thébaud have been unable to find the slightest mention of this form of punishment. Nor has Jean-Yves Le Naour who is currently working on sexist violence during the First World War.

98. 'Brigadier H.E. Hopthrow: First World War trench diary', quoted by Corran Laurens, 'La Femme au turban: les Femmes tondues', H. R. Kedward and Nancy Wood, *The Liberation of France: Image and Event,* Oxford, Berg Publishers Ltd, 1995, pp. 155–80.

99. Georges Simenon, *Pedigree,* 1947, re-edition of *Tout Simenon,* Vol.2, Paris, Presses de la Cité, pp. 883–4. First published in 1947 this novel was written by Simenon between the outbreak of war and 27 January 1943.

100. Francis Balace, 'Les Hoquets de la liberté', in *Jours de Guerre,* Vol.20, Bruxelles, 1995, p. 88.

101. *Ibid.*

102. Martin Conway, 'Justice in Post-War Belgium, Popular Passions and Political Realities', in *Cahiers d'Histoire du Temps Présent/ Bijdragen tot de Eigentijdse Geschiedenis,* No. 2, May 1997, Bruxelles, p. 14.

103. Among others, the collections of the Centre of Etudes et de Documentation (CEGES) at Bruxelles.

104. Claudia Koonz, *Les Mères-patrie du IIIe Reich. Les femmes et le nazisme,* Paris, Lieu commun, 1989, p. 396.

105. Gerd Krüger, 'Straffrei Selbstjustiz: Öffentliche Denunzierungen im Ruhrgebiet 1923–1926', in *Sowiit,* 27, 1998, H.2, pp. 119–25.

106. *Tag,* 27 April 1921, and *Volsfreund,* 11 May 1921, seen by Paul Tirard, *Le France sur le Rhin,* Paris, Plon, 1930, p. 306.

107. In order to reduce tension the French government withdrew all Senegalese troups in June 1921, and north Africans in 1925.

108. Ernest Fraenkel, *Military Occupation and the Rule of Law. Occupation Government in the Rhineland, 1918–1923.* Oxford University Press, 1944, p. 143; cited by Philippe Burrin, *La France à l'heure allemande,* Paris, Seuil, 1995, p. 212. The press refers to such incidents but not to *tontes* specifically. See for example, *L'Illustration,* 12 July 1930; *Le Temps,* July 1930.

109. Anette Warring, *Tyskerpiger – Under besaeltelse og retsopgoger,* Copenhagen, Vertrag beim IV., Nordiskehistorikermode, 1993.

110. Anna Bravo and Anna Maria Bruzzone, *In Guerra senza armi. Storie di donne 1940–1945,* Bari, Laterza, 1995.

111. Marco Dondi, 'Azioni di guerra e potere partigiano nel dopoliberazione', *Italia contemporanea,* No. 188, September 1992, p. 464.

112. Domenico Roy-Palmer, *Processo ai fascisti 1943–1948. Storia di un'epurazione che non c'è stata,* Milano, Rizzoli, 1996. Police reports sent by the prefect of Pisa (Perluzzo) to the Minister of Interior, 18 September 1945, note 33, p. 296.
113. Most of those I have been able to consult are in a special issue of *Gente,* published in March 1961. Captions and details of location have to be treated very cautiously.
114. In Italy, as in France, the image lives on. A woman has her head shaved in one of the last scenes of the film *Novecento.* The poster advertising the conference *Il Guidice, lo Storico, la Società, la Politica. I Processi del Dopoguerra. 1945–1950,* Turin, 1–2 March 1996, has two photographs on it. One of the Nuremberg trials, the other of a woman whose head has been shaved walking through the streets of Milan.
115. Jean-Yves Ruaux, *Vichy sur Manche. Les Îles anglo-normandes sous l'Occupation,* Editions Ouest France, 1994, p.135.
116. Madeleine Bunting, *The Model Occupation. The Channel Islands under German Rule, 1940-1945,* London, Harper & Collins, 1995, p. 235.
117. *Ibid.,* p.258 in Jean-Yves Ruaux, *Vichy sur Manche, op. cit.,* p. 137.
118. *Ce soir,* Paris, 24 August 1944.
119. Kjell Fjortoft, *Oppgjøret som ikke tok slutt.* Gyldendal Forlag, Oslo, 1997, p. 18, describes how a *tonte* took place at Tromso, 8 May 1945. The Norwegian paper *Sunnmøre Arbeideravis,* of 4 September 1945, describes how a woman from Loddefjord had her head shaved in an article entitled 'an amusing act carried out on German girls'. These two examples are quoted by Ebba D Drolshagen, *Nicht ungeschoren davonkommen,* Hamburg, Hoffmann and Campe Verlag, 1998, pp. 151 and 40.
120. Louis De Jong, *Het Koninkrijk der Nederlanden in de tweede Wereldoorlog,* Gravenhage, Martinus Nijhoff, 1980–1982, Vol. 10a, p. 822 (Maastricht), and Vol. 10b, pp. 1431–3 (Amsterdam).
121. Tassoula vervenioti, 'Women after the Resistance in Greece: Personal and Political Experiences', in Mark Mazower, *After the War was Over. Reconstructing the Family, Society,* and the Law in Southern Europe, 1944–1950, summaries of papers to be given at a conference in Brighton, 4-6 July 1996. Typed copy, ten pages.
122. Yannick Ripa, 'La tonte purificatrice des républicaines pendant la guerre civile espagnole', in Danièle Voldman and François Rouquet (eds), 'Identités féminines et violences politiques', *Cahiers de l'IHTP,* No. 31, October 1995, pp. 39–51.

123. *Ibid.* P.39.
124. To be absolutely complete we should add that there were strong rumours of peasant women having had their heads shaved in the Soviet Union before collectivization took place. Rumour had it that their hair would be saved as useful material being prepared for the first quinquennial plan. These rumours were rife in Bilorussia, eastern Siberia and the Urals, and in the provinces of Riazan and Saratov. There is no record of any *tonte* having taken place, however. Sources: N. Eudokimov, *Kolkhozy v klassovyx boïax (Agricultural Collectives and the Class Struggle)*, Moscow, 1930, pp. 27–9. A. Argarov, *Klassovaya bor'ba v derevne i sel'soviet (Class Struggle and Soviet Agricultural Policy)*, Moscow, 1929, pp. 41–5. English sources: R.W. Davies, *The Socialist Offensive. The Collectivization of Soviet Agriculture, 1929–1930*, London, Macmillan, 1980, p. 213. L. Viola, 'Baby Bunty and Peasant Women's Protest During Collectivisation', *Russian Review*, 45 (1), 1986, pp. 28–35.
125. Among the 500,000 Spanish refugees, 120,000 were still there in June 1940. See Denis Peschanski, 'La Résistance immigrée', in Jean-Marie Guillon and Pierre Laborie (eds), *Mémoire et Histoire: la Résistance*, Toulouse, Privat, 1995, p. 202.

Chapter 8 Virile France

1. Pierre Laborie, *L'Opinion française sous Vichy,* Paris, Seuil, 1990, p. 58.
2. Among many we should highlight: Pierre and Marthe Massenet, *Journal d'une longue nuit*, Paris, Fayard, 1971; Jean-Pierre Azéma, François Bédarida (eds), *La France des années noires*, two vols, Paris, Seuil, 1993; Henry Rousso, *Les Années noires. Vivre sous l'Occupation*, Paris, Gallimard, coll. 'Découverte', 1992; Olivier Valade, 'Années sombres . . . Années d'espoir . . . Saint-Martin-d'Hères, 1939–1945', *SMH Histoire-mémoire vive*, No. 1, May 1944.
3. Dominique Veillon, *Vivre et survivre en France, 1939–1947*, Paris Payot, 1995, p. 140.
4. I should like to thank Alain Brossat for having sent me this account which was written in 1944 by one of his readers.
5. Civil court, file No.155 presented by the Liberation committee, 25 May 1945. Departmental Archives, Hérault, 137 W 26.
6. Note from a general information file, 28 February 1945. Departmental Archives, Hérault, 137 W 26.

7. Testimony of the mayor of Marmande, Yves Grassot. National Archives, 72 AJ 158 (I No. 6).

8. Decree of 2 October 1944, *Journal Officiel*.

9. The first portable tape-recorder was only invented by Stéphane Kudelski in 1951.

10. Jehan Despert, 'Il y a 40 ans . . . Mon journal de la Libération de Versailles', in *Revue de l'Histoire de Versailles et des Yvelines*, quoted by Jean-Louis-Norbert Petit, *Et Versailles fut libéré!*, Paris, 1990, p. 217.

11. About 5,800 chapels and churches were destroyed. See Rémi Baudoin, 'La Reconstruction des églises', in *Reconstructions et modernisation. La France après les ruines 1918. . . 1945. . .* National Archives, 1991, p. 282.

12. Testimony of one of the Liberation committee members, police report, Liancourt, 4 February 1945. Departmental Archives, Oise, 998 W 47199.

13. Register '2' of the Creutzwald brigade, 6 June 1945. National Police archives, 210 J6 (Moselle).

14. Imperial War Museum, EA 2976 2. Original caption: 'French women who have collaborated and who have not conducted themselves correctly towards the enemy, according to the code drawn up by the Resistance groups in France, are taken through the streets of Cherbourg on 14 July after their heads have been shaved. Above the lorry it is also possible to read: "The collaborators' cart".'

15. Court of justice, 9 August 1945. Departmental Archives, Oise, 998 W 47203.

16. Report from police headquarters in Knutange, 5 June 1945. Departmental Archives, Moselle, 76 W 496; report, Rochefort, 20 December 1944. Police report, National Police Archives, 100 K3 (Charente-Inférieure); testimony of Claude Jaillet, in René-Charles Plancke, *La Seine-et-Marne 1939–1945*, Vol.4, Le Mée-sur-Seine, Edition Amatteis, 1985, pp. 138–42.

17. H. R. Kedward, 'Introduction: "Ici commence la France libre"', in H. R. Kedward, Nancy Wood, *The Liberation of France. Image and Event*, Oxford, Berg Publishers, 1995, pp. 1–11.

18. Maurice Agulhon, 'La mairie. Liberté, égalité, fraternité', in Pierre Nora (ed.), *Les Lieux de mémoire. La République*, Vol. 1, Paris, Gallimard, 1984, pp. 167–93.

19. Police report, Compiègne, 2 January 1945. Departmental Archives, Oise, 34 W 8467bis.

20. Police report, Pont-sur-Yonne, 10 and 27 September, National Police Archives, 239 H 2 (Yonne).
21. E. Dubois, *Vu pendant la Libération de Paris*, Lausanne, Payot, 1944.
22. *Ce soir*, Paris, 1 September 1944.
23. 322 out of the 624 analysed. In others either places are not mentioned or the *tontes* were carried out behind closed doors and there were no processions.
24. *Les Allobroges*, 25 August and 5 September 1944.
25. Testimony of Mme Yvette Groc, Musée de la Résistance.
26. We are talking of Aumetz and Richemont in the Moselle, Villerupt in Meurthe-et-Moselle, Cherves-de-Cognac in Charente and Craon in Mayenne. For the last of these there is mention only of women being hit, a procession, a rope put around their necks and photographs.
27. Report made by the prefect of the Aveyron to the CCr at Montpellier, 15 June 1945; police report, 20 June 1945. Departmental Archives, Hérault, 137 W 35 and 137 W 27.
28. Chief of police at Hagondange, 30 May 1945. Departmental Archives, Moselle, 77 W 298.
29. Jean-Marie Carbasse, *Introduction historique au droit pénal*, Paris, PUF, 1990, p. 231.
30. P. Demongeot and A. Dulaurens, *Les Hommes de l'ombre*, Autun, Pélux, 1986.
31. René-Charles Pancke, *La Seine-et-Marne 1939–1945*, Vol. 4, Le Mée-sur-Seine, Éditions Amatteis, 1985.
32. *L'Echo de la Corrèze*, Tulle, 14 September 1944. In this cattle-rearing region, once a year in the third week of Lent, bulls decked out with ribbons, escorted by butchers and followed by a crowd cross the town to the slaughter house.
33. *Voies nouvelles*, Périgueux, 8 September 1944. To be made to ride on a donkey is one of the recurrent forms of punishment for adultery. See Pauline Schmitt-Pantel 'L'Âne, l'adultère et la cité', in Jacques Le Goff and Jean-Claude Schmitt (eds), *Le Charivari*, La Haye-Paris, Mouton-EHESS, 1981, pp. 117–22.
34. Alain Brossat, *Les Tondues. Un carnaval moche*, Levallois-Perret, Manya, 1992, p. 258.
35. Jacques Le Goff, Jean-Claude Schmitt (eds), *Le Charivari, op.cit.*: Henri Rey-Flaud, *Le Charivari. Les rituels fondamentaux de la sexualité*, Paris, Payot, 1985.
36. I am borrowing an idea developed by Véronique Nahoum-Grappe concerning rape in ex-Yugoslavia where, because of 'old Balkan

practices', the atrocities of the conflict have not been understood and seen in their full horror. Véronique Nahoum-Grappe, 'Guerre et différence des sexes: les viols systématiques (ex-Yougoslavie, 1991– 1995)', in Cécile Dauphin and Arlette Farge, *De la violence et des femmes*, Paris, Albin Michel, 1997, pp. 159–84.

37. Luc Capdevila, *L'Imaginaire social de la Libération en Bretagne, op. cit.,* p. 651.
38. *Valmy*, 11 September 1944.
39. Laurent Gervereau, 'La thématique vichyste', in Laurent Gervereau and Denis Peschanski (eds), *La Propagande sous Vichy, 1940–1944*, Paris, La Découverte, 1990, p. 144.
40. Headmasters' report drawn up at the request of the education authorities of Seine. National Archives, 72 AJ 62 C.IV.
41. Police archives, 54 C 7 (Nord), report from Condé-sur-l'Escaut, 21 September 1944.
42. See above Chapter VI for further discussion of this incident.
43. Report issued by the commissioner for the Republic, 31 May 1945. National Archives, Fla 4028. My italics.
44. Police report, Agnetz, 20 January 1945. Departmental Archives, Oise, 34 W 8466.
45. Files on individual persons by commune. Police report, Basse-Yutz, 2 June 1945. Departmental Archives, Moselle, 76 W 473.
46. Recalled by M. Siot, general secretary of the town hall at Nantes. National Archives, 72 AJ 148.
47. Danielle Tartakowsky, 'La Province sans Paris ou la Province contre Paris?' in Pierre Favre (ed.), *La Manifestation*, Paris, PFNSP, 1990, pp. 156–77.
48. Luc Capdevila, *L'Imaginaire social de la Libération en Bretagne, op. cit.,* pp. 626–46.
49. Pierre Laborie, *L'Opinion française sous Vichy, op. cit.,* p. 57.
50. Nor is it specific to the enemy. Rather it is a recurring theme in international relations. See Robert Frank and Maryvonne Le Puloch (eds), 'Images et imaginaire dans les relations internationales depuis 1938', *Les Cahiers de l'IHTP*, No.28, June 1994, and in particular the article by Franck Costigliola 'L'Image de la France aux États-Unis' in which he demonstrated how, in the period 1940–58 in the United States, the image of France is feminized. For the First World War we can refer, among others, to François Thébaud, 'La Grande Guerre', in Françoise Thébaud (ed), *Histoire des femmes en Occident. Le XXe siècle*, Vol. 5, Paris, Plon, 1992; Stéphane Audoin-Rouzeau, *L'Enfant de l'ennemi: 1914–1918, op. cit.*

51. Quoted by Laurent Douzou, 'La Résistance, une affaire d'hommes?' in François Rouquet and Danièle Voldman (eds), 'Identités féminines et violences politiques', *Cahiers de l'IHTP*, No. 31, October 1995, pp. 19–20.
52. Significant from this point of view are two famous songs from 1939. 'Excellents Français, excellents soldats' who 'désirent tous désormais qu'on nous foute une bonne fois la paix' sung by Maurice Chevalier. And in 'Petits poilus joyeux' sung by Ray Ventura, it is not a flag but washing that they are going to hang on enemy soil: 'On ira pendre notre linge sur la ligne Siegfried'. The contrast between an activity associated with women and its being attributed to one of Germany's warrior heroes is also extremely pointed.
53. Michael Kelly, 'The Reconstruction of Masculinity at the Liberation', in H. R. Kedward, Nancy Wood, *The Liberation of France. Image and Event, op. cit.,* pp. 117–28.
54. Jean-Pierre Azéma, 'Le choc armé et les débandades', in Jean-Pierre Azéma, François Bédarida, (eds), *La France des années noires,* Vol.1, Paris, Seuil, 1993, p. 97.
55. Francine Muel-Dreyfus, *Vichy et l'éternel féminin*, Paris, Seuil, 1996.
56. Voir Nathalie Dompnier, 'Entre *La Marseillaise et Maréchal nous voilà!,* quel hymne pour le régime de Vichy?', Colloque *La Vie musicale en France pendant la Seconde Guerre mondiale*, 28–29–30 January 1999, Paris.
57. Laurent Gervereau, Denis Peschanski (eds), *La Propagande sous Vichy, 1940–1944, op. cit.,* p. 123.
58. Jean-Paul Sartre, *Situation III*, Paris, Gallimard, 1947, p. 57.
59. Quoted by Jacques Isorni, *Mémoires 1911–1945*, Paris, Robert Laffont, 1984.
60. Pierre Laborie, *Violences et pouvoirs politiques, op. cit.,* p. 214.
61. Tract issued by the Front national, Loire-Inférieure. Date unknown. National Archives, 72 AJ 147.
62. Pierre Laborie uses this expression.
63. Quoted by Laurent Douzou, 'La Résistance, une affaire d'hommes?', *op. cit.,* p. 23.
64. Charles de Gaulle, *Discours et messages. Pendant la guerre, 1940–1946*, Paris, Livre de Poche, 1970, p. 718, quoted by Luc Capdevila, 'Le Mythe du guerrier et la construction sociale d'un "éternel masculin" après la guerre', *Revue française de Psychanalyse*, February 1998, p. 607.
65. Luc Capdevila, 'Le Mythe du guerrier et la construction sociale d'un "éternel masculin" après la guerre', *op. cit.,* p. 614.

66. Declaration made on 10 October 1944 to the *épuration* committee investigating education. National Archives, F17 16734. 'FRANÇAIS' appears in capital letters in the original text.
67. *La IVe République*, Dax, 30 August 1944.
68. Police report, Méru, 10 October 1944. National Police Archives, 68 A 6 (Oise).
69. *Le Patriote de l'Oise*, 30 September and 7 October 1944.
70. *Le Patriote de l'Eure*, 28 July 1945.
71. In Paul Éluard, *Au rendez-vous allemand*, Paris, Éditions de Minuit, 1944. Translation by John Flower.
72. Gabrielle Russier, a philosophy teacher, had an affair with one of her pupils. She was condemned for the corruption of a minor and committed suicide in the summer of 1969. See Corinne Bouchoux, 'L'affaire Gabrielle Russier', *Vingtième Siècle, * No. 33, January–March 1992, pp. 56–64.
73. Jean-Lous Cremieux-Brilhac, *Les Voix de la liberté. Ici Londres (1940–1944), * Paris, La Documentation Française, 1976.
74. *Département*, publication of the CDL in the Indre, 25 August 1944.
75. Paula Schwartz, 'Résistance et différence des sexes: bilan et perspectives', in Françoise Thébaud (ed.), *Clio, Histoire, Femmes et Sociétés*, No. 1, 1995, p. 74.
76. François Rouquet, 'Dans la France du Maréchal', in Christine Fauré (ed.), *Encyclopédie politique et historique des femmes*, Paris, PUF, 1995, p. 676.
77. *Femmes française*, No. 1, January 1944. The first issue of the underground paper of the UFF gives an outstanding example of the protective role attributed to women in an article entitled: 'Mères Françaises défendez vos fils contre les femelles de la Gestapo'.
78. Paula Schwartz, 'Résistance et différence des sexes: bilan et perspectives', *op. cit.*, p. 81.
79. *La Liberté du Pas-de-Calais*, 8 December 1944.
80. 'La Répression des faits de collaboration', in *Notes, Documentaires et Études*, No. 245, série française, LXXX, 26 February 1946.
81. Court of Appeal report, Besançon, 8 January 1945, National Archives, BB[18] 7133.
82. Letter from the prefect of the Vosges to the Minister of Justice, Vosges, 9 March 1945. National Archives, BB[18] 7133.
83. This is not to take account of the amnesty bills voted after the war. The first of these (16 August 1947) concerns minors; the second those inhabitants of Alsace and the Moselle deprived of citizenship. On 5 January 1951 loss of national citizenship was reduced to loss

of civic rights. Finally on 6 August 1953 crimes of collaboration were amnestied. The only exclusions were rape, murder, denunciations, the responsibility by actions or words for the death, deportation or torture of others, cooperation with the armed forces or spying on behalf of the enemy. See Herbert Lottman, *L'Épuration, 1943–1953,* Paris, Fayard, 1986, pp. 523–35.

Appendix: A Paucity of Sources?

In principle, evidence for the practice of *tontes* is not to be found in archives. Not only is it not listed anywhere, but historians and archivists often remain firmly convinced that it did not exist. Allusions are made to it only in passing – in articles describing the liberation of some town or other, in a paragraph in a prefect's report describing how local citizens reacted, buried in testimonies gathered by the police about a woman's behaviour during the Occupation, or in a note in a file dealing with the *épuration*. Because such references are always unexpected a problem is created that cannot be avoided and means that there has to be recourse to documents of all kinds.

In some cases there is little evidence of the practice and since people gave up looking for it at an early stage there was a risk that important references to it would be missed. In Metz, for example, evidence is hard to come by. There are no references to the *tonte* in the local press any more than there are in reports drawn up by the prefect and commissioner for the Republic or in the CHOLF documents in the National Archives. Nor are there any in the many bundles of papers consulted in the Departmental Archives. Various works on the region (including a thesis and an inquiry into the repression of traces of collaboration) and the municipal archives are equally silent. What conclusion should we draw? Was it because Metz, a town of 70,000 people, was first annexed and then experienced a long and violent struggle for liberation from mid September until 22 November 1944? This I would have believed until with the answer to a letter I had written to a local history association, I was sent a photograph, taken by the American army services, of a woman having her head shaved on a platform in the Place St Jean. This showed that the fact that it was not mentioned did not mean that this violent practice had not taken place any more than finding a single reference to it meant that they had all been discovered. In each case difficulties like this meant that it was necessary to consult sources of all kinds, which, even if they were of unequal value complemented each other. Some were contemporary, others from a later period; some first hand, others not. Even though others working on this period may have used them, when read closely, the regional press and reports by prefects and commissioners showed how widespread the practice was.

As a result of reading 233 newspapers which appeared after the Liberation as well as around 60 underground publications I discovered 242 references to the *tonte* in 67 departments. But the interest afforded by the post-Liberation press was more than one of quantity. We should not forget that after several years of censorship there was a resurgence of newspapers (some with two sides only), in the main celebrating freedom but containing as well the declarations and decisions made and taken by the departmental committees coordinating the Liberation, and accounts of *tontes*. As such they are an important source.

Often the clearest indication that the Republic had been re-established was the installation of the prefect or commissioner. However difficult their tasks were the wheels of the local administration began to turn again. Although only fifteen reports by prefects or Republican commissioners held in the National Archives make any reference to the *tonte* they are an invaluable source of information. By their very nature they draw many different sources together. They weigh up and sift information, allowing us to see it as the new authorities did. The fact that prefects' reports make little mention of the *tonte* suggests that it was neither important or noteworthy. At the time of the Liberation it seems to have been an almost normal event. The prefect for the department of the Aude, writing about Troyes on 11 September 1944 observes: 'The Liberation was welcomed with enthusiasm. The working-class population of the town behaved impeccably. Few houses were pillaged and only a handful of women were paraded naked and with their heads shaved. People listened peaceably to the advice and instructions of the authorities.' But if the *tonte* seemed to have little significance in the summer of 1944 by the spring of the following year things had changed. There are more, often repeated, references to the practice as well as worried suggestions that the situation was becoming uncertain and disturbed. Between 28 May and 10 August the prefect for the Jura, for example, noted repeated references, twice pointing out cases of women whose heads had been shaved at Dole, Lons-le-Saunier, Salins, Arbois and Champagnole.

Although they have been hitherto ignored, press accounts of arrests and of trials, and the repeated link made between the 'attitude of local people' and the *épuration*, taken together make the files drawn up on people investigated at the Liberation an indispensable body dealing not only with general cases but individual ones as well. These files in the main were compiled by the *épuration* committees or by the courts of justice. Many of them allow us to get as close as possible not only to the victims but to those who carried out the *tontes* and those who witnessed them as well. They draw together statements, interrogations and testimonies. They provide material for quantitative, statistical analyses based on the registers of the people who were interned (age, addresses, professions, dates of arrest and so on) as well as for qualitative ones as the number of testimonies increased. Such varied accounts enable us to study the reactions of individuals as well as the effect the *tontes* had on the local population as a whole. Written soon after the events had taken place they convey a sense of actuality.

Yet like all other sources they present certain problems. The first concerns the lack of definition of 'group'. If the *épuration* committees could, in principle, compile a list of all persons suspected of collaboration whether or not they had been brought before the courts, the provisional and temporary nature of the committees' role legislated against such lists being exhaustive. Nor was it any better later. The more finely tuned the process became the smaller the number of people investigated. This was so especially in the case of some women who might have had their head shaved but who were not prosecuted. Only some of them found themselves in court. The second problem relates to the testimonies themselves and their transcription. Between people being questioned and their interrogators there were often complex relationships reflecting the local situation, whose implications remain unknown. Those charged with the task of interrogation – members of the police forces, the FFI or the *épuration* committees – cannot be considered interchangeable. They are part of a community with which they have already established all kinds of links. How could a policeman whose conduct during the Occupation had not been blameless react when confronted by the president of the local liberation committee? A large number of statements in files compiled during the *épuration* refer to matters of which the reader is necessarily ignorant. How documents were written up also presents a problem. If the questions asked do not appear in the transcript we cannot judge how spontaneous the testimony was. Is the final version we have a compromise? What value does such a transcription have when we know that it was written several hours after the interrogation took place and when a superior officer made corrections in red pencil thereby reminding us that style mattered as well. The mention of 'read and agreed', necessary for any statement to be valid, sheds no light on the conditions under which it was made.

Nonetheless the files compiled provide a sufficiently coherent body of material for us to be able to study the practice of the *tonte* at this time. Those on women whose heads were shaved together with others on women who escaped punishment and on men as well allow us to make a comparison with everybody accused of collaboration. Testimonies are a direct account of the period of the Occupation and have a directness lacking in mere descriptions. Finally, the fact that there are files on women whose heads had already been shaved show that the subject as a whole can only be approached in the context of the *épuration* as a whole.

The number of police reports in the files is particularly valuable. I was allowed to investigate this little-known source of information in fifteen different departments. During the 1940s the national police force was split into four different territorial sections. How they related to one another can be seen from records and letters; R4 indicated matters relating to the force itself; R2 to others. Such was the disorganization that there was real confusion between the two. If some brigades joined the *maquis*, others were thoroughly investigated at the *épuration*. Many ceased activity altogether during the weeks or days immediately prior to the Liberation. In this case records have, in general, been better preserved. But it is the reports that provide the most valuable information and are to be found in the files on the *épuration* in the departmental archives where they allow us to follow a specific line of inquiry. Since they have been classified chronologically and according to brigade, the facts they contain feature alongside those dealing with other aspects of village life – a broken fence, a theft of coal, a suspected abortion or an accident caused by a horse-drawn vehicle. Unfortunately conservation has been irregular. This may be due to the failure of some brigades to keep records but also to the fact that many documents relating to the Occupation and Liberation were destroyed in the early 1950s – a fact proved by the discovery of a bundle of papers with a note saying 'to be destroyed'. Among the fifteen departments for which permission to consult was granted, seven (italicised in the footnote)[1] proved to contain a rich source of material. Unfortunately two requests were refused.

Taken together the sources I consulted allowed me to trace the practice of the *tonte* in 87 departments. If there was no mention of it how was that to be interpreted? When I looked for an explanation and consulted a number of local histories I discovered new cases and gradually pieced together a map for the whole of France.

In order to understand the period and subject better work carried out by other researchers obviously has to be consulted. Unfortunately many accounts written and published since the Liberation lack the kind of

1. Ardèche, Bouches-du-Rhône, *Charente-Inférieure*, Drôme, *Haute-Garonne*, Indre, *Isère*, Loire, *Moselle*, Nord, *Oise*, Pyrénées-Orientales, Rhône, *Seine-et-Marne*, *Yonne*.

rigour that allows them to be consulted without fear of being misinformed. Rarely are sources given and the distinction between genuine testimony and a reconstructed account is difficult to establish. At the same time despite their limitations they keep the memory of the *tontes* alive when elsewhere there seems to be no trace of them.

Sources

Archives nationales

Dossiers départementaux du Comité d'histoire de la Seconde Guerre mondiale. 72 AJ 90 à 209 : Ain à Territoire-de-Belfort.
Cartons divers du Comité d'histoire de la Seconde Guerre mondiale. 72 AJ 6 : Loiret, correspondance du CDL (CHOLF). 72 AJ 56 : papiers divers sur la Libération de la Haute-Loire. 72 AJ 61 : témoignages sur la Libération de Paris. 72 AJ 82 : direction générale des services spéciaux. 72 AJ 248 : direction générale des services spéciaux, bulletins juin-août 1944. 72 AJ 383 : Libération de la France. 72 AJ 384 : synthèse de la Gendarmerie nationale, 15 septembre 1944–décembre 1946. 72 AJ 521 : papiers Henri Ingrand (commissaire de la République à Clermont-Ferrand) comprenant des papiers divers et de la correspondance à propos des incidents de Cusset. 72 AJ 523 : papiers Henri Ingrand comprenant des rapports de quinzaine. 72 AJ 524 : papiers Henri Ingrand concernant l'épuration. 72 AJ 621 : souvenirs du préfet de la Creuse. 72 AJ 700 : papiers divers du CH2GM. Non coté : fichier chronologique du CH2GM, février 1940–juillet 1947.
Ministère de l'intérieur, objets généraux : sous-série F^{1a}.
Répression de la collaboration avec l'ennemi et des activités anti-nationales. F^{1a} 3299 VII-A, 4, Alsace-Lorraine, rapports de la préfecture de la Moselle. F^{1a} 3300 VII-J : Alsace-Lorraine, répression de la collaboration. F^{1a} 3334 XII-D, 7 : épuration : exécutions sommaires. F^{1a} 3338 XII-E, 1 : camps d'internement XII-E, 1. F^{1a} 3813 : Corse : commission d'épuration.
Service central des commissariats de la République. F^{1a} 4020 à 4028 : rapports mensuels des commissaires régionaux de la République.
Ministère de l'intérieur, esprit public : rapports des préfets. F^{1c} III 1205 à 1233 : Ain à Yonne.
Police générale, série F7. F7 14969 : direction des centres de séjour surveillés, Ain à Tarn-et-Garonne. F7 14970 : direction des centres de séjour surveillés, Var à Yonne.

Ministère de la justice, série BB18. BB18 3618 : exécutions sans juge-
ment après la libération. BB18 7133 : dossiers de personnes soup-
çonnées de collaboration.

Archives de la Gendarmerie nationale

Ardèche. Registre 4 de la compagnie de l'Ardèche. Registres des
sections : Largentière, Privas. Registres des brigades : Le Pouzin,
Privas, Tournon.
Bouches-du-Rhône. Registre 4 de la compagnie des Bouches-du-Rhône.
Registres 4 des sections : Arles, Aubagne, Marseille, Salon-de-
Provence. Registres des brigades : Aix-en-Provence, Marseille-
Blancarde, Marseille-Endoume, Marseille-Mazargues, Marseille-Prado,
Marseille-Valentine.
Charente-Inférieure. Registre 4 de la section Saint-Jean-d'Angely.
Registres des brigades : Château-d'Oléron, Surgères. Procès-verbaux
des brigades : Archiac, Montendre, Montlieu-la-Garde, Rochefort-sur-
Mer.
Drôme. Registre 4 de la compagnie de la Drôme. Registre 4 de la section
de Roman. Procès-verbaux des brigades : Die, Montélimar, Tain-
l'Hermitage.
Haute-Garonne. Registre 2 de la compagnie de Haute-Garonne. Registres
des sections : Muret, Toulouse. Registres des brigades : Aurignac,
Blagnac, Boulogne-sur-Gesse, Cadours, Carbonne, Fenouillet, Luchon,
Montesquieu-Volvestre, Le Plan, Revel, Rieumes, Saint-Béat, Saint-
Félix-Lauragais, Saint-Lys, Toulouse-Saint-Michel, Villefranche-de-
Lauragais. Procès-verbaux des brigades : Bagnères-de-Luchon,
L'Isle-en-Dodon, Saint-Béat, Saint-Martory.
Indre. Registre 2 de la compagnie de l'Indre. Registres de la section de
Châteauroux. Registres des brigades : Blanc, Écueillé, Issoudun.
Procès-verbaux de la brigade de Châteauroux.
Isère. Registre 2 de la compagnie de l'Isère. Registre 2 de la section de
Grenoble. Procès-verbaux des brigades : Clelles, Goncelin, Grenoble,
Moirans, Valbonnais, Vif, Villard-de-Lans, Villard-Bonnot, Vinay,
Virieu, Voiron, Voreppe.
Loire. Registres de la compagnie de la Loire. Registres de la section de
Saint-Étienne. Registres des brigades : Montrond-les-Bains, Roanne,
Saint-Étienne.
Moselle. Registre 4 de la compagnie de la Moselle. Registre 2 de la
section de Thionville. Registre des brigades : Ars-sur-Moselle, Boulay-

Moselle, Château-Salins, Courcelles-Chaussy, Creutzwald, Dieuze, Faulquemont, Hagondange, Hayange, Hettange-Grande, Metzervisse, Phalsbourg, Rémilly, Rombas, Vic-sur-Seille.
Nord. Registres 2 et 4 de la compagnie du Nord. Procès-verbaux des brigades : Berlaimont, Condé-sur-l'Escaut.
Oise. Registre 4 de la compagnie de l'Oise. Registre 4 de la section de Compiègne. Registre 2 de la brigade de Chantilly. Procès-verbaux des brigades : Betz, Choisy-au-Bac, Compiègne, Crèvecœur, Froissy, Lacroix-Saint-Ouen, Liancourt, Margny-lès-Compiègne, Méru, Montataire, Mouy, Neuilly-en-Thelle, Noyon, Saint-Just-en-Chaussée.
Pyrénées-Orientales. Registres 2 et 4 de la compagnie des Pyrénées-Orientales. Registre 2 de la brigade de Perpignan.
Rhône. Registre 2 de la compagnie du Rhône.
Seine-et-Marne. Registre 2 de la compagnie de Seine-et-Marne. Registre des brigades : Fontainebleau, Meaux, Melun, Mormant. Procès-verbaux des brigades : Bray-sur-Seine, Château-Landon, Coubert, Ferté-sous-Jouarre, Lorrez-le-Bocage, Montereau, Nemours, Provins, Souppes-sur-Loing, Tournan-en-Brie, Villiers-Saint-Georges.
Yonne. Registre 4 de la compagnie de l'Yonne. Procès-verbaux des brigades : Avallon, Bléneau, Chablis, Charny, Cruzy-le-Châtel, Guillon, Ligny-le-Châtel, Migennes, Pont-sur-Yonne, Saint-Fargeau, Saint-Florentin, Sens.

Archives départementales de l'Hérault

Commissariat régional de la République. 136 W 5 : Libération, rapports, tracts. 136 W 6 : Libération, incidents, exécutions sommaires. 136 W 7 : rapports bimensuels, 15 novembre 1944–30 septembre 1945. 137 W 3 : rapports sur l'épuration dans les départements de l'Aude, la Lozère, le Gard et l'Aveyron. 137 W 4 et 5 : rapports de police et des Renseignements généraux, janvier–octobre 1945. 137 W 6 : rapports mensuels du secrétaire général de la Police, décembre 1944–juillet 1945. 137 W 25 à 28 : rapports journaliers des Renseignements généraux, septembre 1944–septembre 1945. 137 W 35 : rapports mensuels du préfet de l'Aveyron, octobre 1944–juillet 1945.
Comités départementaux de la Libération. 136 W 9 : CDL du Gard : procès-verbaux des délibérations, 26 août 1944–décembre 1945. 138 W 8 : CDL de l'Hérault, enquêtes sur les personnes coupables d'Indignité nationale. 138 W 17 : CDL de l'Hérault procès-verbaux

des séances, août–décembre 1944. 138 W 18-19-20 : CDL de l'Hérault procès-verbaux des séances, 1945.

Versements sans bordereaux. 19 W 2 : CRR, cour de justice et cour martiale, affaires diverses, 1944–1946. 19 W 3 : CRR, liste des arrestations. 19 W 4 à 9 : CRR, dossiers d'internements pour collaboration : Aude, Aveyron, Gard, Lozère, Pyrénées-Orientales. 19 W 11 : cabinet du préfet, rapports et instructions sur les camps et prisons.

Préfecture de l'Hérault. 161 W 32 : rapports de police journaliers, septembre–décembre 1945. 161 W 33 : enquêtes administratives demande d'emploi. 161 W 66 : rapports de police quotidien mai–juin 1945. 161 W 68 : rapports de police et de gendarmerie, mars–mai 1945. 161 W 73 : rapports de police et de gendarmerie, juin–août 1945. 161 W 92 : rapports de police 25 août 1944–février 1945. 161 W 94 : affaires de police septembre 1944–mai 1945. 161 W 95 : affaires traitées et spéciales de police novembre 1944–avril 1945. 161 W 96 : affaires de police diverses, mai–juillet 1945. 161 W 97 : télégrammes, 1er trimestre 1944. 356 W 55 à 63 : rapports mensuels d'information, synthèses, 1944–1948. 356 W 115 : police, notes de renseignements, janvier–août 1944. 356 W 121 : accidents, explosifs, faits divers, mai 1943–avril 1944. 356 W 130 à 137 : rapports mensuels, août 1944–avril 1946. 356 W 171 : CDL, procès-verbaux de séances rapports annuels, 1944–1945. 356 W 180 : internements administratifs, dossiers individuels.

Sous-préfecture de Béziers. 506 W 316 : libération des internés administratifs. 506 W 317 : Comité local de la Libération. 506 W 318 à 325 : dossiers du comité d'épuration.

Juridiction d'exception, cour martiale. 2 U 53/64 et 65 : cour martiale de Montpellier, 30 août, 4 et 6, 9, 11 et 13 septembre 1944.

Cour de justice. 2 U 53/292 : cour de justice de Montpellier : répertoire alphabétique. 2 U 53/70 à 73 : cour de justice de Montpellier : registre des arrêtés.

Archives départementales de l'Indre

Cabinet du préfet.

Internement administratif. 1279 W 1 : préfet : internements administratifs. 1279 W 2 à 30 : dossiers individuels.

Épuration administrative. 1279 W 31 à 39 : épuration administrative. 1279 W 47 à 50 : internements administratifs. 1279 W 51 et 52 :

rapports mensuels, octobre 1944 – janvier 1946. 1280 W 15 à 17 : internements administratifs.

Fonds du correspondant départemental du cholf. 1281 W 2 : documents du CDL. 1281 W 3 : archives de M. Sadron, correspondant du comité. 1281 W 4 : enquête auprès des communes sur la Libération. 1281 W 6 : Valençay, Saint-Gilles : événements 1944. 1281 W 7 : CLL de Buzançais. 1281 W 8 : CLL de Saint-Maur.

Sous-préfecture du Blanc. 2 Z 2662 à 2664 : événements 1940–1944. 2 Z 2666 : commission d'épuration.

Sous-préfecture de La Châtre. 3 Z 25 : épuration.

Sous-préfecture d'Issoudun. 1 Z 102 : rapports mensuels. Comité départemental de la Libération. 782 W 309 : CDL : charbon, prisonniers, logement. Cour de justice et chambre civique. 999 W 1 à 4 : dossiers de non-lieu. 999 W 12 à 16 : dossiers de non-lieu.

Archives départementales de l'Isère

Cabinet du préfet. 13 R 1000 : commissariat régional de la République. Correspondance et instructions aux cours de justice. 13 R 1009 : commissariat régional de la République. Correspondance, arrêtés, proclamations.

Comité départemental de la Libération. 13 R 1014 : Comité départemental de la Libération. Comptes rendus des séances, janvier–septembre 1944.

Divers. 13 R 1050 : pièces intéressant la Résistance. Affiches, tracts, journaux. 14 R 209 : Fort Barraux, instructions d'internements, 1944–1945. 26 Fi 1-36 : photographies ' Libération de Grenoble '.

Archives départementales de la Moselle

Cabinet du préfet. 151 W 202 à 344 bis (épuration administrative) : dossiers individuels. 151 W 345 à 446 (épuration administrative) : dossiers individuels des instituteurs. 151 W 350 (épuration administrative) : dossiers individuels des agents des PTT. 151 W 365-1 et 2 (Centre de séjour surveillé de Queuleu) : feuilles de mouvement, 21 janvier–30 septembre 1945. 151 W 365 à 372 (épuration administrative) : Camp de Queuleu.

Comité départemental de la Libération. 24 W 1 et 2 (CDL) : procès-verbaux, correspondance, motions, composition. 24 W 10 à 16 : procès-verbaux, correspondance avec les comités locaux de Libération, arrondissement de Metz-campagne. 24 W 17 à 26 : enquêtes sur les personnes. 24 W 27 à 28 : papiers divers, comptabilité. 24 W 29 à 32 : délivrance d'attestations de bonne attitude. 24 W 3 et 4 (épuration) : instructions, motions, correspondance. 24 W 33 à 36 : papiers divers. 24 W 37 à 39 : registre de correspondance, papiers divers ; procès-verbaux de CDL, 1944–1956. 24 W 40 : dossiers des membres des formations nazies. 24 W 5 et 6 : dossiers des détenus de Queuleu, interrogatoires. 24 W 7 à 9 (épuration) : dossiers individuels.

Sous-préfecture de Boulay-Moselle. 73 W 75 à 83 (sous-préfet de Boulay-Moselle) : épuration. 73 W 84 à 99 : épuration, dossiers par communes.

Sous-préfecture de Thionville. 76 W 463 à 522 : épuration, dossiers individuels par commune.

Sous-préfecture de Metz-campagne. 77 W 277 à 295 (sous-préfet de Metz-campagne) : épuration, dossiers individuels par classement alphabétique. 77 W 296 (sous-préfet de Metz-Campagne) : commission d'épuration, instructions, procès-verbaux.

Sous-préfecture de Château-Salins. 1242 W 1 à W5 : dossiers d'épuration par communes.

Cour de justice, sous-section de Metz. 285 W 1 à 285 : affaires n° 1 à 7717. 285 W 286 et 87 : annexe de Thionville, dossiers.

Cour de justice, sous-section de Sarreguemines. 256 W 1 à 27 : cour de justice. 256 W 28 à 118 : chambre civique.

Inspection académique. 1431 W 1 à 3 : épuration administrative. 18 J 248 : Chanoine Morhain, journal manuscrit, août-novembre 1944.

Comité d'histoire de la Deuxième Guerre mondiale. 507 W 1 à 13 : enquête sur la répression à la Libération, fiches individuelles.

Archives privées. J 6356 : souvenirs d'un habitant de Jouy-aux-Arches, 1944.

Archives départementales de l'Oise

Cabinet du préfet. 33 W 8269 à 71 : rapports mensuels, juillet 1944–décembre 1946. 33 W 8406 : Libération 1944, instructions et affiches. 37 W 8692 (CDL) : comptes rendus de séances, octobre 1944–août 1945. 116 W 11.837 : avortement, prostitution. 89 W 10913 : Libération, épuration, rapports hebdomadaires des Renseignements généraux.

Épuration. 34 W 8453, commission d'épuration : dossiers d'enquête. 34 W 8453 bis, commission d'épuration : liste nominative des internés. 34 W 8454, commission d'épuration : blocage des comptes. 34 W

8457, commission d'épuration : fiches de renseignement individuel des internés administratifs. 34 W 8465 à 8472 bis, dossiers individuels des internés. 72 W 199, Maison d'Arrêt de Senlis, instructions, correspondance. 72 W 57, commissariats de Chantilly, Creil et Senlis, rapports mensuels, septembre–décembre 1944. 72 W 58, commissariats de Chantilly, Creil et Senlis, rapports mensuels, janvier–décembre 1945.

Cour de justice de l'Oise. 998 W 47188 à 207, audiences de décembre 1944 à septembre 1945.

Chambre civique. 998 W 47219 à 226, audiences du mois de février 1945 à septembre 1945.

Archives départementales de la Seine

Cabinet du préfet. 1027 W art. 19, préfet : Libération CPL. 1027 W art. 20, préfet : Drancy. 1027 W art. 21, préfet : épuration, liste enquête du CPL octobre 1944. 1011/44/1 art. 25, cabinet du préfet : police 1941–1943. 1011/44/1 art. 37, demandes d'interventions 1942–1943. 1011/44/1 art. 39, dossiers du Comité parisien de libération. 1052/67/1 art. 1, rapports sur l'état d'esprit de la population.

Comité parisien de libération. 1520 W art. 1, ordonnances sur les pouvoirs publics. 1520 W art. 2, CPL : correspondance diverse. 1520 W art. 3, CPL : correspondance administrative. 1520 W art. 4, CPL : compte rendu de réunion septembre–octobre 1944. 10114/64/5 art. 10, CPL : papiers divers. 10114/64/5 art. 11, CPL : nomination des maires. 10114/71/1 art. 3, incidents survenus à l'occasion de l'activité des CLL.

Épuration. 1097 W art. 34, commission épuration du IIe Arrondissement. 1320 W art. 134 et 135, épuration des avocats. 1320 W art. 71, service central des statistiques judiciaires. 901/64/1 art. 342, Comité régional interprofessionnel de l'épuration : spectacle.

Institut d'histoire du temps présent

Archives privées. Fonds Closon : rapports et notes du commissaire de la République à Lille, octobre 1944–décembre 1945. Fonds Massé-Alékan : documents divers sur la Libération de Paris. Fonds Morin-Forestier : photographies sur l'occupation d'Oyonnax par le maquis en novembre 1943 ; rapport sur la libération de Paris.

Témoignages et récits. ARC 02, Fernand-Charles Danchin, notes tenues pendant la libération de Paris. ARC 015, Madeleine Baudoin, recueil de dix témoignages sur la tonte des femmes à la Libération de la France. ARC 038, ' Livre blanc ' de la Principauté de Monaco, septembre 1939–octobre 1945.

Archives du Comité d'histoire de la Deuxième Guerre mondiale. 72 AJ 62 (cote A.N.), direction de l'enseignement de la Seine, rapports fournis par les instituteurs sur la libération de la Seine, septembre 1944. Enquêtes sur la répression de la collaboration à la libération, dossiers départementaux. Dossiers dits de ' propagande ', la libération de la France ; l'après-guerre. OSS équipes Jedburgh en France, juin–novembre 1944. Sheet 87, ' Jedburgh team Tony ' – M2 – Area : Vendée.

Sources imprimées

Presse de l'Occupation. *Au pilori,* Paris, hebdomadaire, juillet 1940–28 juin 1944. *L'Avenir du Plateau Central,* Clermont-Ferrand, quotidien, septembre–décembre 1943 (série lacunaire). *Combats,* Nancy, hebdomadaire de la Milice, novembre 1943 (série lacunaire). *Le Courrier de la Corse,* Lyon, hebdomadaire, septembre–décembre 1943 (série lacunaire). *L'Écho de Nancy,* Nancy, quotidien, septembre–décembre 1943 (série lacunaire). *La Gerbe,* Paris, hebdomadaire, septembre–décembre 1943 (série lacunaire). *Le Matin,* Paris, quotidien, 1er juillet 1943–31 décembre 1943. *L'Œuvre,* Paris, quotidien, 1er septembre–31 décembre 1943.

Presse clandestine. *14 Juillet,* organe de la résistance de la sous-région de Lyon, 15 mai 1944. *44,* organe des FFI des Basses-Pyrénées, 12 août 1944. *Agence d'information et de documentation,* Bulletins d'information presse, 8 mai–3 août 1944. *Agence d'information et de documentation. Les Nouvelles,* publié sous le contrôle du Comité de Libération Régional [Lyon], 8 juin–28 juillet 1944. *Les Allobroges,* organe du FN de l'Isère, mars 1942–15 août 1944. *Alpes Libres,* organe du FN des Hautes-Alpes, août 1944. *Aurore,* organe de la Résistance républicaine, juillet 1943–août 1944. *L'Avant-garde,* organe des JC, décembre 1939–16 août 1944. *Bir-Hakeim,* mars 1943–juin 1944. *Bureau de presse de la France combattante,* octobre 1942–7 août 1944. *Combat,* organe du MLF puis MLN, décembre 1941–juillet 1944. *Défense de la France,* 15 août 1941–1er août 1944. *L'Espoir,* organe du Parti socialiste Populaire du Sud-Est, juillet 1943–avril 1944. *L'Étincelle,* organe du PCF de Bourgogne,

février 1944. *L'Étincelle*, organe PCF de Saône-et-Loire, 23 juin 1941–
1er novembre 1941. *Les Étoiles*, organe du Comité national des
écrivains, août 1943–mars 1944. *La Femme comtoise*, organe l'Union
des femmes pour la défense de la famille et la libération de la patrie,
août 1943. *La Femme d'Eure-et-Loir*, 25 août 1943. *Femmes à
l'action*, organe du Comité des femmes hyéroises, février 1944.
Femmes de la Loire, février 1944. *Femmes de prisonniers*, journal
féminin du mouvement national des prisonniers de guerre et déportés,
mai 1944. *Femmes Française*, organe de l'UFF, janvier–juillet 1944.
Femmes Patriotes, organe comité féminin de la Résistance (MUR),
février 1944. *Flamme*, supplément de *Résistance*, nouveau journal de
l'Ouest, 15 août 1943–5 février 1944. *Forces Françaises*, hebdo du
secteur nord de la Dordogne des FFI, 13 août–17 septembre 1944.
Forces Unies de la Jeunesse, 6 avril–1er octobre 1943. *France
combattante des Côtes-du-Nord*, organe du FN, octobre 1943.
France d'abord, communiqués des FTPF Zone sud, 30 novembre
1943–30 avril 1944. *Hebdo-Maquis*, organe FFI de la Vienne, 14
juillet–1er août 1944. *Libération (nord)-hebdomadaire des Français
libres*, 14 août 1944. *La Marseillaise du Sud-Est*, organe des MUR
(puis du MLN), 1er février–14 juillet 1944. *La Nouvelle République*,
22 novembre 1943–8 août 1944. *Le Nouvelliste*, journal apocryphe
fait par les MUR de l'Ain, 31 décembre 1943. *Le Patriote, organe
français libre*, Le Havre, octobre 1942–septembre 1944. *Le Patriote
d'Auvergne*, organe du FN, avril 1944. *Le Patriote de l'Avesnois*,
organe du FN, décembre 1943. *Le Patriote de l'Oise*, organe du FN
de l'Oise, août 1943–avril 1944. *Le Patriote de la Boucle*, organe du
FN banlieue-est, novembre 1943. *Le Patriote de Saône-et-Loire*,
organe des MUR, juillet-décembre 1943. *Le Patriote des Côtes-du-
Nord*, organe du FN, 28 mars 1943–25 avril 1944. *Le Patriote du Pas-
de-Calais*, organe du FN, octobre 1943–août 1944. *Le Patriote Niçois*,
organe du FN, janvier–14 juillet 1944. *Le Patriote Normand*, organe
du FN, janvier 1943. *Le Pilori*, organe du mouvement France d'abord,
décembre 1943. *Le Populaire de Seine-et-Oise*, organe socialiste,
octobre 1943–février 1944. *Le Populaire du Midi*, organe du Parti
socialiste, juin–août 1943. *Pour la Libération*, organe FN Lille-
Roubaix-Tourcoing, décembre 1943–avril 1944. *Provence libre*,
décembre 1943–30 juin 1944. *Quarante-quatre*, organe des mouvements de Libération de Toulouse, 15 mai–14 juillet 1944. *Résistance*,
journal parisien du MLN, octobre 1942–7 août 1944. *Le Réveil*,
organe FN Gard et Lozère, octobre 1943–janvier 1944. *Rouge Midi*,
organe régional du PCF (Marseille), 23 janvier 1941–1er juillet 1944.

La Voix de la Patrie, organe FN de l'Hérault, mars 1944. *Voix des femmes-zone sud*, novembre 1941–mars 1944.

Tracts clandestins. Rés. G. 1476 IV : tracts clandestins : par catégories de population. Rés. G. 1476 III : tracts clandestins : partis et mouvements de Résistance. Rés. G. 1476 II : tracts clandestins : poésies, chansons facéties. Microfilm M 9967 (417) : tracts clandestins : régionaux ou locaux. Rés. G. 1476 VI : faux tracts clandestins publiés par les Allemands.

Presse de la Libération et de l'après-guerre.

L'Aisne Libre, Soissons, 9 septembre–30 décembre 1944. *L'Aisne Nouvelle*, Saint-Quentin, 3 septembre–8 septembre 1944. *Les Allobroges*, Grenoble, 23 août–22 septembre 1944. *L'Alsace*, Colmar, 24 novembre 1944–31 juillet 1945. *Alsace libérée*, Strasbourg, 29 novembre 1944 – 31 août 1946. *L'Appel de la Haute-Loire*, Le Puy, 20 août–17 décembre 1944. *L'Ardennais*, Charleville, 11 septembre– 12 octobre 1944. *L'Ariège Libre*, Foix, 23 août 1944. *L'Assaut*, Privas, 7 août–25 septembre 1944. *L'Aube*, Paris, 23 août–23 septembre 1944. *L'Aube Libre*, Troyes, 5 septembre–13 octobre 1944. *Avenir de l'Artois*, Béthune, 10 septembre 1944–6 septembre 1945. *L'Avenir Normand*, Rouen, 8 octobre–30 décembre 1944.

Le Bazooka, Châteauroux, 1er septembre–1er décembre 1944. *Bulletin d'information du Maine & Loir*, Angers, 14 août 1944. *Bulletin d'information*, Buchy, 29 septembre 1944. *Bulletin officiel du CDL*, Blois, 24 août–2 septembre 1944. *Le Berry Républicain*, Bourges, 23 septembre 1944. *Le Bien Public*, Dijon, 11 septembre–22 octobre 1944. *La Bourgogne Républicaine*, Dijon, 12 septembre–10 octobre 1944. *Brive Information*, Brive-la-Gaillarde, 20 août–20 septembre 1944.

Le Calvados Libre, Caen, 24 septembre 1944–20 septembre 1945. *Le Cantal Libre*, Aurillac, 13 septembre–14 octobre 1944. *Le Cavaillon Libre*, Cavaillon, 7 septembre–8 novembre 1944. *Ce Soir*, Paris, 24 août–14 septembre 1944. *Le Centre Républicain*, Montluçon, 21 août 1944. *La Charente Libre*, Angoulême, 2 septembre–19 octobre 1944. *Chambéry midi*, Chambéry, 21 août–22 août 1944. *Combat*, Paris, 21 août–11 septembre 1944. *Combat*, Paris, 21 août–11 septembre 1944. *Le Combat du Berry*, Bourges, 7 septembre 1944. *Le Comtois*, Besançon, 9 septembre–30 octobre 1944. *Le Coq Bugiste*, Belley, 23 septembre 1944–13 octobre 1945. *Le Courrier Français du Dimanche*, Bordeaux, 9 septembre–30 septembre 1944. *Courrier de la Mayenne*, Laval, 22 octobre 1944–14 octobre 1945. *Courrier du Maine*, Laval, 3 septembre–15 octobre 1944. *Courrier de l'Ouest*,

Angers, 21 août–21 septembre 1944. *Le Courrier Picard*, Amiens, 16 octobre–4 novembre 1944. *Le Courrier de Saône-et-Loire*, Chalon-sur-Saône, 6 septembre–24 octobre 1944. *La Creuse Libre*, Guéret, 4 septembre–14 octobre 1944. *Le Cri du Peuple*, Saint-Étienne, 5 septembre–5 octobre 1944. *La Croix du Nord*, Lille, 6 septembre–10 octobre 1944.

Dauphiné libéré, Grenoble, 1er mai 1944. *Défense de la France*, Paris, 10 août–25 septembre 1944. *Le Démocrate de l'Est*, Épinal, (devient *Liberté de l'Est*), 4 octobre 1944–10 mars 1945. *Démocrate de Tarn-et-Garonne*, Montauban, 21 octobre 1944–29 décembre 1945. *Le Département*, Châteauroux, 22 août–1er octobre 1944. *La Dépêche de l'Aisne*, Laon, 1er septembre–27 septembre 1944. *La Dépêche Démocratique*, Saint-Étienne, 4 septembre–6 octobre 1944. *La Dernière Heure*, Marseille, 9 septembre 1944. *Les Dernières nouvelles d'Alsace*, Strasbourg, 2 janvier–1er août 1945. *Les Dernières Nouvelles du Haut-Rhin*, 20 février–31 juillet 1945. *Dinan Républicain*, Dinan, 17 août–19 octobre 1944. *La Dordogne Libre*, Périgueux, 11 septembre–13 octobre 1944. *La Drôme en Armes*, 5 septembre 1944.

L'Écho de la Corrèze, Tulle, 7 septembre–14 octobre 1944. *Écho de l'Est*, Strasbourg, 21 décembre 1944–28 septembre 1946. *L'Écho de Lille-bonne et de la Vallée de la Seine*, Lillebonne, 22 septembre 1944–31 août 1945. *L'Écho du Centre*, Limoges, 12 septembre–31 octobre 1944. *Écho du Midi*, Avignon, 9 novembre 1944. *Écho de la Somme*, Amiens, 18 septembre–14 octobre 1944. *L'Éclair*, Clermont-Ferrand, 12 septembre–18 octobre 1944. *L'Éclair de l'Est*, Nancy, 24 septembre–13 octobre 1944. *L'Éclair des Pyrénées*, Pau, 18 octobre–4 novembre 1944. *L'Embuscade*, Guéret, 21 septembre–28 octobre 1944. *En Avant !*, Le Puy, Saint-Étienne, 9 septembre 1944–15 septembre 1945. *L'Espoir de Nice*, Nice, 11 septembre–13 octobre 1944. *L'Espoir*, Saint-Étienne, 3 septembre–20 octobre 1944. *L'Est Républicain*, Nancy, 8 octobre–8 novembre 1944. *L'Étoile du Quercy*, 21 octobre–4 novembre 1944. *L'Eure Libérée*, 2 septembre 1944–27 janvier 1945.

Le Figaro, Paris, 23 août–23 septembre 1944. *La France de Marseille et du Sud-Est*, Marseille, 10 octobre–10 novembre 1944. *Front National*, Montauban, 28 octobre 1944–30 juin 1945. *Front National du Var*, Draguignan, 2 septembre 1944–13 avril 1945.

Le Gers Libéré, Auch, 27 août 1944–27 mai 1945. *La Gironde Populaire*, Bordeaux, 14 septembre–25 septembre 1944.

Haute-Marne Libérée, Chaumont, 27 novembre 1944–18 septembre 1945. *Haute-Saône Libre*, Chaumont, 13 janvier–21 septembre 1945.

Havre Libre, Le Havre, 13 septembre–31 octobre 1944. *L'Heure H,* Criquetot, 9 septembre–7 octobre 1944. *L'Humanité,* Colmar, 10 décembre 1944. *L'Humanité,* Paris, 21 août–22 octobre 1944. *L'Indépendant de Château-Gontier,* Château-Gontier, 8 octobre–22 octobre 1944. *L'Indépendant d'Eure-et-Loir,* Chartres, 22 août–27 octobre 1944. *Les Informations Bolbecaises,* Bolbec, 7 octobre 1944–6 octobre 1945. *L'Information Languedoc,* Montpellier, août 1944–décembre 1945. *Les Informations Dieppoises,* Dieppe, 29 septembre 1944.

Journal d'Elbeuf, Elbeuf, 9 septembre 1944–31 décembre 1945.

Le Libérateur, Bourg-en-Bresse, 28 octobre 1944–21 décembre 1945. *Libération,* Gaillac, 24 août 1944–28 décembre 1945. *Libération,* Paris, 21 août–4 septembre 1944. *La Libération d'Aunis et de la Saint.,* Saintes, 8 septembre–23 septembre 1944. *La Libération du Centre,* Orléans, 9 septembre–14 octobre 1944. *La Libération des Hautes-Vosges,* Épinal, 23 septembre–8 novembre 1944. *Liberté de l'Est,* Épinal, 11 mars–31 décembre 1945. *Libre Poitou,* Poitiers, 9 septembre–11 octobre 1944. *Liberté,* Lille, 5 septembre–14 octobre 1944. *La Liberté,* Arles, 9 septembre 1944. *La Liberté,* Clermont-Ferrand, 10 septembre–27 octobre 1944. *La Liberté,* Lyon, 8 septembre–23 octobre 1944. *Liberté Normandie,* Rouen, 27 octobre 1944. *La Liberté de Normandie,* Caen, 9 juillet 1944. *Liberté des Basses-Alpes,* Digne, 2 septembre–14 octobre 1944. *Liberté du Pas-de-Calais,* Arras, quotidien, 3 septembre 1944. *Liberté roannaise,* Roanne, 23 août 1944. *Le Lorrain,* Metz, 12 décembre 1944–31 décembre 1945. *La Lorraine Libérée,* Metz, 23 novembre 1944–1 mai 1945. *Le Lot Républicain,* Cahors, 25 novembre 1944–7 juillet 1945. *Lozère Libre,* Mende, 10 septembre 1944–9 septembre 1945. *Lyon Libre,* Lyon, 9 septembre–30 octobre 1944.

Le Maine Libre, Le Mans, 8 septembre–28 septembre 1944. *La Manche libre,* Saint-Lô, 10 décembre 1944–16 septembre 1945. *Le Maquis,* Avallon, 12 octobre–16 novembre 1944. *La Marseillaise,* Château-roux, 26 août–25 septembre 1944. *La Marseillaise,* Marseille, 24 août–23 septembre 1944. *La Marseillaise,* Paris 24 août–24 septembre 1944. *La Marseillaise de Lyon et du Sud-Est,* Lyon, 8 septembre–6 octobre 1944. *La Marseillaise de Seine-et-Marne,* Melun, 26 septembre–3 novembre 1944. *Marseillaise de Seine-et-Oise,* Versailles, 28 octobre 1944–15 septembre 1945. *Le Méridional,* Marseille, 9 septembre–12 octobre 1944. *Le Messager Patriotique,* Thonon-les-Bains, 15 septembre 1944–1er juillet 1945. *Le Meusien,*

Bar-le-Duc, octobre–novembre 1944. *Le Midi Libre,* Montpellier, 27 août 1944–31 décembre 1945. *Midi Soir,* Marseille, 7 septembre–17 septembre 1944. *Le Morbihan Libéré,* Vannes, (ou *Liberté du Morbihan*), 6 août–24 septembre 1944. *La Nation,* Clermont-Ferrand, 29 août–24 septembre 1944. *Nord Éclair,* Lille, 10 septembre–22 octobre 1944. *Nord Matin,* Lille, 5 septembre–11 octobre 1944. *Normandie,* Rouen, 1er septembre–15 octobre 1944. *La Nouvelle Aurore,* Villefranche-de-Rouergue, 7 septembre–9 octobre 1944. *La Nouvelle République du Centre-Ouest,* Tours, 7 septembre–27 septembre 1944. *La Nouvelle République des Pyrénées,* Tarbes, 24 août–11 octobre 1944. *Le Nouveau Rhin français,* 20 février–31 décembre 1945. *Les Nouvelles Mayennaises,* Laval, 24 septembre 1944.

L'Oise Libérée, Beauvais, 30 août–14 octobre 1944. *L'Oise Républicaine,* Compiègne, 22 novembre 1944. *Oise Socialiste,* Beauvais, 1er février–1er septembre 1945. *Orne combattante,* Flers, 24 septembre 1944–23 septembre 1945. *Ouest France,* Rennes, 7 août–30 septembre 1944.

Le Parisien Libéré, Paris, 22 août–6 octobre 1944. *Le Partisan du Lot,* Cahors, 1er décembre 1944–1er octobre 1945. *Le Patriote,* Ajaccio, 1er octobre–2 novembre 1943. *Le Patriote,* Blois, 9 septembre–22 octobre 1944. *Le Patriote,* Clermont-Ferrand, 20 août–10 octobre 1944. *Le Patriote,* Marseille, 13 octobre–15 novembre 1944. *Le Patriote,* Lens, 9 septembre–24 septembre 1944. *Le Patriote,* Lyon, 8 septembre–25 octobre 1944. *Le Patriote du Morvan,* Autun, 8 septembre–23 septembre 1944. *Le Patriote de Nevers,* Nevers, 12 septembre–5 octobre 1944. *Le Patriote Niçois,* Nice, 6 septembre–9 septembre 1944. *Le Patriote de l'Eure,* 21 octobre 1944–2 septembre 1945. *Le Patriote de l'Oise,* Beauvais, 9 septembre 1944–1er juillet 1945. *Le Patriote Romanais,* Romans, 8 septembre 1944. *Le Patriote Rouerguat,* Rodez, 10 septembre–3 novembre 1944. *Le Patriote Savoyard,* Saint-Julien-en-Genevoix, 7 septembre 1944. *Le Patriote du Sud-Ouest,* Toulouse, 20 août–9 septembre 1944. *Pays d'Yssingeaux,* Yssingeaux, 27 août 1944–26 août 1945. *Picardie Libre,* Amiens, 16 octobre 1944. *Le Populaire,* Paris, 21 août–22 septembre 1944. *Le Populaire du Centre,* Limoges, 7 août–27 octobre 1944. *La Presse Cherbourgeoise,* Cherbourg, 3 juillet–2 août 1944. *Le Progrès,* Lyon, 8 septembre–16 octobre 1944. *Le Progrès de Fécamp,* Fécamp, 15 septembre–31 octobre 1944. *Le Provençal,* Marseille, 23 août–23 septembre 1944.

Quand même, Belfort, 28 novembre 1944–31 juillet 1945. *Quarante-quatre*, Agen, 21 août 1944–25 août 1945. *La Quatrième république*, Dax, 30 août–22 août 1944.

La Renaissance du Bessin, Bayeux, 23 juin–27 juin 1944. *Renaissance du peuple*, Millau, 27 août 1944–1er mars 1945. *La Renaissance Républicaine du Gard*, Nîmes, 28 août–8 octobre 1944. *Renouveau*, Granville, 24 août 1944–2 mars 1945. *Le Républicain d'Alès*, 10 octobre–25 décembre 1944. *Le Républicain d'Issoudun*, Issoudun, 24 août–13 septembre 1944. *Le Républicain Lorrain*, Metz, 2 février–31 décembre 1945. *La République d'Arles*, Arles, 9 septembre 1944–20 janvier 1945. *La République*, Saint-Étienne, 21 août 1944. *La République de Bordeaux et du Sud-Ouest*, Bordeaux, 14 septembre–11 octobre 1944. *La République du Centre*, Orléans, 27 septembre–18 octobre 1944. *La République de Franche-Comté*, Besançon, 10 septembre–29 octobre 1944. *La République*, Niort, 10 septembre–12 octobre 1944. *La République des Pyrénées-Orientales*, Perpignan, 20 août–31 décembre 1944. *La République du Sud-Ouest*, Toulouse, 21 août–29 septembre 1944. *Résistance*, Rodez, 24 septembre 1944–1er janvier 1945. *Résistance Landaise*, Mont-de-Marsan, 9 septembre–11 novembre 1944. *Résistance de l'Ouest*, Nantes, 17 août–3 octobre 1944. *Le Réveil de Bourgoin*, Bourgoin, 2 septembre–6 septembre 1944. *Réveil du Jura*, Dôle, 1er novembre 1944–12 septembre 1945. *Le Réveil Normand*, Mortagne, 21 octobre 1944–20 octobre 1945. *Réveil de Tarn-et-Garonne*, Montauban, 21 octobre 1944–29 décembre 1945. *Le Rouergue Républicain*, Rodez, 23 août–1er octobre 1944. *Rouge Midi*, Marseille, 24 août–23 septembre 1944.

Savoie française, Chambéry, 1er septembre 1944–1er septembre 1945. *Sud-Ouest*, Bordeaux, édition de Dordogne, 29 août–19 septembre 1944.

Tarn Libre, Albi, 21 août–23 septembre 1944. *Le Travailleur Alpin*, Grenoble, 22 août 1944–30 juin 1945. *Le Travailleur de l'Oise*, Beauvais, 1er octobre 1944–1er juillet 1945.

L'Union, Gap, 21 octobre 1944–25 août 1945. *L'Union Champenoise*, Reims, 30 août–11 septembre 1944. *L'Union Républicaine*, Châlons, 1er septembre–2 octobre 1944. *Unir*, Limoges, 2 octobre–23 octobre 1944. *Unité*, Agen, 26 octobre 1944–1er janvier 1945.

Vaincre, Auch, 17 septembre 1944–28 janvier 1945. *Valmy*, Moulins, 11 septembre–29 septembre 1944. *Le Var Libre*, (devient *La Liberté du Var*), Toulon, 29 août–22 octobre 1944. *Vendée Libre*, La Roche-sur-Yon, 13 septembre 1944–16 septembre 1945. *Vichy Libre*, Vichy, 4 septembre–17 septembre 1944. *La Victoire*, Toulouse, 1er septembre–

24 septembre 1944. *Le Villefranchois Libéré,* Villefranche-de-Rouergue, 2 septembre 1944. *Ville de Versailles,* Versailles, 31 août–10 novembre 1944. *La Voix du Bocage,* Vire, 21 septembre 1944–31 août 1945. *Voix chrétienne,* Bourg-en-Bresse, 24 septembre 1944. *La Voix de la Moselle,* Metz, 2 octobre 1944–31 décembre 1945. *La Voix du Midi,* 18 novembre 1944. *La Voix du Nord,* Lille, 5 septembre–21 septembre 1944. *Les Voies Nouvelles,* Périgueux, 25 août–12 septembre 1944. *La Voix de l'Ouest,* Rennes, 19 septembre–19 octobre 1944. *La Voix de la Patrie,* Montpellier, 27 août–1er octobre 1944. *Volontaire,* Montpellier, octobre 1944–décembre 1945. *L'Yonne Républicaine,* Auxerre, 26 août–27 septembre 1944. *Yonne libre,* Auxerre, 8 octobre 1944–30 mai 1945.

Images filmées et photographies

Photographies. L'ensemble des photographies utlisées dans ce travail proviennent de fonds divers. Une partie des photos sont tirées des périodiques et imprimés. Pour les autres, les fonds consultés sont ceux de : Bibliothèque nationale, Photothèque de la Documentation française, Bibliothèque historique de la ville de Paris, Musée de la Libération de Paris, Imperial War Museum, Keystone, Lapi-Viollet. Vidéothèque de Paris. *Le Défilé de la Libération, 26 août 1944,* actualités 1944, muet, n&b, 8 mn. *La Libération de Paris,* réalisation collective du Réseau Résistance-Cinéma français, documentaire 1944, n&b, 30 mn. *La France libérée,* de Serguei Youtkevitch, documentaire soviétique, 1944, n&b, 1h10. VDP 3839, *Paris liberated !,* réalisation anonyme, documentaire 1944, muet n&b, 7 mn. *Actualités allemandes 1944,* Sélection VdP, n&b, 10 mn. *Libération de Paris,* réalisation collective du Club des cinéastes amateurs, documentaire 1944, n&b, 46 mn. *The Paris Story : scènes historiques de la Libération,* réalisation anonyme, documentaire américain, National Archives of Washington, vo, 1944, n&b, 10 mn. *Paris,* réalisation anonyme, documentaire américain, vo, 1944, n&b, 11 mn. *From D-Day to Germany,* de J. Lieb, documentaire, vo, 1944, couleur, 44 mn. *France libre actualités, septembre 1944,* Sélection VdP actualité 1944, n&b, 32 mn. *France libre actualités, octobre 1944,* Sélection VdP actualité 1944, n&b, 32 mn. *Libération,* de R. Seguin et R. Legrand, documentaire 1944, muet, n&b, 16 mn. *La revue des actualités 1944–1945,* réalisation collective, actualités 1944–1945, muet, n&b, 13 mn. *Libération de Paris,* de Pierre Denoix, documentaire 1944, muet, n&b,

10 mn. *Libération*, de F. Porret, documentaire 1944, n&b, 18 mn. *Libération 1940–1944*, de M. Krébs, documentaire 1944, muet, n&b, 13 mn. *Notre Libération*, de G. Jonesco, documentaire, 1944, muet, n&b, 14 mn. *La Libération*, série *La vie filmée*, de Alexandre Astruc, documentaire, 1975, n&b, 53 mn. (montage d'images amateurs 1944). *Caméras sous la botte. . . !,* de A. Mahuzier et R. Gudin, documentaire, 1944, n&b, 26 mn. *Ici Londres. . . Ici Paris. . . ,* de R. Marcou, documentaire 1945, n&b, 18 mn. *Arrestations de collaborateurs,* actualités américaines, National Archives of Washington, 1944, muet, n&b, 1 mn 36 s. *De l'Occupation allemande à la Libération de Paris,* actualités américaines, National Archives of Washington, 1944, muet, n&b, 10 mn. *Combats poiur la Libération de Paris,* actualités américaines, National Archives of Washington, 1944, muet, n&b, 11 mn. *Défilé des troupes américaines,* actualités américaines, National Archives of Washington, 1944, muet, n&b, 29 mn. *Arrivée des troupes américaines à Paris : 25 août 1944,* actualités américaines, National Archives of Washington, 1944, muet, n&b, 4 mn 27 s. *Scènes de la Libération de Paris 25 août 1944,* actualités américaines, National Archives of Washington, muet, n&b, 4 mn 56 s. *Combats dans les rues de Paris,* actualités américaines, National Archives of Washington, 1944, muet, n&b, 10 mn. *Rue Saint Dominique, 26 août 1944,* actualités, 1944, muet, n&b, 4 mn 31 s. *Vues de Paris, août 1944,* actualités américaines, National Archives of Washington, 1944, muet, n&b, 7 mn. *Arrivée de la 2ᵉ DB à Paris : 25 août 1944,* actualités, 1944, muet, n&b, 9 mn. *Diverses scènes dans Paris : été 1944,* actualités américaines, National Archives of Washington, 1944, muet, n&b, 27 mn. *La journée du 26 août,* sélection VdP actualités américaines, National Archives of Washington, 1944, muet, n&b, 9 mn. *Arrivée des troupes américaines à Paris : 25 et 26 août 1944,* actualités 1944, muet, n&b. *Scènes de la Libération de Paris 25 et 26 août 1944,* actualités américaines, National Archives of Washington, 1944, muet, n&b, 10 mn. *Les journées du 19 au 28 août 1944,* de Jean Baldensperger, documentaire, 1944, muet, n&b, 23 mn. *Montreuil, août 1944,* de Edouard Mills-Affif, documentaire, 1994, couleur, 27 mn. *Paris libéré,* série, reportage n° 79, réalisation anonyme, actualités, 1944, n&b, 8 mn. *1944–1945,* sélection VdP, archives du ministère de la Défense, actualités 1944–1945, n&b, 1h24.

Select Bibliography

Monographs and articles

Women and violence

AUDOIN-ROUZEAU Stéphane, *La guerre des enfants 1914–1918. Essai d'histoire culturelle*, Paris, Armand Colin, 1993, 188 p.

AUDOIN-ROUZEAU Stéphane, *L'enfant de l'ennemi: 1914–1918*, Paris, Aubier, 1995, 223p.

BARD Christine, *Les Garçonnes*, Paris, Flammarion, 1998, 160 p.

BARD Christine (ed.), *Un siècle d'antiféminisme*, Paris, Fayard, 1999, 481 p.

BARROWS Suzanna, *Distorting mirrors: visions of the crowd in late nineteenth-century France*, New Haven: Yale University Press, 1981.

BOUCHOUX Corinne, 'L'affaire Gabrielle Russier', in *Vingtième Siècle. Revue d'histoire*, no. 33, January–March 1992, pp. 56–64.

BOUTIER Jean and JULIA Dominique (ed.), *Passés recomposés. Champs et chantiers de l'Histoire*, Paris, Autrement, 1995, 349 p.

BROWNMILLER Susan, *Against our will: men, women, and rape*, New York, Simon & Schuster, 1975.

CARBASSE Jean-Marie, *Introduction au droit pénal*, Paris, PUF, 1990.

CARBASSE Jean-Marie, '"Currant nudi", la répression de l'adultère dans le Midi médiéval (XIIe–XVe)', in J. POUMARÈDE and J.P. ROYER (eds) *Droit, Histoire et Sexualité*, Paris, L'Espace juridique, 1987, p. 83–102.

CARIO Robert, *Les femmes résistent au crime*, Paris, L'Harmattan, 1997, 191 p.

DAUPHIN Cécile and FARGE Arlette, *De la violence et des femmes*, Paris, A. Michel, 1997, 202 p.

GARÇON Émile (ed.), *Code pénal annoté*, Reedited by Rousselet, Patin and Ancel, Paris, Sirey, 1952, 608 p.

HUGUENEY Louis, 'Crimes et délits contre la chose publique', in *Revue de Science criminelle*, 1947, p. 225–7.

JULIA Dominique, 'La violence des foules: peut-on élucider l'inhumain', in Jean BOUTIER Jean and Dominique JULIA (eds), *Passés recomposés. Champs et chantiers de l'Histoire*, Paris, Autrement, 1995, pp. 208–23.

LE GOFF Jacques and SCHMITT Jean-Claude (eds), *Le charivari*, Paris-La Haye, Mouton-EHESS, 1981, 444 p.

MAALOUF Amin, *Les croisades vues du côté des Arabes*, Paris, J'ai Lu, 1985.

MARTINAGE Renée, 'Les collaborateurs devant les Cours d'Assises du Nord après la très Grande guerre', in *Revue du Nord*, t. 77, no. 309, 1995, pp. 95–115.

MICHAUD Yves, *Violence et politique*, Paris, Gallimard, 1978, 231 p.

MICHELET Jules, *Les femmes de la Révolution*, Paris, Éditions Carrère, 1988, 345 p.

MOSCOVICI Marie, 'Tuer', in *Inactuel* (L'), no. 1, Calmann-Levy, 1994, pp. 111–17

NAHOUM-GRAPPE Véronique, 'Guerre et différence des sexes: les viols systématiques (ex-Yougoslavie, 1991–1995)', in DAUPHIN Christine and FARGE Arlette (eds), *De la violence et des femmes*, Paris, A. Michel, 1997, pp. 159–84.

PERROT Philippe, *Le travail des apparences. Le corps féminin XVIIIe–XIXe siècle*, Paris, Seuil, 1984, 281 p.

PROST Antoine, 'Frontières et espaces du privé', in PROST Antoine and VINCENT Gérard (eds) *Histoire de la vie privée*, Vol. 5, *De la Première Guerre mondiale à nos jours*, Paris, Seuil, pp. 13–153.

PROST Antoine, 'La représentation de la guerre [1914–1918] en France', in *Vingtième siècle. Revue d'histoire*, no. 41, January–March 1994, pp. 23–31.

REY-FLAUD Henri, *Le charivari. Les rituels fondamentaux de la sexualité*, Paris, Payot, 1985, 279 p.

ROBERTS, Mary Louise, *Civilization without Sexes. Reconstructing Gender in Postwar France*, 1917–1927, Chicago – London, University of Chicago Press, 1994, 337 p.

'La Rumeur', in *Le Genre humain*, special no. 5, 1982.

SOHN Anne-Marie, 'Entre deux guerres', in THÉBAUD Françoise, (ed.) *Histoire des femmes*, Vol. 5 'Le XXe siècle', Plon, 1992, pp. 91–113.

TACITE, *La Germanie* XIX, texte et traduction J. PERRET, Paris, Belles lettres, 1949, p. 82.

THÉBAUD Françoise (ed.), *Histoire des femmes en Occident*. Vol. 5, 'Le XXe siècle', Paris, Plon, 1992, 647 p.

THÉBAUD Françoise, 'Femmes et guerres en France au XXe siècle', in MORANT-DEUSA Isabel (ed.), *Mujeres e Historia*, Valencia, Universidad internacional Menendez Pelayo, 1994, pp. 8–32.

THÉBAUD Françoise, 'Deuxième guerre, femmes et rapports de sexe', in *Cahiers d'Histoire du Temps Présent/Bijdragen*, no. 4, 1998, pp. 227–48.

ZDATNY Steven, 'La mode à la garçonne, 1900–1925: une histoire sociale des coupes de cheveux', in *Le Mouvement social*, no. 174, 1996, pp. 23–56.

Postwar, liberation and occupation

ALBINET Josian, *Le pouvoir en Aveyron à la Libération*, mémoire de maîtrise, Université Toulouse Le Mirail, 1989.

ANDRIEU Claire, 'Femmes', in AZÉMA Jean-Pierre and BÉDARIDA François (eds), *1938–1948. Les années de tourmente de Munich à Prague. Dictionnaire critique*, Paris, Flammarion, 1995, pp. 945–56.

AZÉMA Jean-Pierre and BÉDARIDA François (eds), *1938–1948. Les années de tourmente de Munich à Prague. Dictionnaire critique*, Paris, Flammarion, 1995, 1135 p.

AZÉMA Jean-Pierre and WIEVIORKA Olivier, *Les Libérations de la France*, Paris, La Martinière, 1993, 233 p.

AZÉMA Jean-Pierre and BÉDARIDA François, (eds), *La France des années noires*, Paris, Seuil, 1993, 2 volumes.

Vol. 1, 'De la défaite à Vichy', 536 p.

Vol. 2, 'De l'Occupation à la Libération', 517 p.

AZÉMA Jean-Pierre and BÉDARIDA François, *Vichy et les Français*, Paris, Fayard, 1992, 788 p.

AZÉMA Jean-Pierre, *De Munich à la Libération 1938–1944*, Paris, Seuil, 1980, 412 p.

AZÉMA Jean-Pierre, *La collaboration 1940–1944*, Paris, PUF, 1975, 152 p.

BAILLY Jacques-Augustin, *La Libération confisquée. Le Languedoc, 1944–1945*, Paris, A. Michel, 1993, 481 p.

BAILLY Jacques-Augustin, *Aspects de la Libération dans le Languedoc méditerranéen 1944–1945*, Thèse, Montpellier 3, 1991.

BARUCH Marc-Olivier, *Servir l'État français*, Paris, Fayard, 1997, 568 p.

BAUDOIN Rémi, 'La reconstruction des églises', in *Reconstructions et modernisation. La France après les ruines 1918... 1945...*, Paris, Archives nationales, 1991, pp. 282–3.

BAUDOT Marcel, 'L'épuration: bilan chiffré', *Bulletin de l'IHTP*, no. 25, September 1986, pp. 37–53.

BAUDOT Marcel, 'État des recherches sur la répression de la collaboration à la Libération', *Bulletin de l'IHTP*, June 1981, pp. 19–45.

BAUDOT Marcel, 'La Résistance française face aux problèmes de répression et d'épuration', *RH2GM*, no. 81, 1971, pp. 23–47.

BESSE Jean-Pierre, 'L'exemple de l'hôpital psychiatrique de Clermont dans l'Oise', in VEILLON Dominique and FLONNEAU Jean-Marie (eds), 'Le temps des restrictions en France (1939–1949)', *Les Cahiers de l'IHTP*, no. 32–3, May 1996, pp. 433–6.

BESSE Jean-Pierre, 'L'Oise', in Philippe BUTON and Jean-Marie GUILLON (eds), *Les pouvoirs en France à la Libération*, Paris, Belin, 1994, pp. 183–92.

BORDEAUX Michèle, 'Sept ans de réflexion, divorce et ordre social (1940–1945)', in POUMARÈDE J. and ROYER J.P. (eds) *Droit, Histoire et Sexualité*, Paris, L'Espace juridique, 1987, pp. 229–47.

BOUGEARD Christian and SAINCLIVIER Jacqueline (eds), *La Résistance et les Français, Enjeux stratégiques et environnement social*, Rennes, PUR, 1995, 368 p.

BOUGEARD Christian, *Le choc de la guerre dans un département breton: les Côtes-du-Nord des années vingt aux années cinquante*, Thèse d'État, Rennes 2, 1986, 2077 p. dactylographiées.

BOURDERON Roger, 'Jacques Bounin et la restauration de l'État', in *Lendemains de Libération dans le Midi*, Université Paul Valery-Montpellier III, 1997, pp. 67–80. [Actes du colloque de Montpellier 1986].

BOURDERON Roger, *La Libération du Languedoc méditerranéen*, Paris, Hachette, 1974, 283 p.

BROSSAT Alain, *Les tondues. Un carnaval moche*, Levallois-Perret, Manya, 1992, 314 p.

BURRIN Philippe, *La France à l'heure allemande*, Paris, Seuil, 1995, 560 p.

BUTON Philippe and GUILLON Jean-Marie (eds), *Les pouvoirs en France à la Libération*, Paris, Belin, 1994. 592 p.

BUTON Philippe 'L'État restauré', in AZÉMA Jean-Pierre and BÉDARIDA François (eds), *La France des années noires*, Vol. 2, Paris, Seuil, 1993, pp. 405–28.

BUTON Philippe 'La France atomisée', in AZÉMA Jean-Pierre and BÉDARIDA François (eds), *La France des années noires*, Vol. 2, Paris, Seuil, 1993, pp. 377–404.

BUTON Philippe, *La France et les Français de la Libération 1944–1945 vers une France nouvelle*, Paris, Catalogue Musée des deux guerres mondiales BDIC, 1984, 175 p.

CAPDEVILA Luc, 'Le mythe du guerrier et la construction sociale d'un 'éternel masculin' après la guerre', in *Revue française de Psychanalyse*, février 1998, pp. 607–23.

CAPDEVILA Luc and VIRGILI Fabrice, 'Tontes et répression de la collaboration: un antiféminisme?', in BARD Christine (ed.), *Un siècle d'antiféminisme*, Paris, Fayard, 1999, pp. 243–55.

CAPDEVILA Luc, 'La 'collaboration sentimentale': antipatriotisme ou sexualité hors-normes ? Lorient mai 1945', in ROUQUET François and VOLDMAN Danièle (eds), 'Identités féminines et violences politiques', *Les Cahiers de l'IHTP*, no. 31, October 1995, pp. 67–82.

CAPDEVILA Luc, 'La construction du mythe résistancialiste: identité nationale et représentation de soi à la Libération', in BOUGEARD Christian and SAINCLIVIER Jacqueline (eds), *La Résistance et les Français. Enjeux stratégiques et environnement social*, Rennes, PUR, 1995, pp. 347–57.

CAPDEVILA Luc, *L'imaginaire social de la Libération en Bretagne*, Thèse nouveau régime, Université de Rennes 2, Rennes, 1997, 716 p. dactylographiée.

CAPDEVILA Luc, *Les Bretons au lendemain de l'Occupation. Imaginaire et comportement d'une sortie de guerre 1944–1945*, Rennes PUR, 1999.

CHAUBIN Hélène, 'L'Hérault', in BUTON Philippe and GUILLON Jean-Marie (eds), *Les pouvoirs en France à la Libération*, Paris, Belin, 1994, pp. 508–17.

Chroniques en images de la Deuxième Guerre mondiale, Paris, Éditions du Griot, 1995.

CREMIEUX-BRILHAC Jean-Louis, *Les voix de la liberté. Ici Londres (1940–1944)*, Paris, La Documentation française, 1975, 5 volumes.

Vol. 1, 'Dans la nuit, 16 juin 1940–7 décembre 1941', 352 p.

Vol. 2, 'Le monde en feu, 8 décembre 1941–7 novembre 1942', 267 p.

Vol. 3, 'La fin du commencement, 8 novembre 1942–9 juillet 1943', 224 p.

Vol. 4, 'La forteresse Europe, 10 juillet 1943–8 mai 1944', 268 p.

Vol. 5, 'La bataille de France, 9 mai 1944–31 août 1944', 254 p.

DELAUNAY and PIOGER, 'La Libération du Mans', in *La Province du Maine*, 4e série, 1977, pp. 464–7.

DEMONGEOT Pierre and DULAURENS André, *Les hommes de l'ombre*, Autun, EPA, 1986, 357 p.

DENIS Pierre, *La Libération de Metz*, Metz, Serpenoise, 1994, 428 p.

DEVAUX André, *Bapaume pendant la Deuxième Guerre mondiale*, EPA, 1987, 180 p.

DOMPNIER Nathalie, 'Entre 'La Marseillaise' and 'Maréchal nous voilà !' Quel hymne pour le régime de Vichy', in CHIMÈNES Myriam, *La vie musicale sous Vichy*, Bruxelles, Complexe, 2001.

DOUZOU Laurent, 'La Résistance, une affaire d'hommes ?', in VOLD-MAN Danièle and ROUQUET François (eds), 'Identités féminines et violences politiques', *Cahiers de l'IHTP*, no. 31, October 1995, pp. 11–24.

DOUZOU Laurent, FRANK Robert, PESCHANSKI Denis and VEILLON Dominique (eds), *La Résistance et les Français: villes, centres et logiques de décision*, Paris, IHTP, 1995, 547 p. [Actes du colloque de Cachan, 16–18 November 1995].

DUCROS Louis-Frédéric, *Montagnes ardéchoises dans la guerre*, Valence, EPA, 1974–1977, 3 vols, 214 p.; 447 p.; 478 p.

DUFAY Raymond, *1940–1944 La vie dans l'Audomarois sous l'occupation*, Longuenesse, EPA, 1990, 749 p.

DURAND Yves, *La captivité, histoire des prisonniers de guerre français 1939–1945*, Paris, FNCPG, 1980, 548 p.

ECK Hélène, 'Les Françaises sous Vichy', in THÉBAUD Françoise (ed.), *Histoire des femmes en Occident. Le XXe siècle*, Paris, Plon, 1992, pp. 185–211.

FISHMAN Sarah, *We Will Wait. Wives of French Prisonners of War 1940–1945*, New Haven & London, Yale University Press, 253 p. French translation, *Femmes de prisonniers de guerre 1940–1945*, Paris, L'Harmattan, 1996, 284 p.

FLONNEAU Jean-Marie and VEILLON Dominique (eds), 'Le temps des restrictions en France 1939–1949', *Les Cahiers de l'IHTP*, no. 32–3, May 1996, 539 p.

FRANK Robert, (ed.), 'Images et imaginaire dans les relations internationales depuis 1938', *Les Cahiers de l'IHTP*, no. 28, June 1995, 168 p.

GERVEREAU Laurent and PESCHANSKI Denis (eds), *La propagande sous Vichy 1940–1944*, Paris, La Découverte, 1990, 288 p.

GRANDHAY Jean-Claude, *La Libération de Vesoul 12 septembre 1944*, Paris, Erti, 1994, 79 p.

GROS Henri-Jacques, *Août et septembre à Tonnay-Charente et Surgères*, Angoulême, EPA, 1985, 132 p.

GUILLON Jean-Marie, 'La Libération du Var: résistance et nouveaux pouvoirs', *Les Cahiers de l'IHTP*, no. 15, June 1990, 113 p.

GUILLON Jean-Marie, 'La lutte armée et ses représentations', in MARCOT François (ed.), *La Résistance et les Français, lutte armée et maquis*, Besançon, Annales littéraires de l'Université de Franche-Comté, 1996, pp. 147–57 [Actes du colloque de Besançon 15–17 June 1995].

GUILLON Jean-Marie and LABORIE Pierre (eds), *Mémoire et Histoire: la Résistance*, Toulouse, Privat, 1995, 352 p. [Actes du colloque de Toulouse 20–2 December 1993].

HIEGEL Charles, 'La répression de la collaboration et l'épuration en Moselle. Bilan statistique', in LE MOIGNE François-Yves (ed.), *Moselle et Mosellans dans la Seconde Guerre mondiale*, Metz, Éditions serpenoises, 1983, pp. 335–69.

JEANNET André and VELU Marie Hélène, *Le Saône-et-Loire dans la guerre 1939/1945*, Le Coteau, Horvath, 1984, 271 p.

KEDWARD H. R., 'Ici commence la France libre', in KEDWARD Harry R. and WOOD Nancy, *The Liberation of France Image and Event*, Oxford, Berg Publishers Ltd, 1995, p. 1–11.

KEDWARD H. R. and WOOD Nancy, *The Liberation of France Image and Event*, Oxford, Berg Publishers Ltd, 1995, 369 p.

KEDWARD H. R., 'La résistance, l'histoire et l'anthropologie: quelques domaines de la théorie', in *Résistance et mémoire*, in LABORIE Pierre and GUILLON Jean-Marie, Toulouse, Privat, 1995, pp. 109–18.

KEDWARD H. R., *In Search of the Maquis*, Oxford, Oxford University Press, 1993, p. 256. (French translation, *À la recherche du maquis*, Paris, Cerf, 1999, 472 p.)

KEDWARD H. R., *Naissance de la Résistance dans la France de Vichy*, Seyssel, Champ Vallon, 1989, 350 p.

KELLY Michael, 'The Reconstruction of Masculinity at the Liberation', in KEDWARD H. R. and WOOD Nancy, *The Liberation of France Image and Event*, Oxford, Berg Publishers Ltd, 1995, pp. 117–28.

KITSON Simon, 'La reconstitution de la police à Marseille (août 1944 – février 1945)', in *Provence Historique*, fascicule 178, t. 44, 1994, pp. 497–509.

KOYRÉ Alexandre, *La cinquième colonne*, Paris, Éditions Allia, 1997, 52 p.

LABORIE Pierre, 'L'idée de Résistance, entre définition et sens: retour sur un questionnement', in 'La Résistance et les Français Nouvelles approches', *Cahiers de l'IHTP*, no. 37, December 1997, pp. 15–28.

LABORIE Pierre, 'Violence politiques et imaginaire collectif: l'exemple de l'épuration', in BERTRAND Michel, LAURENT Natacha and

TAILLEFER Michel (eds), *Violences et pouvoirs politiques*, Toulouse, PUM, 1996, pp. 205–16.

LABORIE Pierre, 'À propos de la Résistance et de l'opinion française devant la lutte armée', in MARCOT François (ed.), *La Résistance et les Français, lutte armée et maquis*, Besançon, Annales littéraires de l'Université de Franche-Comté, 1996, pp. 141–6, [Actes du colloque de Besançon 15–17 June 1995].

LABORIE Pierre, 'Sur les représentations collectives de la Résistance dans la France de l'après Libération et sur l'usage de la mémoire', in FRANK Robert and GOTOVITCH José (eds), *La Résistance et les Européens du Nord*, Bruxelles, CERHSGM/IHTP, vol.1, 1994, pp. 419–23 [Actes du colloque de Bruxelles 23–5 November 1994].

LABORIE Pierre, 'Vichy et ses représentations dans l'imaginaire social', in AZÉMA Jean-Pierre and BÉDARIDA François, *Vichy et les Français*, Paris, Fayard, 1992, pp. 493–505.

LABORIE Pierre, *L'opinion française sous Vichy*, Paris, Seuil, 1990, 405 p.

LABORIE Pierre, 'De l'opinion publique à l'imaginaire social', in *Vingtième siècle. Revue d'histoire*, no. 18, April–June 1988, pp. 101–17.

LABORIE Pierre, 'Opinion et représentation: La Libération et l'image de la Résistance.', in RH2GM, no. 131, July 1983, pp. 65–91.

LABORIE Pierre, 'Entre histoire et mémoire, un épisode de l'épuration en Ariège: Le tribunal du peuple de Pamiers, 18–31 août 1944' in BRUNET M., BRUNET S. and PAILHES C. (eds), *Pays Pyrénéens et pouvoirs centraux, XVIe–XXe siècles*, Foix, Conseil général, pp. 267–83.

LABORIE Pierre, *Résistants Vichyssois et autres. L'évolution de l'opinion dans le Lot de 1939 à 1944*, Paris, Éditions du CNRS, 1980, 390 p.

LARRIEU Jean, 'L'épuration judiciaire dans les Pyrénées-Orientales', in *RH2GM*, numéro spécial 'Le Languedoc pendant la guerre', no. 112, October 1978, pp. 29–35.

LAURENS Corran, 'La femme au turban: les Femmes tondues', in KEDWARD H. R. and WOOD Nancy, *The Liberation of France Image and Event*, Oxford, Berg Publishers, 1995, pp 155–80.

La Libération du Calvados, 6 juin–31 décembre 1944, Caen, Conseil Général du Calvados-Direction des Archives, 1994, 226 p.

La Libération de la France, Actes du colloque de 1974, Paris, CNRS, 1976, 1054 p.

LEWIN Christophe, *Le retour des prisonniers français*, Paris, Presses Universitaires de la Sorbonne, 1986, 335 p.

LOISEAU Jean-Claude, *Les Zazous*, Paris, Éditions du Sagittaire, 1977, 215 p.

LOTTMAN R. Herbert, *The people's anger: justice and revenge in post-liberation France*, London, Hutchinson, 1986.

LUIRARD Monique, *La région stéphanoise dans la guerre et dans la paix, 1936–1951*, Saint Étienne, Centre d'étude foreziennes, 1980, 1024 p.

MARCOT François, 'La Résistance dans ses lieux et milieux: des relations d'interdépendance', in 'La Résistance et les Français Nouvelles approches', *Cahiers de l'IHTP*, no. 37, December 1997, pp. 129–46.

MARCOT François (ed.), *La Résistance et les Français, lutte armée et maquis*, Besançon, Annales littéraires de l'Université de Franche-Comté, 1996, 549 p. [Actes du colloque de Besançon 15–17 June 1995].

MARTIN Yves, *L'Ain dans la guerre 1939–1945*, Le Coteau, Horvath, 1989, 232 p.

MEDAHI Bernard, *La Moselle et l'Allemagne 1945–1951*, Thèse de 3e cycle, Université de Metz, 1979, 630 p. dactylographiées

MEINEN Insa, 'Wehrmacht und Prostitution – Zue reglementierung der Geschlechterbeziehungen durch die deutsche Militärverwaltung im besetzten Frankreich 1940–1944', in *1999 Zeitschrift für Geschichte des 20 und 21 Jahrhunderts*, Vol. 2, 1999, pp. 35–55.

MICHEL Henri, *La Libération de Paris*, Bruxelles, Complexe, 1980, 184 p.

MILZA Pierre and PESCHANSKI Denis (eds), *Italiens et Espagnols en France 1938–1946*, CEDEI-FNSP, 1992, pp. 237–48. [Actes du colloque international].

MUEL-DREYFUS Francine, *Vichy et l'éternel féminin*, Paris, Seuil, 1996, 385 p.

NOGUÈRES Henri, *Histoire de la Résistance en France*, Vol. 5, 'Au grand soleil de la Libération, 1er juin 1944–15 mai 1945', Paris, R. Laffont, 1967, 923 p.

NOVICK Peter, *The Resistance versus Vichy: The Purge of Collaborators in Liberated France*, Chatto & Windus, London, 1968 ; (French translation, *L'épuration française 1944–1949*, Paris, Éditions Balland, 1985 ; Livre de poche, Paris, Seuil, 1991, 364 p.)

PAXTON Robert O., *Vichy France, Old Guard and New Order, 1940–1944*, (first English edition, 1972), (French translation, *La France de Vichy*, Paris, Seuil, 1973, updated 1997, 460 p.)

'La Résistance et les Français Nouvelles approches', *Les Cahiers de l'IHTP*, no. 37, December 1997, 185 p.

'Résistances et Libérations (France 1940–1945)', in *CLIO, Histoire, Femmes et Sociétés*, special edition, no. 1, 1995, 331 p.

PETIT Jean-Louis-Norbert, *Et Versailles fut libéré!*, Versailles, EPA, 1990, p. 217.

PETITJEAN P-L, *Reims et la Champagne dans la tourmente de 1939–1945*, Versailles EPA, 1959, p. 81 dactylographiée

PLANCKE René-Charles, *La Seine-et-Marne 1939–1945, l'été de la liberté*, Le Mée-sur-Seine, Éditions Amatteis, 1987, 289 p.

RIOUX Jean-Pierre, *La France de la IVe République*, t.1, 'L'ardeur et la nécessité', Paris, Seuil, 1980, 309 p.

RIOUX Jean-Pierre, 'L'épuration en France', in *L'Histoire*, no. 5, October 1978, pp. 24–32.

ROTHIOT Pierre, *Cent-cinquante ans au service du peuple*, t. 2, 'Pour la France et la Liberté', Vittel, EPA, 1979, 282 p.

ROUQUET François, 'Dans la France du Maréchal', in *Encyclopédie politique et historique des femmes*, Paris, PUF, 1995, pp. 663–84.

ROUQUET François, 'Épuration, Résistance et représentations: quelques éléments pour une analyse sexuée', in BOUGEARD Christian and SAINCLIVIER Jacqueline (eds), *La Résistance et les Français. Enjeux stratégiques et environnement social*, Rennes, PUR, 1995, pp. 285–94.

ROUQUET François and VOLDMAN Danièle (eds), 'Identités féminines et violences politiques', *Cahiers de l'IHTP*, no. 31, October 1995, 85 p.

ROUQUET François, *L'épuration dans l'administration française*, Paris, CNRS, 1993, 300 p.

ROUSSO Henry, *Les années noires vivre sous l'occupation*, Paris, Découverte Gallimard, 1992, 192 p.

ROUSSO Henry, 'L'épuration en France une histoire inachevée', *Vingtième siècle. Revue d'histoire*, no. 33, January–March 1992, pp. 78–105.

RUDELLE Odile, 'Le vote des femmes, fin de "l'exception française"', in *Vingtième siècle. Revue d'histoire*, no. 42, April–June 1994, pp. 52–66.

SAINCLIVIER Jacqueline and VEILLON Dominique, 'Sens et formes de la Résistance', in 'La Résistance et les Français Nouvelles approches', *Cahiers de l'IHTP*, no. 37, December 1997, pp. 93–108.

SAINCLIVIER Jacqueline and BOUGEARD Christian (eds), *La Résistance et les Français. Enjeux stratégiques et environnement social*, Rennes, PUR, 1995, 368 p., [Actes du colloque de Rennes 29 September–1 October 1994].

SAINCLIVIER Jacqueline, 'Le pouvoir résistant (été 1944)', in BUTON Philippe and GUILLON Jean-Marie (eds), *Les pouvoirs en France à la Libération*, Paris, Belin, 1994, pp. 20–37.

SARY Monique, 'La vie à Metz sous l'occupation nazie', in LE MOIGNE François-Yves (ed.), *Moselle et Mosellans dans la Seconde Guerre mondiale*, Metz, Éditions serpenoises, 1983, pp. 143–72.

SCHWARTZ Paula, 'Résistance et différence des sexes: bilan et perspectives', in *Clio, Histoire, Femmes et Sociétés*, no. 1, 1995, pp. 67–88.

SILVANI Paul, *Et la Corse fut libérée*, Ajaccio, La Marge, 1993, 246 p.

SILVANI Paul, *La Corse des années ardentes: 1939–1976*, Paris, Albatros, 1976, 267 p.

SWEETS F. John, *Choices in Vichy France*, Oxford University Press, 1986, 306 p. (French translation, *Clermont-Ferrand à l'heure allemande*, Paris, Plon, 1996.)

TARTAKOWSKY Danielle, 'La Province sans Paris ou la Province contre Paris?', in FAVRE Pierre (ed.), *La Manifestation*, Paris, PFNSP, 1990, pp. 156–77.

THÉBAUD Françoise, 'Résistances et Libérations', in *Clio, Histoire, Femmes et Sociétés*, no. 1, 1995, pp. 11–19.

TIRAND Paul, *Castelnaudary: d'Auguste Fourès à Jean Mistler 1870–1945*, Castelnaudary, EPA, 1991, 221 p.

TODOROV Tzvetan, *Une tragédie française été 1944: scènes de guerre civile*, Paris, Seuil, 1944, 248 p.

VALADE Olivier, 'Années sombres. Années d'espoir. Saint-Martin-d'Hères 1939–1945', *SMH Histoire-mémoire vive*, no. 1, May 1994, 54 p.

VALÉE Marc, *Cinq années de vie et de guerre en pays mayennais*, Château-Gontier, IENA, 1962, 314 p.

VEILLON Dominique, *Vivre et survivre en France, 1939–1947*, Paris, Payot, 1995, 371 p.

VIRGILI Fabrice, 'Les tontes de la Libération en France', in VOLDMAN Danièle and ROUQUET François (eds), 'Identités féminines et violences politiques', *Cahiers de l'IHTP*, no. 31, October 1995, pp. 53–66.

VIRGILI Fabrice, 'Les tontes de la Libération le corps des femmes enjeu d'une réappropriation', in *Clio, Histoire, Femmes et Sociétés*, no. 1, 1995, pp. 129–51.

VIRGILI Fabrice, *Tontes et tondues à travers la presse de la Libération*, mémoire de DEA, Paris I – La Sorbonne, 1992, 176 p. dactylographiées.

VOLDMAN Danièle, *Le déminage de la France après 1945*, Paris, O. Jacob, 1998, 184 p. (new edition).

WIEVIORKA Olivier, *Une certaine idée de la résistance: Défense de la France 1940–1949*, Paris, Seuil, 1995, 488 p.

WIEVIORKA Olivier, 'Épuration', in AZÉMA Jean-Pierre and BÉDA-RIDA François (eds), *1938–1948. Les années de tourmente de Munich à Prague. Dictionnaire critique*, Paris, Flammarion, 1995, pp. 933–43.

WORMSER-MIGOT Olga, *Le retour des déportés. Quand les Alliés ouvrirent les portes*, Bruxelles, Complexe, 1985, 341 p.

ZELINGER Barbie, 'La photo de presse et la libération des camps', in *Vingtième siècle. Revue d'histoire*, no. 54, April–June 1997, pp. 61–78.

Other European countries

BALACE Francis, 'Les hoquets de la liberté', in *Jours de Guerre*, t. 20, Bruxelles, 1995, pp. 75–132.

BRAVO Anna and BRUZZONE Anna Maria, *In guerra senza armi. Storie di donne 1940–1945*, Bari, Editori Laterza, 1995, 214 p.

BUNTING Madeleine, *The Model Occupation The Channel Islands under German Rule, 1940–1945*, London, HarperCollins, 1995, p. 360.

CONWAY Martin, 'Justice in Post-War Belgium. Popular Passions and Political Realities', in *Cahiers d'Histoire du Temps Présent/Bijdragen*, no. 2, May 1997, pp. 7–34.

DE JONG, Louis, *Het Koninkrijk der Nederlanden in de tweede Wereldoorlog, t. 10 a, Het Laaste Jaar I*, Gravenhage, Martinus Nijhoff, 1980, 1100 p.

DE JONG, Louis, *Het Koninkrijk der Nederlanden in de tweede Wereldoorlog, t. 10 b, Het Laaste Jaar II*, Gravenhage, Martinus Nijhoff, 1980, 1100 p.

DONDI Marco, 'Azioni di guerra e potere partigiano nel dopoliberazione', in, *Italia contemporanea*, no. 188, September 1992, pp. 454–66.

EDMONDS James E., *The Occupation of the Rhineland 1918–1929*, facsimilé London, HMSO, 1987, 444 p.

FJØRTOFT Kjell, *Oppgjøret som ikke tok slutt*, Oslo, Gyldendal Forlag, 1997, 251 p.

FRAENKEL Ernest, *Military Occupation and the Rule of Law. Occupation Gouvernment in the Rhineland, 1918–1923*, Oxford University Press, 1944.

HOCHHUTH Rolf, *Un amour en Allemagne*, Paris, Ramsay, 1983, 300 p.

KOONZ Claudia, *Les mères patries sous le IIIe Reich les femmes et le nazisme*, Paris, Lieu commun, 1989, 554 p.

KRÜGER Gerd, 'Straffrei Selbstjustiz: Öffentliche Denunzierungen im Ruhrgebiet 1923–1926', in *Sowi*, 27, 1998, H. 2, pp. 119–125.

RIPA Yannick, 'La tonte purificatrice des républicaines pendant la guerre civile espagnole' in VOLDMAN Danièle and ROUQUET François (eds), 'Identités féminines et violences politiques', *Cahiers de l'IHTP*, no. 31, October 1995. pp. 39–51.

ROY-PALMER Domenico, *Processo ai fascisti 1943–1948. Storia di un 'epurazione che non c'è stata*, Milano, Rizzoli, 1996, p. 340.

RUAUX Jean-Yves, *Vichy sur Manche – Les îles anglo-normandes sous l'Occupation*, Rennes, Ouest-France, 1994, 298 p.

VERVENIOTI Tassoula, 'Women after the resistance in Greece: personal and political experiences', in MAZOWER Mark (n.d.) *After the War Was Over. Reconstructing the Family, Society, and the Law in Southern Europe, 1944–1950*, 10 p. dactylographiées. [pré-actes du colloque tenu à Brighton, 4–6 juillet 1996].

WARRING Anette, *Tyskerpiger – Under besæltelse og retsopgør*, København, Gyldendal, 1994, 260 p.

Witness accounts and memoirs

ADLEMAN Robert. H. and WALTON George, *The Champagne campaign*, Boston & Toronto, Little Brown, 1969, 298 p.

ARAGON Charles d', *La Résistance sans héroïsme*, Paris, Seuil, 1977, 220 p.

BADIA Gilbert, *Exilés en France. Souvenirs d'antifascistes allemands émigrés* (1933–1945), Paris, Maspero, 1982, 330 p.

BASSEVILLE Marcel (Abbé), Ouf. . . les lilas ont refleuri, Nancy, Impr. Vagner, 1945, 104 p.

BOUNIN Jacques, *Beaucoup d'imprudences*, Paris, Stock, 1974, 254 p.

BRÉDIER Georges, *Brou pendant la guerre*, Chartres, Impr. de Durand, 1945, 52 p.

DE GAULLE, *Discours et messages. Pendant la guerre, 1940–1946*, Paris, Livre de Poche, 1970.

DUBOIS Edmond, *Vu pendant la Libération de Paris*, Lausanne, Payot, 1944.

ELGEY Georgette, *La fenêtre ouverte*, Paris, Fayard, 1973, 221 p.

ÉLUARD Paul, *Au rendez-vous allemand*, Éditions de minuit, 1944, reissued in, *Œuvres complètes*, Vol. 1, Paris, Gallimard, 1968, pp. 1251–65.

ISORNI Jacques, *Mémoires 1911–1945*, Paris, R. Laffont, 1984, 539 p.

MANOUCHIAN Mélinée, *Manouchian*, Paris, Les Éditeurs français réunis, 1974, 203 p.

MARSHALL Samuel L. A., *Bringing up the Rear*, San Rafael, Presidio Press, 1979, 310 p.

MASSENET Pierre and Marthe, *Journal d'une longue nuit*, Paris, Fayard, 1971, 308 p.

MOOREHEAD Alan, *L'Eclipse*, Paris, Le Sagittaire, 1947, 275 p.

MORE Roger, *Totor chez les FTP*, Paris, 1947, 153 p.

MORGAN William J., *The OSS and I*, New York, Norton, 1957, 281 p.

PENROSE Antony, *Lee Miller, Photographe et correspondante de guerre*, Paris, Du May, 1994, 207 p.

PERRIN Jean-Pierre, *L'honneur perdu d'un résistant. Un épisode trouble de l'épuration*, Besançon, La Lanterne, 1987, 109 p.

RAVANEL Serge, *L'esprit de résistance*, Paris, Seuil, 1995, 444 p.

SARTRE Jean-Paul, 'Qu'est ce qu'un collaborateur', in *Situations III: lendemains de guerre*, Paris, Gallimard, 1949, 317 p.

STEIN Gertrude, *Les guerres que j'ai vues*, Paris, C. Bourgois, 1980, 315 p.

Novels

BEAUVOIR Simone de, *Les Mandarins*, Paris, Gallimard, 1954, 581 p.

BORY Jean-Louis, *Mon village à l'heure allemande*, Paris, Flammarion, 1945, 308 p.

DESFORGES Régine, *Le diable en rit encore*, Paris, Ramsay, 1985, 479 p.

DURAS Marguerite, *Hiroshima mon amour*, Paris, Gallimard, 1960, 155 p.

LEDUC Violette, *La Bâtarde*, Paris, Gallimard, 1964.

MALRAUX André, *L'Espoir*, Paris, Gallimard, 1938, 369 p.

MARGUERITTE, *La Garçonne*, Paris, Flammarion, 1922, 311 p.

SABATIER Robert, *La souris verte*, Paris, Albin Michel, 1990, 222 p.

SIMENON Georges, *Pedigree*, 1947, reissued in *Tout Simenon* t. 2, Paris, Presses de la cité, pp. 883–4.